The Destruction of Jerusalem and the Idea of Redemption
in the *Syriac Apocalypse of Baruch*

Society of Biblical Literature

Early Judaism and Its Literature

Edited by
John C. Reeves

Number 20
The Destruction of Jerusalem and the Idea of Redemption
in the *Syriac Apocalypse of Baruch*

The Destruction of Jerusalem and the Idea of Redemption in the *Syriac Apocalypse of Baruch*

Rivka Nir

Society of Biblical Literature
Atlanta

The Destruction of Jerusalem and the Idea of Redemption
in the *Syriac Apocalypse of Baruch*

Copyright © 2003 by the Society of Biblical Literature

All rights reserved

No part of this work may be reproduced or transmitted in any form or by any means, electronic or mechanical, including photocopying and recording, or by means of any information storage or retrieval system, except as may be expressly permitted by the 1976 Copyright Act or in writing from the publisher. Requests for permission should be addressed in writing to the Rights and Permissions Office, Society of Biblical Literature, 825 Houston Mill Road, Atlanta, GA 30329, USA.

Library of Congress Cataloging-in-Publication Data

Nir, Rivka.
   The destruction of Jerusalem and the idea of redemption in the Syriac Apocalypse of Baruch / by Rivka Nir.
       p. cm. — (Early Judaism and its literature ; no. 20)
   Includes bibliographical references.
   ISBN 1-58983-050-4 (pbk.)
   1. Syriac Apocalypse of Baruch—Criticism, interpretation, etc. 2. Redemption—Judaism. 3. Redemption—Christianity. 4. Eschatology, Jewish. 5. Eschatology. 6. Temple of Jerusalem (Jerusalem) I. Title. II. Series.
BS1830.B4 N57 2002b
229'.913—dc21

2002152549

This book is printed on recycled, acid-free paper.
09 08 07 06 05 04 03 — 5 4 3 2 1
Manufactured in the United States of America

To my esteemed teacher, Prof. Joshua Efron

Contents

Introduction 1

PART ONE: THE HEAVENLY JERUSALEM IN THE *SYRIAC APOCALYPSE OF BARUCH* 17

1. This Is Not the City I Have Engraved on the Palms of My Hands (*2 Bar.* 4:1–7) 19
2. The Hiding of the Temple Vessels 43
   - 2.1. *Syriac Baruch* 6:7–10 43
   - 2.2. The Jewish Tradition 48
   - 2.3. *Paralipomena Jeremiou* 56
   - 2.4. *Jeremiah Apocryphon* 59
   - 2.5. *Vitae Prophetorum* 66
   - 2.6. *Liber Antiquitatum Biblicarum* 71
3. The Abandonment of the Temple 79
   - 3.1. "The Watchman Has Abandoned the House" (8:1–5) 79
   - 3.2. The Keys of the Temple (10:18) 83
     - a. The Christian Tradition 83
     - b. The Jewish Tradition 88
   - 3.3. The Virgins Weaving in the Temple (10:19) 100

PART TWO: THE IDEA OF ESCHATOLOGICAL REDEMPTION 119

4. Description of the Appearance of Messiah (*2 Bar.* 24–30) 121
   - 4.1. The Catastrophes of the Eschaton 121
   - 4.2. The Eschatological Feast 132
   - 4.3. The Beginning of the Messiah's Revelation 138
   - 4.4. The Full Appearance of the Messiah 151
   - 4.5. The Resurrection of the Dead and the Final Judgment 158
5. The Vision of the Forest, the Cedar, the Vine, and the Spring (*2 Bar.* 36–40) 165
6. The Vision of the Bright Waters and the Dark Waters (*2 Bar.* 53, 56–74) 183
   - 6.1. Description of the End and the Appearance of the Messiah 194

CONCLUSION 199
APPENDIX: The Tidings of the Christian Resurrection and Its Conditions
    in *Paralipomena Jeremiae* 203
ABBREVIATIONS 239
BIBLIOGRAPHY 241
INDEX OF SOURCES 281
INDEX OF MODERN AUTHORS 307
SUBJECT INDEX 313

INTRODUCTION

Several pseudepigraphic works are associated with the name of Baruch son of Neriah, the prophet Jeremiah's scribe (Jer 32, 36, 43, 45), among them the *Syriac Apocalypse of Baruch*, known to scholars as *2 Baruch*.[1] This work is extant in its entirety only in the Syriac language, an Aramaic dialect widely used in the Eastern Christian church; hence its name, the *Syriac Baruch*. It is included among the biblical pseudepigraphical works, that is, those anonymous works whose composition is attributed to some ancient biblical personality, a group that includes *Enoch*, the *Assumption of Moses*, the *Martyrdom of Isaiah*, the *Psalms of Solomon*, the *Testaments of the Twelve Patriarchs*, *4 Ezra*, etc. In keeping with this literary conceit, the overt content of the present book is placed at the end of the First Temple period, the period during which Baruch and Jeremiah lived and which was marked by Jerusalem's conquest by Nebuchadnezzar, the destruction of the temple in 586 BCE, and the Babylonian exile. However, there is general agreement that this overt plot is no more than a literary device used to allude to the destruction of Jerusalem and the Second Temple in 70 CE. The work incorporates three apocalyptic visions describing the end of the world, the founding of the new world, and the coming of the Messiah; it concludes with an epistle sent by Baruch to the nine and a half tribes beyond the river, constituting a kind of précis of the ideas expressed in the work as a whole.

This epistle was already known from the year 1645, when it was published in the ninth volume of the *Paris Polyglot* (a Bible including the text in several languages), and afterwards in 1657 in *Walton's Polyglot* in London.[2] Over the

---

[1] The other works whose composition was attributed to Baruch are the apocryphal book of Baruch (1 Baruch), the Greek *Apocalypse of Baruch* (*3 Baruch*), and *The Other Words of Jeremiah the Prophet* (*Paralipomena Jeremiae Prophetae*), which, according to its Ethiopic fragments, was known as *The Remaining Words of Baruch* (*4 Baruch*). See R. H. Charles, *Apocalypse of Baruch* (London, 1896), xix–xxii; R. J. Harris, *The Rest of the Words of Baruch, A Christian Apocalypse of the Year 136 A.D.* (London, 1889), 9–11; P. Bogaert, *Apocalypse de Baruch, Introduction, Traduction du Syriaque et Commentaire* (2 vols.; Paris, 1969), 1:451–57; L. H. Brockington, "The Syriac Apocalypse of Baruch," in *The Apocryphal Old Testament* (ed. H. F. D. Sparks; Oxford, 1984), 835. In this book, this text will be referred to as the *Syriac Apocalypse of Baruch*, *Syriac Baruch*, or *2 Baruch*.

[2] In the Ambrosian MS, the only complete version of the work that has survived in Syriac, the epistle appears both separately and as an integral part of the apocalypse, from which its independent existence may be inferred. This epistle has survived in thirty-eight manuscripts. On the translation of the epistle, see Bogaert, *Apocalypse*, 1:28.

course of some two centuries, various voices asserted its Christian origins. Thus, Pierre Daniel Huet (1630–1721), bishop of Avranches, argued that *Baruch* was written by a Syrian monk, while Augustin Calmet (1672–1757) wrote that: "the Syrians have quite a lengthy epistle bearing the name *Baruch*, but the author of this epistle speaks of the angels in such a way as to make one suspect that he is a Christian." Fabricius, who translated the epistle into Latin in 1723, continued this tendency.[3]

In 1866 the entire work, of which the epistle was one part, was published in Latin translation by the priest M. Ceriani (1828–1907). In 1871 he published the Syriac text on the basis of the only extant Syriac manuscript, which was discovered at the Ambrosian library in Milan and dated to the sixth or seventh century CE.[4] Upon the publication of the full work, the predominant

---

[3] P. D. Huet, *Demonstratio Evangelica* (Leipzig, 1694), 450–51; A. Calmet, *Commentaire Litteral sur tous les Livres de l'Ancien et du Nouveau Testament* (Paris, 1726) 6:324; J. A. Fabricius, *Codex Pseudepigraphus Veteris Testamenti, Collectus, Castigatus Testimoniisque, Censuris et Animadversionibus Illustratus* (2 vols.; Hamburg, 1722–27), 2.145–55; and cf. J. G. Eichhorn, *Einleitung in die apokryphischen Schriften des Alten Testaments* (Leipzig, 1795), 395; H. Ewald, *Geschichte des Volkes Israel bis Christus*, III, Letzte Hälfte (Göttingen, 1852); G. A. Deissmann, *Bibelstudien; Beiträge zumeist aus den Papyri und Inschriften, zur Geschichte der Sprache, des Schrifttums und der Religion des hellenistischen Judentums und des Urchristentums* (Marburg, 1895), 234 n. 2.

[4] A. M. Ceriani, "Apocalypsis Syriaca Baruch," *Monumenta sacra et profana ex codicibus praesertim Bibliothecae Ambrosianae* 5.2 (Milan, 1871), 113–80. The Ambrosian MS includes the Old Testament, *4 Ezra*, Book 6 of Josephus's *Jewish War*, and the *Apocalypse of Baruch*, three works related to the conquest of Jerusalem by the Romans in 70 CE. The number of the manuscript is Codex Ambrosianus 13.21 inf (folio 257a–265b). On the dating of the MS, see Bogaert, *Apocalypse de Baruch*, 1:33–37. A photolithograph facsimile of the entire Ambrosian Manuscript was published in 1876–1883, and another edition of *Syriac Baruch* was published by M. Kmosko in *Patrologia Syriaca*, 1907. For a review of this edition, see T. W. Willett, *The Eschatologies in the Theodicies of 2 Baruch and 4 Esra* (Sheffield, 1989), 78. For the modern, updated edition of chs. 1–77 used in the preparation of this book, see S. Dedering, *Apocalypse of Baruch* (Peshitta Institute, Part IV, Fasc. 3; Leiden, 1975). Parts of the apocalypse are found in two Syriac manuscripts of thirteenth-century Jacobite origin found in the British Museum: W. Baars, "Neue Textzeugen der Syrischen Baruch," *VT* 13 (1963): 477. There is also a Greek fragment among the papyrii discovered in Oxyrhyncus in Egypt: B. P. Grenfell & A. S. Hunt, *The Oxyrhyncus Papyri* (London, 1903) 3:3–7; cf. A. M. Denis, *Fragmenta Pseudepigraphorum quae supersunt graeca* (PVTG 3; Leiden, 1970), 118–20. This fragment suggests that the work was translated into Syriac from the Greek, as suggested by the heading in the Ambrosian MS: "The book of revelations of Baruch son of Neriah, translated from Greek to Syriac." On the various MSS, see Bogaert, *Apocalypse de Baruch*, 1:33–55. There is also an Arabic MS that was discovered at the library of the Santa Catherina monastery:

scholarly opinion supported its identification as a Jewish work. This tendency was first articulated in 1885 by the Jewish scholar F. Rosenthal, who connected the apocalypse to the school of Rabbi Akiva, and by Louis Ginzberg, who asserted its Jewish and Pharisaic character in his entry on "Baruch" in the 1903 *Jewish Encyclopaedia*.[5]

In 1892 R. Kabisch and E. De Faye raised the issue of the unity of the work, asserting that it was comprised of various sources that were unified into one work by a later redactor; both noted certain textual corruptions and corrections that had been made in a Christian spirit.[6] In their wake, Charles admitted that there were numerous points of contact between *Baruch* and the New Testament, and even compiled a detailed list of parallels between the two.[7] By means of fragmenting and breaking down the work, these scholars were able to explain the Christian manifestations without challenging the overall Jewish provenance of the work.[8]

Notwithstanding the extensive opposition elicited by their suggestion,[9] this did not upset in the slightest the view, popular to this day, that the *Syriac Apocalypse of Baruch* was composed by a Jew living in the land of Israel between the years 70 and 135 CE,[10] and that it represented the Pharisaic outlook during

---

F. Leemhuis, A. F. J. Klijn, G. J. H. Van Gelder, *The Arabic Text of the Apocalypse of Baruch* (Leiden, 1986).

[5] F. Rosenthal, *Vier Apokryphische Bücher aus der Zeit und Schule R. Aqiba's: Assumptio Mosis, Das Vierte Buch Esra, Die Apocalypse Baruch, Das Buch Tobi* (Leipzig, 1885); L. Ginzberg, "Baruch, Apocalypse of (Syriac)," *JE* 2 (1903): 551–556.

[6] R. Kabisch, "Die Quellen der Apokalypse Baruch," *JPT* 18 (1982): 66–107; E. de Faye, *Les Apocalypses Juives* (Paris, 1982).

[7] Charles, *The Apocalypse of Baruch*, lxxvi; idem, "II Baruch," in *The Apocrypha and Pseudepigrapha of the Old Testament* (2 vols.; Oxford, 1913), 2:479–80.

[8] On the various suggestions for division that have been raised by these scholars, see de Faye, *Les Apocalypses Juives*, 192–204; Charles, "The Apocalypse of Baruch," xvi-lxv; and Bogaert, *Apocalypse*, 1:57–91.

[9] B. Violet, *Die Apokalypsen des Esra und Baruch* (GCS 32; Leipzig, 1924), xc; Ginzberg, "Baruch" 554–55; Bogaert, *Apocalypse*, 1.57–61, 80–81; A. F. J. Klijn, "The Sources and Redaction of the Syriac Apocalypse of Baruch," *JST* 1 (1970): 65–67; G. B. Saylor, *Have the Promises Failed? A Literary Analysis of 2 Baruch* (SBLDS 72; Chico, Calif., 1984), 5, 38, 87; Brockington, "The Syriac Apocalypse," 837; Charlesworth, "From Jewish Messianology to Christian Christology: Some Caveats and Perspectives," in *Judaisms and Their Messiahs at the Turn of the Christian Era* (ed. J. Neusner, W. S. Green, and E. S. Frerichs; Cambridge, 1987), 246.

[10] For various conjectures concerning the date of composition of this work within this range of years, see Bogaert, *Apocalypse*, 1:270; idem, "Les Apocalypses Contemporaines de Baruch, d'Esdras et de Jean," in *L'Apocalypse Johannique et l'Apocalyptique*

the years following the destruction of the Second Temple. Thus, for example, P. Bogaert, author of the most comprehensive and up-to-date study of this work, writes: "The author lived in the land of Israel. The importance of the theological message that he brings to the Diaspora communities, and the very great Jewish Orthodoxy of that message enable us to see him as one of the most prominent personalities in post-70 Palestinian Judaism."[11] He even suggests a certain similarity between the author of the book and R. Joshua b. Ḥananiah.[12] Those isolated voices that continued to assert its Christianity remained marginal to the predominant view and did not enjoy serious or deep attention.[13]

While most modern scholars have noted the proximity to *Syriac Baruch* of various Christian ideas and concepts, finding parallels between it and the books of the New Testament and other early Christian writings,[14] none of them has questioned its being a fundamentally Jewish work; at best, they have under-

---

dans le Nouveau Testament (ed. J. Lambrecht; Louvain, 1980), 49; E. Schürer, *The History of the Jewish People in the Age of Jesus Christ (175 B.C.–A.D. 135)* (ET, rev. and ed. by G. Vermes and F. Millar; Edinburgh, 1987), 3:752–53.

[11] Bogaert, *Apocalypse*, 1:334 (my translation).

[12] Ibid., 1:443; Charles, *Apocalypse of Baruch*, vii; W. O. E. Oesterley, *Books of the Apocrypha: Their Origin, Teaching and Contents* (London, 1915), 222; M. Rist, "Baruch, Apocalypse of," *IDB* 1:362; R. J. Harris, *The Rest of the Words*, 6–9; M. J. Lagrange, "Note sur le Messianisme au Temps de Jesus," *RB* 14 (1905): 510–11; A. F. J. Klijn, "2 (Syriac Apocalypse of) Baruch," *Old Testament Pseudepigrapha* (ed. J. H. Charlesworth; 2 vols.; London, 1983–85), 1:617, 620; Brockington, "The Syriac Apocalypse," 837; J. J. Collins, *The Apocalyptic Imagination* (New York, 1987), 178; G. Alon, *Toldot ha-Yehudim be-ʾErez Yisraʾel betequfat ha-Mishnah veha-Talmud* (2 vols.; Tel-Aviv, 1976), 1:32. In accordance with this view—namely, that the work was of Palestinian provenance—there are those who argue that it was translated into Greek from the Hebrew or Aramaic. See Bogaert, *Apocalypse*, 1:353–80 and 353 n. 2, for a list of scholars and their position regarding the original language of the work; Schürer, *History*, 3:753 n. 8.

[13] See Bogaert's critique of Zahn's position in *Apocalypse*, 1:446; cf. Th. Zahn, *Die Offenbarung des Johannes* (KNT, 18.1; Leipzig, 1924), 1:130–44. Similar to Bogaert, see Brockington, "The Syriac Apocalypse," 837.

[14] Harris, *The Rest of the Words*, 25; J. B. Frey, "L'Apocalypse Syriaque de Baruch," *Dictionnaire de la Bible, Supplément* (ed. L. Pirot, A. Robert, U. Cazelles, A. Feuillet; Paris, 1928), 421–22; Klijn, "2 Baruch," 614; Lagrange, "Note sur le Messianisme," 510; Sayler, *Have The Promises Failed?* 159. Bogaert himself admits to extraordinary similarities between the apocalypse and the NT, but states categorically that the text of the apocalypse does not allow us to determine the relation of its author to the Christian communities. See Bogaert, *Apocalypse*, 1:477. In his paper "Les Apocalypses Contemporaines" he states that Revelation was based upon *Syriac Baruch*.

stood certain sections as interpolations. In the present study, I have attempted to reexamine the central aspects of this closeness, with the aim of uncovering the theological identity of the work and the source of its theological inspiration. I have focused upon those traditions depicting the destruction of Jerusalem and the three apocalyptic visions portraying the eschatological redemption. These two foci, around which the plot of the work is constructed, may also serve as a litmus test for the identity of the work. This is so because the place of Jerusalem and the temple during the Second Temple period and the question whether to accept the Christian Messiah and the redemption that he was meant to bring to his believers lay at the center of the controversy between Judaism and Christianity. Hence, it was regarding these subjects that the differences in principle between the two religions were most likely to find expression. In addition, one expects to find overt or hidden Christian threads and expressions, especially in the "messianic" texts, as R. A. Kraft concluded: "Some Christians seem to have felt it important to have 'predictive' texts (especially apocalyptic) in which aspects of the career and function of their messiah were somehow noted, even if only cryptically or in passing."[15]

The author of *Syriac Baruch* made extensive use of the Bible and of the Jewish tradition. But this fact is in itself insufficient to serve as a conclusive argument as to the identity of its author, given that the Hebrew Bible, as is well known, became an integral part of the New Testament and occupied a central place in the Christian exegetical tradition. Hence, all Christian literature, especially that of the early period, was based upon what were originally Jewish traditions. As M. de Jonge states in relation to the *Testaments of the Twelve Patriarchs*:

> One should be cautious in using the labels "Jewish" and "Christian." If, for instance, the testaments use biographical material taken from the Old Testament or from Jewish Haggadic tradition, this does not prove that the testaments are Jewish, but only that the author knew the Old Testament and had access to Jewish traditions, either directly or indirectly.[16]

---

[15] R. A. Kraft, "The Multiform Jewish Heritage of Early Christianity," *Christianity, Judaism and other Greco-Roman Cults* (FS Morton Smith; ed. J. Neusner; Leiden 1975), 180.

[16] M. de Jonge, *Jewish Eschatology, Early Christian Christology, and the Testaments of the Twelve Patriarchs* (NovTSup 63; Leiden, 1991), 263–64. On the use Christians made of the Jewish writings, of Jewish liturgy, of the eschatological hopes that took shape within Judaism, and of Jewish customs, see R. A. Kraft, "The Pseudepigrapha in Christianity," in *Tracing the Threads; Studies in the Vitality of Jewish Pseudepigrapha* (ed. J. C. Reeves; Atlanta, Ga., 1994), 61.

Although the author took the materials for his work from Judaism, he reworked them in accordance with his own theological tendencies, giving them other meanings and incorporating them within a new composition that was well-fashioned and compact from a literary and ideological viewpoint. Like all pseudepigraphic and apocalyptic works, the present work is surrounded by a layer of mystery, expressing its ideas in symbolic and typological language. In examining the different traditions, I have sought to uncover and decipher the symbolic significance of these, to trace their early roots as they are reflected in the Jewish traditions, and to discover through a critical comparison of the parallel materials, what changes they had undergone in the course of their reworking.

Even though this study is concerned with theological and ideological aspects, it is essentially a historical study. Its methodology is based upon the assumption that one may only arrive at a full understanding of ideas and traditions, to uncover the soil upon which they draw and their means of development and transmission, on the basis of a consistent distinction among the different sources that have come down to us, their place and time of composition, and the identification of the social and ideological milieu within which they flourished. This distinction is particularly important in clarifying traditions that were conveyed verbally and underwent processes of reworking and editing that might alter their original meaning.

In keeping with this assumption, I have distinguished among three main blocs of sources:

1) **The explicitly Jewish sources.** These were composed during the Second Temple period or close to it, some of them being contemporary with *Syriac Baruch*. These sources reflect the dominant beliefs and approaches among the Jewish people in the land of Israel and in the Diaspora during that period. They include:

• the Bible, which served as the basis for various kinds of faith and spiritual creation, reflecting the Judaism of the First Temple period, the Babylonian exile, the return to Zion, and the beginning of the Hasmonean rebellion (Daniel);

• the apocryphal books—the Book of Hasmoneans (Maccabees), Ben Sira, Judith, Tobit, 1 Ezra, 1 Baruch, Additions to Daniel, Additions to Esther, Wisdom of Solomon, and the Prayer of Manasseh. These works, which were incorporated in the Greek scriptures (the Septuagint), were composed by Jews during the Second Temple period and faithfully reflect the concepts and beliefs widely held among the Jews of Palestine and of the Diaspora during this period.[17]

• the works of Josephus, the Jewish historian who lived and was active in Palestine during the first century CE and whose works, notwithstanding their shortcomings and tendentiousness, present a comprehensive and detailed view of all aspects of Second Temple Jewry;

• the writings of Philo of Alexandria, the writer and philosopher who lived in Egypt (20 BCE–50 CE) and gave expression to his Judaism by means of the Greek language and culture. And, finally:

• the early strata of the Palestinian talmudic literature (*Mishnah, Jerusalem Talmud,* and the early Palestinian midrashim: *Genesis Rabbah* and *Leviticus Rabbah*), which reflect Second Temple period Judaism.

In terms of the use of talmudic tradition as a historical source, I have followed in the footsteps of my mentor, Prof. Joshua Efron, who gives explicit preference to Palestinian talmudic sources over Babylonian sources. These sources preserve within themselves memories from temple times and ancient folk traditions that flourished on the soil of the land of Israel. By contrast, the Babylonian talmudic literature and the post-Babylonian midrashim are more distant in

---

[17] On the Hebrew term *Sefarim Ḥiṣonyim*, see *m. Sanh.* 10.1; *y. Sanh.* 10.1 (28a). No objection is found to works "such as Ben Sira" in terms of the Jewishness of the worldview reflected therein. Rabbi Akiva's statement in the Mishnah, according to which one who reads the external books has no portion in the World to Come, is to be understood in light of the interpretation given in the Palestinian Talmud: "But regarding the books of Homer, and all of the books written from then on, one who reads them is as if he is reading a letter. What is the reason? 'Beyond these, my son, beware . . .' [Eccles 12:12]. They were given for reflection, and not to labor in them." The intention of the JT was explained by Nahman Krochmal in his *Moreh Nevukhei ha-Zeman* (Lemberg, 1851), 101: "'One who reads the external books'—that is, one who reads them in public and expounds their verses and brings arguments from them as if they were among the 24 [canonical] books. 'Books of Homer'—this does not refer only to the story of the well-known Greek poet by that name, but is a general term referring to books in the Greek language not written by Jews. . . . 'One who reads therein is as if he is reading a letter'—that all these are concerned with secular matters, and are not considered the principal thing, and it is not possible to expound or to bring proofs from them." In other words, all those books written after the closing of the biblical canon are to be read in the same manner as one reads a letter, that is, privately, but not in a liturgical context like the Holy Scriptures. *B. Sanh.* 100a gives an inferior reading, and improperly interprets the apocryphal works as heretical writings. See L. Ginzberg, "Some Observations on the Attitude of the Synagogue Towards the Apocalyptic-Eschatological Writings," *JBL* 41 (1922): 115–36.

their time and place of composition, reflecting later internal tendencies and external influences, including Christian ones.[18]

2) **The early Christian writings.** On the opposite pole, one finds the bloc of early Christian writings, especially the New Testament writings,[19] the writings of the apostolic fathers, the apocryphal literature of the New Testament,[20] and that of the patristic exegetes who drew upon the circle of early Christian tradition just as the medieval Jewish exegetes drew upon early Jewish tradition. These sources reflect various aspects of early Christian theology; while they originated in Judaism and were based upon the Bible and Jewish traditions that were well-known during the period in which it took shape, they were filled with christological meanings, overt or covert, that clearly distinguish them from the early Jewish traditions.

---

[18] Efron, "The Hasmonean Kingdom and Simeon ben Shatah," 181–99; idem, "Simeon ben Shatah and Alexander Jannaeus," *Studies on the Hasmonean Period*, 143–47; idem, "The Bar-Kokhba War in Light of the Palestinian Talmudic Tradition," in *Mered Bar-Kohkhba; Mehqarim Hadashim* (ed. A. Oppenheimer and U. Rappaport; Jerusalem, 1984). As I heard from Prof. Efron in his university lectures, *b. Sanh.* 98a already raises the possibility of a suffering Messiah based upon the chapter of the servant of the Lord, esp. Isaiah 53, who sits at the gate of Rome, and of a messiah who will come like the Son of Man on heavenly clouds, as in Daniel 7. These are the two central pillars of Christology, as embodied in the two manifestations of Jesus: his earthly appearance as the suffering servant, tortured and crucified, and his second appearance in heavenly clouds, meant to complete the redemption. Cf. the discussion of the name of the Messiah in *b. Sanh.* 98b; and in *b. Ḥag.* 14a: "one (throne) for him and one for David"; *b. Sanh.* 38b; also the Babylonian testimonies concerning Jesus, and especially *b. Sanh.* 43a. On Christian influences in the Babylonian Talmud, see A. Geiger, "Erbsünde und Versöhnungstod: Deren Versuch in das Judenthum einzudringen," *JZWL* 10 (1872): 166–71. Geiger notes the penetration into the Babylonian Talmud of such Christian concepts as original sin and death as atonement; cf. Klausner, *The Messianic Idea in Israel* (New York, 1955), 405; Efron, *Studies on the Hasmonean Period* (Leiden, 1987), 156 n. 62, 158–60.

[19] The edition of the Greek New Testament used throughout was: K. Aland, M. Black, C. M. Martini, B. M. Metzger, A. Wikgren (eds.), *The Greek New Testament* (2d ed.; New York, 1969).

[20] The apocryphal literature to the NT is concentrated in several collections in English: M. R. James, *The Apocryphal New Testament* (Oxford, 1966); in the updated edition: J. K. Elliott, *The Apocryphal New Testament* (Oxford, 1993); E. Hennecke, *New Testament Apocrypha* (ed. W. Schneemelcher; 2 vols.; London, 1963); W. Schneemelcher, *New Testament Apocrypha* (rev. ed.; 2 vols.; Cambridge, 1991); and the new edition in German: W. Schneelmelcher, *Neutestamentliche Apokryphen* (5th ed.; 2 vols.; Tübingen, 1987, 1989).

3) **The pseudepigraphic-apocalyptic literature.** This includes *Syriac Baruch*, and particularly those works that are close to it ideologically, stylistically, and linguistically, such as the *Apocalypse of Ezra (4 Ezra) Paralipomena Jeremiae*, and to a somewhat lesser extent *Liber Antiquitatum Biblicarum* (Pseudo-Philo). These three works were evidently composed about the same time, utilized common traditions and legends, and grew in a similar theological climate.[21]

These works, alongside the other apocalyptic works, constitute a single literary and ideological unit, which is characterized by several basic guidelines that determine its inner essence and reflect its hidden intentions.

a) It hopes for the end of this world, which is dominated by the powers of evil and sin, and the founding of a new world in its place.

b) The figure of the Messiah, a transcendental miraculous redeemer, who confronts Satan, the polar opposite to Messiah, is at the focus of the drama of the End. The defeat of Satan at the end of times is a precondition for the founding of the new world and the resurrection of the dead, as promised to the believers in this messiah alone.

c) It expresses the hope for the founding of a heavenly Jerusalem to replace the earthly, historical Jerusalem that was condemned to destruction and was found unfit by its very nature.[22]

---

[21] On the proximity between *Baruch* and *4 Ezra*, see Renan, *Histoire des Origines du Christianisme*, 5:517; Violet, *Die Apokalypsen des Esra und Baruch*, lxxxi–xc. However, the issue of the relative chronology of the two apocalypses remains undecided: see Bogaert, *Apocalypse*, 1:25–26; Schürer, *The History of the Jewish People*, 3:753. On the resemblance between *Baruch* and Pseudo-Philo (*L.A.B.*), see Violet, lxxvii–lxxxi; James, *The Biblical Antiquities of Philo* (New York, 1971), 46–54; Gry, "La Date de la Fin des Temps"; Bogaert, *Apocalypse*, 1:247–52; H. Jacobson, *A Commentary on Pseudo-Philo's Liber Antiquitatum Biblicarum*, 1:201. On the date of the *Antiquities*, see James, *Biblical Antiquities*, 7, who dated it in the years following the destruction of the temple; Zeron, "The System of Pseudo-Philo," 233, who dates it between 70 and 150 CE; and J. Hadot, "La Datation de l'Apocalypse," 167–71, who rightly rejects the explanations as if there were a connection between *Syriac Baruch*, the *Antiquities*, and *4 Ezra*, in an environment influenced by the Pharisaic stream (ibid., 157). See Brockington, "The Syriac Apocalypse," 838, who argues that the three works are contemporaneous and reflect the same background and the same theology. Cf. Bogaert, *Apocalypse*, 1:258.

[22] For further characteristics of this literature, definition of terms, and history of research, see Russell, *The Method and Message*, 269; Torrey, "Apocalypse," 669–70; Willett, *The Eschatologies*, 35–47; Smith, "On the History of ἀποκαλύπτω and ἀποκάλυψις"; Flusser, "Apocalypse"; Stone, "Apocalyptic Literature," 392–94; Grinz, "Apocrypha and Pseudepigrapha"; Rist, "Apocalypticism". On the history of research, see esp. Hanson, "Prolegomena to the Study of Jewish Apocalyptic," 389–400; Fritsch, "Apocrypha."

These characteristics, which are interwoven within the unique apocalyptic composition, are inconsistent with the approaches and beliefs of Second Temple Judaism, as expressed in the explicitly Jewish sources enumerated in the first bloc.[23] Those scholars who think that apocalyptic literature has its roots in Judaism note the common elements shared between the apocalyptic works and descriptions in the Bible, such as Ezekiel 38–39, Zechariah, Joel (2:1–11; 3–4), and Isaiah 24–27 (referred to as the Apocalypse of Isaiah).[24] But these sources do not express belief in the figure of a soteriological Messiah; they do not entail a drama of the end of this world and the founding of a new world in its stead; they do not involve a battle between the Messiah and the anti-Messiah at the end of days, nor is there anticipation of a heavenly Jerusalem to replace the earthly temple and Jerusalem. They do not reflect esoteric and sectarian doctrines, but express the hope for a national redemption that will occur on the historical plane and be promised to the Jewish people as a whole.

These elements are likewise not characteristic of the book of Daniel, which is understood in the research as an example of apocalyptic literature and as a transitional link between Jewish and Christian apocalypse. Daniel is not an apocalyptic work in its inner essence and in its intentions: it is entirely rooted in the historical episode of the Hasmonean rebellion and expresses the hopes and anticipations for the success of the rebellion.[25]

---

[23] See Y. Harofe (Troki), *Ḥizzuk 'Emuna* (Amsterdam, 1705; repr., Ashdod, 1975), 145–46, who distinguishes between those works composed by Jews, such as Tobias, Judith, and Ben-Sira, and works that were composed by Christians, who "*invented them from their heart to help themselves,* like the two latter books that they attribute to Ezra, and one book that they attribute to Baruch son of Neriah. . . ." Cf. A. H. Weiss, *Dor dor ve-Dorshav* I (Jerusalem and Tel Aviv, n.d.), 197: "Now let us not leave this until we speak a little bit concerning certain books that originated among Jews in the Land of Israel at this early time. And these are: the Fourth Book of Ezra, the *Book of Enoch,* the *Book of Jubilees.* These three include beliefs and faiths that flourished on the soil of Israel, *even though on the whole they are plantings of foreign vines.*" Cf. G. F. Moore, *Judaism in the First Centuries of the Christian Era,* 1:127–28; Ginzberg, "Some Observations on the Attitude of the Synagogue"; Efron, "Holy War and Visions of Redemption," 55–65. On the application of this method, see his "The Psalms of Solomon, the Hasmonean Decline and Christianity"; W. Schmithals, *The Apocalyptic Movement* (Nashville and New York, 1975), 191.

[24] See, e.g., S. L. Cook, *Prophecy and Apocalypticism* (Minneapolis, 1995).

[25] The Book of Daniel, like the chapters of the servant of God in Second Isaiah, constitute the central axis upon which Christianity based its christology. On this matter, see Efron's studies on the Book of Daniel: "Daniel and His Three Friends in Exile," *Studies,* 67–109; "The Idea of the Servant of God in the Book of Daniel," ibid.,

The fact that the authors of the apocalyptic literature made use of biblical passages, from which they derived the raw materials for the apocalyptic drama, can explain both the external resemblance and the literary dependence existing between the apocalyptic writings and the Bible.

The apocalyptic oeuvre may only be explained against the background of Christian theology, at whose focus is the faith in Christ, who appeared upon the earth in order to bring general redemption to mankind by means of his sufferings and death, and who will appear a second time to complete the redemption that began with his earthly appearance. This second coming will be marked by the sign of the end of this world, the defeat of Satan and his armies, and the founding of a new world, which will be a garden of Eden. This paradise is identified with the heavenly Jerusalem embodied in the Christian church, intended to replace the historical Jerusalem.

The very term "apocalypse" is itself a Christian term; it first appears in the introduction to the Revelation of John, the concluding work of the New Testament ("The Apocalypse [or: Revelation] of Jesus Christ") and the work that provides the most fully developed model for apocalypse in general (cf. the synoptic apocalypse of Mark 13:1ff. and parallels).[26] Apocalypse was born in the bosom of Christianity, which is entirely apocalyptic on all its levels and components. R. A. Kraft has noted the fundamental connection between this literature and Christianity:

> The Christianity of the "pseudepigrapha" is not a hidden ingredient that needs to be hunted out and exposed in contrast to a supposed native Jewish pre-Christian setting. On the contrary, the Christianity of the pseudepigrapha is a given, it is the setting, it is the starting point for delving more deeply into this literature to determine what, if anything, may be safely identified as originally Jewish.[27]

113–20; "Holy War and Visions of Redemption in the Hasmonean Period," ibid., 33–55.

[26] See, e.g., de Jonge's conclusions concerning the *T. 12 Patr.* in *The Testaments of the Twelve Patriarchs*, 117–28; idem, "Two Interesting Interpretations," 221; J. T. Milik, "Le Testament de Levi en Arameen," *RB* 62 (1955), 406; Schürer, *History of the Jewish People*, 770–71; Daniélou, *Theology of Jewish Christianity*, 11–19; Efron, *Studies*, 219–86.

[27] Quoted in D. Satran, "Biblical Prophets and Christian Legend," 149. Thus in R. Kraft's article published on the Internet. The same passage appears in a somewhat more moderate and qualified formulation in Kraft, "Pseudepigrapha in Christianity," 75. There, he adds the qualifying sentence: "On the contrary, when the evidence is clear that only Christians preserved the material, the Christianity of it is the given. . . ." See also R. A. Kraft, "Reassessing the 'Recensional Problem' in Testament of Abraham," 135: "It should not be assumed that a document composed or compiled by a Christian will necessarily contain characteristically 'Christian' contents." Cf. Satran, *Biblical*

These works were in Christian hands, as proven by the quotation from the *Book of Enoch* in Jude 14 (compare Heb 11:5) and the explicit references made to them by the church fathers.[28] The process of their transmission was entirely Christian; parts of them were even incorporated in the liturgy of various minor churches. M. de Jonge pointed out the importance of the transmission process to clarify and understand the theological tendencies of these works:

> The so-called Pseudepigrapha of the Old Testament have to be read primarily as writings transmitted by Christians throughout the centuries. They were transmitted because copyists regarded them as important, and were of the opinion that they could function meaningfully in the communities for which they copied them. Transmission clearly presupposes the enduring relevance of what is transmitted. In early Christianity as well as in the Middle Ages and even later, Christians all over the Christian world were interested in narratives, wisdom books, apocalypses, testaments, etc., centering around figures known from the Old Testament.[29]

On the other hand, unlike the "apocryphal" books, mentioned above, which were composed by Jewish hands during the Second Temple period and which Jews read and quoted,[30] we do not have any internal or external proof that Jews knew these works and acknowledged them at any time in the ancient period.[31] Moreover, it is reasonable to assume that had such works, which include doctrines that challenge the principles of Judaism and undermine the status of Jerusalem and the historical temple, been written by Jews, they would have

---

Prophets in Byzantine Palestine, 76; idem, "The Lives of the Prophets," 60; M. E. Stone, "Categorization and Classification of the Apocrypha and Pseudepigrapha," *Abr-Nahrain* 24 (1986): 171–72.

[28] See the various attitudes of the church fathers in Kraft, "Pseudepigrapha," 63ff. For a possible quotation from 2 Bar. 61:7 in *Barn.* 11:9, see F. Perles, "Les Apocryphes et les Pseudépigraphes," *REJ* 73 (1921) 183. On the role of the *Book of Enoch* in Christian and Gnostic tradition, see M. Gil, "Studies in the Book of Enoch," 192–94.

[29] M. de Jonge, "The So-called Pseudepigrapha of the Old Testament and Early Christianity," *The New Testament and Hellenistic Judaism* (Peabody, Mass., 1997), 59. The suggestion to see these books as "evolved literature" or "developing literature," which "underwent continuous change, by addition, by omission, by corruption and conjecture, as well as by drastic revision" (R. A. Kraft, "The Multiform Jewish Heritage of Early Christianity," 185; R. Baukham, *The Fate of the Dead,* 161), does not change this basic fact. This new terminology does not shed new light on the hidden theological meanings and intentions of this literature.

[30] Thus, e.g., Josephus utilizes 1 Hasmoneans in his *Jewish Antiquities,* and Ben Sira is mentioned as an example of the apocryphal books in the Jerusalem Talmud tradition, *y. Sanh.* 10.1 (28a).

[31] K. Koch, *The Rediscovery of Apocalyptic* (London, 1972), 34.

elicited some sort of reaction on the part of the Sages, who represented the dominant stream at that time, and some record of it would have come down to us.

One may also include within this group the literature of the Qumran sect, which expresses conceptual and linguistic relations and ideological and theological characteristics similar to those of the pseudepigraphic and apocalyptic literature. Like the apocalyptic literature, the Qumran sect's theological focus was on the eschatological anticipation of the approaching end of days, on the war between the forces of light and the forces of darkness, and on the appearance of the expected messianic age. Similar to the apocalyptic literature, the Qumran scrolls expressed absolute negation of the historical Jerusalem and temple. The sect anticipates a new Jerusalem and a new temple in which atonement will be achieved, not by means of the flesh of burnt-offerings and the fats of the sacrifices, but by a spiritual sacrifice "of lips of justice like a righteous fragrance" (1QS ix 4–5).[32] The scrolls of this mysterious sect also include chapters and fragments of works from the apocalyptic literature (such as the *Book of Enoch,* the *Testaments of the Twelve Patriarchs,* the *Book of Jubilees,* etc.), which likewise betray an ideological proximity to the world of Christianity.[33]

---

[32] On the relationship between Qumran and apocalypse, see J. J. Collins, *Apocalypticism in the Dead Sea Scrolls* (Leiden and New York, 1997). The ideological similarity between the scrolls and the apocalypse underlies the Groningen Hypothesis that sees the roots of the Qumran movement and the composition of the scrolls in the apocalyptic tradition of the third century; see F. García Martínez and A. S. van der Woude, "A Groningen Hypothesis of Qumran Origins and Early History," *RevQ* 14 (1990) 537.

[33] Efron, *Studies,* 63; Satran, "Qumran and the Beginnings of Christianity" and the main bibliography there on this subject. Cf. the studies by J. L. Teicher: "The Dead Sea Scrolls—Documents of the Jewish-Christian Sect of Ebionites," *JJS* 2 (1951): 67–99; "The Damascus Fragments and the Origin of the Jewish-Christian Sect," *JJS* 2 (1951): 115–43; "The Teaching of the Pre-Pauline Church in the Dead Sea Scrolls" *JJS* 3 (1952): 111–18, 139–50; 4 (1953): 1–13, 49–58, 93–103, 139–53; "The Habakkuk Scroll," *JJS* 5 (1954): 47–59; "Priests and Sacrifices in the Dead Sea Scrolls," *JJS* 5 (1954): 93–98; *VT* 5 (1955): 189ff.; and "The Essenes," *Studia Patristica* 1 (*TUGAL* 63; 1957), 540ff. Also Y. Baer, "The *Yahad* Scroll" [Heb.], *Zion* 29 (1964): 1ff.; idem, "*Pesher Habakkuk* and its Period" [Hebrew], *Zion* 34 (1969): 1ff.; Efron, *Studies,* 61–62. On the significance of the calendar unique to Qumran and the *Book of Jubilees* and its closeness to the days of the sacred week in Christianity, see A. Jaubert, *La Date de la Cène; calendrier biblique et liturgie chrétienne* (Paris, 1957). This is not the place to discuss the difficult problems involving the identity of the Qumran sect. For our purposes, it suffices to note that the sect separated itself from the Jewish people and

The present book is composed of two central sections, parallel to the two thematic axes of the work. The first section is devoted to a description of the destruction of Jerusalem, in which we discuss the main traditions that may shed light upon the author's position towards the destruction of Jerusalem and the temple: the Divine promise to Baruch that the Jerusalem that is to be destroyed is not the city that He had promised to inscribe upon the palms of His hands; the burying of the temple vessels in the earth until the end of days; the abandoning of the temple by its guard upon its destruction; the call to the priests of the temple to throw the keys up to heaven; and the call to the virgins who weave silk, crimson, and gold to cast their weaving into the fire.

The second half of the book portrays the vision of eschatological redemption, as reflected in the three apocalyptic visions contained in the latter part of the work. The first vision deals with the portrayal of the End, the havoc that precedes it, the eschatological meal, and the two stages in the appearance of the Messiah; next, the vision of the forest, the cedar, the vine, and the well portrays the end of the world and the victory of Messiah over the final ruler; finally, the vision of the bright waters and the black waters, signals the end of the apocalyptic drama with the appearance of the uncorrupted world and the establishment of paradise upon earth.

This research and its methodological principles are based on what I learned from my teacher, Prof. Joshua Efron, who has been my guide and source of inspiration since I began my academic studies. It was at his lectures at Tel-Aviv University during the 1970s that I first heard about the Christianity of the Apocalyptical Literature that constitutes the core of the so-called the "Old Testament Peudepigrapha." He was then a rather isolated voice who used to refer to Marinus de Jonge's work *The Testament of the Twelve Patriarchs* as an example of another modern researcher who had arrived to similar conclusions.

During the last thirty years, there has been a gradual but consistent process of change in the understanding of the theological tendencies of this literature and the ideological soil in which they are rooted. M. D. Eldridge refers to this process as "The New Climate."[34] He points to the influence of M. de Jonge, together with R. A. Kraft, on this process and perceives it as the result of new approaches in reference to three presumptions:

1. The fact that this literature was transmitted throughout the centuries by Christians should be taken into account when considering whether it is Jewish or Christian.

---

challenged the shared religious and ideological basis of all of the Jewish streams of that period.

[34] M. D. Eldridge, *Dying Adam with his Multiethnic Family* (Leiden, Boston & Köln, 2001), 237–38.

2. The old presumption that whatever is not clearly Christian is Jewish has been found to be baseless. A document composed or compiled by a Christian need not necessarily contain obvious "Christian" contents.

3. A text about a Hebrew biblical figure can be a Christian composition ab initio, rather than a Christian editing or reworking of essentially Jewish writing, as was thought earlier.

This process is reflected in recent studies on works like the *Ascension of Isaiah, Lives of the Prophets, Paraleipomena Jeremiae (4 Baruch), Greek Life of Adam and Eve (Asc. Mos.)*, and others. I view the present book as a modest contribution to consolidating this process.

This book is based on my dissertation, which was written in Hebrew under the supervision of Prof. Joshua Efron and Prof. Aryeh Kasher and was submitted to the Senate of Tel-Aviv University in 1996. The English translation was made possible by the support of The Lucius N. Littauer Foundation in New York, "Keren Yaniv" of the School of History at Tel-Aviv University, and the Open University of Israel. The translation was done by Jonathan Chipman.

Rivka Nir
The Open University of Israel, 2003

PART ONE

THE HEAVENLY JERUSALEM IN THE *SYRIAC APOCALYPSE OF BARUCH*

CHAPTER ONE

This Is Not the City I Have Engraved on the Palms of My Hands (*2 Bar.* 4:1–7)

The *Syriac Apocalypse of Baruch* begins with a description of the destruction of Jerusalem in which God appears to Baruch, informing him that, in wake of the people's sins, He intends to bring disaster upon the city and its inhabitants, and asking Baruch to inform Jeremiah and his like to leave the city. Baruch attempts to alleviate the evil decree. Comparing Jerusalem to his mother, he expresses regret that he was born to see its destruction and attempts to convince God that, with the destruction of the city, the name of Israel will no longer be remembered and there will no longer be anyone to spread God's Torah and His praise. But God calms him and says:

> This city will be delivered up for a time, and the people will be chastened for a time, and the world will not be forgotten. Or do you think that this is the city of which I said: On the palms of my hands I have carved you? It is not this building that is in your midst now;[1] it is that which will be revealed with me that was already prepared from the moment that I decided to create Paradise. And I showed it to Adam before he sinned. But when he transgressed the commandment, it was taken away from him—as also Paradise. After these things I showed it to my servant Abraham in the night between the portions of the victims. And again I showed it also to Moses on Mount Sinai when I showed him the likeness of the tabernacle and all its vessels. Behold, now it is preserved with me—as also Paradise. Now go away and do as I command you. (4:1–7)[2]

The Jerusalem that God is about to destroy is not the Jerusalem He promised to engrave on the palms of His hands. That Jerusalem was already prepared in time, and is kept in heaven, next to paradise. The author quotes Isa 49:16, one of the striking chapters of consolation from Second Isaiah, composed at the time of the conquest of Babylonia by Cyrus on the eve of the return to Zion. God promises the captives in Babylonia that He will gather the

---

[1] The Arabic version adds: "a true building." See Leemhuis, Klijn, and Van Gelder, *The Arabic Text,* v. 18.

[2] The English translation of this, and of other passages taken from *Baruch* quoted in this book, are taken from Klijn, "2 (Syriac Apocalypse of) Baruch," in Charlesworth, *OT Pseudepigrapha,* 1:615–52.

exiles and rebuild Jerusalem from its ruins. All the scattered ones of Israel will return to their land, Zion will arise from its destruction, its ruins will be rebuilt, and its enemies routed. As for Zion's suspicions that she has been deserted and forgotten by God, the prophet compares God's love of His people to that of a mother for her children, promising that God will neither forget Zion nor allow her to be forgotten: "Behold, I have graven you on the palms of my hands; your walls are continually before me." The prophet describes God's concern for Jerusalem here in a metaphorical way: He engraves Jerusalem and its walls on the palms of his hands, like one who engraves the image of his beloved on the palms of his hand so that he may remember her constantly.[3] The image of Zion surrounded by walls, the symbol and essence of the concrete, physical reality of the historical Jerusalem, will be constantly before God's eyes, and the redemption that the prophet wishes for his people and for Jerusalem is an entirely earthly redemption, to occur on the real, historical plane. The verse was understood in this spirit by the Jewish tradition: "it is impossible for a man to forget the palms of his hands. Hence these may forget, yet will not I forget thee."[4] Only in the later Jewish tradition is this idea connected to a transcendent, supernal Jerusalem, but there too not connected with the rejection of an earthly Jerusalem but, on the contrary: "from the great love of the lower one, he made another on high."[5]

But the author of the present work explicitly rejects the original intention of the verse, lending it an entirely different meaning. The Jerusalem whose rebuilding from the ruins and whose flourishing with the return to Zion was prophesied by Isaiah—the Jerusalem that God promised to engrave on the palms of His hand is not the Jerusalem that is about to be destroyed, the historic Jerusalem of the Second Temple. Rather, he refers here to another Jerusalem, one kept by God in the heavens, which He himself created before time, alongside paradise—a transcendent and preexistent Jerusalem. Thus, like the city, the earthly temple now being built is not the true temple revealed before God; rather, there exists another temple, prepared by God long ago with paradise and kept with God in the heavens.[6]

---

[3] Cf. Cant 8:6; Isa 44:5; Rashi to Isa 49:16; Radak to Isa 49:16; Luzzatto's *Perush*, 344. For the example of an ornament described as "a city of gold," see *y. Šabb.* 6.1 (7d).

[4] *Pesiq. Rab Kah.* 17.8 (English trans. by W. G. Braude and I. J. Kapstein, Philadelphia, 1974, p. 314; cp. Mandelbaum ed., 292). Cf. *Cant. Rab.* 8.6; *Yalq. Šim.* 2.471 to Isa 49; *b. Taʿan.* 4a; *Pesiq. Rab.* 27 (ed. Ish-Shalom; 134a).

[5] *Tanḥ., Pequdei*, 1, in printed version. On the late date of *Midrash Tanḥuma*, see Zunz, *ha-Derashot be-Yisraʾel*, 111. This tradition does not appear in the manuscripts of *Tanḥuma* used by Buber in his edition. For more on this tradition, see below.

[6] Lohse, "Σιών," 325–26; Murphy, *The Structure and Meaning of Second Baruch*,

CHAPTER 1: This Is Not the City I Have Engraved on the Palms   21

What is the point of this description?

The predominant view in scholarship is that this is one of the ways by which the author deals with the destruction of Jerusalem and the temple. He distracts his attention from earthly city and temple to the heavenly sphere, thereby hoping to comfort the people and to infuse them with hope. Thus, God's promise of the eternity of Jerusalem and His closeness to it, as expressed in Isaiah's prophecy, does not refer to the Jerusalem that was destroyed, but to another, heavenly Jerusalem, alongside which is the eternal temple.[7]

In my opinion, this approach does not square with the true intentions of the author. By means of this verse from Isaiah, the author wishes to express his opinion regarding the inferiority and transience of the earthly Jerusalem and temple.[8] He does not articulate here criticism of the temple, nor does he express hope for any correcting or change of the face of Jerusalem. The author of this book is not at all interested in the rebuilding of the temple and of Jerusalem; indeed, not a word is said in the entire book regarding the hope and anticipation for its future restoration. According to his view, the historical Jerusalem and temple, which were built by man on earth, were from the outset inferior and condemned to a limited life span, as against the heavenly Jerusalem and sanctuary, which were formed by God in hoary antiquity and will enjoy eternal existence.

He identifies the heavenly Jerusalem with paradise, which is also preserved by God in heaven, and which is also preexistent. The pre-creation existence of the temple and of Jerusalem, the fact of their being created by God and not by man, their existence in the heavens, their identity with the garden of Eden and their eternal spirituality, are emphasized by means of the tradition according to which God showed Zion and the temple to Adam before he sinned, as well as

---

103; Stone, "Reactions to Destruction of the Second Temple," 199; Bietenhard, *Die himmlische Welt*, 195; Betz, *Galatians*, 246.

[7] Volz, *Die Eschatologie der jüdischen Gemeinde*, 376; Rowland, *The Open Heaven*, 133; Murphy, *The Structure and Meaning of Second Baruch*, 15; Bogaert, *Apocalypse*, 1:390; Safrai, "The Heavenly Jerusalem," 14; Flusser, "Jerusalem in Second Temple Literature" 286; Klausner, *The Messianic Idea in Israel*, 346; McKelvey, *The New Temple*, 32; Bietenhard, *Die himmlische Welt*, 195; Kuhnel, *From the Earthly to the Heavenly Jerusalem*, 44. It is usual in this context to cite the famous passage from Baruch's dirge, 35:1–5.

[8] For this reason Charles (*II Baruch*, 482) thinks that these verses are interpolations, because in his view the scorn expressed here towards the earthly Jerusalem is opposed to its description in other places in *2 Baruch*. In my opinion, this description is not unusual, and is consistent with this author's overall viewpoint concerning the historical Jerusalem.

to Abraham at the covenant of the pieces, and to Moses, when he showed him the form of the Tabernacle and its vessels.

What are the sources of this tradition?

The ancient Jewish tradition does not know of any pre-creation or pretemporal temple, built by God alongside paradise and located in the heavens, shown by God to Adam, Abraham, or Moses. There is admittedly a Babylonian tradition that lists the temple, alongside the garden of Eden, among the seven things that were created before the creation: "Seven things were created before the world was created, and these were: Torah, repentance, *paradise,* gehenna, the throne of glory, *the temple,* and the name of the Messiah" (*b. Pesaḥ.* 54a; my emphasis).[9] However, in the earliest Palestinian parallel, found in *Genesis Rabbah,* the temple is enumerated among those things which the Creator *thought* of creating, but which were not made into reality until the world was created: "Six things preceded the creation: there were those that were created, and those which were intended to be created. The Torah and the throne of glory were created. . . . The patriarchs and Israel and the temple and the name of the Messiah were intended to be created" (*Gen. Rab.* 1.4 [ed. Theodor-Albeck, p. 6]).[10]

While there does exist a tradition regarding Abraham, enumerating the temple among the four things that were revealed during the deep slumber that fell upon him during the covenant of the pieces—namely, gehenna, the four kingdoms [i.e., that would persecute Israel], the giving of the Torah, and *the temple* (*Gen. Rab.* 44.21 [ed. Theodor-Albeck, 443]; my emphasis).[11] However, it follows from the context that the temple referred to there is none other than the historical temple, upon whose destruction all the sacrifices would be abolished. This is consistent with another tradition, according to which the Holy One, blessed be He, showed Abraham all the historical events to take place in the future to the Jewish people and in the world as whole, including these four things.[12]

---

[9] Cf. *b. Ned.* 39b; *Tanḥ., Naso* 19 (ed. Buber; 17b); *Midr. Mishlei* 8 (ed. Wisotzky; 385); *Pirqe R. El.* 3.2; *S. Eli. Rab.* 29 (ed. Ish Shalom; 160); *Tg. Ps.-J.* to Gen 2:8; ibid., to Gen. 3:24.

[10] Cf. *Midr. Tehillim* 93: 2 (ed. Buber; 414); *Yal. Šim.* 1.20, to Gen 2.

[11] Cf. *Midr. Tehillim* 16.7 (ed. Buber; 122); *Pesiq. Rab Kah.,* 5.2 (ed. Mandelbaum; 80); *Mek. de-Rabbi Yishma'el, Ba-Hodesh* 9 (ed. Horowitz-Rabin; 236); *Exod. Rab.* 51.7; *Tanḥ., Pequdei* 5 (ed. Buber; 65b); *Pesiq. Rab.* 15 (ed. Ish-Shalom; 67a).

[12] Ginzberg, *Legends of the Jews,* 1:235–36; *Tg. Yer.* to Gen 15:12 (ed. Ginsburger; 25). See, similarly to this, the "book of Adam" shown by God to Adam: *b. ʿAbod. Zar.* 5a; *b. Sanh.* 38b; *Gen. Rab.* 24.1–7 (ed. Theodor-Albeck; 231); *ʾAbot R. Nat.,* Version I, ch. 31 (ed. Schechter; 91); Version II, ch. 8 (ed. Schechter; 22); *Eccles. Rab.* 3.11.

CHAPTER 1: This Is Not the City I Have Engraved on the Palms   23

Regarding Moses, the description in *Baruch* bases itself upon the biblical tradition, according to which, when Moses was on Mount Sinai, he was commanded to make a temple for God according to the pattern of the temple and its vessels shown him by God: "and let them make me a sanctuary, that I may dwell in their midst. According to all that I show you concerning the pattern of the tabernacle, and of all its furniture, so shall you make it" (Exod 25:8–9, 40; 26:30; Num 8:4). Some researchers see in this biblical tradition a proof for the existence of an ancient Jewish belief in the existence of a heavenly temple, created by God's hands, of which the earthly temple was only an inferior copy.[13]

In my opinion, this explanation is inconsistent with the overall biblical outlook regarding the sanctuary, evidently being based upon a mistaken interpretation of the term *tavnit* (translated here as "pattern"). In this tradition, the word *tavnit* means the model, pattern, program, or sketch according to which one needs to build,[14] and ought not to be understood as the model or exemplar of a real, concrete building that exists in the heavens. The belief expressed here does not appear in an eschatological context, and its source is in early outlooks that were widespread in the Near Eastern mythology, according to which there is a correspondence or parallel between the heavenly world and the earthly world. According to this outlook, there is a model or pattern of the temple in heaven, which God showed to the king or leader in a vision or dream, commanding him to build an earthly temple according to its model. Thus, Sumerian sources describe how the god Ningursu showed Gudea, the prince-priest of Lagash (ca. 3000 BCE), in night dreams, the model of the temple that he was to build, and gave him the model in writing. Similarly the people of Babylonia, who took pride in the glorious temple of Mardokh located in their city, called Esagla, thought that this temple corresponded to a heavenly temple.[15]

---

[13] See Aptowitzer, "The Heavenly Temple in the Aggadah," 149; Charles, *Apocalypse of Baruch*, 6; McNeile, *The Book of Exodus*, 158.

[14] For interpretation of the word, see *BDB*, 125: "pattern, according to which anything is to be constructed"; Koehler & Baumgartner, *Lexicon*, 1018: "pattern"; Furst, *Handwörterbuch*, 513: "modell, muster"; Steinberg, *Milon Ha-Tanakh*, 878: "the structure of a thing and its form"; Botterweck and Ringgren, *TDOT*, 179: "pattern, model"; and similarly the LXX translates the word *tavnit* in Exodus, at times by the word paradigm: παραδείγμα, and at times as typos: τύπος. On *paradeigma*, see Liddel and Scott, *Greek-English Lexicon*, 595: "a pattern or model of a thing to be executed, an architect's, sculptor's or painter's model or copy of an existing thing." *Typos* (ibid., 824): "the type or model of a thing; an example, an outline."

[15] Mofatt, *Epistle to the Hebrews*, 106; Cassutto, *Perush 'al Sefer Shemot*, 223–24; Levin, "The Prophet Isaiah and His Relation to the Temple," 148. Safrai, "The Heavenly Jerusalem," 13, designates this approach "the correspondence theory." Von

It was in this sense that this verse was also understood by Jewish exegesis of the Second Temple period, such as what was explained by Philo:

> It was determined, therefore, to fashion a tabernacle, a work of the highest sanctity, the construction of which was set forth to Moses on the mount by divine pronouncements. *He saw with the soul's eye the immaterial forms of the material objects about to be made, and these forms had to be reproduced in copies* (μιμήματα), *perceived by the senses, taken from the original draught* (ἀρχέτυπον), *so to speak, and from patterns comprehended in the mind*. . . . *So the shape of the model was stamped upon the mind of the prophet, a secretly painted or moulded prototype, produced by immaterial and invisible forms; and then the resulting work was built in accordance with that shape by the artist impressing the stampings upon the material substances required in each case.*[16]

Regarding this matter Philo bases himself upon an early tradition that was accepted in Israel, a tradition that also finds expression in Josephus.[17]

The early talmudic tradition did not relate to this issue at all;[18] however, the principal biblical exegetes explained it in the spirit of the biblical tradition

---

Rad, οὐρανός, 508, notes a Sidonian inscription which implies belief in this tradition. Cf. Loewenstamm, "Sanctuary," 534; Kaufmann, *Toldot ha-ʾEmunah ha-Yisraʾelit*, 4:82; Hamerton-Kelly, "The Temple and the Origins of Jewish Apocalyptic," 7; Schrenk, ἱερεύς, 240; McKelvey, *The New Temple*, 25; Ego, *Im Himmel wie auf Erden*, 12; Clifford, *The Cosmic Mountain in Canaan and the Old Testament*, 177; Seeligmann, "Jerusalem in Hellenistic Jewish Thought," 206–7; Dimant, "The Apocalyptic Interpretation of Ezekiel at Qumran," 43; M. Weinfeld, "Theology and Wisdom in the Third Millennium BCE Mesopotamian Tradition in Relation to the Bible" [Hebrew] *Shenaton la-Miqra ul-ḥeqer ha-Mizraḥ ha-Qadum* 4 (Jerusalem and Tel Aviv, 1980), 285–87. This approach is widespread in the Hellenistic world as well, and finds expression in Plato, upon which Philo also based himself. Cf. Wolfson, *Philo*, 1:182–84.

[16] Philo, *Mos.* 2.74–76 (LCL; 6:485–87). And see, similarly: Philo, *QE* 52 (LCL; 2:99–100); *QE* 82 (LCL; 2:131–32); *Spec.* 1.12, 66 (LCL; 7:137–38).

[17] Josephus, *Ant.* 3.99–101: "and the Temple shall be made according to the measure (μέτροις) and the vessels that He Himself showed him." Baer, *Yisraʾel ba-ʿAmim*, 82ff.; D. Niemark, *Toldot ha-ʿIqqarim be-Yisraʾel*, 47ff.; idem, *Toldot ha-Philosophia be-Yisraʾel*, 21 n. Also Wis 9:8 ("you commanded to build a temple on your holy mountain and an altar in your royal city, in the form of the holy temple which you prepared from the beginning"), does not depart from this approach.

[18] According to several sources, God showed Moses all of the labor of the form of the temple and its vessels in an image in fire. Thus: *b. Menaḥ.* 29a; *Leqaḥ Tov*, Exod 25 (ed. Buber; 89, 9); *Num. Rab.* 12.8; and cf. the blessing of *Boneh Yerushalayim* for the 9th of Av in *y. Ber.* 4.3 (8a). Jonathan Chipman drew my attention to *Sifre Bamidbar, Behaʿalotkha* 61 (ed. Horowitz; 58), cited in Rashi's commentary to Num 8:4, *vezeh maʿaseh hamenorah*, "that the Holy One blessed be He pointed with his finger, because he [Moses] had difficulty with [understanding] it; hence it says 'and this'" (cf. Exod

CHAPTER 1: This Is Not the City I Have Engraved on the Palms   25

and in that of Philo's interpretation: the "divine sights, which [he saw] are prophetic vision, and not with his eyes" (Ibn Ezra on Exod 25:8).[19] These sources reflect an early belief, widespread in First Temple Judaism, regarding the existence of a model, pattern, or image of the ideal temple in the heaven, according to which Moses was commanded to build the earthly temple. According to Yitzhak Baer: "The most essential principle in the worldview of our forefathers was that the lower world serves only as a reflection of the upper world. There follow from this the details of their human Torah, both universal and individual, and their outlook regarding the place of the Jewish people in history; and one cannot separate between these two aspects" (Baer, *Yisra'el ba'Amim*, 83–84).

The biblical tradition does not imply any contradiction between the plan shown by God to Moses and that Moses wishes to erect. On the contrary, there is an inseparable connection between them. The fact that Moses built the earthly temple according to the heavenly plan that he saw on the mountain is not meant to detract from the importance and status of the former; the plan of the heavenly temple is needed to serve as an ideal model for the earthly temple. Only in later Jewish tradition does there develop an approach connecting this biblical expression to the heavenly temple.[20] Even in the later tradition the earthly temple is not inferior to the temple of God in the heavens but, as in the biblical tradition, constitutes a realization of the ideal plan. This approach fits the outlook found in the Palestinian talmudic tradition, according to which the "Holy of Holies below is aligned opposite the Holy of Holies above," and whatever God created above he also created below (*y. Ber.* 4.5 [8c]).[21] This outlook is consistent with the widespread expectations among the leadership of the Sages and the people during the first generations following the destruction of the temple, which they saw as a temporary reality, hoping for the building of the temple "quickly in our days."[22]

12:2; 30:13). In all of these cases, it is clear that God, as it were, used "means of concretization" for didactic purposes; these were not fixed images in the heavens.

[19] See, likewise, Rashi to Exod 26:30; Abravanel to Exod 25, 417–18.

[20] *Pesiq. Rab Kah.* 1.3 (ed. Mandelbaum; 8); *Tanḥ., Naso* 19 (ed. Buber; 18); *Num. Rab.* 14.3; *Cant. Rab.* 3.11; *Pesiq. Rab.* 5 (ed. Ish Shalom; 22b); *b. Menaḥ.* 29a.

[21] Cf. *Cant. Rab.* 4.4; *Mek. de-Rabbi Yishma'el, Shirah* 10 (ed. Horowitz-Rabin; 150); *Exod. Rab.* 33.4; *Tanḥ., Vayaqhel* 7 (ed. Buber; 62b); and cf. *Tanḥ., Beha'alotkha* 11 (ed. Buber; 25b); *Tanḥ., Pequdei* 2 (ed. Buber; 64); *Tanḥ., Beḥuqotai* 5 (ed. Buber; 55b); *Exod. Rab.* 35.6; *Num. Rab.* 12.1, 12.8; *Tg. Ps.-J.* to Ps. 122:3.

[22] *M. Ta'an.* 4.8; *m. Tamid* 7.3; *m. Pesaḥ.* 10.6; *b. Sukkah.* 41a; *b. Beṣah* 5b; *b. Roš. Haš.* 30a; etc. Cf. G. Alon, *Toldot ha-Yehudim be-'Eretz Yisra'el be-tequfat ha-Mishnah*

Unlike the development of a belief in the existence of a heavenly temple, *there is no image of a heavenly Jerusalem in the early Jewish sources.* The eschatological expectations of the Jewish people, as expressed in Scripture, give expression to the hope for the restoration of the temple, the return of the scattered ones of Israel, and the transformation of Jerusalem as a magnet for all nations; these were the three components of national hopes in Israel, all of which were connected with the historical Jerusalem. A heavenly Jerusalem does not at all appear in Second Temple literature; the same holds true for the early talmudic sources, that is, in the Mishnah, the Jerusalem Talmud, or in the Palestinian midrashim.[23] The talmudic tradition as a whole does not recognize the existence of a heavenly and transcendent Jerusalem, which preceded and is preferable to the earthly Jerusalem, and nowhere in early Jewish tradition is Isaiah's promise to Zion interpreted as referring to a heavenly Jerusalem. The early sources all express hope for the building and restoration of the earthly, historical, and concrete Jerusalem, to which all of the exiles will be ingathered in the spirit of the biblical prophets. In this spirit Ben-Sira asks: "Save us, O God of all; and cast Thy fear upon all the nations. . . . Have compassion upon Thy holy city, Jerusalem, the place of thy dwelling. Fill Zion with Thy majesty, and Thy temple with Thy glory" (Sir 36:1–2, 18–19). Rabbi Akiba concludes the Passover Haggadah with a blessing that expresses the anticipation of an earthly redemption, including the restoration of the historical Jerusalem and the temple: "So, O Lord our God and God of our fathers, bring us to other occasions and pilgrimage festivals which shall come in peace, rejoicing in the rebuilding of Your city and happy in Your service, and may we eat there of the sacrifices and the paschal lambs. . . . Blessed are You, O God, redeemer of Israel" (*m. Pesaḥ.* 10.6). A similar outlook finds expression in the blessing for the rebuilding of Jerusalem in the *'Amidah* for *Tisha b'Av,* as formulated in the *Jerusalem Talmud:* "Have mercy, O Lord our God, with Your great mercy and Your faithful kindness, upon us and upon Your people Israel and upon Jerusalem Your city and upon Zion the resting place of Your glory, and upon the city, that is mourning and ruined and destroyed and desolate, given over to the hands of strangers, trampled with arrogant hands; and it was inherited by legions, and profaned by idolators, and to Israel Your people you have given it as a portion, and to the seed of Jeshurun you gave it as an inheritance, for with fire you have burned it, and with fire you shall in the future built up, as said,

---

veha-Talmud, 1:159; Ben-Shalom, "Processes and Ideology in the Period of Yavneh," 11 and n. 55.

[23] Urbach, "Supernal Jerusalem and Earthly Jerusalem," 156; Ginzberg, *Commentary on the Palestinian Talmud,* vol. 3, on *Berakhot* ch. 4, 403; Seeligmann, "Jerusalem in Jewish Hellenistic Thought," 207–8.

CHAPTER 1: This Is Not the City I Have Engraved on the Palms 27

"For I shall be to it, sayeth the Lord, as a wall of fire around it, and I shall be for glory within it" (*y. Ber.*, 4.3 [8a]).[24]

The expression "the supernal [or: transcendent] Jerusalem" first appears in Jewish sources in a singular tradition in the Babylonian Talmud:

> Rav Nahman said to Rav Yitzhak: What is meant by [the verse], "The Holy One in your midst, and I will not come into the city" [Hosea 11:9]? Because the Holy One is in your midst, I will not come into the city? He replied to him: Thus said Rabbi Yohanan: The Holy One blessed be He has said, "I will not come into the supernal Jerusalem until I come into the lower Jerusalem." And is there [in fact] a supernal Jerusalem? Yes, as it is written, "Jerusalem, built as a city which is bound firmly together" [Ps 122:3] (*b. Ta'an.* 5a; *b. B. Bat.* 75b).

The Talmud's question, "is there [in fact] a supernal Jerusalem?" implies, as Urbach argues,[25] that in the eyes of the interlocutor the very mention of the concept "the supernal Jerusalem" was enough to elicit surprise. This Jerusalem, according to the Babylonian tradition, is located in the heavens, in the fourth heaven called *Zevul*, alongside the temple, and within it is an altar upon which sacrifices were offered (*b. Ḥag.* 12b). The Babylonian Talmud distances itself from the concepts that developed on the soil of the land of Israel, and constitutes a landmark in the development of the idea of a heavenly Jerusalem. But there too, as well as in the post-Babylonian *midrashim*, the "earthly Jerusalem" is not inferior to the heavenly one, and the supernal Jerusalem does not take the place of the earthly Jerusalem which was destroyed. So long as God does not come into the ruined, "lower Jerusalem," he does not enter into the "supernal Jerusalem" either (*b. Ta'an.* 5a). The latter is constructed upon the model of the former, and not vice versa, so that if the one is destroyed there is no place for the other either (*Midr. Tanḥ., Pequdei* 1).

Anticipation of a heavenly Jerusalem that will descend from heaven to supplant the earthly Jerusalem develops gradually in Judaism, attaining full expression in the medieval midrashim of redemption.[26]

---

[24] Cf. *Sifre Devarim*, 43 (ed. Finkelstein; 95); Tobit 13:16–18; ibid, 14:5; Ben Sira 51:12; [1] Bar 5:5–9. On the date of composition of the benediction *Boneh Yerushalayim* according to the Jerusalem Talmud, and the Grace after Meals, in which there is a slightly different text of that same blessing, see Flusser, "Jerusalem in Second Temple Literature," 266, 270, 273; Barrett, "The Eschatology of the Epistle to the Hebrews," 374; de Young, *Jerusalem in the New Testament*, 115–16; Lohse, "Σιών," 326; Bietenhard, Die *Himmlische Welt*, 196; McKelvey, *The New Temple*, 14; Kuhnel, *From the Earthly to the Heavenly Jerusalem*, 34–35.

[25] Urbach, "Supernal Jerusalem and Earthly Jerusalem, 156; Safrai, "The Heavenly Jerusalem," 16.

[26] *Midrash Vayosha'*, in *Bet ha-Midrash*, ed. Jellinek, 1:55; *Tefillat Moshe la-Elohim*;

What, then, are the sources of the tradition in *Syriac Baruch?*

The idea of a preexistent, transcendent, heavenly Jerusalem as a divine, not human, creation appears in the apocalyptic literature related to *Baruch.* Thus, for example, the visionary in *4 Ezra* portrays the heavenly Jerusalem as a city that is today hidden (7:26)[27] but that, upon the coming of the Eschaton and the appearance of the Messiah, will be revealed and seen by all. At that time the mountain carved out without human hands (13:36) (*sicut vidisti montem sculpi sine manibus*) will be visible in place of the building made by human hands, "for no work of man's building could endure in a place where the city of the Most High was to be revealed" (10:54).

Similarly, the *Ethiopic Book of Enoch* portrays the "new house" that God Himself builds in place of the earthly Jerusalem, compared to the "old house" that was removed by him:

> Then I stood still, looking at that ancient house being transformed: all the pillars and all the columns were pulled out; and the ornaments of that house were packed and taken out together with them and abandoned in a certain place in the South of the land. I went on seeing until the Lord of the sheep brought about a new house, greater and loftier than the first one, and set it up in the first location which had been covered up—all its pillars were new, the columns new; and the ornaments new, as well as greater than those of the first, (that is) the old (house), which was gone. All the sheep were within it. (*1 En.* 90:28–29)

As in the *2 Baruch,* in these works too the garden of Eden is identified with the heavenly Jerusalem; it is hidden away with God in heaven and will also be revealed at the end of times.[28] This identification appears explicitly in the *Testament of Dan:* "and the saints shall refresh themselves in Eden, the righteous shall rejoice in the new Jerusalem, which shall be eternally for the glorification of God" (*Test. Dan* 5:12). The identification of the heavenly Jerusalem with Eden may also be seen in the way these works apply the biblical descriptions of Jerusalem and the temple to the garden of Eden. Thus, like Jerusalem, which is pictured in the Bible, primarily in the vision of the end of days, as sitting upon a high and elevated mountain at the end of the north,[29] so too the garden of Eden is seen in the apocalyptic works as located on a high

---

Midrash Alphabeta de-Rabbi Akiva, in ibid., 3:20–21; *Seder Gan 'Eden,* in ibid., 3:137–38; *Sefer 'Eliyahu* and *Pirkei Mashiah, Nistarot R. Shimon Bar Yoḥai,* in ibid., 3:67, 80; *Ma'aseh Daniel,* in ibid., 5:128; and *Yerushalayim shel Ma'alah,* in Even-Shmuel, *Midrashei Ge'ulah,* 20–22.

[27] For exegesis of this verse, see Box, *Ezra,* 114 note c; *4 Ezra* 8:52; *Jub.* 4:24–26; *2 (Slavonic) Enoch* 55:2; *Sib. Or.* 5.414–33.

[28] *4 Ezra* 3:6; 7:36–38.

[29] Isa 2:2; 14:13; Mic 4:1; Ezek 28:14, 16; 40:2; Zech 14:4; Ps 48:3.

mountain, at the far north, at the end of heavens.[30] It is described as the Holy of Holies and as the sanctuary of the Lord, and is located in Jerusalem, in the navel of the earth;[31] at the end of time, the tree of life from the garden of Eden will be planted on a high mountain, where the house of the Lord, ruler of the world, is—that is, in Jerusalem—and it will be the new paradise.[32]

The idea that God showed Adam, Abraham, and Moses a heavenly sanctuary alongside the garden of Eden likewise appears in the pseudepigraphic compositions.[33] Researchers based the attribution of the source of the tradition of a heavenly Jerusalem to Judaism on the ideological similarity between these works and *Syriac Baruch,* on the assumption that these works reflect Jewish approaches that were widely held in apocalyptic circles during the Second Temple period.[34]

---

[30] *1 En.* 39:3; 61:1–4; 70:3; 77:3. See also in the Christian tradition: Ephraem Syrus, *Hymnen de Paradiso und Contra Julianum,* I.4.

[31] *Jub.* 3:12; 8:19; Anderson, "Celibacy or Consummation in the Garden?" 129. It is located in Jerusalem, the navel of the earth: *1 En.* 24:4–25:7; 26:1–3. See J. M. Ford, *Revelation,* 388, on Rev 2:7.

[32] *1 En.* 25:5; *2 En.* 5:3: "and in the middle the tree of life, in the place where the Lord rests whenever He comes to the Garden of Eden"; *Apoc. Mos.* 22:4: "and the throne of God stood fixed in the place where was the tree of life." E. A. W. Budge, *The Book of the Cave of Treasures,* 60. Ezek 28:13–14 already connects the garden of Eden with the holy mountain of God, and depicts the restoration of the earthly Jerusalem using images of the garden of Eden; cf. Anderson, "Celibacy or Consummation in the Garden?" 143. On the lack of clarity regarding the location of the garden of Eden, see Gil, "Studies in the Book of Enoch," 180.

[33] *L.A.B.* 13:8–9; 26:6. God showed Adam the place of the creation and color alongside the garden of Eden. According to Zeron ("System," 169), the place of the creation and color (*locum . . . colorem*) as part of the garden of Eden alludes to the heavenly sanctuary. On the connection between Adam, the garden of Eden, and the future temple, embodied in the concept of "the temple of Adam" in the scroll of the *Damascus Covenant* and the *Florilegium* of the Qumran scrolls from Cave 4, see M. O. Wise, "4QFlorilegium and the Temple of Adam," 126–27, 130. On the secrets of the future revealed to Abraham, cf. *4 Ezra* 3:13–14; *L.A.B.* 23:6; *Apocalypse of Abraham* 9; 29. On the revelation of the heavenly temple to Moses and its proximity to the garden of Eden, see *L.A.B.* 11:15. Zeron ("System," 168), learned of the place of the temple in the garden of Eden because the tree of life was located there, and there too God showed him the likeness (*similitudinem*) of the vessels. Elsewhere, God shows to Moses the paths of the garden of Eden and the measurements of the temple: *L.A.B.* 19:10.

[34] On the basis of the generally accepted Hasmonean date of the *Ethiopic Enoch,* there is a tendency to date the beginning of the development of this approach to this approximate period of time. See Charles, *The Revelation of St John,* 161; Milik, *The*

But in my opinion, the sources for the tradition in *Baruch* regarding the heavenly Jerusalem are to be sought in the Christian approach. Like the proposed exegesis of Isa 49:16 found in *2 Baruch,* the Christian patristic exegesis read that the Jerusalem that God promised to engrave upon the palms of His hands is not to be sought on the earth, in the land of Israel, because the true Jerusalem is not a human creation but rather the work of God's hands, identified with the congregation of the holy—that is, with the Christian church.[35]

Like the tradition in *Syriac Baruch,* the Christian tradition connects the supernal Jerusalem with Abraham and with the covenant between the pieces. In Epistle to the Galatians 4:21–31, the supernal Jerusalem is identified with the congregation of believers in Jesus,[36] allegorically symbolized by Isaac, the son of Sarah, the free wife. Isaac is the prototype of Jesus,[37] who "inherits" the promise given to Abraham in the covenant between the pieces (Gen 15:4; Gal 3:18). In this Christian tradition, as in *Baruch,* a contrast is drawn between "the present Jerusalem" (ἡ νῦν Ἰερουσαλήμ) or "this city" and the supernal Jerusalem (ἡ ἄνω Ἰερουσαλήμ).[38] The use of this expression, rather than the expression that identifies Jerusalem as still "coming"—ἡ Ἰερουσαλήμ μέλλουσα[39]—suggests that, as in *Baruch,* this phrase refers to the Jerusalem that already exists in the heavens and not to a yet-to-be-created Jerusalem. In both traditions the city is now hidden, but will be revealed in the future.[40]

In the Christian approach, particularly as expressed in the Epistle to the Hebrews 8–10, we find the tradition concerning the plan of the sanctuary and its vessels, which Moses was asked to make, at the very focus of the idea of the

---

Books of Enoch, 44–45; McKelvey, *The New Temple,* 23, 25; Schrenk, "ἱερεύς," 239–40; Urbach, "Supernal Jerusalem and Lower Jerusalem," 165–71; Aptowitzer, "The Heavenly Temple," 272; Flusser, "Jerusalem in Second Temple Literature," 265; Safrai, "The Heavenly Jerusalem," 12, 16. A different view regarding the date, origin, and nature of the Book of Enoch is taken by M. Gil. In his opinion, this is a Christian work, written by one author, and expressing the views of one of the Gnostic sects. See Gil, "Studies in the Book of Enoch."

[35] Eusebius, *Comm. Isa.* (PG 24:436–37); Jerome, *Comm. Isa.* (PL 24:469–71).

[36] Cf. Heb 12:23.

[37] Gal 3:16, 19; 4:1–7. The rock of Golgotha, where Jesus was crucified and resurrected, has been identified with the altar upon which Abraham was prepared to sacrifice Isaac, that is, the altar on Mount Moriah. See Wilkinson, "Jewish Influences on the Early Christian Rite of Jerusalem," 352.

[38] Compare this expression in: Col 3:1; Phil 3:14; John 8:23; 3:3, 7, 31.

[39] As in Heb 13:14.

[40] Cf. Heb 9:11ff.; cf. Augustine, *Civ.* 17.3 (LCL; 5:217); E. D. Burton, *Galatians,* 263; H. D. Betz, *Galatians,* 247; Werblowsky, "Metropolis of All the Lands," 175.

"new covenant" (Heb 8:5). It serves as support for the idea that the sanctuary (σκηνή) and its earthly vessels are merely a copy, an exemplar (ὑπόδειγμα), a shadow (σκία), a reflection, and a prefiguration of the true and perfect sanctuary (ἀντίτυπα τῶν ἀληθινῶν) that exists in heaven. In the earthly temple, which was established by humans and is the work of their hands (χειροποίητος; Heb 9:24),[41] there serve "priests who offer gifts according to the law; they serve a copy and shadow of the heavenly sanctuary; for when Moses was about to erect the tent, he was instructed by God, saying, 'See that you make everything according to the pattern which was shown you on the mountain'" (Heb 8:2–6). This sanctuary lies at the focus of the former, old covenant, and symbolizes it, as a corporeal, earthly, external sanctuary, with concrete holy vessels: the lamp, the table, and the shewbread and, in its Holy of Holies beyond the veil, the golden altar, the ark of the covenant, the cherubim, and the kaporet, all of which are formed according to the model of the things found in heaven. The true sanctuary, founded by God (κύριος) and not by man, is "the greater and more perfect tabernacle, not made with hands (ἀχειροποίητος; Heb 9:11),[42] that is, not of this creation." According to this approach,[43] the earthly sanctuary with all its vessels is a mere copy and inferior product, built according to the pattern that God showed him on the mountain, as opposed to the heavenly sanctuary, which is preexistent, eternal, and true. The earthly temple, and the commandments of the Torah, were given until the time of the restoration, and belong to the "old covenant," while the future temple belongs to the "new covenant." The pattern of the sanctuary is interpreted in a similar way in Stephen's speech in Acts 7:44–50. The sanctuary, which Moses was commanded to make according to the pattern he saw, and which was transferred to the temple of Solomon, is not the true sanctuary of God, because "the Most High does not dwell in houses made with hands" (Acts 7:48), but in heaven.[44] The heavenly Jerusalem and sanctuary are embodied in the Christian church as the "body" of the resurrected Jesus and in the Christian church, and they are well anchored in the Christian tradition.

Similar to the tradition in *Syriac Baruch*, according to the Christian approach the heavenly Jerusalem is preexistent and the work of God's hands: "For we know that if the earthly tent we live in is destroyed, we have a building from

---

[41] Mark 14:58; Acts 7:48; 17:24; Eph 2:11.

[42] Mark 14:58; 2 Cor 5:1; Col 2:11.

[43] This approach utilizes terms borrowed from Platonic philosophy. See Mofatt, *Epistle to the Hebrews*, 105–6; Michaelis, σκηνή, 375, 376; McKelvey, "The New Temple," 38–39, 149, 205–6.

[44] This tradition was interpreted in a similar manner by Christian exegetes. See, e.g., Origen, *Hom. Exod.*, Homilia ix, de Tabernaculo (PG; 12:363).

God, a house not made with hands, eternal in the heavens" (2 Cor 5:1).[45] The mixing of this Jerusalem with the garden of Eden is expressed in Revelation 21–22, which depicts "the new Jerusalem" according to biblical descriptions of the garden of Eden.[46] As opposed to Judaism, which awaits the restoration of an earthly Jerusalem, Christianity saw in the heavenly Jerusalem the homeland and mother of the Christians (Gal 4:26). This Jerusalem is located opposite the earthly and historical Jerusalem, that is, opposite the Jewish Jerusalem; it is superior to it and replaces it. The "new Jerusalem" is the embodiment of the prophetic promises, just as the New Testament is the embodiment of the Old. The destiny of the earthly Jerusalem was sealed with the death of Jesus upon the cross, symbolizing the end of the earthly Jerusalem. With the Parousia, Jesus will bring the new Jerusalem down from heaven.

The picture of the heavenly Jerusalem in *2 Baruch* is made clearer by another passage:

> You, however, if you prepare your minds to sow into them the fruits of the law, he shall protect you in the time in which the Mighty One shall shake the entire creation. For after a short time, the building of Zion will be shaken in order that it will be rebuilt. That building will not remain; but it will again be uprooted after some time and will remain desolate for a time. And after that it is necessary that it will be renewed in glory and that it will be perfected into eternity. We should not, therefore, be so sad regarding the evil which has come now, but much more distressed regarding that which is in the future. For greater than the two evils will be the trial when the Mighty One will renew his creation. (*2 Bar.* 32:1–6)

The author depicts the imminent destruction of the temple. God is about to upset the creation, together with destroying the temple. It will be rebuilt, to be destroyed a second time, and after the second destruction Jerusalem will remain desolate "for a time"—that is, for a fixed period of time until the Eschaton. Thereafter Jerusalem will rise anew, shining and completed forever. This latter renewal will be connected with the renewal of creation, involving a tremendous struggle greater than the two upheavals of the destruction. As in

---

[45] Gal 4:26; Phil 3:20; Heb 11:10; 12:22; 13:14; Rev 3:12.

[46] The description of the heavenly Jerusalem as paradise in Rev 22:1–5 is based upon the Christian identification of the river that goes out of Eden to irrigate the garden, in Gen 2:10, with the spring that shall flow out of the house of God in the future, according to the words of the prophets: Ezek 47:1–12; Joel 4:18; Zech 14:8. On this identification, see n. 31 above. In the *Book of the Cave of Treasures* the garden of Eden is identified with the Christian church. The tree of life is a prefiguration of the cross of Jesus the savior, which is the true tree of life, and which was fixed in the navel of the earth, that is, in Jerusalem (Budge, *The Book of the Cave of Treasures,* 62–63). For more on this, see the chapter on the vision of the forest, the cedar, the vine, and the spring below.

the first passage, the author comforts the people by telling them that they ought not to be saddened by the trouble that is coming to it now, nor by that coming in the future, because there is still awaiting it a greater struggle when God will renew the creation.

How are we to understand the two destructions of Jerusalem and of the temple?

Bogaert[47] suggests identifying the first of these destructions with that of 70 CE since, in keeping with the apocalyptic scenario, the author does not distinguish between it and that of 586 BCE. Thus, the former, imminent and temporary restoration is that of the messianic period. The second destruction marks the end of the messianic period and the complete restoration associated with the building of the heavenly Jerusalem of the World to Come.

I accept Bogaert's distinction in relation to the two periods in the eschatological age, which corresponds well with the Christian approach with regard to the End.[48] However, there is no reason to derive from it the existence of an earthly and concrete temple during the messianic period. Such a temple is not implied by the whole composition, by the other apocalyptic works, or by the Christian sources that anticipate a heavenly Jerusalem and temple.

In my opinion, the two destructions of Zion need to be understood in an explicitly apocalyptic framework. Like the two destructions described in chapters 67–68 in connection with the vision of the bright waters and the black waters, they relate to the destruction of the First Temple in 586 BCE and to that of the Second Temple in 70 CE. Thus, the first destruction is depicted in chapter 67 following the description of the age of Josiah. The author emphasizes, in keeping with the explicit chronological background in which the work is embedded, that that destruction is "the disaster which has befallen Zion *now*" (67:1). The period of the second rebuilding describes the period of the Second Temple, during which the people will be immersed in troubles and danger and may expect destruction by the Hellenistic kingdom, but will be saved and overcome their enemies. In the rebuilt Zion, the order of sacrifices will be renewed, the priests will return to the holy service, and the temple will be famed and widely known among the nations (ch. 68). Following the second destruction Jerusalem will be desolate, but only for a limited period of time. At the end of the apocalyptic drama that will take place at the end of time, the

---

[47] Bogaert, *Apocalypse de Baruch*, 1:423–24; and, in wake of Bogaert, García Martínez, "The 'New Jerusalem' and the Future Temple," 210–11; Kuhnel, *From the Earthly to the Heavenly Jerusalem*, 46.

[48] On the two periods in the Eschaton, see Russell, *The Method and Message of Jewish Apocalyptic*, 291; Daniélou, *Theology of Jewish Christianity*, 377, 388–89; Chs. 27–29, 70–74 in *Syriac Baruch*. And see on this in detail in the next chapter.

creation will be renewed and the new, resplendent and eternal, heavenly Jerusalem will be established (chs. 69ff.).

The destiny of Jerusalem and the temple in this chapter may be understood well against the background of similar descriptions in the New Testament. In the synoptic apocalypse, too, the destruction of Jerusalem is a precondition for the coming of the End (τέλος). Only after "there will not be left here one stone upon another, that will not be thrown down" will there come "the end of the world" (Mark 13; Matt 24; Luke 21).[49] The heavenly Jerusalem, which according to Revelation will appear after the End, is not only different from its predecessor, but a city of a new type, having completely new qualities. It will only appear after the former heavens and the former earth are replaced by a new heaven and a new earth. In general, its appearance involves a new creation: "Then I saw a new heaven and a new earth; for the first heaven and the first earth had passed away, and the sea was no more" (Rev 21:1–2).[50] This Jerusalem is connected with a new creation (καινὴ κτίσις), meaning a renewal of humans and the world by God at the end of days;[51] its appearance will be preceded by the great, final confrontation with Satan and his hosts (Rev 20:7–10). There will be no temple in this heavenly Jerusalem, "for its temple is the Lord God Almighty and the Lamb" (Rev 21:22).

This description helps explain the sense of *2 Bar.* 4:1, in which God informs Baruch that he is about to deliver up the city and to chasten the people "for a time," but the world will not disappear (i.e., will not cease to exist), because the destruction of this world will lead to the establishment of a new creation and the appearance of the heavenly Jerusalem during the second and final period of the eschatological age.

The description of the new creation in Revelation is based upon the description of the redemption of Israel in Isaiah: "For behold, I create new heavens and a new earth; and the former things shall not be remembered or come into mind. But be glad and rejoice forever in that which I create; for behold, I create Jerusalem a rejoicing, and her people a joy" (Isa 65:17–18; 66:22). But for the biblical prophet the new heaven and the new earth are only a metaphor, a "parable" for the renewal of man and the people following the

---

[49] This approach is also expressed in Jesus' speech at the Temple: Mark 12:1–12; Matt 21:33–46; Luke 20, as well as in *2 Bar.* 20:2: "Therefore, I now took away Zion to visit the world in its own time more speedily." On the description of the End in the apocalyptic program in *Baruch,* see in extenso below.

[50] Also in Rev 20:11; cf. Rom 8:19–22; 2 Pet 3:10–13.

[51] Gal 6:15; cf. Mark 10:6; Rom 1:20; Matt 19:4; 19:28; Eph 2:10; 4:22–24; Titus 3:5.

CHAPTER 1: This Is Not the City I Have Engraved on the Palms   35

redemption, and not literally a new creation. As Maimonides explains in *Guide for the Perplexed* II.29:

> Thus describing the state of Exile and its various particularities and thereupon the restoration of the kingdom and the disappearance of all those sorrows, he says, speaking in parables: I shall create another heaven and another earth; and those that are now will be forgotten and their traces effaced. Then he explains this in continuity, saying: When I have said "I shall create," I meant thereby that I shall produce for you, instead of those sorrows and hardships, a state of constant joy and gladness so that the former sorrows will not be remembered.[52]

The anticipation of a new and eternal creation, connected to the heavenly Jerusalem and replacing this world, is portrayed in a similar manner in the pseudepigraphic compositions close to *Baruch*.[53] Such a description also appears in the Qumran writings. *4QFlorilegium*[54] describes an eschatological temple to be created[55] by God in the end of days, "the temple of the Lord" (following Exod 15:17), which is the heavenly temple, identified (on the basis of Nathan's prophecy to David in 2 Sam 7) with the seed of David and his royal throne, which God established forever:

> It is the house which [He will create] for [himself at the E]nd of days, as it is written in the book of [Moses the sanctuary of] the Lord, which Thy hands have established. The Lord will reign forever and ever.... (DJD V [1968]: 53)

This combination of ideas likewise appears in the *Temple Scroll*, which describes a temple that will stand until "the day of blessing" (יום הברכה), when

---

[52] English translation of Maimonides from *The Guide of the Perplexed* (tr. S. Pines; Chicago, 1963), 341. Cf. Radak to Isa 65:17 ("For behold—from the great goodness that there will be, as if the world will be renewed, a new heavens and a new earth") and Shadal, *ad loc*.

[53] *4 Ezra* 7:26–36, 75; *1 En.* 72:1; 45:4–5; 91:16; *Jub.* 1:26–29.

[54] Also known as the Midrash on Nathan's prophecy to David in 2 Sam 7. The text was published in J. M. Allegro, "Further Messianic References in Qumran Literature," *JBL* 75 (1956): 174–87; idem, "Fragments of a Qumran Scroll of Eschatological Midrashim," *JBL* 77 (1958): 350–54; and idem, *DJD* V:53. Cf. Y. Yadin, "4QFlorilegium," *IEJ* 9 (1959): 95–98.

[55] This word is absent in the text. The reconstruction is according to Yadin, *The Temple Scroll*, 1:185. For other readings, see Yadin, "4Q Florilegium," 95; Wise, "4QFlorilegium and the Temple of Adam," 104; D. Dimant, "4QGFlorilegium and the Idea of the Community as Temple," 166, 168; Schürer, *History of the Jewish People*, 3:445–46.

God will create his eternal temple.[56] The day of blessing may refer to the *eucharist* (or *eulogy*; εὐλογία), whose literal meaning is thanksgiving, in which case the intent is possibly to refer to the eschatological *eucharist* (which I discuss at length in part II of this book). Elisha Qimron has suggested, rather than יום הברכה "the day of blessing," reading יום הבריה, the day of creation (בריאה),[57] in which case the eternal temple to be created by God is connected with the new creation, exactly as in *2 Baruch* and the Christian tradition.

A further aspect, which complements and confirms my distinctions regarding the image of the future Jerusalem, is presented by the author of *2 Baruch* when it identifies the eschatological Jerusalem with the temple. While in his description of the historic Jerusalem and the temple he distinguishes between the two, in his depiction of the eschatological Jerusalem the two are perceived as being identical. The transition from the description of the historical temple to that of the eschatological city is made in an allusive manner that is barely felt—namely, by means of a change of grammatical gender from masculine to feminine (i.e., the reference shifts from מקדש, "temple," to עיר, "city"). In the first passage (4:1–6), we are informed about the destiny of the historic Jerusalem (feminine). While it will be turned over to its enemies in the future, he calms him by telling him that this is not the city which he promised to engrave on the palms of his hand. The author then goes on to speak of the temple (masculine), as if God's earlier words were said concerning it and as if it were concerning it that Isaiah's words were directed: "It is not this building . . . that was already prepared from the moment that I decided to create Paradise, and I showed it to Adam . . . to my servant Abraham . . . and to Moses." He then turns once again to speak of the city: "Behold, now it is preserved (*natraya,* in the feminine; i.e., referring to the city) with me—as also Paradise."

The same holds true of the second passage, in 32:1–6. "The building of Zion will be shaken (*nttzyʿ*) in order that it will be rebuilt (*ntbnʾ*). The building will not remain (*mqwʾ hw hw*; in masculine); but it will again be uprooted after some time and will remain desolate (*mqwyʾ*; feminine) for a time. And after that it is necessary that it be renewed in glory and that it be perfected into eternity." In relating to the two historical destructions, the author speaks of the building of Zion, that is, of the temple, in the masculine.

---

[56] Yadin, *Megillat ha-Miqdash,* on xxix 7–10; Wise, "4Florilegium and the Temple of Adam," 113. On the day of blessing, see Yadin, *The Temple Scroll,* 1:183–84; 2:128–29. A heavenly temple is also depicted in 4QShirShabb. See Newsom, *Songs of the Sabbath Sacrifice,* 39–58; Ego, *Im Himmel wie auf Erden,* 13–14.

[57] E. Qimron, "On the Text of the *Temple Scroll*" [Hebrew], in *Leshonenu* 42 (1978): 142. Cf. Yadin, *Temple Scroll,* 354; Wise, "4QFlorilegium," 112. On the connection between the Florilegium and the Temple Scroll, see Yadin, *Temple Scroll,* 1:182; Wise, 112–13.

But when he turns to a description of the eschatological future, he speaks of Jerusalem in the feminine, without even mentioning its name, changing the subject by altering the verb from masculine to feminine participle.

How is this to be understood? Is this an accidental stylistic mix-up, or is there some sort of intention concealed behind this change? In my opinion, the implied transition from a description of the temple building (in masculine) to a description of Jerusalem at the end of days (in feminine) is intentional, meant to emphasizes the idea that the future Jerusalem is identified with the temple, because it is itself the temple. The historical Jerusalem contains a temple that is separate and distinct from the city, but after its destruction the renewed Jerusalem will arise without the temple. In the future there will be no need for the temple, because the city as a whole will be the temple. This identification strengthens even further the idea of the heavenly Jerusalem and explains why, in the entire work, no hope is expressed concerning the future restoration of the temple. This identification between the future Jerusalem and the temple finds explicit expression in *2 Bar.* 59:4: God shows Moses the likeness of Zion with its measurements, which is to be made after the likeness (or pattern) of the present sanctuary.

Such an identification between the eschatological Jerusalem and the temple also appears in apocalyptic works close to *Baruch*. Thus, for example, in the vision of the beasts in the *Ethiopic Book of Enoch* Jerusalem is compared to a house, and the tower that is above it to the temple. The historical Jerusalem is thus always symbolized by a house with a tower. On the other hand, the eschatological Jerusalem is described as a house without a tower (*1 En.* 90:26–29; 33–36). The historical Jerusalem has a temple separate and distinct from the city, whereas in the eschatological Jerusalem there will be only the city itself without a separate temple, because at the end of days it will itself be the temple.[58]

A similar view is widely held also among the circles of the Qumran sect. In the *Temple Scroll* Jerusalem is referred to as "the city of the temple," and in several places it is emphasized that the entire temple city needs to be holy and pure. Jerusalem as a whole is understood as the temple, so that the purity of the city needs to be sustained with the same strictures as are demanded for maintaining the purity of the temple itself (11QT^a xlv 13–14; xlvii 3–6, 10–11). The huge dimensions of this temple and its four-square form emphasizes the identity of the city with the Holy of Holies (1 Kgs 6:20; *m.*

---

[58] On Jerusalem as "house," see also *T. Levi* 10:5. On the temple as tower, see *y. Taʿan.* 2.13 (66a); *Tg. J.* to Isa. 5:2. Cf., in like fashion, the church as tower, in Herm. *Sim.* 13 (LCL 24:253). The image is taken from the parable of the vineyard in Isa 5:2; cf. D. Dimant, "Jerusalem and the Temple," and my discussion of Jeremiah's Apocryphon below in the chapter on the hiding of the temple vessels.

Mid. 4.6).⁵⁹ According to this outlook, the restored Jerusalem is itself the Holy of Holies because, as stated, there is no temple in the eschatological Jerusalem, but the renewed Jerusalem and the new temple are one.

Jerusalem is portrayed in similar fashion in a work known as *The New Jerusalem*, which is similar in contents to the *Temple Scroll*.⁶⁰ The Jerusalem to be established in eschatological time by God Himself is portrayed as a heavenly city, in the form of a square having enormous dimensions.⁶¹ According to these works, the eschatological Jerusalem is embodied in the sect itself, which realizes in its life the cultic and sacral framework of the temple city, which is also itself the future temple—that is, the new, spiritual, heavenly, eternal sanctuary, the "temple of the Lord" to be built by God on the day of blessing/creation. This

---

⁵⁹ On the square form of the altar, see Exod 27:1; 30:2; on the breastplate, Exod 28:16; 39:9; Ezek 41:21; 43:16; 45:2; 48:20. On the four-square form of the temple city, see Yadin, *The Temple Scroll*, 1:188–89. Yadin notes the resemblance on this point between the *Temple Scroll* and Josephus's comments in *J.W.* 6.310, according to which there was a widespread belief on the eve of the destruction, based upon written oracles, that the city and the temple would be conquered after the temple would be four-square. According to Yadin (*Temple Scroll*, 1:197–98), Josephus may have received this belief from the *Temple Scroll!* Even though we do not know what writings are referred to (thus H. St. J. Thackeray in Josephus, *J.W.* 7 [LCL 3:466]), it is difficult to assume that Josephus referred to the sectarian *Temple Scroll*. The square bears diametrically opposite significance in the two passages: in the *Scroll* it symbolizes the ideal model of the temple in the eyes of the sect, while in *J.W.* it is associated with conquest and defeat. In addition, as against Josephus, in the *Scroll* it is not the temple that becomes foursquare, but the city as a whole.

⁶⁰ *The New Jerusalem* is a work written in Aramaic that exists in several copies. See Baillet, Milik, and de Vaux, *Les Petites Grottes de Qumran*, 184–93; J. Licht, "An Ideal Town Plan from Qumran—Description of the New Jerusalem," *IEJ* 29 (1979): 45–58. For bibliography on this work, see Wise, *A Critical Study of the Temple Scroll*, 60 n. 21; Dimant, "The Apocalyptic Interpretation of Ezekiel," 46 n. 58; García Martínez, "The 'New Jerusalem' and the Future Temple," 180 n. 1; Schürer, *History of the Jewish People*, 3:427–29.

⁶¹ On the connection between this work and the *Temple Scroll*, see Dimant, *The Apocalyptic Interpretation of Ezekiel*, 46; García Martínez, "'The New Jerusalem,'" 212–13. On the ideological identity between these descriptions and the views of the sect, see García Martínez, "L'interprétation de la Torah d'Ézéchiel," 450–51; he observes the identity between this Jerusalem and the eschatological temple to be built by God Himself (cf. idem, "The New Jerusalem," 201, 211). On the connection between the *Temple Scroll* and the New Jerusalem, see Wacholder, *The Dawn of Qumran*, 96; Wise, *A Critical Study of the Temple Scroll*, 64–86. On the connection between the *Temple Scroll*, the New Jerusalem, and the *Florilegium*, see García Martínez, "The New Jerusalem," 209–10.

CHAPTER 1: This Is Not the City I Have Engraved on the Palms 39

understanding of the sect receives clear expression in the term "the temple of Adam" that appears in the above-mentioned *Florilegium* and is to be understood in light of 1 Pet 2:4–10:

> Come to him, to that living stone, rejected by men but in God's sight chosen and precious; and like living stones be yourselves built into a spiritual house, to be a holy priesthood, to offer spiritual sacrifices acceptable to God through Jesus Christ. . . . But you are a chosen race, a royal priesthood, a holy nation.[62]

What is the source of this identification of the temple with Jerusalem?

Among the biblical prophets of the return to Zion, there are several expressions of the view that the redeemed Jerusalem will be an expanded realm of the temple. It will be ritually pure, and the entire area will be sanctified with cultic holiness by virtue of its being "the holy city."[63] During the Second Temple period Jerusalem assumes a sacred status by virtue of its perception as an extension of the temple precincts themselves.[64] However, both in the Bible and in the early sources of talmudic literature, which reflect the concepts of the Second Temple period, one is dealing with a historical Jerusalem, whose sanctity derives from that of the temple that stands in its center. Only in later Jewish *midrashim* is the heavenly Jerusalem identified with the temple.[65]

In my opinion, both the sources of this idea and its ideological meaning are to be sought in Christianity. In the new, heavenly Jerusalem that Revelation depicts as descending from heaven completely ready, like a bride adorned for her husband, there is no physical sanctuary because "its temple is the Lord God of Hosts [RSV: Almighty] and the Lamb" (Rev 21:2, 22–23). In other words,

---

[62] See also Rev 21:3: "Behold, the dwelling (σκηνή) of God is with men. He will dwells (σκηνώσει) with them, and they shall be his people, and God himself will be with them." The sanctuary of God within man is in effect an incarnation. Thus, according to John 1:14 "the Word became flesh and dwelt (ἐσκήνωσεν) among us"; cf. Augustine, *Civ.* 17.8 (284–85). See also 1QS v 6–7; viii 5–10; ix 3–9; Gartner, The Temple and the Community, 22-26; McKelvey, The New Temple, 47-50; García Martínez, "The 'New Jerusalem,'" 206; Dimant, "The Apocalyptic Interpretation of Ezekiel", 41ff; L. Gaston, *No Stone On Another,* 163–68. For the various proposed identifications given in the research literature for the term "Temple of Adam," see Wise, "4QFlorilegium and the Temple of Adam," 108; D. Dimant, "4QFlorilegium and the Idea of the Community," 184–85.

[63] According to Isa 52:1, it is forbidden for strangers to enter within it; see also Zech 14:21; Joel 4:17; Obad 1:17; and also Isa 61:5–6; 66:20–21. All the inhabitants of the city will be priests of God: see M. Haran, *Bein Rishonot la-Ḥadashot,* 96–101.

[64] *M. Zebaḥ.* 5.8; *m. Kelim* 1.6–9.

[65] Thus, e.g., *Midr. Bereshit Rabbati* 27.17, composed in the eleventh century. See Zunz, *Ha-Derashot be-Yisra'el,* 144–45; Even-Shmuel, *Midrashei Ge'ulah,* 19–22.

Christ and the church are the new temple, the new sanctuary, that is identical to the heavenly Jerusalem.[66] Jerusalem, which the visionary sees brought down from heaven by God and shining with a brilliant, pure light, is the temple. It too, as in the descriptions from Qumran, is a "foursquare city," a cube of enormous dimensions of equal length, breadth, and height (Rev 21:16).[67] "And the city has no need of sun or moon to shine upon it, for the glory of God is its light, and its lamp is the Lamb" (Rev 21:23); the sun and the moon, the luminaries of the original creation (Gen 1:14), have no place in the second creation, in which Christ and his church are the sun and the moon. Concerning this description H. B. Swete says: "There are no words that can prove more clearly the purely spiritual nature of the viewpoint of John regarding the new Jerusalem."[68]

The identity between the new Jerusalem and the temple is also made clear in light of the use that the author of the Apocalypse makes of the description of the future temple in Ezekiel 40–48. The prophet Ezekiel is taken in a vision of God from Babylonia to the land of Israel, where he is placed upon a high mountain. There he sees before his eyes the future temple as "a structure like a city." He is led by an angel holding a measuring reed to measure the building, which is in the form of a square. Like Ezekiel, the visionary in Revelation is also taken to a high mountain, and here too the one speaking to him holds a measuring stick. However, instead of Ezekiel's temple, which is described according to the characteristics of Solomon's earthly temple and, following the model of fortified temples in Babylonia,[69] is to be built on the earth, the visionary sees the heavenly Jerusalem brought down from heaven by the hand of God. Its form, unlike that in Ezekiel, is a perfect square, whose length, width, and height are equal, like the Holy of Holies in Solomon's temple (1 Kgs 6:20), because this is meant to express the harmony and symmetric perfection of the city.

The identification of the city in Revelation with the temple is likewise reflected in the list of precious stones of the walls of the heavenly Jerusalem.

---

[66] See 1 Cor 3:16–17; 6:19; 2 Cor 6:16; Eph 2:19–22; Phil 3:20; Heb 12:22–24; 1 Pet 2:4–8. This outlook also finds expressions in the Gospels: Jesus is the new sanctuary, an identity based on the description of the rending of the veil: Mark 15:38–39 & par.; John 2:21; Augustine, *Civ.* 17.13 (307–9). See also the chapter on the virgins weaving, below, and cf. *1 En.* 90:32–35: the congregation of the righteous constitutes the future temple.

[67] On the possibility that the author of the NT apocalypse knew the Aramaic description of the New Jerusalem, see Baillet et al., *Les Petites Grottes*, 186.

[68] Swete, *The Apocalypse of St. John*, 295.

[69] See Cooke, *The Book of Ezekiel*, 425.

This list is based upon the names of the stones included in the breastplate of the high priest (Exod 28:17–20; 39:10–13), which also suggests the four-square model for the heavenly city.[70]

It is true that *Syriac Baruch* gives no explicit description of the dimensions of the future city that is to arise in the end of days. But it may be that Baruch's words concerning "the likeness of Zion with its measurements which was to be made after the likeness of the present sanctuary" (*2 Bar.* 59:4), and the relation between his description and that of Ezekiel,[71] allude to a four-square city, as in the works from Qumran and in Revelation.

The point of departure for the identification of the heavenly Jerusalem with the temple and with paradise, and for the idea of the heavenly Jerusalem in general, lies in its rejection of the historical, cultic temple, expressing an explicitly Christian outlook. As noted by Simon: "just as the spiritual temple replaced the old temple, so too does the new Israel come in the place of carnal Israel" (Simon, *Christ and the Temple*, 18).

---

[70] See also Ezek 28:13, where there appears a partial list of the precious stones in the garments of the king of Tyre. This description is based in general upon Isa 54:11, and cf. Tobit 13:16. The garden of Eden is described as a place of precious stones by Ephraem Syrus: G. Anderson, "Celibacy or Consummation," 143.

[71] On the basis of Ezek 40:1–2, the *Apocalypse of Baruch* is placed in the twenty-fifth year of the reign of King Jehoiachin: *2 Bar.* 1:1. Similar to Ezekiel, Baruch is also taken up above the walls of Jerusalem (*2 Bar.* 6:4). Many scholars have questioned the significance of this date and noted the difficulties it presents in relation to the historical data implied by the Bible. Primarily, they wished to make use of it in order to determine the date of writing of the work, but without success. Bogaert notes the connection between this date and the prophecy of Ezek 40–48, describing the temple to be rebuilt after the exile from Babylonia. See Bogaert, *Apocalypse*, 1:287–88; Collins, *The Apocalyptic Imagination*, 170. Nevertheless, according to Bogaert this dating is problematic, since Ezekiel is concerned with the building of Jerusalem, whereas the present work focuses on its destruction.

CHAPTER TWO

The Hiding of the Temple Vessels

2.1. Syriac Baruch 6:7–10

The earthly Jerusalem is to be destroyed, in accordance with a predetermined divine plan. Baruch is lifted by a strong wind above the walls of Jerusalem, which are surrounded by Chaldean soldiers; there he sees four angels standing at the four corners of the city, holding in their hands burning torches with which they are about to set it afire. But another angel descends from heaven and delays the execution of the sentence;[1] he has been sent to speak a word to the earth and to deposit therein what he has been told by God. Baruch sees him descending to the Holy of Holies and removing the veil, the holy ephod,[2] the breastplate,[3] the two tablets of the covenant, the holy garments of the priests, the incense altar,[4] the forty-eight precious stones that were worn by the high priest,[5] and all of the holy vessels of the sanctuary. He then says to the earth in a loud voice:

---

[1] See a similar tradition in Rev 7:1–2; 9:14–15.

[2] *'Efoda Qaddisha*. Charles (*II Baruch*, 495), suggests reading here *'aron* ("ark") rather than *'efod* ("ephod"), on the basis of the LXX to 1 Sam 14:18, in which "the ark of God" is translated by the Greek word τὸ ἐφουδ. Likewise Ginzberg, "Baruch, Apocalypse of," 553. They may have felt the difficulty entailed in the ark's not being mentioned here, and therefore assumed a confusion in the text.

[3] In Syriac: *ḥusia*, meaning both breastplace and *kaporet*. Payne Smith (*A Compendious Syriac Dictionary*, 132), Kahana (*Sefarim Ḥiṣonyim*, 1:369), and Bogaert (*Apocalypse de Baruch*, 2:22) also translate this as *kaporet* ("Mercy Seat"), because the breastplate is alluded to further on. But what reason is there to mention the *kaporet* if the ark of the covenant is not mentioned, since the *kaporet* is located above the ark (Exod 25:17–22)?

[4] *Firma*: censer or incense. Payne Smith, *Compendious Syriac Dictionary*, 445; Bogaert, *Apocalypse de Baruch*, 2:22–23.

[5] According to some scholars, this refers to the stones of the breastplate, but the number of stones there was twelve, corresponding to the number of the tribes of Israel, whose names were inscribed upon it: Exod 28:21; Josephus, *J.W.* 5.232–34; *Ant.* 3.166, 216. It is not clear to me why Baruch uses this number; see Charles, *Apocalypse of Baruch*, 11. According to Ginzberg ("Baruch, Apocalypse of," 553), this number is

Earth, earth, earth,[6] hear the voice of the mighty God, and receive the things which I commit to you, and guard them until the last times, so that you may restore them when you are ordered, so that strangers may not get possession of them. For the time has arrived when Jerusalem will also be delivered up for a time, until the moment that it will be said that it will be restored forever.

The earth opens its mouth to swallow these things up, and the angel allows those holding the torches to begin the work of destroying the walls of the city (*2 Bar.* 6:1–7:2).[7]

The hiding of the temple vessels on the eve of the destruction of the First Temple is, as we shall see, a composite tradition that finds expression in the channels of both Jewish and Christian tradition. What are the unique and characteristic features of each of these channels? And to what extent can they help elucidate the theological and ideological meanings of the present tradition?

According to most scholars, the description of the hiding of the vessels found in *2 Baruch* is anchored in Jewish tradition, expressing the author's anticipation of the restoration of Jerusalem and the temple. In the rebuilt temple of eschatological times, it will again be possible to make use of the cultic objects that were consigned to the earth for a limited time, and possibly even to renew the sacrificial service.[8] As I shall attempt to demonstrate below, our author did in fact utilize Jewish tradition, but he reshaped it in accordance with his own theological tendencies and filled it with new ideological meanings. These new meanings can only be understood in light of the Christian tradition, which may be clearly distinguished from the Jewish tradition by definite lines of demarcation. These lines become apparent if one examines the story of the hiding of the temple vessels in light of two criteria: (1) which vessels were hidden, according to each tradition and (2) for what period of time are they

---

composed of the thirty-six bells that surrounded the hems of the priestly garment, and the twelve precious stones, relying upon *b. Zebaḥ.* 88*b*. Bogaert (*Apocalypse de Baruch*, 2:23) suggests understanding this number on the basis of the number of precious stones mentioned in *L.A.B.* 26:12; and thus also Wolff, *Jeremia im Frühjudentum und Urchristentum*, 72. But it is not clear from this passage in Pseudo-Philo why there are specifically forty-eight stones. According to Ginzberg (*Legends of the Jews*, 6:410 n. 61), the Hebrew text reads "four tiers of stones," which the translator erroneously understood as "forty-eight stones." Josephus mentions precious stones on the garments of the high priest (*J.W.* 6.389).

[6] Based upon Jeremiah 22:29.

[7] See also *2 Bar.* 80:3.

[8] Bogaert, *Apocalypse de Baruch*, 1:422; Wolff, *Jeremia im Frühjudentum und Urchristentum*, 65; de Young, *Jerusalem in the New Testament*, 111; Delling, *Jüdische Lehre und Frömmigkeit*, 65; Nickelsberg, "Paraleipomena of Jeremiah," 74; Collins, *The Apocalyptic Imagination*, 172.

CHAPTER 2: The Hiding of the Temple Vessels

hidden? Or: what principle determines the identity of the hidden vessels in each tradition, and what is the eschatological approach expressed thereby?

According to the tradition in *Baruch*, all of the temple vessels are hidden in the earth, but only the veil, the two tablets of the covenant, the incense altar, and the vestments of the high priest containing the ephod, and the breastplate are mentioned by name. Why is it that these, and no other vessels, are specifically mentioned by name? What is the common denominator among these specific vessels?

This selective list cannot simply be explained in light of the historical reality of the Second Temple period because, in addition to the tablets of the covenant, which were not in fact present in the Second Temple, *Baruch* also enumerates many vessels that were certainly present there until its destruction. These include: the veil, the ephod, the breastplate, and the incense altar;[9] hence, these cannot have been hidden on the eve of the destruction of the First Temple.

The answer to this question may be suggested by noting the location of these vessels: according to the tradition at hand, all these vessels were inside the Holy of Holies, and it was from there that the angel took them to be consigned to the earth. This totally contradicts everything that we know from the Jewish sources relating to the Holy of Holies. From the biblical sources, it would appear that during the First Temple period the Holy of Holies contained only the ark of the covenant with the two tablets[10] and the following objects that were kept with it: the anointing oil, the jar of manna, and the staff of Aaron.[11] Following the disappearance of the ark on the eve of the destruction of the First Temple, nothing was left in the Holy of Holies of the Second Temple. According to Josephus' testimony:

> The innermost part of the temple was twenty ells long, and was separated from the outside also by means of a curtain. *In it there was not found a single thing* (ἔκειτο δ' οὐδὲν ὅλως ἐν αὐτῷ). It was forbidden to enter, forbidden to touch, and forbidden to be seen by all, and was called the Holy of Holies. (*J.W.* 5.219)

Unlike what is implied in *Syriac Baruch*, the priestly vestments were never stored in the Holy of Holies, either during the period of the First Temple or in

---

[9] 1 Macc 4:47–52; 2 Macc 10:3–4; Josephus, *J.W.* 5.210–17, 232–34; 6.387–91.

[10] Exod 25:10–22; Deut 10:1ff.; 1 Kgs 8:9; 2 Chr 5:10.

[11] Exod 30:22–31; 16:33–34; Num 17:23–25. The Israelites were commanded to guard the sanctity of these objects and to place them before the ark of the covenant; the jar of manna was to be kept for future generations as a reminder of the bread that God had fed the Israelites in the wilderness. The staff of Aaron with its blossoms and almonds was meant to serve as an admonition to rebels. Accordingly, they were placed within the Holy of Holies together with the ark of the covenant.

that of the second.¹² As for the incense altar, it is explicitly stated that it was located in the Holy Place, in front of the veil separating the Holy from the Holy of Holies, together with the table for the shewbread and the lampstand.¹³ These objects. which were in everyday ritual use, could not have been in the Holy of Holies, which was entered by the high priest alone, once a year.¹⁴

In my opinion, the location of these items in the Holy of Holies is not accidental; a similar tradition, locating the incense altar in the Holy of Holies, appears in Heb 9:4; in both cases, this location reflects explicit theological tendencies. The author of Hebrews distinguishes between the first, external sanctuary, which is called Holy (ἄγια; 9:2, 6, 8), and the second, inner sanctuary, which is called the Holy of Holies (ἄγια ἁγίων; 9:3, 7). The former, containing the lampstand and the table with the shewbread, belongs to the old covenant, to the present era, in which priests offer meal-offerings and burnt-offerings, performing the external commandments of the Torah. The second sanctuary, by contrast, in which there is "a golden altar of incense and the ark of the covenant" (Heb 9:4) belongs to the new covenant, to a future age. The latter is the more perfect sanctuary, not created by human hands, into which the Messiah will enter once and for all in order to attain eternal redemption. This sanctuary is a heavenly one, and the entrance into it signifies the end of the first sanctuary (9:8–10). According to the Christian approach, the Holy of Holies in which these vessels are found is no more than a prefiguration, an anticipatory image of the true Holy of Holies, of the heavenly Jerusalem which is itself entirely a Holy of Holies. The celestial Holy of Holies, embodied in the Christian church, is to be established in the future, in the age of final salvation; the conduct of its cult will require only those vessels that, according to this tradition, were hidden away.

Thus, instead of the veil of the historical temple, which was rent upon the death of Jesus (Mark 15:38 and parallels), the heavenly temple will contain the new veil, the flesh of the Messiah, opening to the believer a new way for identification with his body (Heb 10:20). The two tablets of the covenant are

---

¹² During the First Temple period, the priestly vestments were left in the chambers adjacent to the inner courtyard (see Ezek 42:14; 44:19; Lev 6:4). During the Second Temple period, these garments were left in the *birah* (baris) built by Johanan Hyrcanus north of the temple, for this specific purpose. From the time of Herod on, the garments were kept in the Antonia fortress (Josephus, *Ant.* 15.403–8; 18.93; 20.6–16).

¹³ Exod 25:23–39; 26:33–35; Josephus, *J.W.* 5.5; Philo, *Mos.* 2.101–5; Josephus, *Ant.* 3.147; *Ag. Ap.* 2.106. Cf. Renard, "Autel," 1271–72; Westerholm, "Tabernacle," 702.

¹⁴ Josephus, *J.W.* 5.237; Moffatt, *Epistle to the Hebrews*, 114.

CHAPTER 2: The Hiding of the Temple Vessels   47

the symbol of the old and new covenant together,[15] while the garments of the High Priest will in the future serve the Messiah "through the greater and more perfected tabernacle, not made with hands," when he will enter the Holy of Holies once and for all in order to secure eternal redemption (Heb 9:11–12).[16] Of particular importance is the incense altar, symbolizing the prayers of the holy ones that ascend heavenwards together with the incense (Rev 8:2; Luke 1:9ff.). The rising smoke of the incense symbolizes the link between the believer in this world and paradise, known in the apocalyptic and in early Christian literature by its aromatic spices, which are embodied in Jesus. The incense expresses the longing to enter Paradise once again, through Jesus—the incense sacrifice—and the assurance of attaining the resurrection and eternal life in it in the future.[17]

It is significant that the vessels hidden in the earth did not include the altar for the burnt-offerings, but only the incense altar, upon which it was explicitly forbidden to offer animal sacrifices (Exod 30:1–10; 37:25–28). In the eschatological temple there will be no animal sacrifices, but only the incense offering.[18]

This intention is likewise made clear by the use of the anachronistic term, משכן ("sanctuary" or "tabernacle"). The use of this expression by the author, like its use in the Christian tradition, is intended to emphasize the direct connection between the sanctuary made by Moses in the desert, according to the heavenly pattern he saw and in accordance with God's commandments, and the future heavenly sanctuary. This sanctuary transcends the historical temple built by Solomon, "the temple made by human hands," and is opposed

---

[15] According to Rev 11:19, the ark of the covenant also has a place in the heavenly sanctuary (Wolff, *Jeremia*, 70). The ark of the covenant is a prefiguration of the gospel; see Daniélou, *Sacramentum Futuri*, 235, 242. Cf. the tradition intertwined in *Liv. Pro.*, below.

[16] On the importance of the priestly garments, see *Paralipomena Jeremiae*, below. On the significance of the breastplate in the Christian tradition, see Budge, *The Book of the Cave of Treasures*, 236–37; Ephraem Syrus, *Hymnes sur le Paradis*, 15.7–8 (189–90).

[17] On the use of incense in Christianity, see H. Leclercq, "Encencoir," and my article "The Aromatic Fragrance of Paradise in the *Greek Life of Adam and Eve* and the Christian Origin of the Composition" *NovT* (forthcoming). On spices in paradise, see Part II of this volume.

[18] As follows also from Baruch's dirge in 35:4. See a similar outlook to this in *L.A.B.*: Zeron, "The System of the Author of the *Antiquities*," 177–78; Renard, "Autel," 1278, similar to the "incense brazier" in the Judaean desert sect: see 1QM ii 5; 1QS iii 11; viii 9; 11QTemple xiv 7; xv 13; xvi 10; xxii 8; xxxiv 14; etc. On the place of these cultic vessels in the heavenly temple, see 11QShirShabb, which mentions the sanctuary, the veil, the breastplate, and the ephod; Newsom, *Songs of the Sabbath Sacrifices*, 39–58.

to the Second Temple, which from the outset was seen as improper.[19] In this tradition, the temple for which the vessels are preserved is the heavenly temple, "the sanctuary of God with human beings" (Rev 21:3), identical to the new Jerusalem, which is the Christian church.

This intention becomes fully clear in light of the eschatological perspective. The vessels are consigned to the earth so that it may protect them until "the latter times." The author explains when these times will come: "For the time has arrived when Jerusalem will also be delivered up for a time, until the moment that it will be said that it will be restored forever." As I attempted to demonstrate in the previous chapter, this final and perfect restoration refers to the heavenly Jerusalem, which will be established following the end of this world, upon the second coming of Christ. The vessels are hidden specifically within the soil of Jerusalem, where the second appearance of Jesus is to occur.[20]

2.2. The Jewish Tradition

To what extent is the description of the hiding of the vessels in *2 Baruch* rooted in Jewish soil?

The tradition concerning the hiding of the cultic vessels on the eve of the destruction of the First Temple developed in two branches of Judaism: the Palestinian and the Jewish-Hellenistic. According to the Palestinian tradition, documented in various strata of the talmudic literature, Josiah hid the holy ark so that it would not be carried away to Babylonia; together with it were hidden the "jar of manna and the vial of the anointing oil, the staff of Aaron with its blossoms and almonds, and the case in which the Philistines sent the guilt-offering to the God of Israel."[21]

This tradition developed in wake of the mystery surrounding the destiny of the holy ark, which is not mentioned among those objects taken as booty by the Babylonians upon the destruction of the temple (2 Kgs 25:13–17; Jer 52:17–23), but which was conspicuous by its absence in the Second Temple.[22] Against this background, an etiological legend was woven offering an explana-

---

[19] Stephen's speech, Acts 7:44–50.

[20] See *Paraleipomena Jeremiou* 9:20 for the appearance upon the Mount of Olives; cf. Daniélou, *The Theology of Jewish Christianity*, 1:269, and the appendix to the present volume.

[21] See *m. Šeqal.* 6.1; *y. Šeqal.* 6.1 (49c); *y. Soṭah* 8.3 (22c); *t. Soṭah* 13.1; *t. Yoma* 3.7; *b. Hor.* 12a; *b. Ker.* 5b; *b. Yoma* 52b; 53b; *Baraita de-Melekhet ha-Mishkan* 7 (ed. Ish-Shalom; 49).

[22] According to Haran ("The Disappearance of the Ark," 47), the holy ark was removed and disappeared in the days of Manasseh, who in its place put statues of the Asherah and various cultic objects.

CHAPTER 2: The Hiding of the Temple Vessels 49

tion to this riddle: namely, that the ark was hidden on the eve of the destruction, together with those vessels connected with it. A common talmudic tradition includes the ark of the covenant among those five things that were not found in the Second Temple as opposed to the First Temple: the fire, the holy ark, the Urim and Tummim, the anointing oil, and the Holy Spirit.[23] Unlike *Syriac Baruch*, this Palestinian tradition only speaks of those cultic objects that were in fact missing in the Second Temple, thus reflecting an essentially historical reality, according to which the ark of the covenant disappeared on the eve of the destruction of the First Temple.[24] The explanation offered for this situation likewise reflects a genuine human surprise that was widely felt during the Second Temple period in light of the absence of the ark and related vessels. The fact that this tradition attributes the act of hiding to Josiah also suggests its close connection to the historical story, in which the bringing of the holy ark into the temple by Josiah was explicitly connected with the Passover that he celebrated in Jerusalem (2 Chr 35:3).

In contrast with *Syriac Baruch*, in the earlier, primary talmudic tradition, the hiding of the vessel is not connected with any eschatological context. Such a context only appears in the late, post-Babylonian midrashic tradition, although even there the restoration of the vessels is connected with the earthly temple and the historical Jerusalem:

> When the temple was destroyed the lampstand was hidden, and this was one of five things that was hidden—the ark and the lampstand and the fire and Holy Spirit and the cherubs. And when the Holy One blessed be He will return in His

---

[23] See *y. Ta'an.* 2.1 (65a); *b. Yoma* 21b, 52b; *t. Yoma* 3.7; *Num. Rab.* 15.10; *'Abot R. Nat.*, Version I, ch. 41 (ed. Schechter; 67); Maimonides, *MT, Beit ha-Beḥirah* 4.1. The talmudic tradition contains a dispute among the Sages regarding the destiny of the ark; according to one view, it was exiled to Babylonia together with the holy fire and the Torah, while according to another it was hidden in the chamber of the woodshed: *y. Šeqal.* 6.1 (49c). Cf. Kalami and Purvis, "The Hiding of the Temple Vessels," 680, 685.

[24] An exception to this is the tradition in *'Abot R. Nat.*, Version I, ch. 41, in which the priestly garments and those of the anointed priest are enumerated among the hidden vessels, as in the tradition in *Syriac Baruch*. This detail suggests a late date, leading one to assume that it was already influenced by the Christian tradition. On the late date of the midrash *'Abot R. Nat.*, see J. Efron, "The Hasmonean Kingdom and Simeon ben Shatah," 192–93; idem, "The Bar Kokhba War," 97–98; and Ben-Shalom, "Selected Historical Issues in *Avot de-Rabbi Nathan*," 157–58. According to Kister, even though one is dealing here with a work having a very long history of formation and its origins are very early, "in its present form the work is quite late; centuries separate between the beginning of its editing and Versions I and II in their extant form" (M. Kister, ed., *Aboth de-Rabbi Nathan* [S. Schechter edition; Hebrew; New York & Jerusalem, 1997], 10, 11–12).

mercies and rebuild His house and his sanctuary, he will return them to their place to rejoice Jerusalem. (*Numbers Rabbah* 15.10)[25]

The Jewish-Hellenistic tradition is represented in the 2 Macc 1:10–2:18. In it, the people in Jerusalem send a letter to Aristobulus[26] and the Jews of Egypt, calling upon them to celebrate the holiday of Hanukkah and, in order to emphasize the feeling of miraculous salvation that occurred to the temple during the days of Antiochus Epiphanes, invoking the story of a miracle that happened to Nehemiah during the period of the return to Zion, namely that he succeeded in lighting fire on the rebuilt altar by means of the fire that had been hidden by the priests before going into exile in Babylonia. In the same context, the author of this epistle also cites a tradition concerning Jeremiah, according to which the prophet had commanded the exiles to bring some of this fire with them to Babylonia, as well as asking them to bring the tent and the ark to the mountain from which Moses had seen the promised land. After ascending the mountain he found a cave, in which he placed the holy ark, the tent, and the incense altar and sealed off the entrance. Those who followed him were unable to find the way there, and Jeremiah chastised them, saying that the place would remain unknown until God gathered his people with mercy. Only then would

---

[25] *Tanḥ., Bahaalotkha* 11.44–45 (ed. Buber; 50); *Masekhet Kelim,* in Jellinek, *Bet ha-Midrasch,* 2:88–91. According to this tradition, Baruch and Zedekiah hid away David's harps and lyres so they might not fall into the hands of the enemy, and they remain hidden "until the day that they [Israel] . . . return to their former station and enjoy eternal honor and respect . . . when they find the man, David son of David is his name, and there will be revealed to him the silver and gold, when all of Israel will be ingathered and go up together to Jerusalem." Cf. other traditions: Ginzberg, *Legends of the Jews* 4:320–21; Milik, "Notes de l'épigraphie et Topographie Palestiniennes," 568–71. Later midrashim also contain a tradition connecting the rediscovery of these vessels to Elijah. Cf. *Pirkei Mashiah* and *Yemot haMashiah* in Even-Shmuel, *Midrashei Ge'ulah,* 337; but see in earlier midrashim *Mek. de-Rashbi, Beshalah* 16.15 (ed. Epstein and Melamed; 116); *Mek. de-Rabbi Yishma'el, Beshalaḥ* 5 (ed. Horowitz and Rabin; 172).

[26] This is the second epistle found at the beginning of 2 Maccabees. An entire branch of scholarship deals with the authenticity of this epistle, its date, and its connection with the first epistle. For various opinions, see Kraft & Nickelsberg, *Early Judaism and Its Modern Interpreters,* 320–21; Wolff, *Jeremia,* 20 n. 21. Recently there is a tendency to date both epistles to the time of composition of 2 Maccabees; see Wacholder, *Eupolemus,* 234. In any event, even according to those who date it late, the time of the epistle precedes the tradition of *Syriac Baruch.* Aristobulus is identified with the Hellenistic Jewish philosopher who wrote during the middle of the second century BCE. See Collins, "Aristobulus"; A. Kasher, *Yehudei Mizrayim ha-Hellenistit veha-Romit* (Tel Aviv, 1979), 22, 66.

God disclose these things and show the glory of God and the cloud that had been revealed to Moses (2 Maccabees 2:1–8).

According to the author of the epistle, these traditions were found "in books" (2 Mac 2:1). To what books does he refer? According to the manuscripts,[27] there are two possible ways of reading this verse. According to one reading ("and it was found in the books that Jeremiah the prophet...." [εὑρίσκεται δὲ ἐν ταῖς ἀπογραφαῖς Ιερεμίας ὁ προφήτης ...]), the prophet Jeremiah is the subject of the sentence, while the "books" are anonymous. This has led scholars to conclude that the text alludes to a tradition cited by Eupolemus, the Jewish writer who lived in the mid-second century BCE, parts of whose book, *Concerning the Kings of Judah*, were preserved by Eusebius. According to this tradition, Jeremiah guarded (κατασχεῖν) the ark and the tablets that were in it so that they would not be brought to Babylonia together with the gold, silver, and brass that Nebuchadnezzar (*nabouchodnosoros*) had brought with him as booty after he conquered Jerusalem.[28]

But according to another manuscript version, the reading is "and there were found in the books of Jeremiah the prophet..." (εὑρίσκεται δὲ ἐν ταῖς ἀπογραφαῖς Ιερεμίου τοῦ προφήτου ...), suggesting that the "books" are written by Jeremiah. Hence, the passage may allude to an apocryphal book ascribed to Jeremiah, upon which the tradition drew or whose author made use of a widespread tradition about Jeremiah.

There is, however, a certain similarity between the tradition of Eupolemus and that of 2 Maccabees, in that both traditions attribute the concern for the temple vessels to Jeremiah rather than to Josiah, as is done in the Palestinian

---

[27] W. Kappler and R. Hanhart, *Maccabaeorum Liber II* (Göttingen, 1959), 51.

[28] Eusebius, *Praep. ev.* (PG 21, ix, col. 757); M. Stern, *Greek and Latin Authors on Jews and Judaism*, 160. Eusebius cites the tradition concerning Eupolemus from the first century BCE Greek historian, Alexander Polyhistor. On Polyhistor's degree of reliability for the sources he cited, see Stern, *Greek and Latin Authors*, 157; Wacholder, *Eupolemus*, 44–51; Fallon, "Eupolemus," 861; Giblet, "Eupoleme et l'Historiographie," 550; Efron, "Daniel and his Three Friends," 70. According to many scholars, Eupolemus is to be identified with Judah Maccabee's messenger to Rome mentioned in 1 Macc 8:17ff. and in 2 Macc 4:11 (Josephus, *Ant.* 12:415; Fallon, "Eupolemus," 862–63; Wacholder, *Eupolemus*, 4–25; Goldstein, *II Maccabees*, 182; Guttman, *Ha-Sifrut ha-Yehudit ha-Hellenistit*, 75–78; Hengel, *Judaism and Hellenism*, 932–93; Giblet, "Eupolemus," 552). According to Wacholder, the same Eupolemus may have been the author of the epistle in 2 Maccabees that was sent from Judaea, the Gerousia, and all the Jews in Judah to the Jews in Egypt, but was actually written to Aristobulus by a Greek author in the name of Judah Maccabee (see Wacholder, *Eupolemus*, 234; idem, "The Letter from Judah Maccabee to Aristobulus," 122–32).

tradition.²⁹ But this similarity may derive from the fact that both traditions come from the common soil of the Jewish-Hellenistic tradition rather than because of any reliance of the tradition in 2 Maccabees upon that of Eupolemus.

On the other hand, the differences between these two traditions are even greater. Eupolemus' tradition is a rather limited one, according to which Jeremiah only held the ark and the tablets; it does not refer at all to their hiding. By contrast, the tradition in 2 Maccabees is far more developed: it mentions, in addition to the ark (without the tablets), the tent and incense altar, it specifies the hiding place of the vessels and the act of hiding by Jeremiah; and it determines the period of time until which the vessels are to be hidden. The tradition in 2 Maccabees thus differs both from that of Eupolemus and from the Palestinian tradition, whether in terms of the identity of the hidden vessels or in terms of the existence of an eschatological aspect.

As for the identity of the vessels, in addition to the ark, the tradition in 2 Maccabees mentions the tent of meeting and the incense altar. Like the ark of the covenant, the destiny of the tent of meeting (σκηνή) was unknown. After it served Israel as a portable sanctuary during its wanderings, Solomon brought it to the temple in Jerusalem (1 Kgs 8:4; 2 Chr 5:5), but there is no sign of its presence during the period of the First Temple, nor is it mentioned among the temple vessels during the Second Temple period. Like the ark of the covenant, traditions developed surrounding it, explaining its absence by having it also hidden away; according to the talmudic tradition, it was already hidden upon the construction of the First Temple,³⁰ whereas according to the extant

---

²⁹ Unlike the Palestinian Jewish tradition, the Hellenistic tradition attributes the hiding of the vessels to Jeremiah and not to Josiah. But it seems to me that the Palestinian tradition is the original one. The Bible does not know anything about the hiding of the ark by Jeremiah; according to what is related in it, Jeremiah, who was chained when Nebuzaradan arrived in Jerusalem, would have been unable to save it (Jer 39:14; 40:4). Jeremiah's prophecy about the days in which "they shall no more say, 'The ark of the covenant of the Lord.' It shall not come to mind, or be remembered, or be missed; it shall not be made again" (Jer 3:16) does not refer to an actual hiding of the ark or a rejection of the cult, as has been suggested by some scholars, but must be understood against the background of the prophet's demand for a spiritual metamorphosis of Israel. Jeremiah describes here the period following the redemption, in which a spiritual change will occur and, instead of the ark of the covenant, the concrete object that symbolized the throne of God, all of Jerusalem will become a kind of throne of the Lord and all the nations will stream to it in the name of the Lord. One may assume that the connection of this tradition to Jeremiah originated in the bosom of Egyptian Jewry, in whose consciousness the prophet Jeremiah, who was exiled and died there, enjoys a special place.

³⁰ *T. Sota* 13.1; *b. Sota* 9a; and cf. *'Abot R. Nat.*, Version I, ch. 41 (ed. Schechter; 67).

CHAPTER 2: The Hiding of the Temple Vessels

Hellenistic tradition it was hidden by Jeremiah. Its mention does not deviate from the principle found at the basis of the Palestinian tradition, that includes only those vessels that were not actually found in the Second Temple.

An exception to this is the incense altar, whose presence in the Second Temple is well documented (1 Macc 1:21; 4:47–52; Josephus, *J.W.* 5.216). In my opinion, there is reasonable ground for assuming that this is a late addition, possibly added by a Christian copyist with the aim of adjusting the tradition in 2 Maccabees to Christian traditions. Support for this assumption is to be found in the fact that the incense altar is not mentioned at the beginning of this tradition, which mentions the tent and the ark alone: "and it was in the book that the prophet commanded by the word which came to him, concerning the tent and the ark, that they go together after him" (2 Macc 2:4).[31]

The tradition in 2 Maccabees is unique among the Jewish traditions on this subject in terms of the eschatological viewpoint that it expresses. But unlike the tradition in *Syriac Baruch*, it does not connect the destiny of the vessels to the end of time or the appearance of the Messiah. According to this tradition, the vessels will be hidden until "God will gather his people" (ἐπισυναγωγὴν τοῦ λαοῦ)—that is, until the ingathering of the exiles takes place. Thus, the eschatological aspect in 2 Maccabees gives expression to the anticipation of realization of national, earthly redemption on the historical plane. The earthly dimension of this expectation is further emphasized by the context in which it is incorporated in this tradition; notwithstanding the fact that it emphasizes the miraculous element in this event, it appears within the framework of a letter calling upon the Jews of Egypt to celebrate the holiday of Hanukkah, which is entirely rooted in the historical dimension and symbolizes the joy of national and religious victory over Hellenism and paganism. The victory over Antiochus Epiphanes and the purification of the temple led to anticipation of the beginning of the redemption and the ingathering of the Exiles: "and we waited upon God, that he would quickly have mercy on us and gather us from all the lands under heaven to the holy place, for he will redeem us from great evils, and the place he will purify" (2 Macc 2:18).

---

[31] See Wolff, *Jeremia*, 24. One must remember that this work, along with the LXX as a whole, was preserved within the walls of the church and that the Christians did not refrain from interspersing additions and altering readings. In *Josippon*, based upon 2 Maccabees, only the ark is mentioned (see below, n. 32); this may preserve the original tradition of 2 Maccabees. See also the surprise felt in this connection, regarding the mention of the incense altar, by Kalimi and Purvis, "The Hiding of the Temple Vessels," 680 n. 4.

A version similar to that in 2 Maccabees, albeit much later, appears in the *Book of Josippon* (Josephus Gorionides).[32] In describing the building of the altar during the return to Zion, he incorporates the tradition of the discovery of the holy fire that had been hidden by Jeremiah before he went into exile, unlike the ark, which he had hidden in a cave on Mount Nebo. The main difference between this tradition and that in 2 Maccabees pertains to the eschatological aspect. Jeremiah replies to the priests who pursued him, "that the place will not be known until I come with Elijah the servant of God. Then we shall return the ark to its place to the Holy of Holies, under the cherubs." This tradition seems based primarily upon the story in 2 Maccabees, but it also draws upon the later talmudic tradition, in which eschatological anticipations are connected with the appearance of Elijah.

A tradition concerning the hiding of the vessels from temple times is also attributed to the Samaritans. Josephus (*Ant.* 18.85–87) tells of a Samaritan prophet during the period of Pilate's procuratorship who promised to reveal the location of the holy vessels that had been hidden on Mount Gerizim by Moses. The commotion that resulted was forcibly suppressed by the Roman leader, who was held accountable for this in Rome. The most striking difference between this tradition and that in 2 Maccabees is that the hiding of the holy vessels is connected with the name of Moses rather than with that of Jeremiah. It follows that the Samaritan tradition does not refer to the vessels that were used in the First Temple, but to those used in the desert sanctuary, which were hidden, not on Mount Nebo, but on Mount Gerizim.

But like 2 Maccabees, the Samaritan tradition also involves an eschatological aspect: the discovery of the vessels on Mount Gerizim is connected with a redemptive act that the Samaritan prophet wishes to bring about, explaining both the massive response to his call and Pilate's firm reaction. On the other hand, the response of both the masses and the Roman leader emphasizes the earthly significance of this redemption, anchored in a definite historical context. Hence there is reasonable basis for assuming, as suggested by Kalimi and Purvis,[33] that this was originally a Jewish tradition, which the Samaritans utilized in their polemic with Judaism, altering it accordingly.

---

[32] Flusser, *Sefer Josippon*, 7:43–46. The *Josippon* was composed in southern Italy during the tenth century; see Zunz, *ha-Derashot be-Yisrael*, 68–69; Flusser, *Josippon*, 5:13–20. Among other things, the author relied upon Josephus's *Antiquities*, the apocryphal literature, and aggadic tradition (Flusser, *Josippon*, 24; Zeitlin, *Second Book of Maccabees*, 39–40). For the Arabic source of this work, see S. Sela, "*The Book of Josippon* and Parallel Sources in Arabic and Judeo-Arabic" [Hebrew], Doctoral Dissertation, Tel Aviv, 1991.

[33] Kalimi & Purvis, "The Hiding of the Temple Vessels," 684–85.

From the sum total of these traditions, it follows that there were widespread stories in Judaism during the Second Temple period concerning the hiding of the temple vessels,[34] similar to widespread traditions in the ancient Near East generally concerning the hiding or burying of cultic vessels.[35]

What is the relation of the tradition in *Baruch* to the Jewish tradition?

The tradition in *2 Baruch* seems to be based upon the Jewish tradition concerning the hiding of the temple vessels on the eve of the destruction of the First Temple, particularly upon the Jewish-Hellenistic tradition as it finds expression in the Second Book of Maccabees. These two traditions connect the act of hiding the vessels with the circle of Jeremiah stories rather than those of Josiah, as in the talmudic tradition, and both traditions give expression to the eschatological aspect.

On the other hand, there is a profound difference between the two traditions in terms of their ideological identity, as reflected in the two above-mentioned aspects. In the Jewish tradition, only those temple vessels that were missing in the Second Temple are hidden, their disappearance being explained by their being hidden by Jeremiah on the eve of the destruction. The excitement felt in the Hellenistic diaspora in wake of the Hasmonean victory and the purification of the temple may have engendered a flowering of eschatological hopes for the restoration of the ark of the covenant and the tablets that had been lacking in the temple. By contrast, the Jews of the land of Israel, who were closer to the arena of events and were participants or direct witnesses to the historical action, remained rooted upon the firm soil of concrete reality, and were reconciled to the lack of the ark and the tablets and a certain inferiority of the Second Temple compared to its predecessor. However, even the eschatological elements present in the Jewish-Hellenistic tradition relate to hopes for an earthly and national redemption, hopes that were widespread among the Jewish people during the period of the Second Temple and focused upon the ingathering of the exiles. We find nothing in these ancient Jewish tradition connecting the restoration of the temple vessels with the longed-for Eschaton or with the full and final establishment of the heavenly Jerusalem, such as appear in *Syriac Baruch*.

But the major difference between the two traditions relates to their historical context. The Jewish tradition is anchored in the historical reality of the Second Temple period, during which people struggled with the absence of the ark and the tablets of the covenant; the explanation given for this puzzle is likewise rooted in the possible historical reality of the First Temple period. For

---

[34] Cf. 1 Macc 4:46; B. Z. Luria, *Megillat ha-Neḥoshet;* Collins, "The Hidden Vessels," 112–16; Goldstein, *II Maccabees,* 182.

[35] Herzer, *Die Paralipomena Jeremiae,* 49.

that reason, the hiding of the vessels is associated in the Jewish tradition with such historical figures as Josiah and Jeremiah. The context in which the tradition is incorporated in 2 Maccabees (in an epistle that reports the hope of victory and that relates to the miracle of the freeing of the temple) exemplifies the author's point of view: notwithstanding that the Second Temple lacks certain central cultic vessels, it still remains the temple chosen by God, who saved it and shall in the future restore what is lacking there. On the other hand, the tradition in *Syriac Baruch* is integrated within an imaginary pseudo-historical drama unrelated to historical reality. The cultic vessels mentioned there could not have been hidden on the eve of the destruction of the First Temple, since most of them were present in the Second Temple. This tradition has nothing to do with the historical reality of the temple or its vessels during the Second Temple period; it is focused entirely on its theological significance and intention. These vessels were deliberately chosen on the basis of their location and their being needed in the heavenly Jerusalem, which Christians believed would be established at the End of Time and identified with the "Holy of Holies." Moreover, the overt plot is intended to create the impression that the vessels used in the historical temple in Jerusalem during the Second Temple period were unfit, as the original vessels had been concealed on the eve of the destruction of the First Temple. Their remaining hidden until the Eschaton thus creates a kind of historical and ideological continuity between the First Temple and the heavenly temple.

This tradition, like its predecessor, expresses an outlook that delegitimates the religious validity of the cult in the Second Temple and transfers the national hopes and expectations associated with the temple vessels from the historical plane to transhistorical expectations, involving an age of salvation that will come about with the Parousia and the establishment of the heavenly Jerusalem. In brief, the tradition contained in *Baruch* is evidently based upon Jewish tradition, but has been altered in accordance with its own purposes. The intentions and meanings alluded to in it shall become clear in light of the Christian traditions that developed on the same theological soil and in the same ideological climate.

2.3. Paralipomena Jeremiou

The tradition closest to that of *2 Baruch* appears in a Christian work known as *Paralipomena Jeremiou* ("The Remaining Words of Jeremiah"),[36] rooted in the same literary and historical context. At God's command, Jeremiah and Baruch ascend the walls of the city at night and from there see angels from heaven holding torches in their hands, about to destroy the city.

---

[36] On this work, its Christianity, and its relation to *2 Baruch*, see the Appendix.

Jeremiah appeals to the angels to delay their plan until he can speak to God. As the city is about to be delivered to its enemies and the people to go into exile in Babylonia, Jeremiah turns to God and asks, "What do you want me to do with the holy vessels of the service?" God responds that he should deliver them to the earth (and to the altar),[37] saying:

> Hear, Earth, the voice of your Creator, who formed you in the abundance of waters, who sealed you with seven seals for seven epochs; and after this you will receive your ornaments. Guard the vessels of the temple until the coming of the beloved.

Jeremiah and Baruch then enter the holy place and, after taking the holy cultic vessels, place them in the ground (and the altar) as they were instructed by God (3:7–8, 14).

There is great similarity between these two traditions: in both, the scene occurs against the background of the destruction of Jerusalem and the appearance of the four angels, and in both cases the vessels are placed in the earth, with the instruction to keep them there until the Eschaton. The tradition in the *Paralipomena* differs from that in *Syriac Baruch* in only a few details: instead of the angel hiding the vessels, in the *Paralipomena* the act of hiding is attributed to Jeremiah himself.[38] As against the enumeration of the hidden vessels in *Baruch*, in the *Paralipomena* "the holy vessels of the cult" are only mentioned in a general way; there is also a fairly extensive speech by Jeremiah to the earth before turning over the vessels that is entirely absent in *Baruch*. In my opinion, these differences are insufficient to lessen the strong relationship

---

[37] Thus according to the Ethiopic MS (eth): καὶ τῷ θυσιαστηρίῳ. The word καί is to be understood as an explicative. Thus Herzer, *Die Paralipomena Jeremiae*, 11, 51; Harris, *The Rest of the Words*, 49; Kraft and Purintun, *Paralipomena Jeremiou*, 17 n. 10; Thornhill, "The Paraleipomena of Jeremiah," 823 n. 2. According to Basset's translation of the Ethiopic MS, the vessels were consigned to the earth and to the temple (R. Basset, "Le Livre de Baruch," 8).

[38] Like the tradition in 2 Maccabees. On the basis of this similarity, scholars have suggested that the author of *Paralipomena* was influenced by 2 Maccabees. Thus Harris, *The Rest of the Words*, 23; Herzer, *Die Paralipomena Jeremiae*, 49, 77; Ginzberg, *Legends of the Jews*, VI. 410 n. 61. Nickelsberg ("Narrative Traditions," 64–65) concluded from this that this tradition preserved earlier elements than that in *Baruch*; cf. the critique by Herzer, *Die Paralipomena Jeremiae*, 76–77, of this approach. According to Robinson ("4 Baruch," 415, 417), all four traditions—that in 2 Macc, *Syriac Baruch*, *Liv. Pro.*, and the *Paralipomena*—are based upon an earlier source, which is to be identified with "the books" in 2 Maccabees.

existing between the two traditions, indicative of a common cultural and ideological milieu.[39]

Jeremiah hides the vessels in the holy soil of the altar, or places them on the altar, thereby allowing "the Lord" (κύριος) to take them to heaven. It seems to follow from this that he gave the vessels to heaven.[40] Hence they need to be guarded for the heavenly temple, and will remain there until "the coming of the beloved": ἕως τῆς συνελεύσεως τοῦ ἠγαπημένου.[41] The compound word συνέλευσις, which generally means "gathering, assembly, connection, sharing, cooperation," is to be understood here as ἔλευσις—that is, "coming," referring to the future appearance of the Messiah, or to the second coming of Christ, i.e., the Parousia[42] that will take place at the end of time, in "the final times."

"The beloved" (ἠγαπημένος—perfect passive participle) is a title of Jesus.[43] His second coming will take place after the opening of the seven seals with which the earth is sealed, at the end of seven times. The seals are none other than an expression of the eschatological scheme of salvation to take place before the coming of the End, and they appear in this sense in Revelation (5:1, 2, 5, 9; 6:1; 8:1; 10:4; 22:10) and in other Christian works.[44] The vessels are

---

[39] Riaud, "Les paralipomena jeremiae dependent-ils de ii baruch?" 115, 125–28 (on this, see also the Appendix).

[40] Ibid., 123 n. 103.

[41] Thus according to MS Eth. According to MS c from the tenth century "until his gathering." According to the Armenian MS (arm), "until his perfection/realization" (see Harris, *The Rest of the Words*, 29–30).

[42] See Kilpatrick, "Acts vii.52 eleusis," 140–41, 144. In keeping with the Ethiopic and Armenian MSS, the simple form was transformed in several MSS to συνελεύσεως. Cf. Harris, *The Rest of the Words*, 49; Thornhill, "The Paraleipomena," 823; Collins, "The Hidden Vessels," 103. Similar to that: *Ascen. Isa.* 3:13; *2 Bar.* 30:1; Acts 7:52—"the coming of the righteous one"; *1 Clem.* 17:1; Pol. *Phil.* 6:3; Ireneus, *Haer.* 1.2.

[43] See Eph 1:6 (cf. this title in the plural for Jesus' followers [believers]: 1 Thess 1:4; 2 Thess 2:13; Col 3:12; Jude 1); *Barn.* 3:6; *Ascen. Isa.* 1:3, 7; 3:13, 18; 4:6; etc.; *Odes Sol.* 3:5. Cf. ἀγαπητός: Mark 1:11; Matt 3:17; Luke 3:22; Mark 9:7; Matt 17:5; 2 Pet 1:17; Matt 12:18; Mark 12:6; Luke 20:13; and Delling, "Jüdische Lehre und Frömmigkeit," 66. Kalimi and Purvis ("The Hiding of the Temple Vessels," 681) see this as a messianic reference. Licht ("Paralipomena Jeremiah," 6, 8) translated "until Jeshurun shall be gathered," based upon the LXX to Deut 32:15; 33:5, 26; hence, the term refers to the people of Israel. Similarly Bogaert (*Apocalypse de Baruch*, 1:204) in reference to *2 Bar.* 21:21, although there it reads "beloved people," without the definite article.

[44] The seven seals are identical to the seven times (see Herzer, *Die Paralipomena*, 50, 53). On the seals, see the Appendix; Charles, *Revelation of St. John*, 138, 158–59; and Fitzer, "σφραγίς," 950. See also *T. Benj.* 7:1–5. On the combination of the seal

consigned to the earth, which was created by God during the first initial creation, and which was sealed by him seven times until the new creation at the End of Time. The "fruition" or "beauty" that the earth will receive at the end of this aeon indicates the eschatological aspect of the new creation, as opposed to the first creation of the earth. This aspect is further emphasized by the use of the future tense (λήψῃ), which stands out against the background of the addressing the land with imperative language.[45] And, just as in Revelation only the Lamb, that is, Christ alone, is able to open the seals with his blood, so too in this tradition the vessels will remain in the sealed earth until the coming of the beloved. According to this tradition, it follows that, as in *Baruch,* the vessels consigned to the earth and to the altar are intended for the heavenly temple, where they are to remain until the Parousia of Jesus.

This interpretation is consistent with the place of the tradition of the hiding of the vessels in the overall context of this work: the conquest of Jerusalem, the Babylonian exile, and the return from it under the leadership of Jeremiah, are prefigurations of the new Exodus, which anticipates, according to the Christian understanding, the making of the new covenant with the sacrifice of Jesus and the beginning of the age of salvation. This period will achieve its fullness upon the second appearance of Jesus, when the bodily and individual resurrection that the work promises to its believers will occur, and when the heavenly Jerusalem, for whose own sake these holy vessels are preserved, will be established.

2.4. *Jeremiah Apocryphon*

Confirmation of this interpretation is to be found in another Christian work dedicated to Jeremiah and the conquest of Jerusalem by the Babylonians, one that is based upon the *Paralipomena* but explains and interprets its intentions.[46] In the *Jeremiah Apocryphon,* Nebuchadnezzar, who has come at God's

---

with water as an expression for Christian baptism, see the Appendix on the *Paralipomena,* in connection with the crossing of the Jordan. For a similar description of the creation of the earth with an abundance of water, see the Gnostic work from *Nag Hammadi,* "Concept of Our Great Power," 37: 1–12, in *Nag Hammadi Studies* (ed. M. Krause, J. M. Robinson, and J. M. Wisse; Leiden, 1979), 11:294. The seven times symbolize the seven days of creation: *4 Ezra* 7:30–31; *Barn.* 15 (LCL 24:393–97). In the *Gospel of Peter,* Jesus' tomb is closed with seven seals (*Gos. Pet.* 8:33, in Elliott, *The Apocryphal New Testament,* 156).

[45] Herzer, *Die Paralipomena Jeremiae,* 24. On various suggestions for translating the Greek word ὡραιότης, see Philonenko, "Simples observations sur les Paralipomènes de Jeremie," 162.

[46] A. Mingana, "A New Jeremiah Apocryphon," 329–42, 352–95. For the Coptic version, see E. Amélineau, *Contes et romans de l'Égypte chrétienne* (2 vols.; Collection de

command to conquer Jerusalem, tries to find Jeremiah and to ask about the ark of God containing the tablets written by God's finger, which went before the people. Jeremiah appears before Nebuchadnezzar and informs him that the ark no longer exists (or, in another version, cannot be found); it has disappeared in the mountains of Jericho, because of a large quantity of dust that was heaped upon it by the wind; moreover, Zedekiah took its handles for the cult of Baal and Ashtoreth.

After the people's fate had been sealed to go into captivity, Jeremiah goes into the "house of God," where the holy garments were preserved. He removes the vestments of the high priest, climbs onto to the roof of the temple, and turns toward the cornerstone, with the following words:

> To thee I say that thou hast been a great honor to all those that surround thee and thou hast consolidated them (another version: *to all those that sin against thee and thou hast saved them*), and thou art like the eternal Son of God who shall come into the world: the faithful king, and the Lord of the two testaments, the old and the new; for this reason I shall say to thee that this temple shall only be demolished up to the place of the cornerstone; this is the reason why thou hast received this honour. Open now thy mouth and receive the garment of the High Priest and keep it with thee until the time God wishes and brings back Israel, his people.[47]

---

chansons et de contes populaires, 13–14; Paris, 1888), 97–151; Kuhn, "A Coptic Jeremiah Apocryphon," 95ff. This is a Syriac work that came down to us in a "Garshuni" version—that is, written in the Arabic language (spoken, not classical), but in Syriac letters; there is also an extant Coptic version. The accepted explanation is that the Syriac was preceded by a Greek version (see Harris, "A New Jeremiah Apocryphon," 331; Kuhn, "A Coptic Jeremiah Apocryphon," 104; Wolff, *Jeremia*, 53). The *Apocryphon* is dated in the third–fourth century CE, on the basis of its clear relation to the *Paralipomena* mentioned below and to the the *Infancy Gospel of Thomas*. Par. 32 of the *Apocryphon* relates that Ezra used his garment as a pitcher to carry water. The same miracle is also attributed to Jesus in the *Inf. Gos. Thom.* (which includes stories of miracles performed by Jesus when he was 5 to 12 years old); see ch. 11 of the Greek text and ch. 9 of the Latin text. See James, *The Apocryphal New Testament*, 52, 63; Eliott, *Apocryphal New Testament*, 78, 82 (in another Greek version); Hennecke, *New Testament Apocrypha*, 1:396; Kuhn, "A Coptic Jeremiah Apocryphon," 104; Marmorstein, "Die Quellen des Neuen Jeremiah-Apocryphons," 337; Wolff, *Jeremia*, 54. Cf. Licht, "The Book of the Deeds of Jeremiah," 7. On the Christainity of this work, see Harris, "A New Jeremiah Apocryphon," 331; Kuhn, "A Coptic Jeremiah Apocryphon," 102; this work contains specific references to the Christian Messiah and to belief in the Trinity, and it incorporates ideas and approaches from the NT. It was preserved by the Christian church; the extant Coptic version was copied in a Christian monastery, and was part of the Christian liturgy.

[47] Mingana, "New Jeremiah Apocryphon," 376.

CHAPTER 2: The Hiding of the Temple Vessels

Immediately the stone opens its mouth and receives the embroidered coat of the priesthood from the prophet Jeremiah.[48] He then removes the frontlet upon which is written the name of God Sabaoth the Omnipotent,[49] which Aaron and his sons placed upon their headdress during the divine service. Lifting it to heaven, he says to the sun:

> To thee, I say, O owner of the great light, and the hidden [*heating or protecting*] chief, I cannot see the like of thee in all the creatures of God, be therefore the keeper of this head covering on the sides of which is written the name of God the Omnipotent, keep it till the day in which God brings back from captivity the children of Israel to this place. (Mingana, 376)

He throws the headdress upward, and a ray of light lifts it on high. Jeremiah then hides the remaining things belonging to the house of God.[50] Immediately thereafter the scene of the throwing of the keys is portrayed, as in the *Paralipomena*.

The *Jeremiah Apocryphon*, in a manner that is clearly based upon the *Paralipomena*, explains the two aspects we are examining in connection with the tradition of the hiding of the vessels.[51] However, unlike the very general language used in the *Paralipomena*, it enumerates those items that were hidden. These no longer include the ark and the tablets that appeared in the earlier Christian tradition.

---

[48] In the Coptic version: "He went up to the roof of the Temple (and) stood. He said: I have said to thee, corner stone, take the likeness of a great and honoured person, for thou hast held firm the two walls (and) hast kept them straight. Thou hast taken the character of the son of God who is to come into the world at the End of Days and will have authority over the throne of the Jews and be lord of two covenants, the new and the old. Therefore this whole temple shall be destroyed except this corner stone. Listen to me: open thy mouth, receive to thee the garment of the high priest (and) guard it until the day when the Lord will turn the captivity of his people. (Then) shalt thou give them and they shall serve the Lord therewith. Immediately the corner stone burst open its midst, received them from his hand (and) closed as before" (Kuhn, "A Coptic Jeremiah Apocryphon," 302–3).

[49] From the biblical idiom, "The Lord of Hosts" (*ṣaba'ot;* צבאות ה׳) This expression was not translated into Greek and appears in the LXX transliterated as κύριος σαβαώθ; similarly in the NT: Romans 9:20; James 5:4. Cf. Cross, *The Oxford Dictionary of the Christian Church*, "Sabaoth," 1216.

[50] Mingana, "New Jeremiah Apocryphon," 376–77.

[51] Ibid., 376 n. 6; Harris, "A New Jeremiah Apocryphon," 334, 337; Kuhn, "A Coptic Jeremiah Apocryphon," 101. On the parallels between the *Apocryphon* and the *Paralipomena*, see Wolff, *Jeremia*, 53.

According to this tradition, the ark will never again be found, as its time has passed. It has become superannuated and been covered with dust on the hills of Jericho, in the spirit of Heb 8:13: "In speaking of a new covenant, he treats the old as obsolete. And what is becoming obsolete and growing old is ready to vanish away." In this sense, this tradition reflects a later stage, in which there is really no longer any place for the ark.[52] On the other hand, continuing a tendency whose beginnings may already be seen in *Syriac Baruch*, the *Jeremiah Apocryphon* emphasizes the hiding of the vestments of the high priest, the ornamented robe and headdress, which become increasingly important in Christian ritual.

From this tradition one learns explicitly that these were the only items to be hidden, as they alone were needed by Jeremiah and the high priest to carry out the ritual in the new temple in the heavenly Jerusalem upon their return from exile. In order to understand the significance of this tradition, it is particularly important to answer the question, how and in whose hands were these objects left?

The garments of the high priest (his robe) were given on the temple roof to the cornerstone. The cornerstone, around which all the other stones gather, is identified by the author with Jesus, "the eternal Son of God who shall come into the world: the faithful king, and the Lord of the two testaments, the old and the new." This identification is based upon the New Testament, is which "Christ Jesus himself being the cornerstone, in whom the whole structure is joined together and grows into a holy temple in the Lord; in whom you also are built into it for a dwelling place of God in the spirit" (Eph 2:20–22).[53] The cornerstone receives the garments of the high priest, because he is the true high priest who, according to Heb 7, shall serve in the new spiritual temple. The frontlet upon which is written the name of the Lord Sabaoth, used by the Aaronides during the performance of the temple ritual, is given over to the sun, which is also identified with Jesus.[54]

---

[52] This tradition speaks explicitly only about the ark, although it is possible to understand that as also referring to the tablets therein. This obfuscation seems to be deliberate, as the tablets represent the old covenant which, despite the fact of their having become antiquated, are part of the new covenant.

[53] Mark 12:10; Matt 21:42; Luke 20:18; Acts 4:11; on the basis of Ps 118:22 and Isa 28:16; 1 Pet 2:4–6. See Jeremias, "λίθος," 274–75; Mingana, "New Jeremiah Apocryphon," 376 and n. 5; Kuhn, "A Coptic Jeremiah Apocryphon," 102, 303 n. 93; Wolff, *Jeremia*, 57.

[54] On the Christianity of these verses in the *Apocryphon*, see Mingana, "New Jeremiah Apocryphon," 376 n. 4. On the identification of Jesus as the sun, see below, ch. 3, n. 23.

Chapter 2: The Hiding of the Temple Vessels

What is even clearer in this work is the eschatological aspect of the Christian tradition. As against all the other traditions, this is the only one that portrays, not only the hiding of the vessels until the time of salvation, but also their being taken again with the coming of this age. After Jeremiah returns from captivity, the prophet enters the temple, turns toward the doorpost (or, according to the Coptic version, toward the column) and asks the threshold of the house of God to return the keys that he had placed in its hands. He then ascends to the roof of the house of God, stands upon the cornerstone, and says: "To thee I say, O stone, Open thy mouth and bring out thy trust: the garment of the High Priest, because we are in need of it."[55] It brought out the garment, which Jeremiah gave to the high priest. He then turns to the sun, and says: "To thee, I say, O sun, the great luminary of heaven, bring out the mitre which I confided to thee and on which is the name of the Lord, the Holy One, because the Lord had mercy on His people, and we are in need of it for the service of the altar."[56] The prophet stretches his hand toward the rays of the sun and the frontlet comes down from it to him, and he gives it to the high priest. He does likewise with the other vessels of the house of God, which he had taken with him to Babylonia. The head of the priests puts on the garment of the priests with the headdress, while the prophet Jeremiah puts on the garments of the prophet, which God had ordered him to remove while in exile, and which were placed in the temple until his return. He proceeds to the Holy Place of the Lord, which is filled with divine glory, and there the two of them, together with the people, observe the festival of the twenty-fifth of April.

It is clear from this scenario that the description of Jeremiah's return from captivity alludes to the beginning of the new period of salvation that will come after the end of the world. The conquest of Jerusalem is described in the *Apocryphon* in apocalyptic terms of the end of the world that opens the age of redemption in the New Testament. Nebuchadnezzar together with all the heads of the army had subjugated all of Judah and the cities surrounding Jerusalem. They wanted to wage war against the Hebrews, since all the other peoples were at war with them. The people of Israel were before Nebuchadnezzar like women in their birth pangs: "He who was on the roof did not come down except with bonds, and he who was in the sown field did not enter the city except with fetters, and each one of them was seized in the spot where he was, and none was left who did not come to King Nebuchadnezzar who had fixed his throne at the gate of Jerusalem, the ramparts of which he had ordered to be demolished instantly."[57] At that very moment, when Cyrus and

---

[55] Ibid., 392.

[56] Ibid., 393.

[57] Ibid., 372.

Amsis, the first general of the Chaldeans, set forth to wage war and to oppress the Jews, cloud and thick smoke appeared, the earth shook with a great tremor, the wind grew stronger, an eclipse of the sun took place in the middle of the day, and darkness covered the earth. Those dwelling on the face of the land were mixed up with one another, horsemen with the masses, and the feet of the horses sank deep into the ground like pegs.[58] This description is based upon the signs of the end of the world and the coming of Jesus in the New Testament, which is described as a time of wars, famine, earthquakes, and slander: "Let those who are in Judea flee to the mountains; let him who is on the housetop not go down, nor enter his houses; and let him who is in the field not turn back to take his mantle. Alas for those who are with child and for those who give suck in those days . . . the sun will be darkened, and the moon will not give its light" (Mark 13:5–27 [here, 14–17, 24 RSV]; Matt 24:4–31; Luke 21:8–28).

This work likewise portrays the departure from the Babylonian exile like the Exodus from Egypt, which is a prefiguration of the making of the New Covenant. Those exiled from Babylonia, like the people of Israel in Egypt, will also work with clay and bricks;[59] God commands the angel Michael, as he had commanded Moses, to free the people from the captivity and promises to unleash his rage against the Babylonians should they refuse. Jeremiah, like Moses, is sent to take the people out of Babylonia, and twice Scripture explicitly compares the destiny of the Babylonians, if they refuse, to that of Pharaoh. Like Pharaoh, Cyrus first hardens his heart and does not allow the Jews to go out.[60] After they leave their captivity, silence reigns over the entire cosmos[61] and the sun alone gives light over the earth. Jeremiah rides upon his horse wearing royal garments and a crown on his head, accompanied by horses, mules, camels, and supplies for the journey, with twelve servants, together with all the Hebrews who *go up* to Jerusalem, reciting prayers of gratitude and supplication. They arrive in Jerusalem during the month of Nissan,[62] that is,

---

[58] Ibid., 387.

[59] Ibid., 379. Cf. Exod 1:14.

[60] Ibid., 386–87.

[61] Similar to "primeval silence" in *4 Ezra* 7:30; Rev 8:1.

[62] On the twenty-fifth day thereof: thus Mingana, "New Jeremiah Apocryphon," 393. In the Coptic version this was on the twelfth day of Pharmouthi, according to the calendar customary in Alexandria, that is, 7 April. Kuhn, "Coptic Apocryphon," 322. This date is identified with the date of Jesus' crucifixion. See A. Strobel, *Ursprung und Geschichte*, 70; Leclercq, "Paques," 1554, on 25 April as the date of Easter according to the Alexandrian calendar.

CHAPTER 2: The Hiding of the Temple Vessels

on the Eve of Passover, and they enter Jerusalem with palm branches and carrying wreathes of fragrant bushes and olive branches.

The description of Jeremiah's entry into Jerusalem is based on the festive and royal entrance of Jesus into Jerusalem prior to the Passover festival, as described in John 12:13–15, in which he is shown riding upon a donkey-foal, with palm branches waving to greet him,[63] accompanied by his twelve disciples.

Notwithstanding the fact that it had earlier portrayed the destruction of the temple by the Babylonians, this work describes Jeremiah's entrance into the temple as if it still stood. And indeed, the temple did stand: not the historical temple, but the heavenly temple in the heavenly Jerusalem, established after Jesus' second coming. This interpretation is also consistent with the story of Abimelech's sleep. This sleep is not described as death, but as a sleep of rest (ἀνάπαυσις), an intermediate state in which, according to the Christian approach, the dead who believe in Jesus remain until the resurrection.[64] His awakening after seventy years symbolizes the Christian resurrection. Abimelech's sleep, like the length of the exile of Jeremiah and of the people in Babylonia, must last for seventy years, on the basis of Jeremiah's prophecy of "seventy years," after which the rule of Babylonia will be completed and the people will return to their land (Jer 25:8–14; 29:10). But according to this work, rather than the historical return to Zion referred to by Jeremiah, there will be an age of eschatological-cosmic redemption and the heavenly Jerusalem will be founded. For that reason the coming of Jeremiah and his people to Jerusalem is described as an ascent. This idea receives explicit confirmation in

---

[63] Cf. Rev 7:9–10.

[64] Based upon Ps 95:11; Matt 11:28. Thus is portrayed as well the death of the believers in the Lord: Rev 14:13–14; 6:11; and cf. the parallel term, κατάπαυσις: Heb 3:11–4:12; Acts 7:49. This is a temporary death prior to the resurrection, expressed in the wearing of robes that were washed in the blood of the Lamb: Rev 7:9–17; *L.A.B.* 3:10; 19:12; 28:10; *4 Ezra* 7:32, 75; *Jub.* 23:31; *1 En.* 91:10; 92:3; 100:5; *2 Bar.* 30:1; 85:11. Death as sleep also appears in the Bible: Isa 26:19; Jer 51:39, 57; Ps 13:4; Job 3:13; Dan 12:2, but only as a metaphor. The legend of Abimelech's sleep is based upon a widespread motif in Jewish and Greek tradition concerning the protracted sleep of people who found a changed world upon awakening and did not know where they were. But it betrays a particular resemblance to the tradition in the Jerusalem Talmud, *y. Ta'an* 3.10 (66d), concerning the sleep of Honi the Circle-Drawer. According to this version, Honi the Circle-Drawer (a distant ancestor of the well-known Honi the Circle-Drawer of late Second Temple times) was privileged, thanks to his righteousness, to sleep through the seventy dismal years of destruction. But unlike Abimelech, Honi awoke to see with his own eyes the historic return to Zion and the rebuilding of the Second Temple. See Efron, "The Hasmonean Kingdom and Simeon ben Shatah," 240–41.

Jeremiah's words to Abimelech at their encounter in Jerusalem: "the Lord has overshadowed you with His holy arm and placed you in a refreshing sleep till you saw Jerusalem reconstructed and glorified for the second time."[65] Only after the establishment of the new Jerusalem and together with it the spiritual temple does Jeremiah give the vestments[66] and headdress to the high priest in order to celebrate Passover in the "holiness" of the Lord. The garment worn by the high priest is an Edenic garment, symbol of the white "holy" and "shining" garments, the pure garments that Adam and Eve removed after they sinned and which they wear following their baptism, upon their entrance into paradise—the heavenly Jerusalem.[67]

From the *Jeremiah Apocryphon*, it is clear beyond all doubt that the vessels that were hidden according to Christian tradition were intended to serve in the new temple in the heavenly Jerusalem. Thus, this work clarifies the hidden intentions of the tradition in *Syriac Baruch* and provides further basis for its tendencies and the significance of the tradition in the *Paralipomena*.

2.5. Vitae Prophetarum

An additional tradition concerning the hiding of the vessels, which is closest to that of *Baruch* and the *Paralipomena*, appears in a passage devoted to Jeremiah in a Christian work known as *Vitae Prophetarum* ("The Lives of the Prophets") consisting of traditions, mostly legendary, concerning the biblical prophets.[68] According to this tradition, Jeremiah hid the ark of the covenant

---

[65] Mingana, "New Jeremiah Apocryphon," 391. In the Coptic version: "Until Jerusalem will be destroyed and resettled"—Kuhn, "Coptic Apocryphon," 294. A further allusion to the heavenly Jerusalem appears in the description of the Levites' playing on the harp before Cyrus: the earth suddenly lifted up all those who were upon it, and raised them as if to cause the Israelites to fall upon their land, and their voices were heard on that same day in Jerusalem. Mingana, "New Jeremiah Apocryphon," 383.

[66] The robe of the high priest is identical to the robe of the Christian believer. See Mark 16:5; Rev 6:11; 7:9, 14.

[67] Ephraem Syrus, *Hymnen de Paradiso* 6.7–9; Daniélou, "Terre et Paradis," 464–65, and further bibliography there.

[68] *Life of Jeremiah*, 5–9. The primary edition of the Greek text is T. Schermann, ed., *Prophetarum vitae fabulosae. Indices apostolorum discipulorumque Domini, Dorotheo, Epiphanio, Hippolyto, aliisque vindicata* (Leipzig, 1907); see also idem, *Propheten und Apostellegenden nebst Jungerkatalogen des Dorotheus und verwandter Texte* (TU 31/3; Leipzig, 1907). And prior to that: E. Nestle, "Die dem Epiphanius zugeschriebene Vitae Prophetarum in doppeleter griechischer Rezension," in *Marginalien und Materialen* (Tübingen, 1893), 1–64. See the English translations: Torrey, *The Lives of the Prophets*, 21–22; Hare, "The Lives of the Prophets," 386–88; and see also *Life of Habakkuk*. I chose to discuss this tradition prior to *L.A.B.* because it is related to the cycle of

and the things it contained before the destruction of the temple, thereby causing them to be swallowed up in the stone. He told those who were present with him, "the Lord has gone away from Zion[69] into heaven and will come again in power (ἐν δυνάμει). And this will be for you a sign of his coming (σημεῖον τῆς παρουσίας αὐτοῦ), when all the Gentiles worship a piece of wood (ξύλον)." According to this statement, no one except Aaron will discover this ark, and the tablets within it will not be opened by any of the priests or the prophets except Moses, the chosen one of God (ὁ ἐκλεκτὸς τοῦ θεοῦ). At the resurrection of the dead, the ark will appear first. When it emerges from the stone, it will be placed upon Mount Sinai, and all the holy ones will gather to it while they await the Lord and flee from the enemy who wishes to kill them.

He sealed (ἐσφράγισε) the name of God upon the stone with his finger, and the impression (τύπος) was like a seal of iron. A cloud covered up the name, and no one was able to see the place or read the name until this day and until the End (συντελείας). The stone is located in the desert, at the place where the ark was originally, between two mountains upon which lie the bodies of Moses and Aaron. At night there is a cloud resembling fire, like the earlier model (τύπος), for the radiance of God will never cease from his Law.

---

traditions concerning Jeremiah. This collection is usually considered as a Jewish source from the first century CE, composed in Greek or Hebrew in the Land of Israel and possibly even in Jerusalem before the destruction of the temple. However, everyone agrees that the work as extant includes Christian interpolations, the most striking of which are those found in *Life of Jeremiah* and in the tradition of the hiding of the vessels, with which we are concerned here. Thus, e.g., Jeremiah's stoning to death by the Jews (on the Christianity of this tradition, see the appendix about the *Paralipomena*); the tradition about the sawing of Isaiah in half by Manasseh (*Liv. Pro.*, Isaiah, 1), a tradition connected both to the *Paralipomena* and to the *Ascent of Isaiah*, but primarily the belief in the virgin and in her son in the manger (*Life of Jeremiah*, 7–8), who are obviously Jesus and Mary. According to Satran, this is a fourth-century Christian work: Satran, "Biblical Prophets and Christian Legend," esp. 149; idem, "The Lives of the Prophets," 60, 96–97; idem, *Biblical Prophets in Byzantine Palestine*, 76, 120. As opposed to his original analysis of the tradition of Daniel, Satran more or less accepted the dominant position in relation to the tradition of the hiding of the ark, stating that it originated in the Second Temple period and that it was taken from a mélange of traditions from this period (Satran, *Biblical Prophets in Byzantine Palestine*, 61); thus also according to Schwemer (*Studien zu dem frühjüdischen Prophetenlegenden Vitae Prophetarum*, 236–37), this tradition constitutes an earlier stage than that expressed in *Syriac Baruch*, the *Paralipomena*, or the talmudic tradition.

[69] Thus according to the earliest Greek MS included in the Marcelianus Codex (Q) from the sixth or seventh century. According to other manuscripts, the reading here is "Sinai" rather than "Zion."

Comparison of the tradition of the hiding of the vessels in *Vitae Prophetorum* to that in 2 Maccabees indicates several points of similarity. In both traditions Jeremiah hid the ark of the covenant in a cave or rocky cliff; on the occasion of the hiding he is accompanied by people; he announces that the way to the place is unknown; the place is in some way connected with Moses; and, most important, in both traditions there is an explicitly eschatological aspect.[70] This similarity gives expression to the common relation of both traditions to Egypt, in which the figure of Jeremiah, who went down to Egypt after the murder of Gedaliah son of Ahikam (Jer 43–44), occupies a special place.

But these points of resemblance cannot obscure the differences between the two traditions, nor the explicitly Christian elements connected with the eschatological aspect of this work. The rock upon which the ark is placed alludes to the tomb of Jesus, hewn into the rock,[71] from which he rose to life and ascended to heaven. Jesus' heavenward ascent from Zion (*anabasis*: ἀνάβασις) concludes his earthly life, which began with his descent to earth (*katabasis*: κατάβασις); the Christians anticipate his second coming, the Parousia, which shall take place in glory and in power. The wood (ξύλον; Latin: *lignum*) symbolizes the cross, an identification made clearer from several complementary manuscripts: ἁγία, that is, the holy wood.[72] According to the Christian approach, Jesus will return a second time when *all* the nations will convert to Christianity. The cross anticipates his coming and will be the first sign of the Parousia.[73] Moses, "the chosen of God," is the prototype of Jesus,

---

[70] On the basis of this resemblance, scholars have suggested 2 Maccabees as a basis for the tradition in *Liv. Pro.* (see Wolff, *Jeremia*, 64; Torrey, *The Lives of the Prophets*, 10; Collins, "The Hidden Vessels," 103; Zeitlin, *Second Book of Maccabees*, 111; Goldstein, *II Maccabees*, 183; Bohl, "Die Legende vom Verbergen der Lade," 66; Schwemer, *Studien*, 203).

[71] Joseph of Arimathea placed Jesus' body in a grave hewn out of the rock and rolled a stone over the door of the tomb: Mark 15:46; Matt 27:60; Luke 23:53; and cf. 1 Cor 10:4, "and the rock was Christ." Cf. Budge, *The Book of the Cave of Treasures*, 237; and ibid., 109–10, for a similar tradition to that in *Liv. Pro.*

[72] The wood of the cross is described in Greek as ξύλον, meaning a tree that has been cut down, and not δένδρον, meaning a living tree. Likewise in the NT: Acts 5:30; 10:39; 13:29; Gal 3:13; 1 Pet 2:24; Rev 2:7; 22:2. According to Wolff, *Jeremia*, 37, in cod. barb. there is an addition: τοῦ χριστοῦ—"of the messiah."

[73] Eph 4:9–10; John 16:28; *Paralipomena* 9:20; H. Leitzmann, *A History of the Early Church* (London, 1967), 62. See the tradition in the *Paralipomena* on Jesus' return to the Mount of Olives. According to Matt 24:30 "Then will the sign (σημεῖον) of the Son of Man be seen in the heavens." Cf. *Did.* 16.6; *Apoc. Pet.* 1, in Elliott, *The*

CHAPTER 2: The Hiding of the Temple Vessels 69

who is also the chosen of God (ὁ ἐκλεκτὸς τοῦ θεοῦ),[74] and he alone will be able to open the tablets.

The ark, that will come to life first, is none other than the cross. The Greek term ἡ κιβωτός, meaning a box of wood, refers to the ark of the covenant, but also to Noah's ark, symbolizing the salvation and eternity of the church; the wood from which it is made symbolizes the cross.[75] It is located on Mount Sinai, because it comes in place of the Torah that was given to Moses on Sinai, and all the saints who will gather to it are the patriarchs from the Old Testament, the Christian believers, and the martyrs who will be the first to rise to life.[76] They wait for his coming so that he may defeat the enemy that pursues them, that is, the Satan, in the war to be conducted between the Messiah and the powers of the Satan when the End comes (Rev 20:7–10).[77] The "name" engraved by Jeremiah on the stone, which no one can read and

---

Apocryphal New Testament, 600; Daniélou, *The Theology of Jewish Christianity*, 1:268–70, 276.

[74] Luke 23:35; 1 Pet 2:4; Koester, *The Dwelling of God*, 52. The expression "the chosen of God" has messianic overtones.

[75] Noah's ark is a symbol of the Christian church that saves its believers, the remnant that will remain from the flood, symbolized by the waters of baptism; see Daniélou, *Sacramentum Futuri*, 55–94; Matt 24:38–39; Luke 17:27; Heb 11:7; 1 Pet 3:20. This may also be the intention in Rev 11:19; Daniélou, *Theology*, 1:277; Justin, *Dial.* 138 (PG 6:793); Daniélou, *Primitive Christian Symbols*, 67–68; Hippolytus (*Frag. Dan.* 2.6 [PG 10:648]) identifies the ark of the covenant with Jesus. Budge (*Book of the Cave*, 228) states that the cross of Jesus was from the ark of the covenant: the pieces of wood that carried the tablets of the covenant also need to carry the master of the covenant.

[76] Rom 16:15; 2 Cor 13:12; Phil 4:22; Schwemer, *Studien*, 224, 329. And see the chapter on the resurrection of the dead, below.

[77] See also *2 Bar.* 4; *4 Ezra* 14:29–38. According to the Christian tradition, this war must be conducted in Jerusalem. The author may have based himself upon Rev 12:13–18, which describes the fleeing of the woman, the symbol of the church, to the desert because of the serpent, that symbolizes the Satan (Schwemer, *Studien*, 225). See also below, in the chapter on "The Vision of the Forest, The Cedar, the Vine and the Spring." *Life of Habakkuk* 12–14 mentions the pillars of the temple, which, upon the destruction, will be taken by angels into the desert to the site where the tent of meeting was originally placed; according to this tradition as well, its place was hidden. In *1 En.* 90:28 the pillars of the temple are thrown to a place in the south of the land (cf. *1 En.* 1:4). The desert is connected with the kingdom of Satan, and Behemoth is found there (*1 En.* 60:7–9, 24–25). The Qumran sect saw the desert as the site of the imminent appearance of the Messiah (1QS viii 13; F. Bohl, "Die Legende vom Verbergen der Lade," 67). This is also associated with the activity of John the Baptist in the desert (Mark 1:3–4 & par.).

which is on the order of a secret, represents the name of Jesus, which is identical to the "Divine Name," the Tetragrammaton.[78] This name is considered a mystery,[79] and will only be revealed at the Parousia, as implied by the Greek word (συντέλεια, "End"), which is connected in the New Testament with the end of the world and the second coming of Jesus.[80] The description of the engraving of the name like an engraving in iron alludes to the "engraving" of the names of the twelve tribes upon the stones of the ephod and the breastplate.[81] These precious stones will also be used in building the wall and foundations of the heavenly Jerusalem, according to Rev 21:18–20. The cloud covering the name is God, who is revealed in the pillar of cloud that goes before the people of Israel in the desert by day. He is also the pillar of fire that illuminates their path at night to show them the way,[82] as stated explicitly in this tradition, as well as the cloud upon which the Son of Man is carried.[83]

As we have seen, despite the fact that this tradition displays considerable closeness to Hellenistic Jewish traditions in terms of the identity of the hidden vessels, it also goes further in terms of its Christian eschatological aspects.[84]

---

[78] Acts 2:21; 4:12; Rom 10:13; Herm. *Sim.* 9.14.5; Daniélou, *Theology*, 1:152, 158. Therefore the belief in Jesus is for the sake of his name: in his name are performed the signs and wonders, and sinners receive forgiveness and merit to redemption: Matt 10:22; Luke 21:12; John 15:21; Matt 18:5; 19:29; 24:5; Mark 9:38; Luke 24:47; John 14:13; 20:31; Acts 3:6; 4:7; 4:30; 9:27; 10:43; 1 Cor 5:4; 6:11; Phil 2:10; 1 John 2:12; Rev 2:3; etc.

[79] Rev 2:17; 19:12–13. This aspect is particularly emphasized in the Gnostic writings: see Daniélou, *Theology*, 1:157–58; but cf. John 1:18.

[80] Matt 13:39, 40; 24:3; 28:20; Heb 9:26; Thayer, *Greek-English Lexicon*, 606.

[81] The term γλυφή is used in the LXX to translate the expression פתוח or מילואים connected with the names of the tribes of Israel engraved upon the jewels of the breastplate and the ephod (Exod 28:21; 25:6; 35:9; 2 Chr 2:6, 13; Exod 28:9; E. Hatch and H. A. Redpath, *A Concordance to the Septuagint* [Graz, 1954], 1:271).

[82] Exod 13:21; 19:9; 24:16; 33:9–10; 40:34–38; Num 12:5; Deut 31:15; Ezek 10:4; Ps 99:7.

[83] Matt 24:30; Mark 13:26; Luke 21:27; Acts 1:9; 1 Thess 4:17; Rev 1:7; 14:14.

[84] See also *Life of Habakkuk* 10–14 (Torrey, *The Apocryphal Literature*, 29, 43–44). According to this tradition, Habbakuk gave an omen to the people in Judah that they would see a shining light in the temple and thus would know the brilliance of the temple. In relation to the end of the temple, he prophesied that it would be destroyed by a Western kingdom. Then, he said, the inner holy veil would be torn to shreds (or, in another version, into two pieces, as in Matt 27:51) and the heads of the two columns would be taken and no one would know where they were. They would be taken by angels to the desert, to the place where the tent of meeting had originally been located,

2.6. Liber Antiquitatum Biblicarum (L.A.B.)

Another tradition concerning the hiding of the vessels appears in the *Liber Antiquitatum Biblicarum* of Pseudo-Philo, a work that is a kind of paraphrase of what is written in the Bible, from Adam through the death of King Saul.[85]

---

and through them there would eventually be revealed the presence of the Lord (κύριος), because they will enlighten (φωτίσουσιν; another version uses the singular form φωτίσει, thereby referring the verb to the Lord) to those who are pursued by the serpent in the darkness, as in the beginning. Like the tradition concerning Jeremiah, that concerning Habakkuk is also an explicitly Christian tradition. Like the prophecy about the veil that will be rent with the destruction of the temple, the veil is rent with the death of Jesus on the cross: Mark 15:38; Matt 27:51; Luke 23:45. Jesus and the apostles are columns (Gal 2:9; Rev 3:12; and cf. Flusser, "The Isaiah Pesher and the Idea of the Twelve Disciples," 56), and through them the Lord will finally be revealed, at the Eschaton. The Lord is the light, who will illuminate the path of those who are in darkness, that is, will show the way to the children of darkness who are still in the realm of Satan (Luke 22:53; John 3:19; Acts 26:18; Rom 2:19; 13:12; 2 Cor 4:6; 6:14; Eph 5:8, 11; 6:12; 1 Thess 5:5; 1 John 1:6–7). They are pursued by the serpent, who is the Satan, who stands against the Messiah (Matt 7:10; Luke 11:11; Mark 16:18; Luke 10:19; 1 Cor 10:9; 2 Cor 11:3; Rev 12:9, 14, 15). All this is similar to the tradition about Jeremiah, according to which all the saints will gather at Mount Sinai upon the resurrection of the dead and will await the Lord while fleeing from their enemies who seek to destroy them. According to both traditions the second coming of Jesus will take place in the desert, as opposed to the main Christian tradition.

[85] This work has only come to us in the Latin, and has been mistakenly attributed to Philo of Alexandria. The earliest MSS are of German or Austrian origin and date from the eleventh through fifteenth centuries; however, nearly all scholars think that the original language of the work was Hebrew and that the extant Latin version is a translation from the Greek. On the history of the work, its manuscripts, and various versions, see Zeron, "The System of Pseudo-Philo," 1–45. Scholars disagree as to the date of its composition; the main difficulty relates to the fact that, unlike *Syriac Baruch* and *4 Ezra*, the work is not rooted in the background of the conquest of Jerusalem and the destruction of the temple in 70 CE. On the basis of this fact, and the interpretation of chronological hints in the work itself (19:7), there are those who date *L.A.B.* to the period preceding the destruction. Bogaert (*Apocalypse de Baruch*, 1:246, 257), relying upon the author's mode of use of the Bible, dates the work between Eupolemos (ca. 160 BCE) and Josephus, and in any event prior to 70 CE (Harrington, "Pseudo-Philo," 299). Other scholars date it after the destruction of the temple, primarily on the basis of its ideological closeness to *Syriac Baruch* and to *4 Ezra*. James (*Biblical Antiquities*, 32–33) suggests placing it at the end of the first century CE. Zeron ("The System," 51) dates it after the destruction, between the Bar Kokhba rebellion and before the eighth century, but is unable to decide whether it belongs to the period between the destruction and 150 CE or later—all this on the basis of the Latin nature of the work and its closeness to late midrashim. Brockington, "The Syriac Apocalyse of Baruch," 838 and n. 115;

According to this tradition, God commands Kenaz, one of the key figures in the work, to take precious and brilliant stones, found by people from the tribe of Asher in the temples of the Amorites, and place them on the top of the mountain near the new altar. An angel will then take them and throw them into the depths of the sea, so that they may be swallowed up; in their stead the angel will place twelve other stones upon the top of the mountain, upon which are engraved the names of the tribes and the names of the stones, which Kenaz needs to place upon the robe opposite the twelve stones placed by Moses on the breastplate. Kenaz does as he is commanded. In place of the seven impure stones from the Amorite idols, he finds twelve new stones on top of the mountain, engraved in the form of eyes. The names of the tribes are written upon these stones, each one of which resembles a precious jewel. The first one is like a sardius, the second like a topaz, the third like a carbuncle, the fourth like an emerald, the fifth like a sapphire, the sixth like a diamond, the seventh like a jacinth, the eighth like an agate, the ninth like an amethyst, the tenth like a beryl, the eleventh like an onyx, and the twelfth like a jasper.[86] God orders Kenaz to place them in the ark of the covenant of the Lord together with the tables of the testimony given to Moses. Then:

> They will stay there until Yahel, who will build a house in my name, will arise, and then he will set them before me upon the two cherubim, and they will be before me as a memorial for the house of Israel. And when the sins of my people have reached full measure, and enemies begin to have power over my house, I will take those stones and the former stones [that were on the breastplate][87] along with the tablets, and I will store them in the place from which they were taken in the beginning. And they will be there until I remember the world and visit those inhabiting the earth. And then I will take those and many others better than they are from where eye has not seen nor has ear heard, and it has not entered into the heart of man, until the like should come to pass in the world. And the just will not lack the brilliance of the sun or the moon, for the light of those most precious stones will be their light.

After Kenaz took the stones,

> It was as if the light of the sun was poured over them and the earth glowed from their light. And Kenaz put them in the ark of the covenant of the Lord with the

---

Nickelsburg, "The Book of Biblical Antiquities," 109; Jacobson, *A Commentary on Pseudo-Philo's Liber Antiquitatum Biblicarum*, 1:209–10.

[86] On the stones of the breastplate, see Exod 28:17–20. Cf. Philo, *Spec.* 1.86–87 (LCL 7:149–50); Josephus, *Ant.* 3.168 and *J.W.* 5.234; *Exod. Rab.* 38.8–9; *Num. Rab.* 2.7. Cf. Feldman, "Prologemenon," cxiii–cxiv.

[87] Perrot and Bogaert, *Les Antiquites Bibliques*, 158.

tablets, as it had been commanded him, and they are there to this day. (*L.A.B.* 26.12–15)

This description displays certain points of similarity to the tradition in the *2 Baruch:* in both descriptions it is God or his angels, rather than any historical personality such as Jeremiah or Josiah, who hide the vessels; the hiding of the vessels comes in the wake of the people's sin and is intended to save them from their enemies; the overt plot associates the hiding with the First Temple;[88] in both traditions the hiding of the "tablets" is mentioned alone, without the ark of the covenant. However, what is particularly important for our purposes is the fact that both of them speak of the hiding of the precious stones connected with the stones of the breastplate, the urim and tummim, thereby revealing the eschatological aspect that is their focus.

The tradition in *Liber Antiquitatum Biblicarum* speaks of several kinds of stones. The first twelve stones, which Kenaz needs to place on the robe opposite the stones of the breastplate, are inscribed with the names of the tribes of Israel and the names of the stones. The twelve other stones, which Kenaz must hide in the ark of the covenant, also have the names of the Israelite tribes engraved upon them. These stones, along with the first ones, are restored by God to the place where they were originally. Only in the future, at the end of days, when he will remember the world and visit the inhabitants of the earth, will God take them and many other precious stones to provide light to the righteous instead of the light of the sun and the radiance of the moon. One is thus speaking of a total of twenty-four specific stones: those that Moses had placed in the breastplate, and those that Kenaz is commanded to place in the ark of the covenant, together with many others whose number is not specified.

This description betrays a definite eschatological aspect. The first twelve stones, whose "engraving is as if eyes were opened in them," were intended for building the new temple, similar to the one stone which has "seven facets," "the top stone" and "single stone" of Zechariah 3:9; 4:7, 10.[89] This image in

---

[88] The stones that were hidden by God in *L.A.B.* were in the house built by Yahel (Iahel, Iabel, Iachel), identified with Solomon. Thus Ginzberg, *Legends of the Jews,* 6:183 n. 13, sees this name as a distortion of Athiel, one of the ten names of Solomon. Cf. Gaster, *The Chronicles of Jerahmeel,* 22, 57; Harrington, *Pseudo-Philo,* 338, 169; Perrot and Bogaert, *Antiquites Bibliques,* 2:158. Others identify him as the angel Yuhal, according to *Apoc. Abr.* 10:4, 9; 16:11; Wolff, *Jeremia,* 64 n. 5; Harrington, "Pseudo-Philo," 338; Feldman, "Prologomenon," cxiv. Zeron ("The System of Pseudo-Philo," 189–90) identifies the angel Yahel with Metatron.

[89] Meyers and Meyers, *Haggai, Zechariah 1–8,* 205–6. There are those who connect this stone in Zechariah with one of the stones that adorned the garments of the high priest, on the basis of Exod 28 (see H. G. Mitchell, M. P. Smith, and J. A. Bewer, *A Critical and Exegetical Commentary on Haggai, Zezhariah, Malachi, and Jonah* [ICC;

Zechariah, together with the mention of the sin of the people, is connected with and precedes the redemption. God will hide these stones, together with the others and the tablets, in the place from which they were originally taken; that is, he will return them to the garden of Eden, for they originated in "the land of Havilah,"[90] from which they were originally taken, and there too God will also conceal them a second time. Concerning one of the stones, it is explicitly stated that it was taken from *excelso Syon,* that is, from Zion located in the heights of the heaven (*L.A.B.* 26.11). The stones will remain in the garden of Eden until such time as God will visit the world, that is, until the end of all time, which will be the time of full redemption at the end of days in the apocalyptical sense.[91]

It follows from the text that the description is directed towards the heavenly Jerusalem, which is located in the garden of Eden, and on whose behalf the stones and tablets are preserved. In the heavenly Jerusalem these precious stones will provide light for the righteous, and there will no longer be need for the light of the sun or the radiance of the moon. At the times of the complete redemption, at the end of days, that Jerusalem will descend to earth and be established forever, exactly as in *Syriac Baruch.*

Here the author clearly makes use of passages from the Bible, basing his portrait on the description of the breastplate in Exod 28:15–21, the description of the stones of Jerusalem at the end of days found in Isa 54:11–12, and Ezek 28:13, which connects the stones of the breastplate to the garden of Eden. But the author of *Liber Antiquitatum Biblicarum* gives these descriptions a new interpretation, thereby turning the focus toward the heavenly Jerusalem. This new exegesis becomes very clear when one compares the tradition in *Liber*

Edinburgh, 1912]), 157). In Christian exegesis the stone is interpreted as Jesus (M. F. Unger, *Zechariah* [Grand Rapids, 1963], 66–68).

[90] *L.A.B.* 25:11, based on Gen 2:11 and Ezek 28:13.

[91] Zeron, "The System of Pseudo-Philo," 16 n. 4; 77; 77–78. The expression "the end of days" is well integrated into the story of Kenaz, as if it belonged to the days of Kenaz, i.e., the period of the judges. But the reference to the last days is intended in the apocalyptic sense. Thus Kenaz relates before his death, "Behold now, the Lord has shown to me all his wonders that he is ready to do for his people in the last days" (*L.A.B.* 28:1). This passage does not make explicit what these wonders are, but from the context of the story of the precious stones it follows that Kenaz saw the secrets of paradise, and learned that the origin of the stones was in paradise and that they shall provide light for the righteous at the end of days (see Zeron, "The System," 220). Bogaert thought that the other stones are directed toward the nations of the world, to whom God will reveal them at the end of days (*Apocalypse de Baruch,* 2:123; see Murphy, *Pseudo-Philo,* 124).

Antiquitatum Biblicarum with the description of the heavenly Jerusalem in Revelation, which reflects a special closeness to it.

In the heavenly Jerusalem, as described in Rev 21, there are also twenty-four stones that bear a direct relation to the stones of the breastplate. The names of the twelve tribes of Israel are written upon the gates in the wall of the city (based upon Ezek 48:31), while the names of the twelve apostles of the Lamb, written upon the foundations of the city walls and decorated with various precious stones, are none other than the stones of the breastplate.

As in *Liber Antiquitatum Biblicarum,* this city has no need for the sun or the moon to give it light,[92] because in it resides "the glory of God, its radiance like a most rare jewel, like a jasper, clear as crystal . . . for the glory of God is its light, and its lamp is the Lamb; by its light shall the nations walk . . . and there shall be no night there" (Rev 21:11, 23–25). Based on Revelation, it follows that the stones hidden by God in *Liber Antiquitatum Biblicarum,* like all the stones in all of these traditions, are connected with the Christian typology of the stone. There, it symbolizes the Christian church and its Messiah, which are the "house" and the "tower," the "shining stones" and the "cornerstone" of the heavenly Jerusalem, that will descend to earth in the future from the garden of Eden upon the coming of the age of redemption. The precious stone is none other than "that living stone, rejected by men but in God's sight chosen and precious" (1 Pet 2:4–8).[93]

These implications of the tradition in *Liber Antiquitatum Biblicarum* and the points of similarity between it and Revelation become clear from a

---

[92] After Isa 60:19.

[93] This significance is also made clear by the language used by the author in describing the beauty of the stones: "For in those days God will take these stones and many others, more beautiful than them, whose like no eye has seen and no ear has heard, and it has not occurred to any heart, that their like exist in the world." This expression is clearly based upon 1 Cor 2:9. It also appears in a fragmentary way in the HB (Isa 52:15; 64:3; 65:17), but in all those places it may be interpreted in a christological manner. Josephus (*Ant.* 3.215–18) also interprets the urim and tummim in terms of light; he even states that the stones in the ephod and the twelve stones of the breastplate radiated light. The former gave light when God was present in the holy service; the latter, when God intended to inform the people who were about to go to war of their victory. According to him, the breastplate and the urim and tummin ceased to yield light two hundred years earlier, because God was angry at the non-performance of the laws (*Ant.* 3.215–18). Cf. A. Shalit, Yosef ben Mattityahu, *Qadmoniot ha-Yehudim,* Vol. III, n. 153, p. 70; Josephus, *Ant.* 3.216–18 (LCL, IV:418 n. *c*), but Josephus's words do not have an eschatological cast.

fragment of the *Isaiah Pesher* from the fourth cave in Qumran (4QpIsa^d [=4Q164] frg. 1):[94]

> "[I will make] all your battlements [of rubies]" [Isa 54:12]. Its interpretation concerns the [chiefs of the priests who] illuminate with the judgment of the Urim and the Thummim . . . .[95]

In this *pesher,* as well, Isaiah's prophecy is seen as relating to the precious stones of the breastplate, to the urim and tummim. Here too the precious stones are interpreted as shining stones[96] connected to the eschatological Jerusalem, identified with the Qumran sect.[97]

The tradition in *Liber Antiquitatum Biblicarum* clarifies the eschatological aspect of the tradition of the hiding of the vessels in *Syriac Baruch.* The vessels are hidden in the garden of Eden and are preserved, not for the historical temple, but for the heavenly Jerusalem, which will descend to earth at the end of all times. The fact that these stones were taken from the temple of Solomon and hidden until the Eschaton emphasizes the inferiority of the Second Temple.

In conclusion, the inner significance and hidden intentions of the tradition of concealing the vessels in the *Syriac Apocalypse of Baruch* become clear in light of the parallel traditions that developed and became interwoven within the Christian tradition, finding their expression in the *Paralipomena,* in the *Jeremiah Apocryphon,* in the *Vitae Prophetarum,* and in the *Antiquitatum Biblicarum.* All these traditions emphasize the eschatological aspect, connecting the concealing of the vessels to the end of days and the establishment of the heavenly Jerusalem, for whose sake these vessels were preserved. This

---

[94] The text was published by J. M. Allegro, "More Isaiah Commentaries from Qumran, Fourth Cave," *JBL* 77 (1958): 220–21; *DJD* 5:164; *Commentary on Isaiah,* 27–28 (Oxford, 1968); Yadin, "Some Notes on the Newly Published Pesharim of Isaiah."

[95] *The Dead Sea Scrolls Study Edition* (ed. F. García Martínez and E. J. C. Tigchelaar; Leiden, New York & Köln, 1997), 1:326–27.

[96] Flusser, "The Isaiah Pesher," 53, 58. According to Flusser's reconstruction, "illuminating by the law/way of the urim and tummim" is connected, not to the priests, as Yadin proposes, nor to the luminaries, as suggested by Allegro, but to "the precious stones."

[97] Yadin, "Some Notes," 42; Flusser, "The Isaiah Pesher," 52ff.; cf. Enoch 18:6–8: ". . . seven mountains of precious stones. . . . As for those toward the east, they were of colored stones—one of pearl stone, and one of healing stone [jacinth]; and as for those toward the south, they were of red stone. The one in the middle was pressing into heaven, like the throne of God, which is of alabaster, and whose summit is of sapphire" (*OTP* 1:23).

eschatological aspect is entirely absent from the Palestinian Jewish tradition, which presents the original tradition regarding this matter; but neither does the Hellenistic Jewish tradition deviate from the hopes of redemption that were predominant among the Jewish people during the Second Temple period. While the tradition of hiding the vessels in *Syriac Baruch* is in fact based upon the Jewish tradition, it reshapes that tradition in accordance with its theological tendencies and fills it with new meanings that can best be understood in light of the Christian tradition.

CHAPTER THREE
The Abandonment of the Temple

3.1. "The Watchman Has Abandoned the House" (8:1–5)

It is related that, after the temple vessels were consigned to the earth till the end of days, the angels began to shake the corners of the wall and to break it up. After it fell, a voice emerged from the inner part of the sanctuary: "Enter, enemies, and come, adversaries, because he who guarded the house has left it" (8:1).[1] The Babylonians then occupied the temple and its environs, took the people into captivity, killed some of them, bound King Zedekiah in irons, and sent him to the king of Babylonia.[2]

Who is the watchman of the house, and how is his abandonment of it to be understood?

Josephus reports that on the eve of the destruction of the Second Temple there were visible, early signs of the approaching calamity. Among these, he mentions that the Nikanor Gate, the eastern gate of the inner court of the temple, which usually required twenty people to close it, suddenly opened of its own accord during the sixth hour of the night. This was taken as a sign that the security of the temple had been breached, and that it was about to be given over to its enemies. On the Festival of Pentecost, the priests, upon entering the inner part of the temple, "were conscious, first of a commotion and a din, and after of a voice as of a host, 'We are departing hence'" (*J.W.* 6.293–300).[3]

According to Jewish tradition, as reflected in Josephus and in talmudic sources, the angelic entourage, a heavenly voice, or the Shekhinah, symbolizing the divine presence, abandoned the temple on the eve of its destruction as a concrete expression of the approaching destruction. Tacitus cites a similar

---

[1] *OTP* 1:623.

[2] Based upon 2 Kgs 25:1–7; Jer 39:1–9; 52:4–11; cf. the parallel tradition in *Pesiq. Rab.* 26 (ed. Ish-Shalom; 131), based upon *Syriac Baruch*. On *Pesiq. Rab.* and its relation to the pseudepigraphic tradition, see below, pp. 96, 115–16.

[3] Based upon Ezek 11:23. Similarly in the talmudic tradition, *Pesiq. Rab Kah.* 13.11 (ed. Mandelbaum; 234). "The Shekhinah moved ten stops . . . and the Glory of the Lord went out from above the threshold of the temple." *B. Roš Haš.* 31a; *ʾAvot R. Nat.*, Version A, ch. 34 (ed. Schechter; 102); *Lam. Rab., Petihta* 1.25; this tradition alludes to Jer 12:7.

testimony in connection with the miracles that heralded the destruction of Jerusalem: "Contending hosts were seen meeting in the skies, arms flashed, and suddenly the temple was illumined with fire from the clouds. Of a sudden the doors of the shrine opened and a superhuman voice cried: 'The gods are departing.' At the same moment the mighty stir of their going was heard" (Tacitus, *History*, 5.13).[4] Tacitus's testimony, evidently based upon that of Josephus,[5] reflects a tendency of Roman propaganda; such traditions were used to make it easier for Roman soldiers to conquer places that had an immanent holiness, and that it was forbidden to destroy so long as they served as a dwelling place of the god. If the God who dwelt in the Jewish temple and protected it had left it, then its sanctity was terminated and there was no longer fear of conquering it.[6] In all these testimonies, the divine presence willingly abandoned the temple even before the Romans began to lay siege to it.

The tradition in *Syriac Baruch* evidently relies upon the same report, although giving it a totally different interpretation. Instead of the entourage of angels, a divine voice, or gods, it speaks of the "watchman" who abandons the house. It particularly emphasizes that the voice that called to the enemies originated in the inner part of the temple, that is, from the Holy of Holies, and that the departure of the watchman did not take place prior to its destruction, but during its course. The author stresses that the guard only left after the wall fell, leaving the Babylonians nothing to do but to take possession of the temple and its environs.

Careful examination of early Christian tradition suggests a direct relation between the tradition discussed here and the exegesis given to the rending of the veil of the temple upon Jesus' death (Mark 15:38; Matt 27:50; Luke 23:45). Thus, for example, *T. Benj.* 9:3–4 relates that, upon the crucifixion of the Lord, the veil of the temple (τὸ ἅπλωμα τοῦ ναοῦ) shall be rent and the

---

[4] Tacitus, *The Histories* (ET by C. H. Moore, in *Tacitus* [LCL; London and Cambridge, Mass.; 1969], 3:197–99). Unlike Josephus, Tacitus speaks of gods, in the plural, in accordance with pagan conceptions. Cf. Eusebius, *Hist. eccl.* 3.8.1–9 (LCL 153:221–25).

[5] J. Levy, "Tacitus' Words on the Antiquities of the Jews," 154. Eusebius also relies on this tradition; see *Comm. Luc.* (PG; 24:605b). Cf. de Jonge, "Two Interesting Interpretations," 226.

[6] Levy, "Tacitus' Words," 151–55. See there on the ancient pagan custom of *evocatio deorum*, according to which the Romans were accustomed before every battle to invoke the gods of the enemy to invite them to abandon their place and join their gods. See M. Beard, "Evocatio," *The Oxford Classical Dictionary* (Oxford and New York, 1966), 580; Kaufmann, *Toldot ha-Emuna ha-Yisra'elit*, 8:22.

CHAPTER 3: The Abandonment of the Temple

Spirit of God (τὸ πνεῦμα τοῦ θεοῦ) will pass to (or descend upon) the nations, like fire poured out.[7]

According to this tradition, upon Jesus' death the veil was rent and the spirit of God abandoned the temple in order to dwell among the nations who had accepted belief in him. In this context the "spirit of God," represented in some sources by a divine angel, symbolizes the presence of the Godhead in the temple, while its abandonment is a sign of its imminent destruction.

Likewise, we read in the early Christian work *Didascalia Apostolorum* (23.5.7)[8] that God left the Jewish people and the temple and came to the church of the Gentiles. When He did so, He also abandoned the temple, leaving it desolate. He tore the veil, removed the Holy Spirit, and put it upon the believers among the Gentiles, as is said by Joel (3:1): "I will pour out my spirit on all flesh." He thereby removed from the people the Holy Spirit, its power of the word, and its entire mission, establishing these in His church.[9] Hence, the tradition in *Syriac Baruch* emphasizes that the voice emanated from the inner part of the sanctuary—i.e., the Holy of Holies in which the veil is

---

[7] On the basis of this tradition there also developed the holiday of Pentecost, the festival of the founding of the Christian church, which is described, following Joel 3:1–5, as the pouring out of spirit upon all flesh with "blood, and fire, and vapor of smoke" (Acts 2.3, 17; 10:45); see on this also below; cf. de Jonge, *Studies on the Testaments of the Twelve Patriarchs,* 236. On the Christian origins of the term ἅπλωμα as a term for the veil, see de Jonge, "Two Interesting Interpretations," 222–23. On the same term in *Life of Habakkuk* 12, see Torrey, *Lives of the Prophets,* 29, there too in a Christian context. On the rending of the veil, cf. below. On the Christianity of the testaments, see de Jonge, *Testaments of the Twelve Patriarchs,* 125–28; idem, "Two Interesting Interpretations," 221; Kee, "Testaments of the Twelve Patriarchs," 827. This work is dated by de Jonge between 190 and 225 CE, that is, close to the time of *Syriac Baruch.*

[8] The work is dated in the third century CE and devoted to the arrangements of the church in various areas of life. See Connolly, *Didascalia Apostolorum,* xxvi, lxxxvii ff.

[9] Funk, *Didascalia et Constitutiones Apostolorum,* 312–13; Connolly, *Didascalia,* 199. Cf. Ephraem Syrus, who interprets the rending of the veil and the abandonment of the Holy Spirit as a sign of impending destruction: Ephraem Syrus, *Commentaire de l'Evangile Concordant,* 21.4–6 (SC 121:376–78). Tertullian relies upon Isa 1:8; 5:2 in describing the temple veil as being rent by the angel who broke outside and abandoned the daughter of Zion, leaving her as a booth in a vineyard, like a lodge in a cucumber field (Tertullian, *Marc.* 4.42 (ed. E. Evans; Oxford, 1972; p. 500). So also Eusebius, in his interpretation of Isa 1:8 (PG; 24:92–93); and *T. Levi* 10:3. For further examples of this tradition, see Daniélou, *The Theology of Jewish Christianity,* 15, 145–46; de Jonge, "Two Interesting Interpretations," 221–31; Kuhnel, *From the Earthly to the Heavenly Jerusalem,* 55.

found—and that it was heard only after the wall had fallen down, that is, after Jesus had breathed out his soul on the cross.

This idea already appears in the Gospels: in his prophecy of the destruction of the temple, Jesus states, "Behold, your house is forsaken [and desolate]. For I tell you, you will not see me again, until you say, 'Blessed is he who comes in the name of the Lord'" (Matt 23:38–39 and Luke 13:35, based on Ps 118:26). The temple will be abandoned until the second coming of Jesus, alluded to in the blessing for his coming (Rev 22:6–21). Immediately thereafter, it is related that he left the temple and went on his way (Matt 24:1), thereby sealing its fate. Upon leaving the temple he went to the Mount of Olives, where the Parousia is to take place at the end of days.[10] Thus, specifically at this stage, after the prophecy of the destruction of Jerusalem and the temple and having himself abandoned the temple, he is asked by his disciples for a sign of his coming and of the End of the world. His leaving the temple symbolizes its destruction and is a precondition for the End and for the second coming (Mark 13:2ff.; Matt 24:2ff.; Luke 21:5ff.). But Jesus also literally appears as the "watchman of the house." In John 20:15, Mary Magdalene thought that the resurrected Jesus was the "keeper of the garden" (ὁ κηπουρός)[11] in which his new grave had been dug and in which he had been buried, wrapped in shrouds and spices. The description of the garden is reminiscent of the garden of Eden planted with trees having a special fragrance, where man had been placed by God to work it and keep it (according to Gen 2:15).[12] The garden of Eden symbolizes the heavenly Jerusalem, the new and true temple, and Jesus, the new man, is the watchman of this temple, as opposed to the earthly temple, whose watchman has abandoned it.

---

[10] On the basis of Ezek 11:23; Zech 14:4; cf. *Pesiq. Rab Kah.* 13 (ed. Mandelbaum; 234). The Christian tradition interpreted the testimony of Josephus similarly; thus Rabanus Maurus, *Comm. in Ezechielem* (PL 110:645). On the Mount of Olives as the site of the Parousia, see *Paralipomena* 9:20. Jesus' ascent to the heavens from the Mount of Olives and his return there are alluded to in the NT: Luke 24:50; Acts 1:12. Cf. Limor, "Christian Traditions of the Mount of Olives," 129–30.

[11] In Syriac: *gnana*, "the gardener or owner of the garden"; in the Vulgate: *hortulanus*. In the ancient Near East, it was usual to describe the gods as gardeners. The Teacher of Righteousness is so described in the *Thanksgiving Scroll* (1QH viii 4–11); see J. H. Charlesworth, "Jesus as the 'Son' and the Righteous Teacher as 'Gardener,'" in *Jesus and the Dead Sea Scrolls* (New York, 1992), 146–47.

[12] Among the Manichaeans the first man is portrayed as guarding the garden of life, and is understood as "the 'gardener.'" See G. Widengren, *Mesopotamian Elements in Manichaeism* (Uppsala, 1946), 25.

3.2. The Keys of the Temple
a. The Christian Tradition

The description of the watchman leaving the temple upon its destruction is closely related to two other traditions: that of the throwing of the keys of the temple heavenward by the priests, and of the throwing of the veil into the fire by the weaving virgins following the destruction of the city and the temple. These traditions are incorporated in the dirge recited by Baruch over the destruction of Zion, in which he also refers to those who serve in the temple.

> You, priests, take the keys of the sanctuary and cast them to the highest heaven and give them to the Lord, and say "Guard your house yourself because, behold, we have been found to be false stewards."[13] And you virgins who spin fine linen and silk with gold of Ophir, make haste and take all things and cast them into the fire so that it may carry them to him who made them. And the flame sends them to him who created them so that the enemies do not take possession of them. (*2 Bar.* 10:18–19)

These verses are the focus and climax of the dirge, and elucidate its intention. The priests are asked to take the keys of the temple, to throw them heavenwards, and to give them to the Lord, so that He may guard the temple instead of them; unlike the priests of the historical temple, who are shown to have been false guardians, he is the true steward. According to the Arabic version, this temple was from the very outset given to these priests as a charge.[14] This statement is consistent with the Christian claim that the temple was only given to the Jews for a limited time period, so that it might become a house of prayer for all the nations; they, however, stole it and turned it into a den of robbers (Mark 11:17; 12:1–12 and parallels). It was therefore decreed that it was to be destroyed. The throwing of the keys heavenward by the priests was not intended to save it; hence this scene is described as taking place *after* the temple had already been destroyed.

---

[13] רבי בתא דגלא, evidently a translation of the Greek expression: ἐπίτροπος ψεύδους (see Bogaert, *Apocalypse de Baruch*, 1:237 n. 1). This expression appears subsequently in the *Paralipomena*, in *'Abot R. Nat.*, Version B (*apotropsin*), and in *Pesiq. Rab.*, in the sense of "guard/watchman," administrator (of the fiscus) (Jastrow, "Apitropus," *Dictionary*, 102).

[14] Leemhuise, Klijn, and Gelder, *Arabic Text*, 44. The extant Arabic manuscript is tentatively dated to the tenth or eleventh century, but is based upon a much earlier manuscript. On the basis of linguistic and stylistic signs, it is possible to determine that the translation of the work into Arabic is early (ibid., 4–5).

The text distinguishes between the historical "sanctuary," whose keys the priests needed to give over, and "the house,"[15] that is, the heavenly temple, identical to the heavenly Jerusalem, which the Lord must protect. The keys are thrown heavenward because the heavenly Jerusalem is located there, alongside paradise. There, in the seventh or eighth heaven, is also located the Lord, who will return in the Parousia, and it is there that the true spiritual cult, of which the earthly cult is a mere pale imitation, is conducted.[16]

The departure of the "guardian of the house" is in this work directly connected to the tradition of the throwing of the keys heavenwards by the priests. Unlike the loyal steward Jesus, the priests of the historical, ruined temple were false stewards; thus they need to deliver the keys of the temple to the true priest who serves in the true sanctuary, established by God and not by man (Heb 8:2).

These intentions are explained more fully in the Christian traditions similar to or related to *Syriac Baruch*. Thus, the *Paralipomena*[17] relates that Jeremiah, after lifting up the keys to the temple, goes outside of the city and throws them before the sun, saying: "I say to you, sun, take the keys of Temple of God and keep them until the day in which the Lord will question you about them. Because we were not found worthy of keeping them, for we were false stewards" (*Paralipomena* 4:4–5).[18]

The similarity between these two traditions is quite clear, emphasizing their connection in terms of both contents and ideas. However, it is the differences between them that shed light upon the intentions of the tradition alluded to in *2 Baruch*. The tradition in *Paralipomena* differs from it in several respects: from a literary viewpoint, it is not incorporated within the dirge; rather than the imperative language used by *Baruch*, it uses the narrative literary

---

[15] "You priests, take the keys of the *sanctuary*," as opposed to "Give them to the Lord and say, 'Guard your *house* yourself."

[16] *Asc. Isa.* 8:7ff.; *1 En.* 2:3–20; Daniélou, *Theology*, 174–79. For this reason, in early Christian tradition the appearance of the eschatological cross in heaven precedes the Parousia (Daniélou, 269–70, and the examples presented there). The tradition concerning the firmaments in the heaven, usually seven in number, is also widespread in talmudic literature: see *Midr. Tehillim* to Ps 114; *'Abot R. Nat.*, Version A, 37 (ed. Schechter; 110); *Pesiq. Rab.* 5 (ed. Ish-Shalom; 18b); *Tanh., Naso* 24 (ed. Buber; 19a); *b. Ḥag.* 12b.

[17] The Christianity of this work has already been noted by J. R. Harris, who published a critical edition with English translation in 1889 under the title *The Rest of the Words of Baruch: A Christian Apocalypse of the Year 136 A.D.* (London, 1889). Cf. Bogaert, *Apocalypse de Baruch*, 1:216–17, and recently Philonenko, "Simples Observations," 157–77.

[18] Trans. S. E. Robinson, in *OTP* 2:419.

genre; instead of the priests throwing the keys, there appears the figure of Jeremiah;[19] the keys are given to the sun and not to God; the tradition specifies the period of time during which the keys will be preserved by the sun—that is, until God asks for them; and the act of delivering the keys occurs during the actual time of the destruction of the temple.

The appearance of Jeremiah rather than the priests makes sense in light of his central role in this composition and the function that he fulfills therein as high priest (5:18; 9:2, 8). However, the following two distinctions are of greater importance:

(1) The composition of the *Paralipomena* confirms the identity of God, to whom the keys are given, with Jesus, who is metaphorically described in this tradition as the sun. While in the [Hebrew] Bible the sun appears as a metaphor for the God of Israel (Ps 84:12; Isa 60:1–3; Mal 3:20), in Christianity it becomes a symbol for Jesus, who is identified with the "sun of righteousness," as in the prophecy of Mal 3:20: "But for you who fear my name the sun of righteousness shall rise, with healing in its wings."[20] The term צמח ("Plant" or "Branch"), found in such biblical expressions as "the man the Branch," "my servant the Branch," "the righteous Branch" (Zech 6:12; 3:8; Jer 23:5) and associated with the offshoot of the Davidic line, is translated into Greek as ἀνατολή, meaning also "east" or "rising sun." This expression, with its double meaning, is referred to Jesus, who is both an offshoot of the house of David and the sun who rises in the east (Matt 2:2; 24:27; Luke 1:78; Rev 7:2; 16:12).[21] Thus, in the *Odes of Solomon*, which is the earliest extant work in

---

[19] In this context, the fact stands out that *Paralipomena Jeremiah* speaks in the plural, even though he alone gave over the keys. This may indicate that the tradition in *Paralipomena* is secondary and that its author made use of *Syriac Baruch*, although he did not rework it in a consistent way.

[20] Eusebius, *Dem. ev.* 4.10 (PG 22:280); 7.3 (ibid., cols. 560–61); cf. Ps 72:5, 17; 19:6–7; 104:19.

[21] Justin Martyr connects the idiom in Zech 6:12 (with the Greek verb ἀνατέλλω in the LXX) to Num 24:17, understanding the coming of Christ as a rising star: Justin *Dial.* 100 (PG 6:709); 106 (ibid., col. 724); 121 (ibid., col. 757); 126 (ibid., col. 769); Melito of Sardis, frg. VIIIb 4 (SC 123:232). See also the Greek verb ἀνατέλλω, used to translate the verbs צמח and זרח in connection with Messiah: Heb 7:14; 2 Pet 1:19; Ign. *Magn.* 9.1 (LCL 24:205). On the significance of these terms see H. Schlier, ἀνατέλλω, ἀνατολή, *TDNT*, 1:351–53. Cf. *T. Judah* 24:1; *T. Levi* 18:3–4; *T. Zeb.* 9:8. In the Qumran writings, the Davidic Messiah (i.e., the Prince of the Congregation) is identified with "the shoot of David," based upon the interpretation of Isa 11:1 in *Pesher Isaiah*, 4QpIsa[a] 8–10; 11–24 (4Q161, *DJD* 5:13–14); 4Q*Serek HaMilhamah* (4QSM = 4Q285) 5 1–6; *Pesher Bereshit* 4QpGen[a] 5 1–7 (4Q252); 4QFlor. 1 11–13 (*DJD* V:53);

Syriac, Jesus is compared to the sun: "He is my sun, and his rays have lifted me up and his light has dispelled all darkness from my face" (*Odes Sol.* 15:2–3; 11:13).[22] Jesus comes instead of the radiant sun and moon (Rev 1:16; 12:1; 21:22–24),[23] and for that reason is compared to light. He is "the true light that enlightens every man" (John 1:9) and he is "the light on high" (ἀνατολὴ ἐξ ὕψους) who comes "to give light to those who sit in darkness and in the shadow of death" (Luke 1:78–79, after Isa 9:1); those who believe in him are the "sons of light" (υἱοὶ φωτός; 1 Thess 5:4–5).[24]

(2) From the period of time until whose end the keys are given over, one is to understand that they are given for a limited period of time[25] and that they will be asked for in the future. What is this period of time until which the keys will be guarded? The answer to this question is clarified by the *Jeremiah Apocryphon*. In this work the prophet delivers the keys of the temple, not to the Lord, as in *Syriac Baruch*, nor to the sun, as in the *Paralipomena*, but to the doorposts of the temple, or to the lintel or tower, all of which are clearly Christian symbols.[26] It may be clearly seen from the *Apocryphon* that the keys

---

cf. Pomykala, *The Davidic Dynasty Tradition*, 180–216. Cf. on the similarity of this figure to that of the righteous teacher (Tepler, "The Teacher of Righteousness," 92–94).

[22] Harris and Mingana, *The Odes and Psalms of Solomon*, 1.31, 35. On the antiquity of this work, see ibid., 69; Murray, *Symbols of Church and Kingdom*, 24.

[23] Hence Jesus was born, according to Christian tradition, on a Wednesday, the day on which the sun was created, and was resurrected on a Sunday, the day on which light was created. Sunday was also the day dedicated to Helios in the Hellenistic pagan world. Christians, adopting the widespread terminology, referred to the Day of the Lord as Sunday, the day of the sun (dies solis; ἡμέρα ἡλίου); Tertullian, *Apol.* 16 (PL 1:371); Justin, *1 Apol.* 67 (PG 6:429). On the rays of the sun as a symbol of the cross, identified with Jesus, see Daniélou, *Theology*, 275; Lampe, *A Patristic Greek Lexicon*, 605. The importance of the mystery of the sun embodied in Jesus also finds expression in the Christian cult of Easter and in the two holidays in which they celebrate the birth of Christ: Epiphany and Christmas. On them, and for more on the image of Jesus as sun, its sources and its significance in Christian cult and theology, see Rahner, *Greek Myths and Christian Mystery*, 89–154. Among the Manicheans there is an identity between the sun and Christ: Bogaert, *Apocalypse*, 1:237.

[24] The image of Jesus as light also underlies the vision of the bright water and black water in *2 Bar.* 53:56–74.

[25] Like the temple vessels: *2 Bar.* 6:7–10; *Paralipomena* 3:7–8.

[26] The doorposts and lintels are ancient symbols for the cross, based upon the sign placed on the doorposts and lintels of Israelite homes to keep away the destructive angel at the time of the Exodus (Exod 12:7, 13). See Justin, *Dial.*, 111:4 (PG 6:732); Daniélou, *Theology*, 272. For the tower as symbol of the church, see Herm. *Vis.* 3.2.4 and Herm. *Sim.* 9, in *The Apostolic Fathers* II (LCL 25) pp. 31, 217ff.); *Jub.* 29:17, 19;

CHAPTER 3: The Abandonment of the Temple

are being kept for the new, heavenly Jerusalem, to be established in the age of salvation to follow the end of the world.

After Jeremiah's song of praise to the new Jerusalem, he enters through the door of the temple and says to the doorpost: "To you I say, O threshold of the house of God, bring out the keys which I had confined to thee." After he is given the keys, he opens the door of the temple and enters it together with all the people, and they serve the Lord.[27] The keys are thus kept for the spiritual sanctuary, which will be in the new, heavenly Jerusalem. In this way the work explains the intentions of the tradition in *Syriac Baruch*, and further establishes the basis for the significance of the tradition in the *Paralipomena*.

This Christian tradition and the place occupied therein by Jesus also explain the meaning of the keys: the keys are meant to open the gate to the heavenly temple, the kingdom of heaven which will be established at the end of days, and to the future heavenly Jerusalem, which is identical to paradise. The one holding the keys in his hands has full control, and the power to prohibit or to allow entry. All these are in the hands of Jesus, who likewise holds the keys of Death and of Hades (Rev 1:18; 9:1). He is also the true Holy One in whose hands is "the key of David, who opens and no one shall shut, who shuts and no one opens" (Rev 3:7).[28] The key of David is that held by Christ in his hand as the promised scion of David and his descendants (Rev 22:16), giving him unlimited control over the future world. He alone rules over mercy and justice, and he alone decides whether a given person will merit salvation at the end of times or not.[29]

31:6. On Abraham's house, which is parallel to the tower, see *Jub.* 22:24; 31:4; 32:22. See also Jeremias, λίθος, 280.

[27] Mingana, "New Jeremiah Apocryphon," 392.

[28] Hippolytus, *Frag. Dan.* 2.20 (PG 10:656). This description is based upon what was prophesied of Eliakim son of Hilkiah when he would be appointed royal treasurer: "I will place on his shoulder the key of the house of David; he shall open, and none shall shut; and he shall shut, and none shall open" (Isa 22:22). But a messianic interpretation of this verse is unknown in Judaism: see Jeremias, κλείς, 748. In Isa 22:22, "the key of the house of David" refers to the royal palace in Jerusalem.

[29] Jeremias, κλείς, 748–49. Thus Jesus leaves the keys to the kingdom of heaven in the hands of Peter: "and whatever you bind on earth shall be bound in heaven, and whatever you loose on earth shall be loosed in heaven" (Matt 16:19). Cf. *3 Bar.* 11:2; *T. Levi* 18:10–11; Ephrem de Nisibe, *Sermons on Paradise* 2.2; 7.1: "the cross is the key to paradise." See N. Séd, "Les Hymnes sur le Paradis de Saint Ephrem et les Tradition Juives," *Le Muséon* 81 (1968): 490; 1QS x 4; Brownlee, "Messianic Motifs," 208.

b. The Jewish Tradition

The motif of the rending of the keys against the background of the destruction of the temple appears in the talmudic tradition as well. The earliest version of this tradition appears in the Jerusalem Talmud, *Tractate Sheqalim* (6.3 [50a]).[30] Unlike that in *Baruch,* this early Palestinian talmudic tradition is rooted in the concrete historical background of the destruction of the First Temple. The figures of the Babylonian king Nebuchadnezzar, Jehoiachin king of Judah, and of the nobles of Judah,[31] play a central role in the description of Jehoiachin's surrender and exile to Babylonia in the year 597 BCE, together with many of the social elite of Jerusalem (2 Kgs 24:12–16). The lot of the temple was sealed upon Nebuchadnezzar's arrival in Daphne in Antioch.[32] A Judaean delegation meets with him to inform him that the time has come for the temple to be destroyed. Nebuchadnezzar is willing to suffice with Jehoiachin's surrender: "he whom I have anointed king you must give me, and I will go away."[33] Once Jehoiachin is told that he is wanted by Nebuchadnezzar,

---

[30] This tradition is incorporated in the original text of the Jerusalem Talmud as it appears in Codex Leiden, Scal. 3, Facsimile edition of the MS, Jerusalem, opening volume of *Tractate Shabbat,* 544; *Seridei ha-Yerushalmi* (from the Genizah), ed. L. Ginzberg (New York, 1909), 135–36. While the text is fragmented, the extant portion is identical to MS Leiden. On the nature of MS Leiden to *Sheqalim* and the genizah versions, see Y. Sussman, "Traditions of Study," 23ff.

[31] The nobles of Judah and Jerusalem appear in Jer 27:20 as having been exiled by Nebuchadnezzar together with Jehoiachin. According to Jer 39:6, upon the conquest of Jerusalem in 586 BCE the nobles of Judah were slaughtered by Nebuchadnezzar in Riblah, and were not exiled to Babylonia. Cf. Jer 52:24–27; 2 Kgs 25:18–21; Josephus, *Ant.* 10.140, 149–50. This may be the basis for the development of the tradition concerning their suicide.

[32] For the different readings: *rifni, dafne, dofna,* see *Tractate Sheqalim* (New York, 1954), ed. A. Sofer, 74. Daphne was a suburb of Antioch: see R. Vilk, "The Jews of Seleucid Syria" [Hebrew], Doctoral Dissertation, Tel Aviv, 1987, 115–16. Cf. *y. Sanh.* 10.6 (29c): "Israel was exiled in three exiles . . . and one to Daphne of Antioch." Daphne does not appear in the Bible. Its appearance in this tradition depicting the destruction of the First Temple is anachronistic, as is also the reference to the Great Sanhedrin. See Hüttenmeister, *Übersetzung des Talmud Yerushalmi; Sheqalim,* 131; Hoenig, *The Great Sanhedrin,* 143.

[33] The present tradition mixes the description of the exile of Jehoiachin with that of Zedekiah. While it was Jehoiachin who willfully surrendered and gave Jerusalem to the Babylonians, Zedekiah, his uncle, was the king anointed by Nebuchadnezzar and whose name was changed by him from Mataniah to Zedekiah; see 2 Kgs 24:17; Jer 37:1. During Zedekiah's reign Jeremiah warned that "this city shall surely be given into the hand of the army of the king of Babylon and be taken" (Jer 38:3). This prophecy,

CHAPTER 3: The Abandonment of the Temple

he takes the key [*sic*] of the temple,[34] climbs onto the roof of the sanctuary, and says to God: "Master of the Universe, in the past we were faithful to You, and Your keys were given to us. Now that they are not faithful, here are Your keys given back to You." After the nobles of Judaea saw this, they climbed up to their roofs, jumped off, and were killed.

This tradition reflects a characteristic Jewish approach, according to which the destruction of the temple is the result of a divine decision, the Babylonian king being merely the rod of God's anger.[35] For this reason it is the Jewish Sanhedrin that informs him that the time has come for the temple to be destroyed. The delivery of the keys expresses the religious and national responsibility of the people and its leaders to guard the integrity and security of the temple, the dwelling place of God. Once it is no longer within their power to fulfill this task, they return the keys. The earlier tradition is not at all interested in the destiny of the keys or to whom they were given. Thus is added to it the exegesis of two *amoraim* who disagree among themselves: one of them states that Jehoiachin threw them heavenwards and they did not fall down, while another says that he saw a kind of hand taking them from his hand. The giving of the keys is a symbolic act, intended to express the failure of the leadership who were unable to prevent the destruction, and hence are no longer to be entrusted with the keys to the sanctuary. Jehoiachin is the one to return the keys, but his use of the plural form reflects the Jewish approach, widespread in Palestinian talmudic sources, that responsibility for the failure is collective, and not imposed upon one or another individual, but upon the people as a whole.[36] The suicide of the nobles of Judaea gives further expression to this feeling of guilt. The story in the Jerusalem Talmud relies upon the passage in Isa 22:1–2: "The oracle concerning the valley of vision. What do you mean that you have gone up, all of you, to the housetops, You who are full of shouting, tumultuous city, exultant town? Your slain are not slain with the sword or dead in battle." In keeping with this biblical source, the rooftops play a central role in the story: Jehoiachin goes up to the roof of the sanctuary to return the keys to the Almighty, and the nobles of Judah "go up to their rooftops, and fall down and are killed." In this tradition the death of the nobles

---

stating that the destruction of the city was the result of a divine decision, is even placed in the mouth of Nebuzaradan in his words to Jeremiah (Jer 40:3–4).

[34] Thus according to *y. Šeqal.* (ed. Sofer), 74. In MS München, 1st ed., Venice, 1522–23, the reading is מפתחות ("keys").

[35] According to Isa 10:5–7.

[36] Like the collective guilt in the Palestinian talmudic sources following the Bar Kokhba rebellion: *y. Taʿan.* 4.2 (69a). See Efron, "The Bar-Kokhba War," 63, 70; Ben Shalom, "The Support of the Sages."

of Judah is not at all connected to the temple, as they fall from "their rooftops"; the use of these verses from Isaiah is intended to emphasize that their death does not occur by sword or by battle.

Unlike the tradition in *Syriac Baruch,* in the Palestinian Jewish tradition the scene takes place entirely *before* the destruction of the temple, and not thereafter. Those responsible for the existence of the temple, the king and the nobles, turn over the keys, and there is still hope to save it.

The ancient Palestinian midrash, *Leviticus Rabbah* (19.6; ed. Margaliot, 2:432–437)[37] presents a more colorful and detailed tradition, albeit similar in general outlines to that in the Jerusalem Talmud.[38] This version is likewise rooted in the background of the historical events that preceded the destruction of the First Temple and the Babylonian Exile, but it expands the narrated time period, beginning with a description of the destiny of Jehoiachin's father, Jehoiakim,[39] and concluding with Jehoiachin's exile to Babylonia. This tradition also explains the justification for the returning of the keys, for the first time, by the fact that those serving in the temple had not carried out their task faithfully: "We did not merit to be faithful stewards (גזברין נאמנין)." From here the later talmudic tradition developed the attitude to the priests as the explicit guardians of the temple. Rather than the nobles of Judah, who climbed onto the roofs and died, בחורין של ישראל: "the youths of Israel" appear here. David Goodblatt, who argues for the antiquity of the tradition referring to the priests, suggests that rather than בחורין של ישראל, "the youths of Israel," we read בחירי ישראל, "the chosen ones of Israel," to be understood as a poetic expression for the priests. That is to say, those chosen for the priesthood are "chosen ones," and may be identified with the Zaddokites in the scroll of the *Damascus Document*. According to his view, the tradition in *Leviticus Rabbah* is consistent with that of *Syraic Baruch* and the Babylonian Talmud as well, attributing the act to the priests and not to the nobles of Judah, whose mention in the Palestinian Talmud Goodblatt sees as a secondary development.[40] This interpretation seems to me forced. While in the talmudic tradition the word

---

[37] On the antiquity of this midrash, see Zunz, *Ha-Derashot be-Yisra'el,* 343 n. 104; H. Albeck, "Midrash Vayiqra Rabbah" [Hebrew], in *Sefer ha-yovel likhevod Levi Ginzberg* (ed. S. Leiberman et al.; New York, 1946), 27ff.; M. Margaliot, *Mavo Nispahim u-maftehot la-MidrashVayiqra Rabbah* (Jerusalem, 1972), xxxii–xxxiii.

[38] On the similarity between this midrash and the Yerushalmi, see Margaliot, xvii, xxvii–xxxiii.

[39] The section that speaks about Jehoiakim is taken from another source; see Albeck, "Midrash Vayikra Rabbah," 31.

[40] Goodblatt, "Suicide in the Sanctuary," 16–17.

CHAPTER 3: The Abandonment of the Temple

בחורין also appears in the sense of "chosen,"[41] it never does so in the sense of "the chosen of Israel." By contrast, this expression appears in similar contexts in other talmudic passages in the sense of young people.[42] Second, the strong and evident connection between the tradition in *Leviticus Rabbah* and that in the Jerusalem Talmud indicates that the same Palestinian tradition is present in both. "The nobles of Judah" is the original expression appearing in all manuscripts and versions of the Jerusalem Talmud.[43] Thus, both the change made in this midrash and the justification given for the giving of the keys indicate the beginning of the process of distancing of the Jewish tradition from its sources and its transposition to the destruction of the Second Temple, in which there is no longer any place for "the nobles of Judah."[44]

The Babylonian tradition reflects a further stage in the development of the Jewish tradition (*b. Taʿan.* 29a; *Yal. Shimʿoni* 2.249, 421). True, the subject here is still the destruction of the First Temple ("after the temple was destroyed the first time . . ."), and the reference to Isa 22:1–2 is maintained. But it is already mixed with a mélange of traditions that speak of disasters that visited the Jewish people, including the destructions of the First Temple, the Second Temple, and Betar.[45] The actual historical background of the destruction of the

---

[41] Albeit in the singular: *b. Šabb.* 105a: "I have made you chosen בחור among the nations"; *Gen. Rab.* 76.1: "The chosen בחור among the patriarchs and the chosen among the prophets. . . ." Cf. J. Levy, "bahur," in *Wörterbuch über die Talmudim und Midraschim* (Berlin & Vienna, 1924), 1:209.

[42] See *b. Giṭ.* 57b; *b. Sanh.* 92b; there is also an expression בחורי ישראל (*b. Ber.* 43b; *b. Šabb.* 62b; *b. Yoma* 9b; *b. Pesaḥ.* 87a; cf. Levy, *Wörterbuch*, 210). While in the Bible the word בחור admittedly appears as a passive participle of בחר, it only appears there in a military context, and one may assume that it comes in the sense of a young man, as is its regular meaning. It is used numerous times as a parallel to בתולה, "virgin" (Deut 32:25; Jer 51:22; Isa 23:4; Ps 148:12), or as a term for those serving in the army. In any event, the word בחיר, *electus*, has a totally different meaning, referring in the Bible to one who has been chosen by God; this title relates to the servant of God, identified with the people of Israel and its leaders, such as Samuel, Moses, etc.: 2 Sam 21:6; Isa 42:1; 43:20; 45:4; Ps 89:4; 106:23; etc.

[43] *Šeqal.* (ed. Sofer); Sussman, "Tradition of Study"; Goodblatt, "Suicide in the Sanctuary," 16 n. 17.

[44] As we have seen, the original tradition already contains anachronisms connecting it to the Second Temple period. The tendency of the Sages to relate to the destruction of the Second Temple while using scriptures and traditions that speak of the destruction of the First Temple is widespread in talmudic literature (see Ginzberg, *Legends of the Jews*, 6:391 n. 24).

[45] The tendency to confuse the traditions of the destructions also exists in the Yerushalmi, *y. Taʿan.* 4.8 (68d–69b).

First Temple disappears completely: the scene no longer refers to Nebuchadnezzar, Daphne, and Jehoiachin, and the negotiation between the Sanhedrin and the Babylonian king is completely missing. It no longer speaks of the "nobles of Judah" or of the "chosen ones of Israel" who climbed upon the roofs and died; instead, readers are introduced for the first time to different groups of young priests who go up to the roof of the sanctuary, throw the keys heavenwards, and throw themselves into the fire:

> When the First Temple was about to be destroyed, bands upon bands of young priests with the keys to the temple in their hands assembled, and mounted the roof of the temple and exclaimed: "Master of the Universe, as we did not merit to be faithful treasurers, these keys are handed back into your keeping." They then threw the keys towards heaven, and there emerged the figure of a hand and received the keys from them, whereupon they jumped and fell into the fire.[46]

In the Babylonian Talmud, unlike the Palestinian tradition but similar to *Syriac Baruch* and the *Paralipomena,* this scene takes place *after* the destruction of the temple—a detail that changes the meaning of the tradition as a whole. In the Palestinian tradition, even though the destiny of the temple has been decided, Jehoiachin attempts to reverse the sentence: he returns the keys to God and hands himself over in the hopes of saving the temple. This intention is likewise reflected in Nebuchadnezzar's unwillingness to destroy it, a refusal that finds clearer expression in *Leviticus Rabbah*. In the Babylonian tradition, the returning of the keys can no longer help to save the temple, and the action thereby becomes further removed from its significance in the earlier Palestinian tradition. Instead of the nobles of Judah, a well-established social stratum during the days of the First Temple, the young priests appear—that is, young priests who were responsible for guarding the temple during the Second Temple period, and who may also have been charged with keeping the keys.[47] Their appearance here is evidently based upon a firm tradition connecting the death or suicide of the priests and the young priests with the destruction of the First and Second Temples.[48]

---

[46] *B. Taʿan.* 29a; ET from the *Soncino Talmud: Seder Moʿed,* IV (London, 1938), 155.

[47] *M. Tamid* 1.1; *m. Yoma* 1.7; *m. Sanh.* 9.6; *b. Sanh.* 82b.

[48] The priests are included among those executed by Nebuchadnezzar at Riblah (2 Kgs 25:18–21; Jer 52:24–27; Josephus, *Ant.* 10.140, 149–50). According to the talmudic tradition, the young priests were killed by Nebuzaradan: *y. Taʿan.* 4.8 (69a-b); *b. Sanh.* 96b; *Lam. Rab.* (ed. Vilna), 4:16. The death of the young priests is connected with the murder of Zechariah son of Jehoiada (2 Chr 24:20–22; cf. Lam. 2:20; 4:13), incorporated by *Tg. Esth. II* within the tradition of the throwing of the keys (see *Tg. Esth. II* 1:3). On the suicide of the priests and their jumping into the fire upon the

The Babylonian Talmud continues the process of moving the tradition to the Second Temple, a process that already began in *Leviticus Rabbah* and that finds definite expression in *'Abot de Rabbi Nathan* (Version A, 4, ed. Shechter, p. 24; Version B, 7, ed. Shechter, p. 21).[49] In this midrash the tradition is removed to the days of Rabban Yohanan ben Zakkai—that is, after the destruction of the Second Temple—and is incorporated within the legends of the destruction. The reference to Isa 22:1 disappears and in its place appears another biblical source, one more suitable to the historical background in which this tradition is rooted: "Open your doors, O Lebanon, that the fire may devour your cedars!" (Zech 11:1).[50] Rather than the young priests of the Babylonian tradition, *'Abot de Rabbi Nathan* mentions the "high priests" (in Version A) or the "sons of the high priests" (in Version B). Instead of the "loyal stewards" (*gizbarin ne'emanin*) appearing in *Leviticus Rabbah* and in the Babylonian Talmud, *'Abot de Rabbi Nathan* uses an expression borrowed from the Greek: "loyal guardians" (*apotropsin*), a term that does not correspond to any defined function in the temple. In this respect, it is similar to the pseudepigraphic apocalyptic tradition and to the *Pesiqta Rabbati*, as discussed below. In both versions of *'Abot de Rabbi Nathan* the reason for the surrendering of the keys is that "we were not loyal stewards, [deserving] to perform the labor of the king and to eat at the royal table" (Version A) or "to eat from the treasure houses of the king" (Version B).[51]

In Version B an additional tradition concerning the destruction is appended to the story of the throwing of the keys, and both are attributed to Rabbi Hananiah, the Vice Priest (*segan ha-kohanim*): "Forty years before the temple was destroyed and the Sanctuary was burnt the people of Jerusalem would lock the doors [of the temple], and wake to find them open, as is said: 'Open your doors, O Lebanon.'" The reference here to Rabbi Hananiah the

---

destruction of the Second Temple, see Josephus, *J.W.* 6.280; Cassius Dio, *History of Rome* 66.6.3. On the relations between the Babylonian tradition and Josephus, see Efron, "Simeon ben Shatah and Alexander Jannaeus," 176ff.

[49] On the late date of *'Abot R. Nat.* and its composite nature, see p. 49 n. 24 above.

[50] Lebanon is interpreted as referring to the temple because the cedar wood used in its construction was brought from Lebanon: 1 Kgs 5:20ff.; 7:2: "the House of the Forest of Lebanon." See, e.g.: *Mek. de-Rashbi, Beshalah* 17.14 (ed. Epstein-Melamed; 124); *Sipre, Pinhas* 134 (ed. Horowitz; 181); *b. Yoma* 39b, and also all of the traditions about R. Yohanan ben Zakkai's departure from Jerusalem; *Lam. Rab.* 1.5 (ed. Buber; 37); *b. Giṭ.* 56b; *'Abot R. Nat.,* Version A, 4 (ed. Schechter; 22, 24); Version B, 6 (19).

[51] Version A, it is true, preserved from *Lev. Rab.* and the Bavli the phrase גזברין נאמנים ("faithful stewards"), but it omits the jumping from the roof of the sanctuary, mentioned in Version B (ראש ההיכל). Version A also does not identify the suicide of the priests.

Vice Priest and the incorporation of the traditions brought in his name reveals something of the associative method of this midrash. The choice of Rabbi Hananiah the Vice Priest to convey these traditions suits his statement in tractate *'Abot:* "Pray for the peace of the rulers, for were it not for the fear of them, every person would swallow up his neighbor" (*m. 'Abot* 3.2).[52] It is likewise consistent with the conciliatory spirit towards the Roman Empire that permeates all the legends of destruction in this midrash. The story concerning the gates of the sanctuary opening by themselves already appears, as we have noted, in Josephus among the signs that preceded and heralded the approaching destruction,[53] and it is mentioned in similar manner in the ancient Palestinian talmudic tradition:

> They taught: Forty years before the destruction of the temple the Western lamp [of the candelabrum] was extinguished, and the crimson-colored ribbon [placed on the head of the scape-goat on the Day of Atonement] turned red, and the lot for the Lord [on the Day of Atonement] came up in the left hand. And they would lock the gates of the Sanctuary in the evening, and wake up to find them open. Rabban Yohanan ben Zakkai said to them: "Sanctuary, why do you alarm us? We know that your end is to be destroyed, as said, 'Open your doors, O Lebanon, that the fire may devour your cedars!'" (*y. Yoma* 6.3; 43c)

The Babylonian Talmud (*b. Yoma* 39b) also brings this tradition and, notwithstanding various changes, deletions, and additions, it preserves the main

---

[52] This dictum is included with a characteristic correction to this midrash in ch. 31 (ed. Schechter; 68): "Rabbi Nehunyah [*sic*] the Vice Priest, says, 'Pray for the peace of the government, that rules us all the days, for were it not for its fear, we would each swallow up his neighbor (בלענו) instead of (בלעו)." The name of Rabbi Hananiah the Vice Priest is here replaced by Rabbi Nehuniah, under the influence of Rabbi Nehuniah son of Hakanah, whose dictum appears immediately thereafter, and is also mentioned in *m. 'Abot* 3.5. On the basis of the words of Akaviah son of Mahallalel in the Mishnah ("From whence do you come? From a putrid drop. And whence do you go? To a place of dirt, maggots, and worms") God rebukes Titus: "Rotten evildoer, putrid, worm, and maggot." The name of Akaviah son of Mahallalel, whose dictum precedes that of Rabbi Hananiah the Vice Priest in *'Abot* (3.1–2), evidently underlies the associative homilies on the expression "*Hillel Brosh*": "Wail, oaks of Bashan," from Zech 11:2. Similarly, the mention of "sons of the high priests" in *m. Ketub.* 13.1 in relation to the law pertaining to one who goes out "to the maritime provinces" led to the appearance in the present midrash of "the sons of the high priests" in the story following the rampage of Titus and his setting out "to be praised in the maritime provinces" (see Efron, "Bar Kokhba War," 100–101).

[53] See above, p. 79.

CHAPTER 3: The Abandonment of the Temple   95

elements of the ancient tradition.[54] But in the midrash (Version B) the story of the doors of the sanctuary is removed from the original context in which it appears in the two Talmuds, and is attached in an associative manner to the story of the throwing heavenwards of the keys of the temple. This combination creates a patently anachronistic combination: whereas the tradition of the opening of the gates of the sanctuary describes a situation prior to the destruction ("forty years before . . ."), that of the returning of the keys, here directly connected with it, describes a situation that occurs after "the temple was destroyed and the sanctuary burned." Thus, the discussion of the tradition in both versions of *'Abot de Rabbi Nathan* exemplifies the anthological nature of this collection, which is compiled of "a mosaic of sayings gathered in a post-talmudic interweave."[55]

The final stage in the development of the talmudic tradition about the turning over of the keys of the temple finds its expression in *Pesiqta Rabbati*, which presents an eclectic version, based upon an amalgam of both the talmudic and the Christian traditions (*Pesiqta Rabbati* 26, ed. Ish-Shalom, p. 131).[56] Although here the event occurs in the days of Jeremiah, that is, on the eve of the destruction of the First Temple, the main heroes of the story are not Jehoiachin, the young priests, or the sons of the high priest or of the high priests, but, as in the *Targum Sheni* to Esther,[57] the high priest himself. It is he who throws the keys, and the text emphasizes that this took place "when the high priest saw that the temple had been burnt"—i.e., *after* the destruction of the temple. The cooperation between the conquerors and the Jewish delegation is further heightened by the description of the enemies sitting on the dais on the Temple Mount and taking counsel with the elders as to how to burn the temple. The central motif of the story thus becomes the death of the religious leadership and those serving in the holy place, and all of the various figures serving in the temple who appeared in the earlier traditions are here gathered together under one roof: the high priest and his daughter, the priests, and the Levites, who commit suicide together with their musical instruments, as in the *Targum Sheni to Esther*. Unlike the earlier Jewish tradition, here the high priest

---

[54] In the Babylonian Talmud, these traditions are connected with Rabbi Hananiah the Vice Priest; we may assume that this fact also influenced the preacher to choose him as the one transmitting both traditions.

[55] Efron, "Bar Kokhba War," 101 n. 247; Kister, *'Aboth de-Rabbi Nathan*, 12.

[56] On the late date of the *Pesiqta*, see below.

[57] Above, n. 48.

who surrenders the keys is slaughtered together with his daughter on the altar, the place where he used to offer the perpetual offering.[58]

On the other hand, it is clear that the *Pesiqta* makes use of the pseudepigraphic apocalyptic tradition. The story of the throwing of the keys appears here in the same context and is combined within the same frame story: the four angels stand at the four corners of the sanctuary (or of the city, as in *Syriac Baruch*) and wish to burn it, as against the lone angel who descends from heaven.[59] The destruction of the temple is performed by the angels and not by the enemies, and for the same reason: so that the enemies will not be able to brag that they destroyed the temple—"A conquered city you have conquered, a dead people you have killed."[60] The conquerors are called upon to enter the temple, since "the guard has left it and gone"; as in the tradition of *Syriac Baruch*, here too the keys are thrown heavenwards, and the high priest, evidently parallel to Jeremiah in the *Paralipomena*, says the very same words: "Here are the keys of your house; I have been a faithless steward of it."

What is the relationship between the tradition in *Syriac Baruch* and the talmudic tradition? Is it possible to identify relations of dependence between them, and if so, which one represents the authentic tradition?

---

[58] The slaughter of the high priest may have been influenced by the slaughter of 4000 priests by Nebuchadnezzar related in the *Targum Sheni of Esther*, a motif based upon the slaughter of the young priests in the tradition of the murder of Zechariah son of Jehoiada. The story of Zechariah's murder may have also influenced the locale of the murder of the high priest, near the altar. The tradition in *Pesiqta Rabbati* reveals lines of similarity to the version in *Targum Sheni* of Esther: both of them speak of the high priest in the singular, in both the servants of the temple commit suicide together with their musical instruments, and both link this story to the murder of Zechariah son of Jehoiada (although in the *Pesiqta* this is only by way of allusion). Nevertheless, the *Targum* does not explicitly mention the throwing of the keys, but speaks of "guards" in the plural, and brings a detailed tradition concerning the murder of Zechariah son of Jehoiada. *Targum Sheni* to Esther is dated at the end of the seventh century or the beginning of the eighth century CE. See Komlush, *ha-Miqra be-Or ha-Targum*, 97.

[59] But the functions were switched: in *Syriac Baruch* the single angel delays the destruction until the hiding of the temple vessels, while in *Pesiqta Rabbati* he, and not a voice emanating from the sanctuary, is the one to break through the wall and to declare that the master of the house has abandoned it.

[60] As in the Babylonian Talmud (*b. Sanh.* 96b), where it is also in the context of the destruction of the temple, but without any connection to the tradition of the throwing of the keys heavenwards.

CHAPTER 3: The Abandonment of the Temple   97

In a recently published book, Anat Israeli-Taran argues the antiquity and authenticity of the tradition in *Syriac Baruch*,[61] basing her argument on the widely accepted dating of *Syriac Baruch* and the *Paralipomena* at the end of the Second Temple period. The presence in these works of the motif of the giving over of the keys testifies to the motif's originating close to the destruction, as part of a dirge that was *supposedly* recited over the destruction of the First Temple. In her opinion, this tradition constitutes the earliest layer upon which the talmudic tradition developed. The amoraic traditions in the Jerusalem Talmud and in *Leviticus Rabbah* preserved the pseudo-historical context of the tradition within the period of the First Temple and further tightened this connection by substituting figures from the First Temple period for the "priests," who serve as the heroes of the story in the apocalyptic tradition, and by adding the act of suicide. The Babylonian Talmud continued to adhere to this pseudo-historical context, but by attributing the key-throwing to the priests rather than to the protagonists of the destruction of the First Temple, it too connected this tradition to the destruction of the Second Temple, thereby returning to the point of departure of *Syriac Baruch*. Israeli-Taran correctly notes the relation of the *Pesiqta Rabbati* to the tradition of *Syriac Baruch*, on the one hand, and to the early talmudic tradition, on the other. However, in her opinion it was specifically the later tradition of *'Abot de Rabbi Nathan* that preserved the original literary and historical context of the legend: the tradition of the throwing of the keys is integrated there, as it is in *Syriac Baruch*, within the dirge, and is explicitly connected to the destruction of the Second Temple. "This chronological 'conversion' in practice removes the pseudo-historical dress with which this legend had already been enveloped in the apocalyptic literature, as from the outset this legend was created against the background of the second destruction and not the first."[62]

The explanation for the development of this tradition is rooted, according to Israeli-Taran, in the motif of the suicide of the priests added to the talmudic tradition. The deletion of this motif from the tradition in *Syriac Baruch* and in the *Paralipomena* reflects the polemic within Jewish society between the priests,

---

[61] A. Israeli-Taran (*'Aggadot ha-Ḥurban* [Tel Aviv, 1997], 92–94 [Hebrew]), who follows in the footsteps of Goodblatt ("Suicide in the Sanctuary," 22–23). According to Goodblatt, the early Palestinian talmudic tradition presents a secondary version by comparison to the Babylonian talmudic tradition, which connects the story of the suicide and the throwing of the keys to the priests ("Suicide," 16–17). Goodblatt's conclusion is surprising in light of the criteria that he himself established in his various studies of the criticism, classification, and sorting of the talmudic sources (cf. D. Goodblatt, "Tannaitic Support or Priestly Influence" [Hebrew], *Cathedra* 29 [1984]: 7; idem, *The Monarchic Principle*, 78, 104).

[62] Ibid.

who saw suicide as a supreme expression of loyalty to the temple, and that of the Sages, who were opposed to this extreme ideology and therefore sought to suppress these traditions. Even when this motif arose in the Jerusalem Talmud and in *Leviticus Rabbah* it did so in borrowed identity and context. However, this "internal censorship" did not withstand the distancing in time and the strong impression of these acts, so that specifically in the later talmudic sources the mask concealing this motif would be removed and the tradition uncovered in its fullness in the Babylonian Talmud, in the *Pesiqta Rabbati,* and in the *'Abot de Rabbi Nathan.*

But the alleged convoluted development of this tradition as described by Israeli-Taran and her explanation of it raise a number of questions. The author seems to take as self-evident that *Syriac Baruch* and the *Paralipomena* were composed in the land of Israel, where they absorbed motifs related to the destruction of the Second Temple, and that there is a direct line of development by which these motifs devolved until their incorporation in the Palestinian talmudic literature. In my opinion there is no real basis for this assumption, since there is no proof that *Syriac Baruch* was in fact composed in the land of Israel. To the contrary, the Jewish traditions used therein betray an ideological and stylistic proximity specifically to non-Palestinian works.[63] The assumption is even more doubtful in relation to the *Paralipomena,* which is painted in clearly Christian colors, and took shape among eastern Christian Gnostic circles.[64] Except for *Pesiqta Rabbati,* a late medieval midrash that evidently knew *Syriac Baruch* and other apocalyptic works by means of its connections with Christians in southern Italy,[65] we have no proof that the third and fourth century Palestinian Amoraim knew *Syriac Baruch* or any other apocalyptic works.

In surveying the development of the talmudic tradition, the above-mentioned author maintains the distinctions accepted by scholarship in reference to the talmudic sources, which she discusses in chronological order: the Jerusalem Talmud, *Leviticus Rabbah,* the Babylonian Talmud, and *Pesiqta*

---

[63] Thus, e.g., the tradition of the hiding of the vessels (*2 Bar.* 6:6–10) is closer to the Jewish Hellenistic tradition that finds expression in *2 Hasmoneans,* and not to the Palestinian talmudic tradition. Both traditions connect the act of hiding away the vessels to the circle of stories of Jeremiah, who was a much-admired figure among the Jews of Egypt, and not to Josiah, as in the talmudic tradition; both traditions express the eschatological aspect. The author of *Syriac Baruch* also reveals a certain closeness to such works as the *Protevangelium of James* and the *Jeremiah Apocryphon,* which were not composed in Palestine.

[64] Above, n. 17.

[65] See below, in the discussion of the virgins who weave the veil.

CHAPTER 3: The Abandonment of the Temple   99

Rabbati. However, her conclusions turn these distinctions on their head. In her opinion, it is precisely the late talmudic sources—*Pesiqta Rabbati* and *'Abot de Rabbi Nathan*—that preserved the authentic tradition, rather than the early Palestinian sources such as the Jerusalem Talmud and *Leviticus Rabbah*.

The reason why the tradition in *Syriac Baruch* and in the *Paralipomena* of the heavenward key-throwing is in fact rooted in the background of the destruction of the First Temple is self-evident, stemming as it does from the pseudepigraphical character of these works. But why should this "pseudo-historical" facade also be maintained by the Palestinian Amoraim, who went so far as to replace the priests by authentic figures from the First Temple period? And why did the Babylonian Talmud again change the identity of the heroes, but continue to preserve the pseudo-historical background?

Israeli-Taran's answer to these questions, surprisingly, is that it was precisely the early sources, which were relatively close to the events, that succeeded in concealing and forgetting the act of suicide of the priests, but, as these events became obscured in the historical memory of the nation, the powerful impression left by them actually became greater and brought about a situation where they could be related to with their proper identity! This explanation involves a reversal of the basic rules of study of historical sources, whose degree of reliability is generally determined by their proximity in time and place to the events depicted! The claim that the powerful impression of these events could not withstand the progress of time is particularly weak in relation to the talmudic literature, which was set down in writing relatively late in relation to the events mentioned.

In addition, it is difficult to believe that *'Abot de Rabbi Nathan*, specifically, preserved the original tradition. M. Kister states of this work that "the book—in its present form—is not a tannaitic work, and it is doubtful whether one may [even] say that in its present form it is amoraic; rather, it is best seen as a post-talmudic work. *It is distant and inferior, shallow and cliched, and frequently suffers from exaggerated secondary developments that damage the ancient form of the traditions as well as our ability to understand what is being said.*"[66]

The original tradition of the throwing of the keys is in fact that reflected in the early talmudic literature, even if it was perhaps recorded later than the apocalyptic tradition. It was originally associated with the period of the First Temple, as is indicated also by the context in which this tradition is included in the Jerusalem Talmud, of which the suicide of the nobles of Judah constitutes an integral part. The tradition in *Syriac Baruch*, notwithstanding its incorporation in a dirge over the destruction of Zion, was not intended to portray

---

[66] Kister, *'Aboth de-Rabbi Nathan*, 12.

the destruction or to weep over it. It seeks to emphasize the end of the earthly temple and of the function of those who serve there. The fact that the temple was destroyed is the decisive proof that the priests were false wardens, who therefore need to transfer the keys to the true warden who can guard the temple—that is, the heavenly Jerusalem and the heavenly temple. Hence the tradition in *Baruch* emphasizes, as does the Christian tradition as a whole as opposed to the Jewish tradition, to whom the keys were given and the identity of the true guardian. The only thread connecting *Syriac Baruch* and the early Palestinian Jewish tradition is the motif of the giving over of the keys. With regard to the other elements, *Baruch* resembles more the post-talmudic Jewish tradition of *'Abot de Rabbi Nathan* Version B and *Pesiqta Rabbati*. All these traditions relate the story to the destruction of the Second Temple; they speak of the priests who were revealed as "false wardens," and in all of them the keys are given over after the destruction of the temple and after all hopes to save it were lost. The fact that the motif of suicide does not appear in *Syriac Baruch* does not indicate the antiquity of this tradition, as argued by Goodblatt and Israeli-Taran. This motif is to be found on all levels of the talmudic tradition, constituting its ideological and educational core. The early Palestinian tradition in the Jerusalem Talmud and in *Leviticus Rabbah* seeks to emphasizes the collective responsibility of the leadership (King Jehoiachin and the nobles of Judah), who did not succeed in preventing the destruction and were prepared to pay the price for it. The suicide of the priests in later Jewish tradition is intended to restore to this class, whose prestige was clouded on the eve of the destruction of the Second Temple, its past glory and to emphasize the responsibility of the high priests, the sons of the high priests, and the young priests, for the destruction—the same responsibility that Jehoiachin and the nobles of Judah felt for the First Temple. The motive of the suicide is deleted from *Syriac Baruch* because it is opposed to the book's tendencies, which are based upon total rejection of the earthly temple and those who serve there. While the tradition in *Syriac Baruch* did make use of the Jewish tradition, it only did so using those elements that served its needs and its tendencies.

The intention of this tradition is likewise confirmed by the context in which it is incorporated, as I shall attempt to demonstrate in the discussion of the virgins who weave the curtain.

3.3. *The Virgins Weaving in the Temple (10:19)*

After Baruch addresses the priests and prods them to throw the keys of the temple heavenwards, he addresses the "virgins who weave (spin)[67] fine linen,

---

[67] *D'zlan*. The verb *'zl* mean to spin. Thus in Peshitta to Matt 6:28; Luke 12:27. See Kiraz, *Concordance to the Syriac New Testament*, 3:2150; Sokoloff, *Dictionary of Jewish Palestinian Aramaic*, 401; Hirshberg, *Hayyei Tarbut be-Yisra'el*, 133.

CHAPTER 3: The Abandonment of the Temple 101

and silk with gold of Ophir," ordering them to "make haste and take all things, and cast them into the fire, so that it may carry them to Him who made them . . . so that the enemies do not take possession of them" (*2 Bar.* 10:19).

Who were these virgins, and what were they weaving? What is the significance of this tradition, and what are its sources?

This tradition was first connected to talmudic traditions by Adolf Büchler, who attempted to prove that women inside the temple were engaged in weaving the veil.[68] In this context, S. Krauss cited the mishnah in *Šeqal.* 8.5:[69]

> Rabban Simeon the son of Gamaliel said in the name of Rabbi Simeon, son of the chief of the priests: The veil [*parokhet*] was a handsbreath in thickness, and was woven on seventy-two cords, each cord made up of twenty-four threads. It was forty cubits long and twenty cubits broad, and *was made up of eight-two times ten thousand threads.* Two veils were made every year, and three hundred priests were needed to immerse it [in the purifying bath].[70]

This mishnah is transmitted by Rabban Simeon ben Gamaliel II in the name of Rabbi Simeon son of the Vice Priest (*segan*), a third-generation *tanna*—that is, the son of R. Hanina the Vice Priest, who was evidently conversant with matters pertaining to the temple by virtue of his position.[71] In the course of its discussion of a temple veil that had been rendered impure, this mishnah elaborates on the making of the veil, its thickness, of how many threads it was woven, its length and width, the number made each year, and the number of priests needed to immerse it in water.[72]

S. Krauss, on the basis of an emendation of the word רבוא (here translated "tens of thousands") to ריבות ("maidens")—a change already suggested by some medieval Jewish commentators[73]—infers that the curtain was woven by

---

[68] Büchler, "Die Schauplätze des Bar-Kochbakrieges," 201 n. 1. Büchler cites in this context *t. Šeqal.* 2.6; *b. Ketub.* 106a; *y. Šeqal.* 4.3 (48a); *Cant. Rab.* 3.6, and related to this tradition the *Pesiq. Rab.* 26. On these sources, see below.

[69] Krauss, *Synagogale Altertümer,* 377–78.

[70] See the parallels to this mishnah: *y. Šeqal.* 8.4 (51b); *b. Tamid* 29b; *b. Ḥul.* 90b.

[71] A. M. Hyman, *Toldoth Tannaim ve'Amoraim* (Jerusalem, 1964) 3:1172. All of the traditions cited in his name relate to matters of the temple: thus in *m. Šeqal.* 8.5; *m. Ketub.* 2.8; *m. Menaḥ.* 11.9. In all three places the tradition is cited in his name by R. Simeon b. Gamaliel.

[72] English from: *The Talmud* (London: Soncino, 1938), *Moʿed* (vol. 7, p. 34).

[73] Commentary to *b. Tamid* 29b, attributed to the Rabad of Posquières (R. Abraham ben David, 1125?–1198), sometime erroneously identified as belonging to Rashi. Cf. similarly: R. Asher to *Sheqalim, naʿarot shehayo osot otan,* the main interpretation there; R. Obadiah of Bartenura to *m. Sheqalim,* one of the interpretations; *Tosafot*

eighty-two maidens.⁷⁴

S. Lieberman accepted the altered reading, in the wake of Büchler and Krauss, and interpreted the word ריבות as referring to young girls who had not yet reached their menarche, and were chosen to engage in this task because of their freedom from menstrual impurity. He identified these with the virgins in *2 Baruch* and concluded that "a college of eighty-two noble virgins below the age of puberty participated in the weaving of the temple veil."⁷⁵

In my opinion, the suggested connection between the tradition in *Baruch* and this mishnah is without basis.

First, even if we accept the suggested correction and read ריבות rather than רבוא, it does not seem reasonable to me that the task of weaving the veil, requiring considerable skill and experience, would be left in the hands of young girls simply because they had not yet menstruated. In all talmudic sources the word ריבה denotes a young woman or maiden who is already nubile, and not a young girl who has not yet menstruated.⁷⁶ This interpretation is consistent with what we know about the work of weaving throughout the ancient world, and particularly weaving for ritual purposes, which was performed by grown women.⁷⁷

Yom Tov to *m. Sheqalim,* one of the interpretations; Kahouth, *'Arukh Ha-Shalem,* 7:240, second commentary; Ratner, *Ahavat Zion ve-Yerushalayim: Sheqalim,* 52, "like another thought"; Albeck, to *m. Šeqal.* 8.5.

⁷⁴ Krauss, *Synagogale Altertümer,* 377–78, relied upon the corrected reading as suggested by R. Obadiah of Bartenura and the *'Arukh.* Krauss was also the first to connect this tradition to the *Protevangelium of James,* on which see below.

⁷⁵ Lieberman, *Hellenism in Jewish Palestine,* 168. He likewise based himself on Epstein, who accepted this correction (see Epstein, *Mavo le-Nusah ha-Talmud,* 952). See also Manns, "Une ancienne tradition sur la jeunesse de Marie," 107–8; Alon, "The Halakhah in the Epistle of Barnabas," 297 n. 3; Ilan, "The Status of the Jewish Woman in Palestine," 254–55.

⁷⁶ Jastrow, *Dictionary,* 1472; Sokoloff, *Dictionary* 513, *rabi.* See *t. Nid.* 1.9; *b. Niddah* 9b; *b. Yebam.* 59b; *y. Nid.* 1.1 (48d), 1.5 (49b); *b. Sanh.* 109b; *b. Ber.* 18b; *b. Šabb.* 127b; *b. Ketub.* 66b.

⁷⁷ Zeus, the father of the gods, commanded the virgin Pallas Athena to learn and to teach the skill of weaving: Hesiod, *Works and Days,* 64, in *The Homeric Hymns and Homerica* (LCL, pp. 6–7); idem, *Theogony,* 573–75 (ibid., 120–21). "The weaving daughters of the gods" is also a common motif in early Greek epic poetry. Thus, e.g., Homer, *Odyssey* 10.223ff., 254 (LCL; 1:360–61); 7.104–11 (LCL; 1:239–41); Homer, *Illiad,* 6.490 (LCL; 1:296–97). In Athens, the Athenian women wove the *peplos* (πέπλος), the garment of Athena, that was made every four years and carried in the Pan-Athenic processions. Lieberman tried to find support for his stance regarding the young age of the virgins who weave the curtain by comparing them to the weavers of the *peplos*

CHAPTER 3: The Abandonment of the Temple   103

Moreover, according to the talmudic sources, the task of weaving the curtain was assigned to women, who received payment from the temple treasury, in a manner analogous to the family of Beit Garmo, who were charged with the baking of the shewbread, or that of Abtinas, who were responsible for the incense (*t. Šeqal.* 2.6; *y. Šeqal.* 4.3 [48a]; *b. Ketub.* 106a; *Cant. Rab.* 3.6.). It may be that these women also belonged to a particular family that specialized in this work, similar to the families of Garmo and Abtinas.[78]

It nevertheless appears from the extant sources that in the Jewish temple there were also men involved in the weaving of the veil, such as Eleazar, who was responsible for the weavers of the veil (*m. Šeqal.* 5.1; *y. Šeqal.* 5.1 [49a]).[79]

(Leiberman, *Hellenism,* 168–69). Similarly, Mach connected the pure virgins in the *Protevangelium* with the maidens who wove the *peplos* (Mach, "Are There Jewish Elements in the Protevangelium Jacobi?" 217). Ilan compared the function of the virgins to "the virgins in the temples of the goddess Athena in Athens" ("The Status of the Jewish Woman," 254 n. 246). While it is true that the weaving of the *peplos* was begun by two or four girls (ἀρρηφόροι; carriers of the holy vessels), between seven and eleven years of age, who were chosen once a year from among the families of the aristocracy so as to carry out various religious functions, other women (ἐργαστίναι) from respected families continued in the weaving and embroidering of the *peplos*. The *arrēphoroi* were too young and few in number to make the *peplos* by themselves. Only these four young maidens, who received this honor, lived for a certain period in the house of the *arrēphoroi* located on the Acropolis (see Deubner, *Attische Feste,* 11–13, 31; Pomeroy, *Goddesses, Whores, Wives, and Slaves,* 76; Keuls, *The Reign of the Phallus,* 306–8). Moreover, the spinning of the *peplos* by the young girls, like their involvement in other ritual areas, is not connected with their menstrual purity but with the preparation of the young virgin girls, who had not yet married, for communal life and for their function therein in the future (Golden, *Childhood in Classical Athens,* 46–50).

[78] Ilan, "The Status of the Jewish Woman," 254. Cf. on the place of weaving and spinning as women's labor: Exod 35:25; Prov 31:19; *m. Neg.* 2.4; *y. Soṭah* 3.4 (19a).

[79] He may be identified with Eleazar, who is mentioned in Josephus as being in charge of the temple veil: *Ant.* 14.106-7. The role of the men in weaving the curtain is also implied by *Lam. Rab.* (Vilna ed.) 2.4: "Hundreds of shops of weavers of the curtain were in Kfar Nimrah." In the parallel in the Jerusalem Talmud (*y. Taʿan.* 7.8 [69a]), we read: "eighty shops of weavers of the *palgas.*" *Palgas* is a distortion of the Greek word *pinoles, phainoles, phailones, paenula,* which were a kind of trouser or travelling coat, wrapping, and covering. Thus, the weavers of *palgas* are weavers of cloth for the *paenula* (see Jastrow, *Dictionary,* 1165; Kahouth, *'Arukh ha-Shalem,* 6:338). Even if the tradition in *Lam. Rab.* regarding this matter is not precise, it is sufficient to reflect the awareness that there were also men who were engaged in the weaving of the veil. During the biblical period, weaving and spinning were characteristic labors of women, but special items, such as the weaving of fine linen, were woven by artisans who worked especially in this field (see Exod 35:35; 1 Chr 4:21; Yisraeli, "Labor," 1003).

This labor evidently required scrupulous observance of the rules of purity, although nothing is said in the talmudic sources to indicate that maidens and women in their child-bearing years were disqualified from engaging in this activity due to menstrual impurity. Moreover, in the talmudic sources the term בתולה does not refer to a girl who has not yet menstruated, but is used for a woman who has never had sexual relations (as opposed to a בעולה) and, by extension, to refer to anyone or anything that in some respect remains unaffected by human involvement.[80]

Second, in my opinion the reading רבוא is in any event the preferable one, being confirmed by the majority of good manuscripts of the Mishnah and Talmud; the alteration of the mishnaic text from רבוא to ריבות is only based upon a few manuscripts of the Babylonian Talmud.[81] In all other manuscripts and printed editions of the Mishnah and of both Talmuds, *without exception,* the word appears in the form רבוא or in its variant spellings—i.e., ריבוא / ריבוה / רבוא / ריבוא.[82] The word רבוא fits in well from both the syntactical point of

---

[80] See *y. Nid.* 1.4 (49a); *t. Šeb.* 3.14; *b. Yebam.* 61b; *y. Yebam.* ch. 9.1 (10a); Jastrow, *Dictionary,* 200; Kasovsky, *Thesaurus Mishnae,* 1:417; idem, *Thesaurus Talmudis,* 8. 846; Kosovsky, *Otsar Lashon Talmud Yerushalmi* (Jerusalem, 1982), 2:592. A married woman who has not yet born a child is occasionally described as a בתולה; see M. M. Kasher, *Torah Shelemah* (New York, 1958), 12:273. Leiberman conjectured that one is speaking here of a "virgin for blood," based on *m. Nid.* 1.4: "Who is a virgin for blood? Whoever has never seen [i.e., discharged] blood in her lifetime, even if she is married." But in this case one is speaking, not of a child, but of a grown maiden "whose time has come to see"; thus Meiri's commentary.

[81] MS München (95) to Sheqalim (*Zera'im-Mo'ed*), photo ed., p. 227, בשמונים ושתים ריבות; MS Hamburg 169 to *b. Ḥul.*, p. 123: ומשמונים ושתים ריבות נעשות. Likewise in a late addition added between the lines of MS München to the Bavli, *b. Ḥul.* 90b (*Qodashim-Toharot*), 890. Cf. Epstein, *Mavo le-Nusaḥ ha-Mishnah,* 952; likewise *Diqduqei Sofrim* to *Ḥul.*, 122. While the origin of *Sheqalim* is in the Talmud Yerushalmi, once it became part of the curriculum of students of the Babylonian Talmud it underwent a long and extensive process of "babylonization," particularly in the version that was printed with the BT, which is "not only a garbled and eroded version, as a result of the routine of students of the Bavli and their glosses added over the generations, but was evidently a version that was reworked by force, with deliberate intention" (Sussman, "Traditions of Study," 25). This version changed its form due to the repeated revisions that it underwent, like all the other tractates of the Bavli (ibid., 41–42). The form ריבות, which appears in the JT in MS München alone, is influenced by the BT (ibid., 75 n. 170). Cf. Assis, "On the History of Text of Tractate Shekalim," 145–46.

[82] In manuscripts of the Mishnah: MS Paris, 328–29 (Jerusalem, 1973), Pt. I, 258: רבוא (MS Paris is one of the four earliest surviving manuscripts of the Mishnah); MS Cambridge, ed. W. H. Lowe, I.55b: רבוא. Printed editions: an unknown printed edition (Pissaro or Constantinople), *Seder ha-Mishnah: Zera'im-Mo'ed-Nashim* (Jeru-

CHAPTER 3: The Abandonment of the Temple

view and that of the context of the Mishnah: if one is indeed speaking of "young ladies," the structure of the sentence would have needed to be: ושמונים ושתים רבות עושות אותה[83] (i.e., rather than רבוא, as in our reading).

The meaning of the word רבוא is ten thousand, a myriad, or some other phrase to indicate a very large quantity.[84] This mishnah deals with the dimensions of the veil, and describes in exaggerated terms the large number of threads required for its weaving, or their great monetary value.[85]

---

salem, 1971), 102: רבוא; *Mishnah 'im perush ha-Rambam,* translated from the Arabic by D. Kapah, *Seder Mo'ed* (Jerusalem, 1964), 153, and the first printed edition: רבוא; MS Pharma, fol. 85: ריבו; MS Kaufmann, *Zera'im, Mo'ed, Nashim,* 138: ריבוה. In these last two manuscripts the form is: ריבו (in MS Kaufmann it seems that the final *hē* is added, and may belong to the first word of the following line: היתה). In manuscripts of the Palestinian Talmud (Yerushalmi): MS Leiden: רבוא; 1st ed., Venice: רבוא. MS Leiden is free of Babylonian additions and is a version that is "authentic, clean and generally speaking good," which does not suffer from the phenomenon of "babylonization" and was not gone over by the quills of [innumerable] "correctors" (Sussman, "Traditions of Study," 23–24; Epstein, "On Fine Points of the Jerusalem Talmud," 261; Rabinowitz, "Talmud Jerusalem"; Lieberman, "Introduction to the Leiden Manuscript," 233–34). *Sheqalim,* ed. A. Sofer, 90; MS Off. 726 (=Neubauer 370): ריבוא. Manuscripts of the Babylonian Talmud (Bavli): *b. Ḥul.,* MS München: רבא, in the principal reading, and as opposed to the late addition between the lines. For some reason, this matter is not mentioned in *Diqduqei Sofrim* to *Ḥul.* or by Epstein, *Mavo le-Nusaḥ ha-Mishnah,* 2:952; *b. Tamid* 29b, MS Firenze (which is the earliest complete extant manuscript of the Babylonian Talmud), I:304: רבוא. And likewise in MS Venice (first printing), to *Bavli Sheqalim, Ḥul.* and *Tamid* (see Sussman, "Traditions of Study," 28; 75 n. 170).

[83] See Shlomo Adani, *Melekhet Shlomo le-Masekhet Sheqalim,* ch. 2: רבוא: "There are those who read here ריבות, as is written by R. Obadiah, and R. Menahem De Lonzano wrote that this interpretation is not clear, for if were so, it would need to read 'and eighty-two maidens do it (עושות אותה),' and I have found [the reading] רבואות" (*Shisha Sidrei Mishnayot Vilna ha-Shalem 'im shemonim ve-ahat Hosafot; Seder Mo'ed,* I [Jerusalem: Ma'ayan ha-Hokhmah, 1960], 39).

[84] Jastrow, *Dictionary,* 1140; Levy, *Otzar Lashon ha-Talmud,* 4:413; Sokoloff, *Dictionary,* 513, רבו.

[85] It was also understood thus by the earliest and principal exegetes of the Mishnah and the Talmud: Rashi to *b. Ḥul.* 90b, "threads," as the first interpretation; Maimonides to *Mishnah Sheqalim:* "eighty-two myriads: eight hundred thousand dinar and twenty thousand dinar. And the curtain was made in sections, and whatever was said regarding this veil is simply an exaggeration, and thus was it explained in the Talmud" (in *Mishnah 'im Perush ha-Rambam,* ed. Kapah), *Seder Mo'ed,* 236–37. Likewise in *Mishnah 'im Perush ha-Rambam,* 1st ed.; R. Obadiah Bartenura on Sheqalim: "and eighty-two myriads: This was the number of threads of which it was made; another interpretation, the number of gold coins which were spent on it." Shlomo Adani, *Sefer Melekhet Shlomo le-Masekhet Sheqalim:* "and [eighty] two myriads . . . meaning eighty-two gold talents";

In my opinion, the "virgins who weave fine linen, and silk with gold of Ophir" in *2 Baruch* are not to be identified with the women who wove the curtain of the Jewish temple, because the former tradition does not reflect an internal Jewish historical reality. Its hidden contents and intentions become clear against the background of concepts and folk traditions widespread in early Christianity.

In the pseudepigraphal gospel known as the *Protevangelium of James*,[86] attributed to Jesus' brother James, which describes the birth of Mary, her youth, and the birth of her son Jesus, it is related how the virgin Mary was raised in the temple from the age of three. When she reached the age of twelve, the priests decided, due to their fear of contamination of the temple, to place her with an elderly widower named Joseph, who would take care of her. The priestly council decided to make a veil for the temple of the Lord, and for this purpose the priests assembled "pure virgins from the tribe of David" (10:1).

Among the eight pure virgins found in order to perform this task was the child Mary, who was also "of the tribe of David and was pure before God." A lot was cast among the little girls as to who would weave the gold, who the amiantus, who the linen, the silk, the hyacinth-blue, the scarlet, and the pure purple (10:2). The scarlet and the purple fell to Mary's lot. During the spinning, an angel appeared to her and informed her that she would conceive from God's word, that the child to be born to her would be a holy one and called son of the Most High, and that she would call him Jesus. After preparing the purple and the scarlet, she brought them to the priest and he blessed her: "Mary, the Lord has magnified your name, and you shall be blessed among all generations of the earth." Mary rejoiced and went to her kinswoman Elizabeth.

Perush ha-Mishnah leha-Meiri ([M. Hameiri]; ed. M. M. Meshi-Zahav; Jerusalem, 1971) 2:344: "and from eighty-two myriads it was made: meaning, that the cost of buying it was eight hundred twenty thousand dinar, and in any event they explained in the *gemara* regarding this, that one was speaking in exaggerated terms—that is, that its value was very great" (cf. *Penei Moshe* to *y. Sheqalim*).

[86] *Protevangelium Jacobi*, 10; Tischendorf, *Evangelia Apocrypha*, 1–50; Strycker, *La Forme la plus ancienne*, 108–13; James, *Apocryphal New Testament*, 38–49; E. Hennecke, *New Testament Apocrypha*, 379–80; Schneemelcher, *New Testament Apocrypha*, 421–39. The contents of the *Protevangelium* are incorporated within a work that is extant in Syriac, and is dated to a period prior to the end of the fourth century (E. A. W. Budge, *The History of the Blessed Virgin Mary and the History of the Likeness of Christ* [London, 1899]). In the West, the contents of this work were incorporated within a later work called *Pseudo-Matthew*, written in the eighth or ninth century (Hennecke, *NT Apocrypha*, 405–6).

In this source the virgins who weave the veil are eight very young maidens, "pure virgins," holy from the seed of David, including Mary, the mother of the Christian Messiah.

On the basis of the tradition in *2 Baruch*, generally dated around 80–100 CE, and the identification of the virgins who appear there with the maidens in *Mishnah Šeqalim*, S. Lieberman argued that the tradition in the *Protoevangelium*, which is later than *2 Baruch*, is of Jewish origin. He explains the term "pure virgins" in the *Protevangelium*, on the basis of the above-mentioned mishnah in *Niddah*, as referring to "virgins for blood"—that is, young girls, pure virgins, who had not yet reached nubility, and not yet menstruated. They were less than twelve years of age,[87] the age of puberty, and the task of weaving the curtain was assigned to them.[88]

As I have attempted to prove, it is impossible to understand the tradition of the "weaving virgins" in the temple, as described in *Syriac Baruch*, in light of the talmudic sources concerning the making of the curtain or in light of Jewish law generally. In my opinion, this tradition becomes clearer on the basis of the tradition concerning Mary and the virgins in the *Protevangelium of James*. This tradition did not originate in Judaism, as suggested by Lieberman, but reflects folk concepts and beliefs widespread in the Christian world of the first centuries CE.[89]

The *Protevangelium of James* is a Christian folk work, intended to praise and to testify to the eternal virginity of Mary, and reflects early stages in the

---

[87] This detail is based upon what is related in *Prot. Jas.* 8:2, that when Mary was twelve years old the priests decided to keep her away from the temple so as not to contaminate the temple of the Lord. According to Mach ("Are There Jewish Elements?" 217), it was not the fear of contamination of the temple that led to her distancing, but that she had reached the age of twelve, which is set in Roman law as the age of maturity. In 12:3, the work brings contradictory information regarding Mary's age, implying that she was sixteen. In works parallel to the *Protevangelium*, which were already based upon it, the age given is fourteen or fifteen (James, *Apocryphal NT*, 73, 88).

[88] Lieberman, *Hellenism*, 167–69. Lieberman does not explain the contradiction between the use of the number eight, given in the *Protevangelium*, and the number eighty-two thousand, in the talmudic tradition (for a similar exegesis, see Manns, "Une Ancienne Tradition," 107; Alon, *Toldot ha-Yehudim*, 297; Bogaert, *Apocalypse*, 2:33). S. Krauss was, as mentioned, the first to connect the talmudic tradition with the *Protevangelium* (Krauss, "Addenda et Corrigenda," 177 n. 5; idem, *Synagogale Altertümer*, 378–80).

[89] See Schneemelcher, *NT Apocrypha*, 423; Mach, "Are there Jewish Elements?" 216, and especially his justified criticism of Lieberman.

process of veneration of Mary, the mother of Christ.[90] This work, which seeks to arouse its readers sentiments and to cause them to identify with the figure of the Virgin and what she underwent, was very widespread and popular throughout the Christian world, especially in the Eastern Church, where it occupied an important place in Christian liturgy and iconography.[91] It is dated to the second half of the second century (180–200 CE)[92]—that is, nearly contemporary with the tradition in *2 Baruch.*

It is clear that the text does not refer to every young "virgin" who has not menstruated, as it explicitly states that only seven such maidens were found, and that the priest needed to remember Mary, who was the eighth—indicating that such virgins were not common. Moreover, they also needed to be holy (thus according to the Syriac version) and related to the seed of David! It is therefore clearly difficult to accept the view that one is speaking here of ordinary young girls, who are pure simply because they have not yet menstruated, as in Lieberman's view.

Moreover, the *Protevangelium* emphasizes Mary's virginity without any connection to her age or situation vis-à-vis menstruation, as she remains a virgin even after the birth of her son Jesus.[93] Moreover, it follows from the

---

[90] The process of veneration of Mary and the development of the cult surrounding her image already began in the Gospel of Luke, as reflected in her centrality in the story of the nativity. Already in the Acts of the Apostles she appears among the disciples of Jesus who gather together following his ascension (1:14). There is no doubting the Christianity of the *Protevangelium,* although there are those who claim that it was written by a Jewish-Christian who utilized Jewish traditions, especially those from the Bible and the apocryphal literature. In my opinion, his use of Jewish sources is the same as that made of these sources by the NT.

[91] Testimony to the extensive circulation of this work is to be found in the variety of traditions that have come down to us in numerous manuscripts and in different versions (see Hennecke, *NT Apocrypha,* 370–74; James, *Apocryphal NT,* 38; Schneemelcher, *NT Apocrypha,* 421–22; Cothenet, "Le Protévangile de Jacques," 4254–59). On the role of virginity or celibacy as a central value in the Syrian churches of the 2d and 3rd centuries, see Vööbus, *Celibacy, A Requirement for Admission to Baptism,* 8, 9.

[92] James, *Apocryphal NT,* 38; Strycker, *La forme la plus ancienne,* 9, 418; Strycker, "Le Protévangile," 353; Schneemelcher, *NT Apocrypha,* 423; Cothenet, "Le Protévangile," 4259; Mach, "Are There Jewish Elements?" 215; Stemvoort, "The Protoevangelium Jacobi," 425.

[93] See 19:3–20:1, where the midwife and Salome are called to witness to Mary's virginity after childbirth. When Salome doubts and attempts to examine the matter with her fingers, her hand literally falls off, consumed by fire, but is miraculously healed after she touches the infant Jesus.

CHAPTER 3: The Abandonment of the Temple   109

Christian sources that there was a widespread folk tradition connecting Mary's virginity to the temple and that she was understood as "the temple virgin."[94]

How are we to understand the tradition concerning Mary as weaving the veil? To what veil does this refer? And why was she specifically chosen to weave it?

It seems to me that this tradition, too, like that of the "abandoning by the guard of the house," makes sense in light of the folk beliefs that developed in early Christianity surrounding the rending of the veil upon the death of Jesus: namely, that the rent veil of the sanctuary was interpreted as the garment of an anthropomorphic temple identified with Jesus. The veil rent upon his death reveals the divine identity of Jesus, who is the true temple, the true Holy of Holies, and the new veil.

This approach finds expression in *T. Levi* 10:3. In a description of the sins committed against Jesus by the sons of Levi, priests in Jerusalem, the punishments that will befall them in the wake of these sins, and the prophecy concerning the coming of the new priest, Jesus Christ, we read: "And you will act lawlessly together with Israel, so that he [the Lord][95] will not bear Jerusalem because of your wickedness, but will rend the coverings of the temple (τὸ ἔνδυμα τοῦ ναοῦ), so as not to cover your shame."[96] The veil in whose weaving

---

[94] Origen mentions a tradition according to which the high priest Zechariah allowed Mary, even after the birth of Jesus, to continue to live in the τόπος τῶν παρθένων next to the temple, for which reason Zechariah was killed. This provides indirect testimony to the existence of stories similar to those of the *Protevangelium* that connected Mary to the temple, a connection that was a source for the tradition of Mary as "the Temple Virgin" (Origen, *Comm. Matt.* 25.2 [Matt 23:35; PG; 13:1631]; cf. Stemvoort ["The Protevangelium Jacobi," 412, 414]: "Mary was generally known as a temple-virgin").

[95] This verse is difficult, because it is not clear what its subject is. The reconstruction is according to de Jonge, who cites various suggestions that have been made in research ("Two Interesting Interpretations," 223).

[96] Hollander and de Jonge, *Testament of the Twelve Patriarchs*, 159. In some of the manuscripts, instead of the word ἔνδυμα for veil, καταπέτασμα appears. But the former reading is preferable (de Jonge, "Two Interesting Interpretations," 223; C. Bonner, "Two Problems in Melito's Homily," 185). This approach is closely connected with the tradition according to which the angel or spirit of God left the Holy of Holies upon the rending of the veil, as we have seen in *T. Benj.* 9:4 and other sources (see de Jonge, "Two Interesting Interpretations," 200–231; Manns, "Une ancienne tradition," 114; Hollander and de Jonge, *Testaments of the Twelve Patriarchs*, 80–81. And see, similar to *T. Levi*, Melito of Sardis, *Sur la Pâque*, 98 [SC; Paris, 1966], 118). Melito clearly considers the veil of the temple to be like the garment of the angel who dwells there, as demonstrated by Bonner ("Two Problems," 175–90). A similar idea appears in Tertullian, *Marc.* 4:42 (ed. E. Evans; Oxford, 1972; p. 500), and among other Christian

Mary and the other pure virgins participate is therefore the curtain of the new, heavenly temple, which is in an allegorical manner the flesh and body of Jesus. As stated in Heb 10:19–20, "Therefore, brethren, since we have confidence to enter the sanctuary by the blood of Jesus, by the new and living way which he opened for us through the curtain (διὰ τοῦ καταπετάσματος), that is, through his flesh."[97]

This approach is clearly implied by the present text. When Mary weaves the crimson and scarlet she receives the annunciation of the birth of Jesus from the angel of God (*Prot. Jas.* 11:2): "Do not fear, Mary, for you have found grace before the Lord of all things, and shall conceive by his Word."[98] Immediately upon concluding her labors of weaving and returning the veil to the priest, she is transformed into the mother of the Lord, who is blessed for all generations. This is implied by the words of the priest, who says to her: "Mary, the Lord has magnified your name, and you shall be blessed among all generations of the earth." She then conceives, to indicate that she has woven the body of Jesus which she carries in her womb.[99]

The function of the pure virgins who participate in the weaving of the veil in the *Protevangelium of James* is to be understood in a similar manner. They

---

authors (for the various testimonies, see de Jonge, "Two Interesting Interpretations," 223–24, 228–30). This personification of the temple is characteristic of Christian theology, in which, as noted, the temple is the body of Jesus—and of Qumran, in which the community of the Yahad is the temple (1QS v 6–7; viii 5–10; ix 3–9; and cf. Gartner, *The Temple and the Community,* 22–46; McKelvey, *The New Temple,* 47–50; García Martínez, "The 'New Jerusalem' and the Future Temple," 206; Eisenman and Wise, *The Dead Sea Scrolls Uncovered,* 26; Flusser, "The Isaiah Pesher and the Idea of the Twelve Apostles," 284; D. Dimant, "Jerusalem and the Temple According to the Animal Apocalypse," 192). This approach of the sect finds clear expression in the term "Adam Temple" (4QFlorilegium [=4Q174; Allegro, *DJD* V:53]). See, similarly, 1 Pet 2:4–10; Rev 21:3.

[97] This veil replaces that of the temple, which was rent in two upon Jesus' crucifixion (see Mark 15:38; Matt 27:51; Luke 23:45; Heb 6:19–20; and cf. Moffatt, *Epistle to the Hebrews,* 143).

[98] Based upon Luke 1:30ff.

[99] The fact of her pregnancy is not stated explicitly, but is clear from the continuation, when she comes to the house of Elizabeth. This symbolic detail was understood thus by the early Christian church as well, which gave it artistic expression in the mosaic found upon the triumphal arch in the church of Santa Maria Maggiore in Rome, built by Pope Sixtus III following the council of Ephesus (432–440) to commemorate the incarnation of Jesus and his being born of God to Mary (the "*theotokos*"). The first scene in this ritual series is the annunciation, in which Mary is shown seated, holding in her hand the scarlet fleece and holding close to her body the spindle, while the angel Gabriel appears to her (Schiller, *Iconography of Christian Art,* 33–37).

CHAPTER 3: The Abandonment of the Temple

too are partners in weaving the body of Jesus, because only they, as opposed to the married women, can worry about the things connected with Jesus. They are holy in both body and in spirit and are so-to-speak betrothed to the Messiah. As 1 Cor 7:34 puts it: "And the unmarried woman or virgin [girl] is anxious about the affairs of the Lord, how to be holy in body and spirit; but the married woman is anxious about worldly affairs, how to please her husband." Elsewhere, the Christian community is portrayed as the pure bride who is betrothed to Christ (2 Cor 11:2). The virgins are the models for the maidens who consecrate their virginity to God and follow in the footsteps of Mary. For this reason they need to be not only virgins but also, like her, members of the Davidic family. Their appearance here and in *2 Baruch* matches the tendency and types, beginning in the New Testament—types that progressively developed in the Christian church during the second century CE. They strengthen and exalt virginity and emphasize the function of the virgins in the coming of the Kingdom of God.[100]

This tradition may have originated against the background of the Jewish-Christian polemic, or of an internal Christian polemic against those circles that denied the virgin birth of Jesus. Origen, who was familiar with this work, cites Celsus in stating that the Jews denigrate Jesus by saying that he invented his birth from a virgin, when he was in fact born in Judaea to a local girl: a poor spinster who fornicated with a Roman soldier named Pantira, was sent away by her carpenter husband, and gave birth to Jesus in secret while wandering about.[101] Thus, as opposed to the poor village spinster, Mary is presented in the *Protevangelium* as the daughter of wealthy parents, Hannah and Joachim, who was trained as a temple virgin. It is true that she worked at spinning, but the high priest assigned her the task of spinning the crimson to be used in the

---

[100] See the apocryphal *Acts of Paul* 3:5–6, a popular work that blesses the virgins who are acceptable to God and will receive a reward for their purity, and especially the story of Thecla in that same work (James, *Apocryphal NT,* 272–81; Hennecke, *NT Apocrypha,* 2:353–64; on Thecla, see further W. Wright, *Apocryphal Acts of the Apostles* [Amsterdam, 1968], 116–45). The story of Thecla, the virgin who devotes her life to her Lord, is from the second to third century (Elliott, *Apocryphal New Testament,* 350–51). The widows and virgins became a class enjoying a special status within the church. In inscriptions upon memorials, the Christian virgins appear as married to Christ (Lefkowitz, *Women in Greek Myth,* 129; Cothenet, "Le Protevangile de Jacques," 4267; idem, "Protévangile de Jacques," *DBS,* 1383; S. Krauss, "Sklavenenbefreiung," 61–62). Virginity is also a symbol of purity (Rev 14:4).

[101] Origen, *Comm. Matt.* 10.17 (Matt 13:55; SC 162:217); *Cels.* 1.32 (SC 132:163–65 [par. 32]). Celsus wrote his work about 178–180 CE (Goodspeed, *History of Early Christian Literature,* 248; Chadwick, *The Early Church,* 54; cf. *b. Šabb.* 104b; *b. Ḥag.* 4b).

veil of the temple, and she was chosen by God to be "blessed among all generations of the earth."

This understanding of the tradition also makes sense in light of Baruch's call to the virgins to take the threads of the veil and to throw them into the fire, so as to bring them to Him who created them, so that the enemies may not take possession of them. According to early Christian tradition, as discussed above, upon the rending of the veil of the historical temple, the Holy Spirit, embodied in the new veil, abandoned Jerusalem and spread like fire over the nations. This corresponds to the description of the festival of Pentecost (the 50th day) in the early Christian church: "When the day of Pentecost had come, they were all together in one place. And suddenly a sound came from heaven like the rush of a mighty wind, and it filled all the house where they were sitting. And there appeared to them tongues as of fire, distributed and resting on each one of them. And they were all filled with the Holy Spirit . . ." (Acts 2:1–4a, 17; 10:45).[102]

The connection between the tradition in *Syriac Baruch* and that of the *Protevangelium* also finds expression in the types of threads from which the curtain was woven. According to the Torah, the veil of the temple was woven from four threads: "of blue and purple and scarlet stuff and fine twined linen,"[103] while in *2 Baruch* the virgins weave "fine linen and silk with gold of Ophir." The fine linen is identical to the fine twisted linen (*shesh*) of the veil; but what is the source of the silk and the gold?

The word משי is the Hebrew translation of the Syriac word *shiraya* (*shira*), to be identified with *siricon* (*sericus*; σιρικόν), a kind of silk similar to flax.[104]

---

[102] Based upon Joel 3:1–5. Daniélou, *Theology*, 145; de Jonge, "Two Interesting Interpretations," 223.

[103] Exod 26:31, 36; 36:35; 2 Chr 3:14; Josephus, *J.W.* 5.212; *Ant.* 8.72; Philo, *Mos.* 2.87–88. The *tekhelet*, translated by the LXX as hyacinth, whose color is dark blue or violet. *Argaman* is a weave made of linen dyed scarlet. It is identified with *porphira*, that appears in the classical sources, and its origin is in the name of the mollusk from which was taken the dark red material for dyeing rich cloths. The *tolaʿat shani*, here translated crimson, in the LXX κόκκινος, is a color close to red derived from the aphid that lives on oak trees, the *karmil*. *Shesh*, here translated "fine linen," in Greek βύσσος, is a delicate and highly-praised white-colored linen fiber, and coresponds to the Hebrew בוץ.

[104] Payne Smith, *Compendious Syriac Dictionary*, 554. This is not identical to משי, mentioned in the Bible only in Ezek 16:10, 13. The Peshitta translates the word *meshi* there by two other words: חלא in v. 10 (a word that, according to Payne Smith, 142, is a garment made of fine linen cloth), and תכלתא in v. 13. It is not clear what the *meshi* mentioned in Ezekiel is. According to all, it is not to be identified with the weave made of the fibers of the bulbs of Chinese silk worms, which appeared in the Mediterranean basin only at the beginning of the Roman empire. In *m. Kil.* 9.2 one finds שיריים, and

CHAPTER 3: The Abandonment of the Temple   113

Yet in the *Protevangelium of James,* siricon is mentioned as one of the threads from which the veil was woven, along with the linen (βύσσος καὶ τὸ σιρικόν). The same holds true of the gold thread. Unlike the curtain of the temple, which was not woven with a golden thread at all,[105] gold appears in the *Protevangelium* as one of the seven threads from which the curtain is woven. "The gold veil" also explicitly appears in the *Temple Scroll,* which portrays the ideal temple.[106]

---

in *b. Šabb.* 20b שירא. The term שריא appears in the Peshitta to the Bible elsewere (in Ezek 27:16 and Est 1:6), but in neither place is it used to translate the word *meshi.* As against that, in Rev 18:12, *shiraya* is identified with siricon.

[105] See the description of the tabernacle in Josephus, *Ant.* 3.125–26; that of Solomon's temple in *Ant.* 8.72; and cf. *b. Yoma* 71b; Rashi to Exod 39:3; Maimonides, *Hilkhot Kelei Miqdash* 7.16, who enumerates the list of materials from which the veil was made, which does not include gold (Schiffman, "The Furnishings of the Temple," 626). *Baraita de-Melekhet ha-Mishkan,* ch. 4 (ed. Ish-Shalom; 27), cites a tradition according to which the veil was not woven with threads of gold: "And in the same way as one would weave the veil, so did one weave the ephod and the breast plate, only in these there was one extra thread, of gold." But alongside this there is also an opposed tradition: *Baraita de-Melekhet ha-Mishkan,* ch. 7 (ibid., 49) states "and two veils of gold were spread upon them," making the testimony of the *Baraita* ambivalent. But see Lieberman's remarks quoted in Yadin, *Megillat ha-Miqdash,* 21. This detail may be indicative of the lateness of this midrash, notwithstanding the tendency to date it earlier (cf. Zunz, *Ha-Derashot be-Yisra'el,* 43; *Baraita de-Melekhet ha-Mishkan* [ed. Ish-Shalom], 7).

[106] Yadin, *Megillat ha-Miqdash* (11QTemp vii 13–14), 2:21. He interprets this veil as being in addition to the regular one found in the temple according to *b. Yoma* 5a. Similarly, Lehmann emphasizes the uniqueness of this expression of the scroll, seeing in this a distinction existing between the scroll and the halakhah ("The Temple Scroll as a Source of Sectarian Halakhah," 581). Schiffman explains this expression as being influenced by the description of the ephod in Exod 39:3, that was also made of gold ("Furnishings of the Temple," 626–27). Veils in the heavenly temple are also mentioned in the *Shirot 'Olat ha-Shabbat* (4Q405 15 ii–16; see Newsom, *Songs of the Sabbath Sacrifice,* 286–89; Baumgarten, "The Qumran Sabbath Shirot and Rabbinic Merkabah Tradition," 202). In the Jewish sources, the gold is clearly connected with the veil only in late sources, as *Tractate Kelim* (Jellinek, *Bet ha-Midrasch,* 1:89). Similarly in *Yalqut Shim'oni* (*Pequdei,* §422), it says: "The making of the curtains was of blue and crimson and scarlet and fine woven linen, and the thread was doubled over into four. R. Yossi said: And there was an extra thread of gold in them." According to Ish-Shalom (*Baraita de-Melekhet ha-Mishkan,* 30), it follows from this that in all of them, even the veil, there was a thread of gold in addition to the four kinds of fiber (cf. Avi-Yonah, "The Second Temple," 400, which mentions *Baraita de-Melekhet ha-Mishkan* as a source for the existence of the golden veil; Rabinowitz, *Mahzor Piyyutei Yannai,* 338).

The combination of linen and gold in *2 Baruch* may also allude to the garments of the high priest, which were "skillfully worked," whose weaving needed to be done in the holy place and was performed by particular families that specialized in this (Exod 39).[107] This interpretation is consistent with what is told in the *Protoevangelium,* as the threads of gold, white, linen, silver, hyacinth, crimson, and purple are the colors of the garments of the high priest; it also fits the Christian tradition, according to which Jesus was the true high priest.[108]

According to scholarly consensus, the source of this work is not in Palestine; the ignorance it reveals regarding the geography of the land of Israel and the customs that were widespread in Judaism refutes any possibility that it was written by a Jew or upon the soil of the land of Israel.[109] Some scholars have suggested Egypt or Syria as the venue of its writing.[110]

How, then, did an approach that identified the virgins in *2 Baruch* with the weavers of the veil in the temple penetrate into the world of Judaism and become accepted, as we have seen, by Jewish exegetes from the Medieval period on? It is difficult to assume that they relied directly upon *Syriac Baruch,* which was not current among Jews, but they could have known this tradition through an intermediate source—by means of the midrash, *Pesiqta Rabbati.*

---

[107] The garments of the high priest were made of linen (שש, בוץ); the garments worn throughout the year by the high priest are known as golden garments, because the four garments that were unique to the high priest (the breastplate, ephod, robe, and headplate) were made of gold. The garments worn by the high priest on the Day of Atonement were the "white garments," made of white linen (Exod 28:6–34; 39:22–29; *m. Yoma* 3.4; *b. Yoma* 31b; *m. Yoma* 3.6–7; *b. Yoma* 34b; Josephus, *J.W.* 5.231; Moore, *Judaism,* 2:56). The garments of the high priest were "woven wear"—that is, garments woven from the outset as a kind of full garment except for the sleeves, which were woven separately. The families of Beit Eshboa engaged in "the labor of the linen" (1 Chr 4:21); their weaving needed to be done in the holy place (*y. Yoma* 3.6 [40c]). On the priestly garments, see "*Bigdei kehunah,*" *Encyclopaedia Talmudica* [Heb.], 2. 330–36.

[108] Heb 2:17; 3:1; 4:14–15; 5:1–6, 10; 6:20; 7:15–17, 21, 24, 26–28; 8:1–4; 9:11, 25; 10:21. Rev 1:13 describes him as clothed with a ποδήρης, which was the name for the garments, or tunic, of the high priest (LXX to Exod 28:4; 29:5; Zech 3:4; *Wis. Sol.* 18:23; Josephus, *Ant.* 3.153–56, 159; Bousset, *Die Offenbarung Johannis,* 194; and cf. John 19:23).

[109] His ignorance regarding matters of Judaism finds expression, e.g., in the expulsion of Joachim, father of Mary, because he had no children, and the raising of Mary in the temple.

[110] Strycker, "Le Protévangile de Jacques," 418–21; Cothenet, "Protevangelium," 4267.

CHAPTER 3: The Abandonment of the Temple   115

As we have already seen, chapter 26 of the *Pesiqta Rabbati* presents a tradition parallel to that of *Baruch*. Like *2 Baruch,* this chapter depicts the destruction of the First Temple, the breaking through of the walls of Jerusalem by an angel from heaven, the burning of the sanctuary by the four angels holding torches [in their hands], the abandonment of the temple by the Lord who protects it, and the heavenward throwing of the keys. It also includes the tradition about the virgins weaving in the temple:

> When the virgins who were *weaving the veil* saw the temple was being burned, they fell into the fire and were burned up, so that their enemies might not violate them. (*Pesiq. Rab.* 26, ed. Ish-Shalom, p. 131)

As in *Baruch,* in the *Pesiqta* too this tradition is intertwined with the description of the destruction of Jerusalem and the temple, and follows the key-throwing. The obvious difference between the two traditions is that, unlike *Baruch,* in which the virgins cast all the labor of their weaving into the fire so that the enemies might not take possession of it, in the *Pesiqta* the virgins throw themselves into the fire, so as not to be violated by the enemies. This detail may have penetrated to this tradition under the influence of the motif in the Jewish tradition of suicide of the priests after giving over the keys to the Lord.

One may explicitly infer from the *Pesiqta* that the work of these virgins was connected to the weaving of the veil of the temple. If so, how is one to explain the tradition found in the *Pesiqta Rabbati?* Does it reflect an independent, internal Jewish tradition? And if an independent Jewish tradition of this type indeed existed, would this not help to confirm the internal-Jewish sources of the tradition in *2 Baruch?* In my opinion, the answer is negative. *Pesiqta Rabbati* is a late midrash, whose editing occurred, according to the opinion of the majority of researchers, sometime between the sixth and ninth centuries.[111]

---

[111] Ish Shalom (*Pesiqta,* p. 24), who published this midrash, dates it to the second half of the fourth century, though he notes that it is not a uniform composition and there are late parts in it that do not precede the Geonic period. Zunz (*Derashot,* 118) dated the *Pesiqta* no earlier than the second half of the ninth century, and several scholars followed in his wake. Braude (*Pesikta Rabbati,* 26) dates it to the sixth or seventh century; Lévi ("Notes Critiques," 228), dated it to the eighth century, although he does not rule out the presence of earlier elements. This date is accepted by Bacher ("Notes critiques," 43, 44), though he elsewhere dates it to the latter half of the ninth century (I. Lévi, "Bari dans la Pesikta Rabbati," 281). Cf. Mann, *The Jews in Egypt and in Palestine,* 1:48; Gry, "La Ruine du Temple par Titus," 215; Bogaert, *Apocalypse de Baruch,* 1:222. For a summary of the positions of research on the subject of the date of this midrash, see Strack and Stemberger, *Einleitung in Talmud und Midrasch,* 273–79.

According to I. Lévi, this midrash is composed of two distinct parts: while certain portions were taken on the whole from *Pesiqta de-Rav Kahana*,[112] entire chapters alongside them constitute a separate bloc having a Christian coloration, expressing Christian views and approaches. Chapter 26 is among these and reflects the lines that make it so unique in the most explicit way.[113] While in the other chapters the author suffices with copying the texts he uses, reworking and ornamenting them according to his taste, in the chapters constituting this unit he gave free rein to his own ideas. He gathered stories having a Christian coloration, which were widespread among certain circles and by whose means he also discovered the apocryphal books that were widespread in those circles. In Lévi's opinion, this encounter took place in southern Italy,[114] where there were close relations between Jews and Christian during the Middle Ages, and where the author found apocryphal works and Christian ideas that he adopted indiscriminately. One may assume that the author of *Pesiqta Rabbati* became acquainted with *2 Baruch* and other pseudepigraphical works that concentrated on the destruction of Jerusalem, such as *4 Ezra*, by means of these circles, and that he made use of their ideas.[115]

Hence, the *Pesiqta Rabbati* does not represent an independent, intra-Jewish tradition regarding the virgins weaving the veil in the temple; it made use of the tradition already appearing in *2 Baruch*, and therefore cannot serve as evidence for the ideological identity of this tradition as such. Instead, it may serve to uncover the path through which that same tradition penetrated into

---

[112] *Pesiq. Rab Kah.* is dated by Zunz (*Derashot*, 86) to roughly 700 CE and was composed in his view in the land of Israel. On the antiquity of this midrash, see also *Pesikta de-Rav Kahana* (ed. Mandelbaum), vii.

[113] Cf., e.g., the tradition concerning the meeting between Jeremiah and the woman (=Zion) in *Pesiq. Rab.* 26 (ed. Ish-Shalom; 131b) to the vision of the begrieved woman in *4 Ezra* 9–10. Clear signs of Christian elements may also be found in chs. 36–37 (a Messiah [Ephraim] who preceded the creation; a suffering Messiah, according to the chapter of the Servant of the Lord in Isaiah; a Messiah who ascends to heaven; and more).

[114] Lévi, "Note Critiques sur le Pesikta Rabbati," 484–85; idem, "Bari dans la Pesikta," 281–82; Bacher, "Notes critiques," 43–44. Bogaert (*Apocalypse*, 1:223) also points out the unique origin of ch. 26 and thinks that it is an artificial addition to the collection. Mann (*Jews in Egypt*, 48) suggested that the editor was an Italian who during the first half of the ninth century settled in Jerusalem. According to Zunz (*Derashot*, 118) the midrash was composed in Greece. For other views connecting the midrash to Palestine, see Braude, *Pesikta Rabbati*, 26.

[115] Lévi, "Bari"; Braude, *Pesikta Rabbati*, 22; Bogaert, *Apocalypse*, 1:233, 448; Wolff, *Jeremai*, 77; Gry, "La Ruine du Temple," 219–20.

Judaism and to explain the expression that it found among scholars from the Middle Ages down to our own day.

An analysis of the traditions depicting the destruction of Jerusalem in *Syriac Baruch* has exposed its author's hidden intentions and concealed tendencies. Even though the historical background against which the plot of the work is set is the destruction of the temple, and *Baruch* as-it-were expresses the pain of his people over the destruction of Jerusalem and the temple, there is no authentic anticipation of the rebuilding of the temple or of the historical Jerusalem in the entire work. The author does not await the reconstruction of the earthly Jerusalem, because this was by its very nature considered inferior and destined to be destroyed. The eternal Jerusalem, that which is engraved upon the palm of the Divine hand, is a heavenly, preexistent city, preserved by God in heaven alongside paradise. The historical temple is intended for destruction: the true "guardian of the house" has abandoned it so as to serve in the heavenly temple built by God, not by man; its keys were thrown heavenwards so that they might be used in the heavenly temple, and the veil of this temple, woven by the virgins, is embodied in the body of Jesus. When it was destroyed, the Holy Spirit abandoned the temple and moved over to the nations of the world, who are the true bearers of the Christian message. Hence, the traditions in *Baruch* are inconsistent with those that were dominant in the mainstream of the Jewish world at the end of the first and the beginning of the second century CE, the period of time during which the work is generally dated, and may only be explained against the background of Christian theology.

PART TWO

THE IDEA OF ESCHATOLOGICAL REDEMPTION

CHAPTER FOUR

Description of the Appearance of Messiah (*2 Bar.* 24–30)

4.1. *The Catastrophes of the Eschaton*

The author of the *Apocalypse of Baruch* unfolds his eschatological outlook by means of three principal visions: the description of the appearance of the Messiah in chapters 24–30; the vision of the forest, the cedar, the vine and the spring in chapters 36–40; and the vision of the cloud with the bright waters and the black waters in chapters 53, 56–74. These visions portray the apocalyptic drama to take place at the coming of the End, the disasters that will precede it, the appearance of the Messiah, and the redemption he will bring to those that believe in him. Taken together, these three visions complement one another, articulating a unified and well-fashioned apocalyptic vision; so much so, that a number of scholars have suggested they be viewed as a separate source that was later interpolated into this work.[1]

In what follows, I shall attempt to prove that these apocalyptic visions are an inseparable part of the author's worldview and that, as in the case of other apocalyptic works, they are rooted in an overall ideological and theological system.

The destruction of Jerusalem is a necessary precondition for the occurrence of the apocalyptic drama and for the beginning of the era of redemption. This fact follows, not only from the development of the plot in *Syriac Baruch*, in which the destruction of Jerusalem precedes the apocalyptic vision, but is explicitly stated in the work itself:

> Therefore, behold, the days will come and the times will hasten, more than the former, and the periods will hasten more than those which are gone, and the years

---

[1] E.g., Bousset and Gressmann, *Die Religion des Judentums*, 36. Similarly, scholars have suggested a separate source for these sections, on the basis of the contrast in the apocalyptic drama between the pessimistic portions that bring the world to its end and the optimistic sections concerning the future of the people Israel and the redemption following the end (Charles, *Apocalypse of Baruch*, liii-lxv; idem, "II Baruch," 474–76; Hadot, "La Datation," 84–85; and cf. Bogaert, *Apocalypse de Baruch*, 1:415–16).

will pass more quickly than the present ones. *Therefore, I now took away Zion so I might hasten more and heal the world in its own time.* (*2 Bar.* 20:1–2)²

The destruction of Zion is the precondition allowing God to bring about the end of days and to renew the creation at the time fixed by Him. In order to bring the End in its proper time, God promises to hasten the times. On the one hand, this hastening of the times concretizes the anticipation of the rapid coming of the End, after which is promised the age of complete redemption, but it also expresses the upheavals in the titanic forces of nature that will accompany its coming.³ The coming of the end is heralded by the revealing of certain books:

> For behold, the days are coming, and the books will be opened in which are written the sins of all those who have sinned, and moreover, also the treasures in which are brought together the righteousness of all those who have proven themselves to be righteous. (24:1)

These books will be used in the Last Judgment, to take place at the end of days.⁴ However, this judgement will only take place "when the time of the

---

²Cf. *2 Bar.* 32:1–6; see also *4 Ezra* 7:26, according to the Ethiopic version: "and the city which now appears [i.e., the earthly Jerusalem] shall be hidden" (Box, *The Ezra Apocalypse*, 113–14). This promise to heal the world is realized with the final appearance of the Messiah in the vision of the clear waters and the black waters, *2 Bar.* 53:9, on which see below.

³Cf. *2 Bar.* 48:34–42; 54:1; 83:1, 6; 85:10–13; *L.A.B.* 19:13; *1 En.* 80:2; *2 En.* 17:4; *Apoc. Ab.* 29.

⁴Mention of the books to be opened in the context of the final judgment is based upon Daniel 7:9–10. The Bible only mentions the Book of Life, in which are written the names of all the people. God erases the name of him who sins, and thereby denies him the right to be included in the Book of Life: thus Exod 32:32–33; Ps 69:29. The God-fearing people whose names are written in the book will flee from the trouble that befalls the people on the future Day of the Lord (Isa 4:3; Dan 12:1; Mal 3:16). The biblical approach is a positive one, assuming that all human beings deserve to be written in the book of life until they sin. A similar approach finds expression in the well-known tradition of the Babylonian Talmud, *b. Roš. Haš.* 16b, that speaks of the three books that are open on New Years Day—the books of completely evil people, of completely righteous, and of the intermediate ones, all of whose names are "written and sealed," each one according to his deeds. The books mentioned in *Baruch* only include the list of sins according to which the sinners will be judged. The good deeds of the righteous are not recorded there; these are stored in the treasure house, on which see below. See, in like vein, *1 En.* 89:61ff.; 90:17, 20; 97:5–6; 98:7–8; 104:7. A similar deterministic outlook appears in the NT: in Revelation, the Book of Life stands against the other books in which are recorded the deeds of every human being. The dead are judged

CHAPTER 4: Description of the Appearance of Messiah   123

appearance of the Anointed One has been fulfilled and he returns with glory" (30:1). If so, why is the revealing of the books already mentioned at the beginning of the description of the End?[5] The answer to this question lies in an understanding of the nature of the books. The use of the verb גלה ("revealed") suggests that these were books that were written in hoary antiquity, to be revealed and discovered only on the eve of the End.[6]

The books referred to are identical to the tablets of heaven, written long ago. In these are recorded, not only "all the deeds of humanity, and of all the children of the flesh upon the earth for all the generations of the world," for which they shall be judged at the end of time (*1 En.* 81:1–2), but also all of human history "concerning the children of righteousness, concerning the elect ones of the world, and concerning the straight plant of truth" (93:2) until "the first heaven shall depart and pass away, [and] a new heaven shall appear" (91:16). That is, these books depict the anticipated history of mankind, with all its days and aeons, from the very beginning until the end of the world.[7]

The sign,[8] the signal for of the coming of the end of times, will be "when horror seizes the inhabitants of earth, and they fall into many tribulations and further, they fall into great torments." Only after they lose all hope, then "the time will awake" (*2 Bar.* 25:3–4).

Baruch enumerates the calamities to accompany the awakening of the time by means of a twelve-part typological scheme: in the first part there will be the beginning of the commotions; in the second, the slaughter of the leaders; in the third, many will fall into death; in the fourth, expulsion by the sword; in the fifth, famine and drought; in the sixth, earthquakes and terror; in the seventh, . . . ;[9] in the eighth, a multitude of ghosts and harmful demons; in the ninth,

---

according to what is written in those books, and those not found in the Book of Life are thrust into the pool of fire (Rev 20:11–15).

[5] This order of times also appears in *4 Ezra*: the opening of the books is already mentioned in 4:20; however, the trial itself only takes place after the seven days, during which the world returns to primeval silence (*4 Ezra* 7:31ff.).

[6] See a similar use of this verb below, p. 153. See Charles, *Enoch*, 131–32, regarding *1 En.* 47:3; Charles, *Revelation of John* 2:194. Cf. *4 Ezra* 6:20.

[7] Similarly, in *Jubilees* 4:17–19; *Asc. Isa.* 9:22–27.

[8] σημεῖον; similarly *4 Ezra* 5:1–12; 6:18–28; 9:1–12; *Sib. Or.* 3:796–807.

[9] The seventh part is missing in this manuscript (see Dedering, *Apocalypse of Baruch*, 14); According to scholars, this may refer to the destruction of the temple (thus: S. F. Johnson, "Notes and Comments," *Anglican Theological Review* 22 [1940], 330–31; Bogaert, *Apocalypse*, 1:292–93; 2:60–61; Gry, "La Date de la Fin," 345–56). MacCulloch ("Eschatology," 381) understands from the phrase "that time" that the subject is this world as against the world to come. The above scholars tend to explain

the falling of fire; in the tenth, violence and great wickedness; in the eleventh, injustice and lewdness; and in the twelfth, a mixture of all the things that happened previously.

These parts of time will not come in an orderly fashion, one after the other, but "will be mixed one with another, and they will minister to each other"; hence, the people who will live on the earth in those days will not understand that it is the end of days (27:1–18).[10]

Similar descriptions of signs of the End to precede the coming of the Messiah, presented in similar typological schemes of either twelve or ten parts, are to be found at the focus of other apocalyptic works.[11]

All of the stages depicted thus far serve as a necessary anticipatory prelude to the coming of the end of the world, the revealing of the Messiah, and the appearance of the "new creation," and they express the work's deterministic approach: all the events, from beginning to end, are the result of a guided and predetermined divine plan.

Syriac Baruch even specifies the period of time that the End will continue: "For the measure and the calculation of that time will be two parts: weeks of seven weeks" (*2 Bar.* 28:1–2). This statement, based upon the formula of

---

these catastrophes against the background of the historical events of the Second Temple period. In my opinion, these attempts are to be rejected. While it is true that the End, according to the author's approach, already occurs in the present, the catastrophes of the End do not take place in the historical plane. The destruction of Jerusalem, described in the first part of the work, is the last event rooted in concrete historical reality; it is likewise clear, from the author's use of the future tense, that the final catastrophe has yet to take place. The apocalyptic vision is by its very nature directed toward the Eschaton, which is the end of history. At this stage, I have no satisfactory explanation for the absence of the seventh catastrophe in the manuscript.

[10] See further on the catastrophes of the End: *2 Bar.* 48:34–42; the last black waters in the vision of the cloud (chs. 70–71); and the division there as well into twelve periods (chs. 56–74; 53:11).

[11] On twelve divisions prior to the End, see also *4 Ezra* 14:10–11 on the basis of the Latin text. According to the Ethiopic manuscript of *4 Ezra*, the author enumerated only ten periods (Box, *Ezra Apocalypse*, 310). *Apoc. Ab.* 29:1–12 also enumerates ten parts, but these come after a period of twelve parts (years, hours); similarly in *1 En.* 93:4–10; 92:12–17; *Asc. Moses* 7:2. See ten periods (Jubilees) in The Scroll of Melchizedek [=11QMelch], l. 7; the salvation and the final judgment will be in the tenth jubilee (M. de Jonge and A. S. Van der Woude, "11Q Melchizedek and the New Testament," *NTS* 12 [1966]: 302; Licht, "The Doctrine of Time of the Judaean Desert Sect," 66–68). On a similar division into twelve periods in Persian belief, see Kohler, "Eschatology," 210–11. On the catastrophes of the End, see *Asc. Moses* 10; *4 Ezra* 5:1–12; 13:29–31; *1 En.* 93:4–10; 92:12–17; *Sib. Or.* 2:6ff.; 3:796–807; 7:96ff.; *Ascen. Isa.* 3:22–31.

CHAPTER 4: Description of the Appearance of Messiah   125

"seventy weeks [of years]" counted by Daniel until the redemption (Dan 9:24–26), similar to the division into twelve periods in chapter 27, served as a point of departure for various conjectures concerning the date of the work, on the assumption that these allude to concrete historical events.[12] However, many scholars have justifiably rejected these attempts.[13]

In my opinion, this expression ought in fact to be understood in light of the widespread tradition in the pseudepigraphic literature concerning the period of time until the End. The week of seven weeks refers to the eschatological Sabbath, in which each day of the week is like a thousand years, based upon Ps 90:4: "for a thousand years in thy sight are but as yesterday when it is past." According to this calculation, the period of time until the redemption is 7000 years, assuming that we take one day as the unit of time of the week, and each week as a thousand years. This calculation, like the division of the weeks into two parts, is consistent with a similar tradition found in *L.A.B.* 19:14–15. There, Moses asks God to tell him how much time has passed until his own days, and how much time remains until the end of days. Four and a half days have already passed, and two and a half remain until the End. Here too one is speaking of seven units of time (2½ + 4½), each unit corresponding to a cosmic year: in total seven cosmic years, equivalent to 7000 years.[14]

---

[12] See Gry, "La Date de la Fin de Temps," 345–56; Bogaert, *Apocalypse*, 1:292–93; James, *Biblical Antiquities*, 132. Kahana adds: "two portions *and each one a week of seven weeks.*"

[13] Charles is unable to explain 28:2 (*Apocalypse of Baruch*, 50; idem, *Eschatology*, 324). Schürer (*History*, 3:752 n. 2) rejects any possibility of arriving at a chronological conclusion on the basis of 28:2; according to Klijn, this indication is not clear ("2 Baruch," 628, 630 n. a; cf. ibid., 617; Rowley, *The Relevance of Apocalyptic*, 119–20).

[14] Zeron, "The System of the Author of *Antiquities*," 139–40. Cf. *L.A.B.* 28.8, where a voice reveals to Kenaz that this world will exist for 7000 years (see this reading in Zeron, 140 and n. 1, and also at 118). The pseudepigraphic tradition proposes a different calculation, according to which the length of time until the End is 4900 years (see *Jub.* 50:4–5 and *Asc. Moses* 1:1; 10:12). The Babylonian talmudic tradition recognized both possibilities, which appear alongside one another as a quotation from "a certain scroll that was found among the hidden things in Rome, in which is written, 'four thousand two hundred and ninety-one years from the creation of the world, the world will end.' Among them the battle of the sea monsters, among them the battles of Gog and Magog, and the rest are the days of Messiah." This number corresponds to the position of Rav Aha son of Rabba. Alongside this tradition is the speculation that "the Holy One blessed be He will not renew His world except after seven thousand years" (*b. Sanh.* 97b), or "six thousand" according to Codex Florence, matching the tradition in *b. Sanh.* 97a ("six thousand years shall be the world"). According to the Latin text of *4*

According to the apocalyptic approach taken by *2 Baruch*, the End referred to here is the end of this world as a whole: it will be felt by all those who are alive (29:1) and it is already in fact occurring in the present (19:5; 77:13–14). But only after that which is to occur in the future is completed, only after the period of the calamities is over, will the Messiah begin to be revealed.

What, then, characterizes the description of the End in *Syriac Baruch?*

The end of time means the end of the world as we know it and the coming of a new world; this is the general, cosmic end of the world, which will not take place within the historic realm. It is predicated on the destruction of the historical Jerusalem; its arrival will be preceded by the hastening of the times and by catastrophic occurrences that are signs and signals of the End. The coming of the End will not be known and will not be understood as the end of times by the inhabitants of the land; the End and the awakening of time that accompanies it are not a one-time act, but constitute an ongoing period of time, and the completion of the portions of the End is necessary for the revealing of the Messiah and the appearance of "the new creation."

What are the sources of this description?

It is widely opined among scholars that the source of the apocalyptic drama is found in Judaism.[15] These scholars particularly note the bold descriptions of the Day of the Lord, portrayed by the prophets as a day of disaster, of darkening of the celestial luminaries, of earthquakes, tremors, fear, and terror.[16]

But the biblical descriptions of the Day of the Lord, like the prophecies of the end of days, are rooted in concrete historical and political situations. They do not contain descriptions of the end of the world and the appearance of another world in its stead, nor do they anticipate the end of time, history, or the cosmos. The term אחרית הימים (variously translated as "the end of days,"

Ezra 14:10–11, among the twelve periods into which the world is divided, nine and a half have already passed, and two and a half remain. However, according to Box (*Ezra Apocalypse,* 310) the meaning of this text is ambiguous. These verses are completely missing in the Syriac and Armenian manuscripts and may have been inserted into the text later. According to the Ethiopic manuscript, the text only enumerates ten periods, of which only half of the tenth week remains. This framework also corresponds to the half week of Dan 9:27. There are also differences in relation to the division between the parts that have passed and those that remain (cf. *Sib. Or.* 4:47).

[15] Mangenot, "Fin du mond," 2263; Urbach, *The Sages,* 651; Rowland, *The Open Heaven,* 158; Saylor, *2 Baruch,* 59 n. 38; and the survey of the main scholarly position in Charles, *Eschatology,* x–xiv.

[16] Isa 13; 24–27; Jer 4:23; Ezek 32; 38–39; Joel 3:1–5; 4:9–16; Amos 8; Zeph 1:15; Mal 3; etc.

the "latter days," or "the days to come"),[17] translated in the Septuagint by the Greek word τὸ ἔσχατον, meaning "in the course of time, in future days," which is similar to the talmudic expression לעתיד לבוא (lit. "in the future to come"), does not refer to the end of time.[18] Kaufmann's view on this matter is in my opinion the most penetrating and accurate:

> The biblical vision of the End of Days does not involve a description of the destruction of the world, and hence does not encompass a description of the creation of a new world and a return to the beginning. The prophets portray the calamities that are to take place in vivid and exaggerated colors. They speak of earthquakes, the extinguishing of the luminaries, blood and fire and pillars of smoke, hailstones and flood and sword and famine and plague, etc. But all these are no more than poetic exaggerations, and nowhere is there a prophecy of the world returning to chaos nor of a new creation. Only in Isaiah 65:17 do we find an expression referring to the creation of "new heavens and a new earth," but throughout Isaiah 40–66 there is nothing to justify the assumption that even this is any more than poetic hyperbole. At the center of the vision of the End of Days are found Israel, Zion, the Temple Mount, the ruins of Jerusalem, the ingathering of the exiles, etc.[19]

The biblical term קץ generally means "end" or "extremity."[20] In the well-know verse from Hab 2:3, "For still the vision awaits its time; it hastens to the end—it will not lie," this term means "time," and refers to concrete historical events. Rashi interprets the verse in this light: "'Still the vision awaits its time'—there shall arise a prophet in the future, at the end of many years, to whom there will be revealed a vision of the time of the downfall of Babylon

---

[17] Gen 49:1; Num 24:14; Deut 4:30; 31:29; Isa 2:2; Jer 23:20; 30:24; 48:47; 49:39; Ezek 38:8, 16; Hos 3:5; Mic 4:1; Dan 10:14.

[18] Gvaryahu (*Studies in the Book of Isaiah*, 94) prefers to translate this term as "later days" rather than as "the end of the days." Buber translates: "in der Späte der Tage"; Wildberger in his interpretation of Isaiah uses "in der Folge der Tage." Cf. A. Steudel, "אחרית הימים in the Texts from Qumran," *RevQ* 16 (1993/95), 225.

[19] Kaufmann, *Toldot ha-Emunah* 3:644; thus also Moore, *Judaism*, 2:312; Mowinckel, *He That Cometh*, 130–32. All the Israelite prophets anticipate the reconstruction of Israel following the disaster; this expectation did not leave room for apocalyptics that awaited the end of the world; see Urbach, *The Sages*, 651. Urbach cites there (n. 3) the position taken by G. Scholem (in his essay, "The Messianic Idea in Kabbalah," *The Messianic Idea in Judaism and Other Essays* [New York, 1971], 38) who, in Urbach's opinion, exaggerated in his statement that: "Classical Jewish tradition is fond of emphasizing the catastrophic strain in redemption." The problem, as Urbach properly asks, is exactly who in "classical Judaism" was fond of this?

[20] J. Licht, *Qez* [Hebrew], *Enc. Bib.* 7:211. See, e.g., Gen 6:13; Isa 9:6; Ezek 7:2–8; 21:30, 34; 35:5; Amos 8:2; Ps 119:96; Job 22:5; 28:3; Eccles 4:16; 12:12.

and the redemption of Israel."²¹ It is in this sense that the term קץ appears in the Book of Daniel as well, and there too it relates to concrete political and historical events, some of which are the heritage of the past or were contemporary with the author. These events express Daniel's unique historical interpretation of the past and his hopes for the victory of the people of Israel over the Hellenistic kingdom in the future.²² The term never appears in the sense of the end of the present world or the appearance of another world in its place. The end likewise appears in Ben Sira in a meaning similar to that found in Habakkuk and Daniel: "Hasten the end and ordain the appointed time" (Sir 36:10). The word קץ ("end") is here parallel to the term מועד ("appointed time"); the term does not appear in the Mishnah, a fact consistent with the absence of apocalyptic descriptions in the Mishnah generally.²³ It does appear in the Jerusalem Talmud in connection with redemption (y. Ta'an. 1.1 [63d]), but in the context of a comparison to the redemption of Israel from Egypt,

---

²¹ Likewise R. Abraham Ibn Ezra and Radak (R. David Kimḥi); Abravanel interprets the verse as referring to two visions: the former relates to the fall of Babylon, and the latter to "the end of the nations and their fall, and the end of the exiles and the end of anger" (Licht, "Qez," 212); D. Sivan (*Ugaritic Grammar* [Hebrew; Jerusalem, 1993], 3) explains the word יפח, on the basis of the Ugaritic, in the sense of עד, "witness." מועד is a synonym of קץ, and יפח is parallel to עד; presumably the original text read כי עד חזון למועד: that is, the vision recorded here will serve as a testimony when the time comes. See Prov 14:5, 25; 19:5, 9.

²² E.g., Dan 8:17, 19; 11:13, 40; 12:4, 9; Montgomery (*The Book of Daniel*, 346) on Dan 8:17: "the end is Antiochus," and on Dan 12:4: "until the time of the end"—until the height of the crisis of Antiochus (p. 473). Verse 13 ("But go your way till the end; and you shall rest") announces the death of Daniel. But the book concludes on an optimistic note: "and you shall stand to your destiny at the end of the days," referring to the prophecy in Isa 26:19, which constituted the inspiration for the beginning of Dan 12 and for those readers who follow in his wake. In any event, it is agreed that vv. 11–13 are "later glosses" (Montgomery, *The Book of Daniel*, 477–78; Lacoque, *The Book of Daniel*, 249; Hartman & Di Llela, *The Book of Daniel*, 313–15). On the relation of the Book of Daniel to events of the time, see Efron, "Holy War," 33–44; "Daniel and His Three Friends"; and "The Idea of the Servant of God."

²³ Many scholars have concluded from this that apocalyptic literature was outside of the central stream of Judaism, and therefore cannot constitute a source for the study of Jewish eschatology (Moore, *Judaism*, 1:127; 2:281; Ginzberg, "Some Observations on the Attitude of the Synagogue," 115–36; Buchanan, in Charles, *Eschatology*, xxi). At the end of *m. Soṭah* a tradition appears in which scholars have found apocalyptic elements (thus, e.g., Russell, *Method and Message of Jewish Apocalyptic*, 31). But others explain this as a talmudic *beraita* (see *b. Sanh.* 97a) that was copied from there and attached to the original mishnah (thus Epstein, *Mavo*, 976; Albeck [ed.], *Mishnah*, Appendix to *Seder Nashim*, 394; Urbach, *The Sages*, 677).

CHAPTER 4: Description of the Appearance of Messiah   129

making it clear that the term is used here to refer to historical redemption. This tradition brings out the fundamental difference between the understanding of the End in *Syriac Baruch* and in the early talmudic tradition: in *Baruch*, the coming of the End is inevitable and man is unable to influence it or to alter its course. It is not anchored in historical reality, but in the meta-historical, transcendental realm, and its coming is accompanied by cosmic catastrophe.

In the mainstream Jewish tradition, by contrast, redemption is rooted in the historical dimension. It is a consequence of human acts, and its coming depends upon repentance and good deeds. As R. Eliezer b. Hyrcanus states in the above-mentioned discussion: "If Israel does not repent, they will never be redeemed."

The concept of the End, in a sense close to that of the apocalyptic descriptions, first appears in the Babylonian Talmud and in the post-Babylonian midrashic literature. The discussion in *Pereq Ḥeleq, b. Sanh.* 96b–99a,[24] particularly stands out in this context. This chapter incorporates the concepts of the end of the world and calculations of the End, a description of the catastrophes that will precede the redemption, the hastening of the times, the days of Messiah and the renewal of the world, as well as calculations of the period of time of the days of Messiah—which may be seen as parallel to the calculation of the duration of the periods of catastrophe in *Baruch*. Such concepts, composed in such a fashion, do not appear in Jewish literature of the Second Temple period or in early Palestinian talmudic literature. It should be clear that the Babylonian tradition already reflects an absorption of concepts and approaches that were commonly found in the Christian world. This absorption is in part a result of grappling with the Christian world of ideas, even though the Babylonian tradition does not go to the extent of negating "this world" and anticipating the coming of a new world in its place. Such an ideological transformation only occurs in the Jewish medieval midrashim of redemption.[25]

The description of the end of the world and the disasters to precede it in *2 Baruch* are clearly related to the apocalyptic sections of the New Testament. As in *Syriac Baruch*, so too in the synoptic apocalypse the destruction of Jerusalem and the temple precede the events of the end and constitute a necessary prelude to the coming of the full redemption and the appearance of the kingdom of heaven (Mark 13; Matt 24; Luke 21). In the New Testament, as well, the catastrophes constitute a "sign" (σημεῖον) heralding the coming of

---

[24] On the existence of apocalyptic thought in the Babylonian Talmud, see Lévi, "Apocalypses dans le Talmud," and Ginzberg, "Some Observations on the Attitude of the Synagogue," 119–20.

[25] See these midrashim in Y. Even Shmuel, *Midrashei Ge'ulah,* and in the collections of Jellinek's *Bet ha-Midrasch*.

the End and the second appearance of Christ.[26] One should take note of the fact that here too, as in *Baruch,* the sign appears in the singular and is connected with the end of the world and the appearance of Messiah, a phenomenon without parallel in the Bible.[27]

As in *Syriac Baruch,* so too in the apocalyptic descriptions in the New Testament the hastening of the times is promised for the sake of the elect: "And if those days had not been shortened, no human being would be saved; but for the sake of the elect those days will be shortened" (Matt 24:22; Mark 13:20). The New Testament as a whole gives expression to the recognition that, with the death of Jesus and his first resurrection, the End, which takes place in the present but will be completed with the Parousia, had already begun. The term "end" (τέλος), in the sense of the end of the world, is characteristic of the apocalyptic descriptions of the New Testament,[28] and as in *Baruch,* the age of the Eschaton or the end of days occurs in the present.[29] Nevertheless, unlike the tradition in *Baruch* and in the apocalyptic literature generally, in the New Testament the time of the coming of the End is not known (Mark 13:32); hence Paul rejects any attempt to calculate the End.[30]

---

[26] Matt 12:38; 24:3ff.; Mark 8:11–12; 13:1ff; Luke 21:7ff.; John 2:11–18. Balz and Schneider, *Exegetical Dictionary of the NT,* 239.

[27] In only one place in the Bible is the term מופת ("wonder" or "portent") used parallel to אות ("sign") in relation to the description of the Day of the Lord—in Joel 3:3 ("and I will give portents in the heavens and on the earth, blood and fire and columns of smoke"). But even there the term appears in the plural form, מופתים, and they are given in heaven rather than on the earth. This verse is quoted in Acts 2:19, but with a characteristic Christian addition in the middle: "and signs on the earth beneath," evidently referring to the miracles wrought by Jesus and the apostles (see Balz and Schneider, *Exegetical Dictionary,* 240).

[28] Matt 10:22; 24:6; 1 Cor 1:8; 15:24; Heb 3:6; 1 Pet 4:7; Rev 2:26; 21:6: viz. the end of the world and the appearance of a new world. The term parallel to the biblical אחרית הימים is translated in the NT, as in the LXX, by the Greek ἔσχατος (*eschatos*), which generally refers to the concept of "the last." In only a few cases does the term appear in the sense of the end of the world as in, e.g., John 6:39 and several other times in the same chapter; cf. 1 Pet 1:20; 2 Pet 3:3; 1 John 2:18. The term קץ also occupies a central role in the Qumran writings (Licht, "*qez,*" 211); see, e.g., 1QpHab 2:1–3 (col. vii); and cf. Schürer, *History,* 2:514 n. 3.

[29] E.g., Heb 1:1–2: "In many and various ways God spoke of old to our fathers by the prophets; but in these last days he has spoken to us by a Son, whom he appointed the heir of all things, through whom also he created the world." A similar approach to the Eschaton is also found in Qumran (Steudel, "אחרית הימים in the Texts from Qumran," 226ff.).

[30] 1 Thess 5:1ff.; 2 Thess 2:2; Luke 17:20; Mark 13:5.

CHAPTER 4: Description of the Appearance of Messiah 131

The connection to the Christian tradition is also expressed in the division into twelve catastrophes. This number occupies an important place in *Syriac Baruch*, both in the division of the vision of the bright waters and the dark waters into twelve periods, and in the enumeration of the tribes to whom Baruch sends his epistle in chapters 77–87.

The number twelve is a symbolic number in its own right. It is the lowest number divisible by the three consecutive numbers 2, 3, and 4, and the sum of its own factors (3 and 4) is 7, which is a symbol of wholeness. Twelve indicates the number of the months of the year and the constellations, and possibly also the hours of the day. But this number also bears explicit eschatological significance: on the basis of the location of the twelve tribes of Israel in Scripture, Christianity anticipated the return of the twelve tribes, identified with the masses of the nations, who will in the end of days accept upon themselves Christianity. This is likewise the significance of the number in *2 Baruch*.[31]

The period of disaster preceding the End and the coming of the Messiah is compared in Christian sources to the birth pangs of a woman, and is described by means of the same word, ὠδίνες, meaning birth pangs.[32] Although it is true that this image developed against the background of the Septuagint's translation to the biblical writings (Isa 66:7–8; Hos 13:13; Mic 4:9–10; 5:2), nowhere in Scripture outside of the New Testament is it connected with the end of days and the subsequent appearance of the Messiah. This concept is totally unknown in the Palestinean talmudic sources, in the Mishnah, in the

---

[31] See Geyser, "The Twelve Tribes in Revelation"; idem, "Some Salient NT Passages"; L. Goppelt, *Typos: The Typological Interpretation of the Old Testament in the New*, 108; McKelvey, *The New Temple*, 144; Bogaert, "Les Apocalypses Contemporaines de Baruch, d'Esdras et de Jean," 54; cf. *Prot. Jas.* 1:1; Acts 26:7; Matt 19:28; Luke 22:30; Rev 7:5–9; 12:1; 21:12–14; twelve tribes, each one of which has twelve thousand seals. Pines, "Notes on the Twelve Tribes," 153–54. The genealogy of Jesus in Luke 3:23–38 also seems to be built on a pattern of eleven periods, each one of which contains seven names, until the end, in which Jesus opens the twelfth period (Brown, *The Birth of the Messiah*, 91–93, esp. n. 72). *T. Naph.* 5:4 states the superiority of Levi and Judah over the twelve tribes in the context of the double messiahship. On the significance of the number, see A. Jaubert, "La Symbolique des Douze," *Hommages à André Dupont-Sommer* (Paris, 1971), 453–60; G. Vermes, "The Impact of the Dead Sea Scrolls on the Study of the New Testament," *JJS* 27 (1976): 109.

[32] Ἀρχὴ ὠδίνων ("the beginning of the birth pangs"): Mark 13:8 and Matt 24:8; cf. Gal 4:19; 1 Thess 5:3.

Jerusalem Talmud, or in the early Palestinean midrashim; it first appears in Jewish sources only in the Babylonian Talmud.[33]

4.2. The Eschatological Feast

Following the description of the catastrophes of the End, the manner of revelation of the Messiah is described:

> And it will happen that when all that which should come to pass in these parts has been accomplished, the Anointed One will begin to be revealed. And Behemoth will reveal itself from its place, and Leviathan will come from the sea, the two great monsters which I created on the fifth day of creation and which I shall have kept until that time. And they will be nourishment for all who are left. The earth will also yield fruits ten thousandfold. And on one vine will be a thousand branches, and one branch will produce a thousand clusters, and one cluster will produce a thousand grapes, and one grape will produce a cor of wine. And those who are hungry will enjoy themselves and they will, moreover, see marvels every day. For winds will go out in front of me every morning to bring the fragrance of aromatic fruits and clouds at the end of the day to distill the dew of health. And it will happen at that time that the treasure of manna will come down again from on high, and they will eat of it in those years because these are they who will have arrived at the consummation of time.
>
> And it will happen after all these things, when the time of the appearance of the Anointed One has been fulfilled and he returns with glory, that then all who sleep in hope of him will rise. And it will happen at that time that those treasuries will be opened in which the number of the souls of the righteous were kept, and they will go out and the multitudes of the souls will appear together, in one assemblage, of one mind. And the first ones will enjoy themselves and the last ones will not be sad. For they know that the time has come of which it is said that it is the end of times. (29:3–30:3)

The Revelation of the Messiah in *2 Baruch* opens the new era, "that time," "the end of times," "when all that should come to pass in these parts has been accomplished," after the twelve calamities which precede the end of times. Then Behemoth and Leviathan will appear, to be served as food for those who will remain; the ground will yield myriad of fruit; and the vine will produce an abundance of grapes, from each of which a huge amount of wine could have been produced. Morning winds will bring fragrances of fruit, and by evening

---

[33] In the Babylonian Talmud it also appears in the singular form: חבלו של משיח, "the birth pang of Messiah" (thus in *b. Sanh.* 98a; *Šabb.* 118a; *Pesaḥ.* 118a). MS München and MS Rome to *b. Ketub.* 111a read חבלי דמשיח, but the printed versions have חבלא דמשיחא, and in MS Leningrad-Firkovitz משיח. Likewise in the Genizah MS: דמשיחא without the term חבלים at all. See *Masekhet Ketubot, Talmud Bavli 'im shinuyei nushaot*, ed. M. Hershler (Jerusalem, 1977), 542; Moore, *Judaism*, 361 n. 4; Klausner, *The Messianic Idea*, 260 n. 1.

CHAPTER 4: Description of the Appearance of Messiah 133

they will distill dew of health and the treasure of manna will come down from high. But this is only the beginning of the Revelation of the Messiah. In his last appearance he will come back in glory. Then will be the resurrection of the dead, the storehouses in which the righteous souls are held will be opened, and the last judgment will occur.

How is this description to be understood, and what are its sources? The description presents Behemoth and Leviathan, the two great monsters created by God on the fifth day of creation (according to Gen 1:21), as two primeval creatures, one of which lives in the sea and the other on the dry land. Their appearance is clearly related to the appearance of the Messiah; like him, they are primeval beings that have existed since the creation. These two primeval creatures have been set aside for these last times, to serve as food for all those who remain.

Hence, the passage refers to a feast to be conducted after the apocalypse, at the end of times, after the *beginning* of the Messiah's appearance, in which *those few who remain* until his coming[34] will take part, and at which the Behemoth and Leviathan will serve as food.

To what extent does this tradition have roots in Judaism?

The word בהמות (*behemoth*) is ordinarily used in the Bible to refer to a number of animals or beasts, rather than as a singular nominal form.[35] Hence, the word does not refer to any particular kind of monster or primeval beast; indeed, it does not appear at all alongside the leviathan, but rather alongside other groups of living creatures, such as צאן ("flock"), עוף ("birds"), חית יער ("beasts of the forest").[36] Notwithstanding this, the predominant scholarly opinion identifies Behemoth with a mythological beast that appears alongside the Leviathan, based primarily upon Job 40:15–24: "Behold, Behemoth, which I made as I made you . . . ," in which the verbs referring to *behemoth* are in the third person singular, followed by a description of Leviathan (Job 40:25–41:26).[37]

---

[34] *Meštaḥrin*—in Syriac, "the remnant." See Rom 11:5; 1 Thess 4:15, 17; cf. Kiraz, *Concordance*, 4:2875.

[35] Thus in the LXX, θηρία as the plural of τὸ θηρίον, and in the Aramaic Targum "*b'irya*" (Tur-Sinai, "Beasts," 39–40; idem, *The Book of Job* [Hebrew; Jerusalem, 1941], 2:464). In the Babylonian tradition the word בהמות still *always* appears as the plural of בהמה.

[36] Ps 8:8; 50:10; Jer 12:4; Job 12:7; 35:11: Mic 5:7.

[37] Scholars find a parallel to this description in Ugaritic texts (Pope, *Job*, 321–22; Day, *God's Conflict with the Dragon and the Sea*," 80, 82; Jacobs, "Elements of Near Eastern Mythology," 10; Driver and Gray, *The Book of Job*, 326; Caquot, "Leviatan et Behemoth," 120). Behemoth is identified as a monstrous land creature, similar to *Shor*

Leviathan, by contrast, is presented in the Bible[38] alongside such antediluvian creatures as the serpent, the sea-dragon, and Rahab, which originated in ancient Canaanite or Babylonian myths that penetrated into the Bible[39] and which, like the tradition under discussion here, are connected to the sea.

Nevertheless, these creatures are stripped in the Bible of their mythological significance and become a symbol of the power of evil or of hostile enemy kingdoms such as Egypt and Assyria; their defeat or slaying is an expression of God's power and His rule over the cosmos.[40] Nowhere in Scripture are the sea monster and the other creatures mentioned alongside him or the Behemoth connected to any apocalyptic description. They do not symbolize metaphysical and demonic forces that stand against the rule of God, nor are they associated with the appearance of the Messiah. They are not related to any feast that will be conducted for the righteous in the world to come, and certainly not to a feast to take place together with Messiah in the new creation. Those biblical passages, on the basis of whose exegesis it might have been possible to develop a tradition associating Leviathan with an eschatological feast, are few and tenuous.[41]

The Jewish tradition connecting the pair of Behemoth and Leviathan to the righteous in any sort of eschatological context appears in the midrash

---

ha-Bar (the "Wild Ox" of legend); Guttmann, "Leviathan, Behemoth and Ziz," 225. Cf. *b. Ḥul.* 80a; *Tg. Ps.-J.* to Ps. 50:10; Ibn Ezra to Job 40:15: "the name of a large animal, than which there is no larger on the dry land." The identification of Behemoth with a mythological beast may have been influenced by its pairing with Leviathan in apocalyptic works.

[38] Isa 27:1; Ps 74:14; Ps 104:26; Job 3:8; 40:25ff.

[39] There are those who explain the origin of this tradition in the Babylonian creation myth, while others seek its roots in Canaanite or Ugaritic myth (Box, *Ezra Apocalypse*, 90; Charles, *Revelation of St. John*, 2:205; Russell, *Method and Message of Jewish Apocalypse*, 123–24; Cassutto, "Leviathan," 485; idem, *The Goddess Anath*, 54–57; Day, *God's Conflict*, 2, 4, 7, 181).

[40] Isa 51:9; Ps 74:13–14; 89:11; 104:6–9; Job 7:12; 9:13; 26:12–13. See Rashi on Isa 27:1: "'Leviathan the fleeing serpent' is Egypt, 'Leviathan the twisting serpent' is Assyria, and 'the dragon that is in the sea' dwells in the heart of the sea and is called the islands of the sea" (Ezek 29:3; 32:2). Cf. J. Priest, "A Note on the Messianic Banquet," in J. H. Charlesworth (ed.), *The Messiah* (Minneapolis, 1992), 235. In the two above-cited passages, the eschatological theme has been adapted to the historical situation: the slaughtered enemy is Pharaoh and, by extension, Egypt as a whole.

[41] See Ps 74:14; 104:26. In several manuscripts, there is a mythological reference to the flesh of the Leviathan that was meant to be given as food to Israel at the end of days, but this is a late gloss (see Briggs, *The Book of Psalms*, 155; and cf. Exod 24:11; Isa 25:6; 55:1–3; 65:11–13; Zech 9:15; Priest, "Messianic Banquet," 235–36).

CHAPTER 4: Description of the Appearance of Messiah   135

Leviticus Rabbah, where Behemoth and Leviathan are presented as game animals or as combat animals that serve as entertainment for the righteous in the future: "Whoever has not seen the beasts of chase[42] of the nations of the world in this world will be privileged to see them in the world to come" (*Lev. Rab.* 13.3; ed. Margalioth, 277).[43] On the basis of Ps 50:10, Behemoth is presented in the talmudic tradition as a mythological beast dwelling in the thousand mountains alongside the Leviathan (*Pesiq. Rab Kah.* 6; ed. Mandelbaum, 112–113), while in the Babylonian tradition the flesh of the leviathan is connected for the first time with the feast that the Holy One blessed be He will make for the righteous.[44] But this meal is not connected to Messiah or to any new creation.

A similar tradition to that in *Baruch* appears in Fourth Ezra (6:49–52) and in *1 Enoch* (60:7–9, 24–25; 62:7–16). Even though these two works bring a more detailed text, it seems clear that the three works utilized an identical tradition, according to which these creatures were kept in reserve for an eschatological feast.[45]

The detailed tradition in *4 Ezra* and in *Enoch* includes various details that do not appear in *Syriac Baruch*. It mentions the separation between the two monsters: Leviathan is intended to dwell in the depths of the sea and Behemoth is sent to a dry place—"the thousand mountains," according to *4 Ezra,* and an

---

[42] *Kenigin:* Jastrow, *Dictionary,* 1392, derives it from the Greek κυνήγιον; Kohut, *'Arukh ha-Shalem,* 6:132.

[43] Also *y. Sanh.* 10.6 (29c); *y. Meg.* 1.3 (72b), 3.2 (74a); *Pesiq. R. Kah., Parasha Aheret* (ed. Mandelbaum; 455–57); *b. B. Bat.* 74b; *Pesiq. Rab.* 16 (ed. Ish Shalom; 90b); *Lev. Rab.* 22.9; *Num. Rab.* 21.18. One should note that the tradition concerning Leviathan and Behemoth in an eschatological context is not mentioned at all in the Mishnah. R. Akiva's dictum "And everything is prepared for a feast" (*m. 'Abot* 3.16) does not allude to any messianic feast. Rather, it appears in the context of man's responsibility for his actions and the reckoning that he needs to give for them, not only in this world, but also in the world to come. The feast is the reward of the righteous in the world to come, according to Albeck, or it is the feast reserved for both the righteous and the wicked, each according to his deeds (R. Obadiah of Bartenura; *Perush ha-Mishnah la-Meiri*). Even if this saying does allude to the feast of the righteous in the world to come, it does not refer to a messianic feast to be held at the end of time.

[44] See *b. B. Bat.* 75a; *b. Pes.* 119b; and cf. *Tg. Ps.-J.* to Ps 50:10 and to Gen 1:21; *Pirqe R. El.* 11; Jellinek, *Bet ha-Midrasch* 6:150ff. And cf. Ibn Ezra to Dan 12:2; *Tanh., Beshalah* (ed. Buber; 34b); *Midrash Shoher Tov* 23:7 (ed. Buber; 202); Guttmann, "Leviathan, Behemoth, and Ziz," 225, 229–30.

[45] According to Black, *The Book of Enoch,* 227, the tradition in *Enoch* is the original one, upon which the other two are based.

invisible desert, according to Enoch;[46] and it specifies the sex of the monsters: the Leviathan is a female sea-monster, while the Behemoth is male.[47] But of particular importance for clarifying the intentions of this tradition is the parallel tradition in *Enoch,* which connects the dwelling place of Behemoth and Leviathan with paradise. Behemoth is located in a desert, whose name varies in the Ethiopic manuscripts: Donodein, Dondein, Dadein, etc., located east of the garden of Eden, in the place where the chosen ones and the righteous will dwell (*1 En.* 60:8). It may be that this desert is to be identified with the desert in Dudael mentioned in *1 En.* 10:4, the place of darkness, where the angel Raphael was commanded to throw Azazel and to place upon it hard and sharp rocks.[48] He will be kept there in the future without seeing light forever, until the great day of judgment in which he will be flung into the fire. Azazel is the Satan, from which it follows that the dwelling place of Behemoth is the place of Satan; for that reason, these two monsters are counted among the hidden things, and are located next to the "garden of the righteous" (*1 En.* 32:3; 60:23; 77:3). It follows clearly from this tradition that the two monsters were preserved for the messianic banquet intended for the righteous on the great day of the Lord: "These two monsters, prepared for the great day of the Lord, will provide food"[49] or, according to another reading: "These two monsters are prepared for the great day of the Lord (when) they shall turn into food" (1 En. 60:24).[50] This banquet will occur at the end of time and the final judgment "which the Lord of Spirits has prepared" (60:6). There also follows from *Enoch*

---

[46] On this translation, see Caquot, "Leviatan et Behemoth," 117; on the desert, Black, *Book of Enoch,* 227ff.

[47] In *Apoc. Mos.* 15:3, the garden of Eden was divided between Adam and Eve. In the territory of Adam, located in the northeast, were the male animals, while in that of Eve, located in the southwest, were the female animals (on this see also in the Jewish tradition *Gen. Rab.* 7.4; *b. B. Bat.* 74b).

[48] It is identified with *Beit Hadudei* which, in the talmudic sources, *m. Yoma* 6.8 refers to the desert to which the scapegoat was sent; *Tg. Ps.-Jon.* to Lev. 16:21–22: *Beit ḥarurei.* The source of the name in Greek, "Dudael," is from *Ḥadudei El;* i.e., the high mountains of God (thus Milik, "The Dead Sea Scrolls Fragments of the Book of Enoch," 395; Black, *The Book of Enoch,* 134; Kahana, on Enoch 10:4; M. A. Knibb, *The Ethiopic Book of Enoch* [Oxford, 1978], 87). Charles identified it with "the land of Nod" (Gen 4:16), which is also "east of Eden," which in the LXX is called Ναιδ (Charles, *Enoch,* 115; Klausner, *The Messianic Idea,* 299 n. 48).

[49] Thus according to MS D from the fifteenth century (but which follows the ancient Ethiopic Manuscript, Eth. I). The passage as a whole is corrupt, but it clearly refers to a feast to be conducted at the end of time (see Knibb, "1 Enoch," in Sparks, *Apocryphal Old Testament,* 241).

[50] E. Isaac, "1 (Ethiopic Apocalypse of) Enoch," *OTP* 1:42.

a certain connection between these two monsters and the tradition in the book of Revelation. Enoch asks the angel to show him "how strong these sea monsters are, how they were separated on this day and were cast, the one into the abysses of the ocean, and the other into the dry desert" (*1 En.* 60:9). Similarly, the beast that ascends from the sea in Rev 13 is to be identified with Leviathan, and the other creature ascending from the land with Behemoth. Like the sea monster (δράκων), which in Revelation embodies the Satan, the *diabolos,* and the antichrist, is thrown into the pit for a thousand years, and at the end of days is defeated and thrown into the lake of fire (Rev 20:1–6), so too the sea monster in *Enoch* dwells in "the desert that is in Dudael," where Azazel had been thrown. The latter is the embodiment of the Satan, with his arms and legs bound so that he might dwell there for ever, to be thrust into the fire on the day of judgment. It follows from *Enoch* that Leviathan and Behemoth's role in the eschatological meal, and their perception as the embodiment of the anti-Christ in Revelation, belong to the same tradition, rather than being seen as different stages in the development of this tradition.[51]

Additional details concerning this feast appear in another chapter in *Enoch,* which also reveals great closeness to the apocalyptic description in *Baruch.* The Son of Man had been hidden since long ago, and God protected him so that he might be revealed to the chosen ones at the end of days, upon the final judgment and the birth pangs of the catastrophes. The righteous and the chosen ones will flee on that day, will eat together with the Son of Man, and will fall asleep to awaken forever and ever (*1 En.* 62:13–16). This tradition expresses a definite Christian theological perception. "The Son of Man" is widely used in the New Testament as a synonym for Jesus.[52] The righteous and the chosen who will eat together with Jesus are the remnant that remains until that time, together with the martyrs, who "had been beheaded for their testimony to Jesus" (Rev 20:4–6). The feast to be conducted at the end of days prior to the resurrection is none other than the Eucharist—that is, the final meal that heralds the second coming of the Messiah, and for whose sake the Behemoth and Leviathan were preserved. At this feast the righteous and the martyrs will eat together with Messiah, at the eternal resurrection.

---

[51] Contra Black, *The Book of Enoch,* 227, 230–51.

[52] Against M. Hooker's definitive statement that "there is no hint that the picture of the Son of man owes anything to Christian theology" (*The Son of Man in Mark,* 48). She admits that "there are similarities between 1 Enoch and the eschatological 'Son of Man'" sayings in the Gospels. The image of Enoch, in my opinion, should be seen as a prefiguration of Jesus.

4.3. The Beginning of the Messiah's Revelation

The new aeon to be founded following the Eschaton is described in clearly Christian terms in *2 Baruch*. The abundance of grain, of fruit of the land, and of wine,[53] the fragrance of the sweet fruits that will be brought by the morning winds and the healing dew carried by the evening clouds, all characterize paradise, which according to the Christian view is embodied in the church.[54]

The healing dew is identified in Christian sources with the "dew of the Lord," as depicted in the early Syrian work, *Odes of Solomon:* "And the Lord (is) like the sun upon the face of the land. My eyes were enlightened, and my face received the dew; and my breath was refreshed by the pleasant fragrance of the Lord. And he took me to his paradise, wherein is the wealth of the Lord's pleasure" (*Odes Sol.* 11:13–16).[55]

Inside paradise are trees, including the tree of life, whose leaves and fruits do not wilt, the like of whose goodly fragrance has never been known, and which are "the healing of the nations" (Rev 22:2). Christ is the tree of life and a healing sun (after Mal 3:20). The partaking in his flesh at the Last Supper assures healing from death and provides eternal life, as stated by Ignatius in his *Letter to the Ephesians* 20:2, describing the bread that is broken at the Eucharist as a "medicine of immortality."[56]

---

[53] Grain is explicitly mentioned in the Arabic version (Leemhuis, Klijn, and van Gelder, *The Arabic Text,* 46); it is not mentioned in the Syriac version, but is known there as the fruit of the earth. See Exod 23:10; Lev 23:39; 25:19ff.; 26:4–5; Isa 30:23; Ps 85:13; 107:37; Neh 9:36–37. The combination of grain and wine is very common in the Bible (see, e.g., Deut 33:28; 2 Kgs 18:32; Isa 36:17; Hos 7:14; 9:1; 14:8; Mal 3:11). This idiom is based upon Gen 27:28 ("and much grain and wine"). See, similarly, *1 En.* 10:16–20, which suggests a tradition very similar to *Baruch,* but in which wine appears before grain, and including oil. These three elements—grain, wine, and oil—appear a great deal in the Bible to express the abundance of fruit of the earth (see, e.g., Deut 11:14; 28:51; Hos 2:24; Hag 1:11; 2 Chr 32:28). However, in all the biblical passages the order is generally grain, wine, and oil, and not as in *Enoch*. This period of time is depicted in *Enoch* as being after the Flood, but the Flood can be understood here as the end of the world, after which comes a new creation (Stanton, *The Jewish and Christian Messiah,* 313–14; Daniélou, *Sacramentum Futuri,* 59; cf. *Jub.* 5:11–12; *L.A.B.* 3.10; *Sib. Or.* 3:619–23; 3:743–60; Irenaeus, *Haer.* 5.33.3 [SC 153:411]).

[54] Daniélou, *Sacramentum Futuri,* 4–5, 8, 16–17; Murray, *Symbols of Church and Kingdom,* 125.

[55] The expression "healing dew" is based upon the LXX to Isa 26:19. Cf. *Odes Sol.* 35:1, 5; 36:7.

[56] *The Apostolic Fathers* (LCL) 1:194. Ephraem Syrus: "Blessed be even the cluster of grapes that is like a source of life" (*Hymnen de Nativitate* [= *Hnat.*; CSCO 186, Syr. 82] 3.15; *Hymnen de Virginitate* [CSCO 223, Syr. 94], 31.13). And cf. *4 Ezra* 7:123;

CHAPTER 4: Description of the Appearance of Messiah

The perfume and pleasant fragrance characteristic of the trees of paradise are connected with Jesus, who heralds the new paradise. Thus, Mary anoints his feet with pure and expensive nard, and the house is filled with the fragrance of the ointment (John 12:3). She anointed his body for burial, by which his messiahship is revealed (Mark 14:8), and for that reason Jesus is buried with perfumes in his new grave in the garden (κῆπος) that commences the new world, the heavenly paradise to be established upon his resurrection (John 19:39–40).

In a manner similar to that of the present description, Ephraem Syrus also describes paradise with its abundance of fruits, its dew for bathing, its moist and healing breezes, and the fragrance of the garden of Eden, all of which are connected with the feast conducted in paradise:

> Who has seen such a feast in the heart of the forest, with fruits of all flavors easily available! One by one they approach at your choice: fruits for food and drink, dew in which to bathe, and leaves with which to dry oneself. All this abundant treasure belongs to our Lord, who is rich in all. Seated among the trees, in the fresh air, with flowers beneath them, fruits above them, their heaven—made from the fruits of the earth and the earth beneath them—a bower of flowers. Who has heard or seen such a thing? A cloud of fruits shades their heads, and a cloud of flowers falls down and is spread beneath their feet. A brook of pleasure—when that tree takes leave of you, another one beckons to you. They all rejoice, for you partake of the fruit of one, and drink the drink of the second, and bathe in the dew of another and perfume yourself. You anoint yourself with the juice of this one, breathe in the fragrance of that one, and hear the song of the other—blessed is he who has given such joy to a human being. Perfumed winds waft with all flavors, and like Martha and Mary who hasten to prepare (the feast), because the guests at the feast never cease arriving....
>
> Winds of Paradise rush before the saints. One blows satisfaction, another spreads healing. From the blowing of one is fruitfulness, from the breath of the other satisfaction. Who has seen such winds, that bring gusts that are good for food, another for drink, one blowing dew, another oils. The winds sustain the souls in a spiritual manner. This is a *feast* without tiredness: the hand does not tire, nor do the teeth become weary, nor the belly heavy. He who sits at the table rejoices without effort, and is satisfied without food, and is quenched without drinking. The gentle breeze refreshes him, and another satisfies his hunger.... The

---

Paralipomena 9:1–3; Rev 22:2, based on Ezek 47:12; *1 En.* 24:3–5; 25:4–6. One should take note that the tree of life, whose fragrance is incomparable and whose fruit gives life to the elect, is not the name of an isolated tree but is a collective term, as in Gen 1:11, and as opposed to Gen 2:9; 3:22, facilitating its description as a grove of trees (*Paralipomena* 9:3; *1 En.* 28–30; 32:3–4; 36:1; *T. Levi* 18:11; *2 En.* 5:1–6; *4 Ezra* 8:52; Rev 2:7; *Sib. Or.* 3:702–96: see Andersen, *2 Enoch*, 114–15; *Greek L.A.E. (Apoc. Mos.)* 28–29; 40:7; Budge, *The Book of the Cave of Treasures*, 75). In works related to *Baruch*, the manna is also connected to paradise (*L.A.B.* 19:10; *Sib. Or.* 7:149).

fragrance of Paradise serves as food instead of bread, and the breath of life serves as drink. This breath of life substitutes for drink while the senses are scented with waves of pleasure, that come in each type to all; with the power of joy they stand out without burden, rejoicing each moment in the miracles of the splendid Almighty.[57]

According to the extant tradition in *2 Baruch*, the land will give an abundance of grain, one vine will have a thousand branches, each branch will have a thousand clusters, each cluster will bear a thousand grapes, and each grape will produce a vat of wine. This image of abundance of grain and wine is to be understood in the context of that same messianic feast for whose sake Behemoth and Leviathan were preserved—the feast that is to occur in paradise upon the second appearance of Messiah.[58]

According to the Bible (2 Kgs 18:32; Isa 30:23; 36:17; Ezek 48:18) grain is also bread, but in Christianity bread becomes the symbol of the body of Jesus.[59] The image of Jesus as bread lies at the focus of the sacrament of the Eucharist, finding expression in the breaking of bread: the body of Christ is the bread, and whoever partakes of it is satisfied.[60] The manna, which will again come down from heaven, symbolizes the heavenly bread of life. Scripture describes manna as a wondrous bread that God rained upon his people from heaven during the forty years when they were in the desert (Exod 16:4, 35),[61] for which reason it is called "bread from heaven" (Ps 105:40) or "the bread of the mighty" (Ps 78:25).[62]

---

[57] Ephraem Syrus, *Hymnes sur le paradis*, ix.3–9, 17 (CSCO, vol. 174, Scr. Syri 78, pp. 36–37, 39).

[58] Indeed, the biblical prophecies also describe the future as a time in which the earth will yield an abundance of fruit (Amos 9:13–14; Hos 2:24; Isa 7:15; Isa 35; 41:18ff.; Ezek 47:1–12; Moore, *Judaism*, 2:365; Kaufmann, *Toldot ha-Emuna*, 3:646). Notwithstanding their hyperbole, these passages depict in a colorful and concrete way the goodly future anticipated for the people of Israel in its land, and have nothing in common with the end of days and the appearance of Messiah and paradise. In only two places is the future age of redemption compared with the garden of Eden: in Ezek 36:35 and in Isa 51:3, but in both it is only used as a metaphor (see Moore, *Judaism*, 2:365).

[59] Matt 6:11: "Give us this day our daily bread." Cf. Luke 11:3. He comes instead of the shewbread that was in the old temple (Matt 12:4 & par., and esp. the miracle of the bread and fish: Mark 6:38ff.; 7:27; 8:4–8).

[60] Mark 14:22; 1 Cor 10:16–17 ("Because there is one bread, we who are many are one body, for we all partake in the one bread"); 11:23; Acts 2:42, 46; 20:7, 11; 27:35.

[61] Josephus, *Ant.* 3.30.

[62] *Wis. Sol.* 16:20. Philo interpreted the manna allegorically, identifying it with the word of God, the Logos, which was the bread from heaven. This interpretation enabled

CHAPTER 4: Description of the Appearance of Messiah   141

In talmudic sources manna is considered as the food of the angels,[63] on the basis of Ps 78:25 (LXX), in which *lehem abirim* is translated as "bread of the angels." This is one of the cultic items that Elijah will prepare for Israel in the future: "the dish of manna, the vial of the purifying water, and the vial of anointing oil, and there are those who say, also the staff of Aaron, with its almonds and flowers" (*Mek. de-Rabbi Yishma'el, Masekhta Vayehi Beshalah,* 5; ed. Horowitz and Rabin, 172).[64] Manna is mentioned in a later tradition as the food of the righteous, to be ground in the mill located in the third heaven, in the sky (*b. Hag.* 12b), and is also connected to the appearance of the Messiah.[65] However, no Jewish source expresses the expectation that manna will once again descend in the new world following the End; indeed, Judaism does not even know of the concept "the storehouse of manna."

Christian tradition identified manna, the bread from heaven, with the body of Jesus. But unlike the corporeal manna eaten by the Israelites in the desert, which failed to provide them eternal life, Jesus is "the bread of life," the "spiritual food" (1 Cor 10:3), the true manna that symbolizes his flesh; one who believes in him and shares in his body will no longer be hungry or thirsty and will enjoy eternal life. Like "I am the true vine" is Jesus' declaration "I am the bread of life (ἐγώ εἰμι ὁ ἄρτος τῆς ζωῆς). He who comes to me shall not hunger; and he who believes in me shall never thirst" (John 6:27–35, 48). Jesus is "the living bread which came down from heaven"; whoever eats of him "will live forever" (John 6:51). "*This is the bread which came down from heaven, not such as the fathers ate and died; he who eats this bread will live forever*" (John 6:54–58). The expression "the living bread" or "bread of life" is thus interpreted as alluding to the sacrament of Eucharist.

In the Gospel according to John, the manna is explicitly identified with the bread that was at the focus of the last supper that Jesus conducted upon earth—a meal that became the model for the founding of the eucharistic

---

the Christians to identify the manna with Jesus, who according to the Gospel of John was the Logos (see Philo, *Leg.* 2.86 [LCL 1:279]; 3.176 [LCL 1:419]; *Mut.* 258–60 [LCL 5:275]; *Det.* 118 [LCL 2:281]; *Fug.* 137 [LCL 5:83], etc.). On the interpretation of the manna in Philo in comparison to that of John, see Borgen, *Bread from Heaven.*

[63] Relying upon the LXX to Ps 78:25, where *lehem abirim* is translated as "bread of angels." Cf. *b. Yoma* 75b, and *Mek. de-Rabbi Yishma'el, Masekhta Beshalah* 3 (ed. Horowitz and Rabin; 167): "Do not read אבירים but איברים"; *Tanh., Beshalah* 22 (ed. Buber; 67); *Seder Eliyahu Rabbah* 23 (ed. Ish-Shalom; 129).

[64] *B. Pesah.* 54a, enumerates the manna among the ten things that were created on the eve of the first Shabbat; *t. Sotah* 11.10; *b. Ta'an.* 9a.

[65] *Pesiq. Rab.* 15 (ed. Ish-Shalom; 73); *Cant. Rab.* 2.9; *Num. Rab.* 11.2; *Qoh. Rab.* 1.9. The talmudic traditions relating to the manna are based upon Mic 7:15 and Hos 12:9.

sacrament.⁶⁶ The Syriac term *ozra* ("storehouse") is used by the New Testament to translate the Hebrew word *'asam*, the "grain storehouse" to which Jesus will gather the grain—i.e., the wheat, a symbol for the believers—as opposed to the chaff or wild wheat, which shall be burned with fire (Matt 3:12; 13:30). A similar meaning is given to "the hidden manna" to be given to the believers in the messianic kingdom, together with the tree of life and the white stone upon which will be written a new name—that of Jesus (Rev 2:7, 17).

The vine (ἡ ἄμπελος) or vineyard (ὁ ἀμπελών) are also symbols for Jesus. In the Hebrew Bible, the vine and the vineyard symbolize the people of Israel;⁶⁷ Jesus, who according to the Christian approach embodies the true

---

⁶⁶ The Gospel according to John does not explicitly describe the act of founding the eucharistic sacrament, but most scholars connect the miracle of the bead, which in this gospel occurs when "the Passover was at end" (John 6:4), and Jesus' speech concerning the bread of life in ch. 6, as well as that concerning the true vine, ch. 15, with the Eucharist (J. Coppens, "Eucharistie," *DBS*, 2:1146–1215, esp. at 1189; Brown, *Gospel According to St. John*, 272–74; Brooks, "The Johannine Eucharist," 296; C. T. Craig, "Sacramental Interest in the Fourth Gospel," *JBL* 58 [1939]: 38–40; Cullmann, *Early Christian Worship*, 93ff.). Cullmann also connects with both the Eucharist and the eschatological feast the story of the wedding in Cana and the miracle of the transformation of water to wine (ibid., 66–71).

The issue of the sacramental allusions in the Fourth Gospel generally, and in John 6 in particular, is subject to debate among scholars. Some think that 6:51–58 is an interpolation inserted by an editor with an ecclesiastical orientation (see, e.g., Bultmann, *Theology of the New Testament*, 1:147–48; 2:54). On this debate in Johannine studies, see Borgan, *Bread from Heaven*, 25–26, 189–92; R. E. Brown, "The Johannine Sacramentary Reconsidered," *ThS* 23 (1962), 183–88. In terms of our subject, it does not matter if these elements were added at a later stage in the shaping of the gospel. As Brown observes, the fact that an editor added them at a later date does not mean that they are less ancient than materials that found their way to the first versions of the Gospel. In his words, "we do not believe that the redactor's purpose was to insert sacramental references in a non-sacramental Gospel, but rather to bring out more clearly the latent sacramentalism already in the Gospel" (Brown, *Gospel According to John*, xxxvii–xxxviii).

Cf. *Did.* 9.4; H. Lesêtre, "Manna," *DB* (Paris, 1912) 4.I.662–63. Manna appears as a symbol of the Eucharist in the catacomb paintings, and the idea finds expression also in an ancient communion vessel with the inscription φάγε μάνα: "eat manna" (R. Meyer, "Μάννα," *TDNT* 4:465 and n. 31). For outlooks challenging the connection between the last supper and the Eucharist, see Riggs, "The Sacred Food of *Didache* 9–10," 256–83.

⁶⁷ As vine: Isa 5:1–9; Hos 10:1; 14:8; Jer 2:21; 6:9; Ps 80:9–17; Ezek 15:1–6; 17:5–10; 19:10–14. As vineyard: Isa 27:2–6; Jer 5:10; 12:10–11. A vine of gold with clusters of grapes hanging down was one of the prominent decorations in the temple because of its size and its craftsmanship (thus Josephus, *Ant.* 15.395; *J.W.* 5.210;

CHAPTER 4: Description of the Appearance of Messiah   143

Israel, inherited the image of the vine, which in turn became a symbol of the Christian Messiah and his flock, occupying an important place in the theological symbolism of the early church. Jesus is the true vine, as he himself declares:

> I am the true vine (ἐγώ εἰμι ἡ ἄμπελος) and my Father is the vinedresser. Every branch of mine that bears no fruit, he takes away, and every branch that does bear fruit he prunes, that it may bear more fruit. You are already made clean by the word which I have spoken to you. Abide in me, and I in you. As the branch cannot bear fruit by itself, unless it abides in the vine, neither can you, unless you abide in me. I am the vine, you are the branches. He who abides in me, and I in him, he it is that bears much fruit, for apart from me you can do nothing. If a man does not abide in me, he is cast forth as a branch and withers; and the branches are gathered, thrown into the fire and burned. (John 15:1–6)[68]

The vine and branches, shown overflowing with fruit in *2 Baruch*, describe Jesus and the congregation of believers in the new era that will follow the appearance of Christ, and they well illustrate the metaphor in John 15. The vine described in *Syriac Baruch* is the true vine belonging to the heavenly order, since God his Father is the vinedresser. Its branches receive their life from the vine, and their connection to it is a condition for the abundant yield of fruit. Just as the manna is "heavenly bread" so is the vine "the tree of life."

The vine described in John 15 is a sacramental symbol that clearly refers to the Eucharist. The fruit of the vine is wine (Mark 14:5; Matt 24:29; Luke 22:18), a symbol of the blood of Jesus, blessed in the ceremony of the Eucharist, in which the believer by drinking it identifies with Jesus' crucifixion and sacrifice. The vine similarly appears in the same connection in a blessing recited at the Eucharist, preserved in the *Didache*: "We bless you our Father, for the holy vine of David your servant which you have revealed to us through Jesus your servant" (*Did.* 9.2).[69]

In the work discussed here, the vine is also connected to the image of paradise. The vine is identified with the tree of life located in paradise (Rev 2:7; 22:2) and constitutes an archetype for Christ as the source of life of the church

---

m. Mid. 3.8). On the vine as a symbol of Judaism, see Brown, *Gospel According to John*, 674–75; Murray, *Symbols of Church and Kingdom*, 96–104.

[68] See the exegeses that connect the image of the vine to Jesus, based upon Ps 80:9, 18 and Ezek 17 (Brown, *Gospel According to John*, 670–71); cf. *4 Ezra* 5:23; Aphraates, *Sermon* 23 (SC 359:875ff.). Ephraem Syrus compared the cluster of grapes brought by the spies upon returning from Canaan (Num 13:23) to Christ upon the cross (CSCO 186, Syr 82; *Hnat.* 1.3; see Murray, *Symbols*, 104–30).

[69] Cf. Ignatius, who speaks about Jesus' blood as alluding to the Eucharist (Ign. *Rom.* 7.3; *Phld.* 4.1; *Smyrn.* 7.1); Brown, "Johannine Sacramentary," 203.

and its sacraments.[70] The bread and wine thus symbolize the flesh and blood of Jesus and are at the focus of the Eucharist sacrament.

The description of the fullness of grain, manna, and wine completes and explains the meaning of the meal, associated with the beginning of the appearance of Messiah, for whose sake the Leviathan and Behemoth have been preserved. This Messianic feast is based upon the last supper, in which the Lord is blessed (εὐχαριστεῖν, εὐλογεῖν) by means of bread and wine, symbolizing the new covenant. This meal is the realization of Jesus' promise, given at the Last Supper, that he would no longer drink of the fruit of the vine "until that day when I drink it new in the kingdom of heaven."[71] The kingdom of heaven is here the kingdom of paradise expected upon the second coming of Jesus, expressed in the eucharistic sacrament: "For as often as you eat this bread and drink the cup, you proclaim the Lord's death until he comes" (1 Cor 11:26).[72] The anticipation of the second coming also appears in several places in Aramaic: "*Marana ta:* Our Lord, come!" (1 Cor 16:22; Rev 22:17–20; *Did.* 10.6). This is an ancient prayer, recited at the ceremony of the holy meal associated with the day of Jesus' resurrection. Just as on the day of the resurrection Christ appeared to his disciples at the time of the meal, so too will he reappear at the meal to take place at the End: "therefore *Maranatha* is above all a prayer that belongs to the Eucharist."[73] Hence in the ancient Christian approach the Eucharist expressed the eschatological anticipation of the return of the Lord following his resurrection, and the believer's eating and drinking with him at his table in the new world. The daily meal of the early church was thus an act of eschatological joy in anticipation of the coming redemption, and a kind of enjoyment in advance of the messianic feast at the end of time.[74]

The Last Supper conducted by Jesus with his disciples, in which he himself instituted the sacrament of the Eucharist, is understood as a prefiguration of the great messianic meal to be conducted at the end of time with the Messiah

---

[70] Aphraates begins the history of the blessing hidden within the grape, based upon Isa 65:8–9, in speaking about paradise. Although he does not say so explicitly, it is implied there that the grape itself comes from paradise (Aphraates, *Sermon* 23, concerning the seed of the grape [SC 359:875ff.]). Similarly, Ephraem Syrus describes the cluster of grapes as giving life to all (*Hymnes sur le paradis*, 6.8 [R. Lavenant and F. Graffin, SC 137 (Paris, 1968), 85]).

[71] Mark 14:25; Matt 8:11ff.; 26:29. Matthew adds "with you"; Luke 13:29; 14:15; 22:16–18.

[72] Mark 14:22–25 & par.; 1 Cor 10:3–4, 16–21; *Did.* 10.2; Ign. *Eph.* 20:2; Justin, *1 Apol.* 66 (PG 6:428–29).

[73] Cullmann, *Early Christian Worship*, 13–14.

[74] Ibid., 16, 71; Kuhn, "The Lord's Supper," 67–86.

CHAPTER 4: Description of the Appearance of Messiah 145

and the saints who are to enter the messianic kingdom. Just as the Eucharist was part of the act of accepting Christianity and of sharing in the lot of Jesus and the believers, so too the eschatological Eucharist is an act of acceptance into the kingdom of heaven and participation in the accompanying blessings.[75]

The eschatological feast to take place in paradise is in place of the eating of the tree of knowledge in the original paradise. Just as the eating of the tree of knowledge in the garden of Eden led to the origin of sin in the world, so will the feast conducted by Jesus, the "new Adam," in the spiritual garden of Eden together with his believers, atone for his sin.

It was this expectation that led an apocalyptic work such as *Syriac Baruch*, in describing the eschatological Eucharist, to place the emphasis upon the fullness of the fruit of the vine that Jesus had promised to drink in the kingdom of heaven, and not upon the bread, the fruit of the earth, to which this tradition only devotes a short sentence.

Just as in the Eucharist the believers "eat their food in joy," ἐν ἀγαλλιάσει (Acts 2:46)[76] and are satisfied,[77] so too the believers who partake in the messianic feast described in *Syriac Baruch* are satisfied and no longer hungry; they are joyous and again see (*neḥzun*) miracles (*tedmurta*) every day.[78]

---

[75] For further hints of the messianic feast in the NT, see Rev 19:9, 17–18; Luke 22:28–30. This subject may also be connected to the stories about miraculous eating (Mark 6:30–44; Mark 8:1–10; John 6:5–14). These descriptions involve a projection of the Eucharist or of the messianic feast into the historical life of Jesus. Another allusion to the messianic feast appears in Jesus' answer to his mother in John 2:4: "my hour has not yet come." Jesus refers here to the day on which he will be able to provide the wine at the messianic feast (cf. Cross, *The Ancient Library of Qumran*, 168–69). For a similar description to that of *Baruch*, see Aphraates, *Sermons*, 6.6 (PS, vol. 1, vv. 265–68; SC 349:381): "the curse is fixed on the cross, and the sword was removed from the tree of life, which was given as food to the believers. Paradise is promised to the righteous, to the virgins and the saints, and the fruits of the tree of life are given as food to the believers and to the virgins who perform the will of God. The door is opened and the way is clear, the spring flows and satiates the thirsty, the table is set and the feast is prepared. The fattened calf has been slaughtered and the cup of salvation is mixed. The feast has been prepared and the bridegroom comes in order to take his place next to the table. The messengers have made the invitations, and many are called."

[76] Cf. Acts 16:34; John 5:35; 1 Pet 4:13; Jude 24; *Jub.* 22:4 ("a feast of joy"); 31:22; 45:5; Lietzmann, *Mass and Lord's Supper*, 176–77; Kuhn, "The Lord's Supper," 87; Black, "Qumran Baptismal Rites," 105.

[77] Mark 6:42: "they all ate and were satisfied" in the miracle of the loaves and fish (cp. Mark 8:4–8 & par.).

[78] Acts 2:11; on seeing as a path toward faith in the Gospel of John, see Cullmann,

The description of the meal in *Baruch* corresponds to the accepted order in the Eucharist ceremony, in which the blessing over the bread precedes that of the wine (Mark 14:22–25; Matt 26:26–29; 1 Cor 11:23–26),[79] reflecting the original version, based upon the bread and wine taken to Abraham by Melchizedek (Gen 14:18–20).[80] The tradition in *Syriac Baruch* therefore describes the ceremony of the Eucharist to take place in paradise before the second coming of Jesus at the end of days.

A similar eschatological feast is described in the Qumran writings. The *Rule of the Congregation* ii 11–22 (1Q28ᵃ)[81] describes a meal to take place at the end of days[82] when *the coming* of the Messiah *will be revealed*[83] and they will

---

Early Christian Worship, 38ff. This seeing relates to the characteristic theophanic sights from the past that are realized in the spiritual theophany (Borgen, *Bread from Heaven*, 175).

[79] It follows from many versions that the breaking of bread was the only ceremony performed. Thus Acts 2:42; 20:11; Luke 24:30; *Ps.-Clem.* 14.1 (PG 2:345); cf. Lietzmann, *Mass and Lord's Supper*, 195ff.; Cullmann, *Early Christian Worship*, 14. A later tradition places the wine before the bread (Luke 22:17–20; *Did.* 9.2–4, although *Did.* 9.5 acknowledges the accepted order); cf. the comment on Irenaeus below. For further sources, see Lietzmann, *Mass and Lord's Supper*, 162–63. According to Lietzmann, the placing of the wine prior to the bread is a later stage in the tradition, done under the influence of the Jewish blessing, in which the Kiddush over wine is the first and primary blessing, and only thereafter follows that on the bread. On the order of blessings in Judaism, see *Mekhilta de-Rabbi Yishma'el, Masekhta de-ba-Hodesh* 7 (ed. Horowitz and Rabin; 229), which interprets the verse "remember the Sabbath day": "To sanctify it with a blessing: from this, we learn that one sanctifies it over wine at its entrance." *B. Pesaḥ.* 106a: "Our Rabbis taught: 'Remember the Sabbath day to sanctify it'—Remember it over the wine." According to Flusser ("The Last Supper and the Essenes," 116–19), the formula of Luke 22:17–20, placing wine before bread, is the original formula (but omitting Luke 22:19b–20). Hence, Jesus and the Christian group within which the *Didache* was written behaved like all Jews, and recited the blessing over the wine before the blessing over the meal.

[80] Melchizedek is the prototype of Jesus, according to Ps 110:4. The wine is the blood, based on Deut 32:14; the sacrifice in the Bible is called בשר (flesh), a word also used for bread: the bread is the sacrifice, and the libation is the wine. The combination of flesh and blood also follows from the description of the manner of offering the sacrifice (Lev 17:5ff.). The combination of flesh and blood likewise appears in the Mishnah (*m. Naz.* 9.5; *m. Soṭah* 8.1).

[81] See D. Barthélemy and J. T. Milik, *DJD* I (Oxford, 1955), 107–30; J. Licht, *The Rule Scroll* (Jerusalem, 1965), 269–70.

[82] Ibid, 1:1. On this term as designating the end of time see *Pesher Habakkuk* ii 5; ix 6; *CD* iv 4; vi 11.

[83] This has been suggested by Puech ("Préséance Sacerdotal et Messie-Roi," 359–

CHAPTER 4: Description of the Appearance of Messiah   147

bless the *beginning* of the bread and the wine, and thereafter break bread. This unique eschatological-cultic meal will be conducted upon the coming of the Messiah, that is, at the Parousia. The use in this context of the expression, "his coming will be revealed" (Hebrew: יתגלה בואו), indicates the similarity between this tradition and that of *Baruch,* which uses identical terminology to describe the appearance of Messiah. Only the high-ranking members of the sect, "men of renown, those summoned to the gatherings of the community council" (to identify these, compare 1Q28ᵃ i 27–ii 3), will participate in this meal; first they will bless the bread and wine, as at the Christian feast, and thereafter break the bread:

> For he is the one who blesses the first-fruit of bread and of the new wine and stretches out his hand towards the bread before them. Afterwards, the Messiah of Israel shall stretch out his hands towards the bread. And afterwards, they shall bless all the congregation of the community.

As in the Christian Eucharist, the common meals of the members of the sect conducted upon earth in the present, at which they bless the bread and the wine, are no more than an anticipation of the eschatological meal to take place when the Messiah will appear among them (1QS vi 2–5).[84]

Support for our interpretation that the description in *Baruch* relates to an eschatological meal to be conducted at the end of days, upon the coming of Messiah and the establishment of the new world in the image of paradise, may also be found in an explicitly Christian source. In his exegesis of the blessing with which Isaac blessed Jacob, "May God give of the dew of heaven, and of the fatness of the earth, and plenty of grain and wine" (Gen 27:28), Irenaeus states that this refers to the days of the messianic kingdom, when the righteous will rule after their resurrection. At that time the renewed and liberated creation will yield an abundance of food of all kinds, from the dew of heaven and the fruit of the earth. He invokes a saying that Jesus used to say in connection with those times:

> Let there come days in which the vines will spring forth, and on each one of them there will be tens of thousands of branches, and on each branch ten thousand

---

60), who rejects the widespread reading in wake of Barthélemy and Milik: יוליד or יוליך. See the list of scholars who followed them and the various changes proposed by them in Puech, "Préséance," 354–55; for different suggestions, see Burrows, *More Light on the Dead Sea Scrolls,* 300–304.

[84] See Priest, "The Messiah and the Meal in 1QSa," 95, 98–100; Schiffman, *Halakhah,* 310; Kuhn, "The Lord's Supper," 70. The Messiah (with the definite article) is here identified with the Christian Messiah by Sutcliffe, "The Rule of the Congregation," 544. Cf.: Black, "Qumran Baptismal Rites," 104; Priest, "A Note on the Messianic Banquet," 228–29.

twigs, and on each twig ten thousand shoots, and on each shoot ten thousand clusters, and on each cluster ten thousand grapes, and each grape, when it is squeezed, will yield twenty-five measures of wine. And when one of the saints will pluck a cluster, another will cry out: "I am a better cluster, pick me, and *bless the Lord through me.*" Similarly, every seed of wheat will yield ten thousand stalks, and each stalk ten thousand seeds, and each seed will yield five litra of flour. And all the other fruits and seeds and grasses will do likewise. (Irenaeus, *Haer.* 5.33.3–4 [SC 153:411–19])[85]

Irenaeus cites this tradition in the name of the Presbyters (the elders) who heard it from Jesus' disciple John. It was testified to by Papias from Hierapolis in Phrygia, who according to Irenaeus was a disciple of John, a friend of Polycarp, and an ancient figure who composed five books, this tradition appearing in his fourth book. The tradition in *Syriac Baruch* is the same as that brought by Irenaeus. If this tradition may indeed be attributed to Papias who, as related by Irenaeus and Eusebius, lived during the first half of the second century, then both of these traditions came from the same time.

The vine is cited by Papias in a clearly eucharistic context: one thereby blesses the Lord, and following the description of the vine the tradition describes the abundance of grain, that is bread.[86] But unlike the case in *Syriac Baruch,* Irenaeus places the wine before the bread.[87] Irenaeus describes the abundance of the wine by the number ten thousand, which *Baruch* only uses with regard to the fruits of the earth, and he writes at greater length than does

---

[85] Cf. Eusebius, *Hist. eccl.* 3.39 (LCL 153:291). This tradition also appears in *Visio Pauli* 21–22 (Elliott, *Apocryphal New Testament,* 629), again in connection with the advent of the Messiah at the end of this world and the establishment of "the promised land," and in connection with this description of paradise to which Paul is taken. A similar formulation of the same tradition is found in *1 En.* 10:19. Hence the thesis that I propose in this book is that *Enoch* belongs to the same theological and ideological complex as does *Syriac Baruch,* and therefore does not reflect a Jewish tradition prior to that of *Baruch.*

[86] Cf. Hippolytus, *Christ and Antichrist* 11 (PG 10:736–37): "With the blood of which grape? Rather, his flesh alone is hanging on the cross like a cluster of grapes." Cyril, *On Easter:* "The vine is the Christ who comes to us. He offers us his clusters of grapes with love" (*Hymni et Sermones, Syriac* [ed. G. Bickell; *ZDMG* 27 (1873): 581]; cf. Murray, *Symbols of Church and Kingdom,* 124).

[87] In this he is close to the tradition in Luke and the *Didache.* It seems that the tradition in *Syriac Baruch* also originally placed the wine before the bread, referring to the combination of vine and manna, in accordance with the order of Irenaeus. This was, perhaps, afterwards adjusted to the Orthodox Christian order by the brief addition of the fruit of the earth.

CHAPTER 4: Description of the Appearance of Messiah   149

Baruch about the abundance of wheat. It nevertheless seems clear that we have here an identical tradition.

The basis for the thousand used in describing the yield of wine and grain in Irenaeus and in *Syriac Baruch* is found in the use of the word *rov,* "much," in Isaac's blessing of Jacob (Gen 27:28), interpreted as ריבוא (i.e., ten thousand). This gives expression to the Christian belief in the thousand year kingdom (*chiliasmus,* according to the Greek, or *millenarianism,* as derived from the Latin). According to this, upon Jesus' second coming, that is, the Parousia, he will establish a temporary earthly kingdom of a thousand years, in which the resurrected saints will rule together with him.[88] According to Daniélou, these views were widespread among many circles, especially in Asia Minor. Irenaeus attributes them first of all to the *Presbyters* ("elders"), adding that they are also found in Papias. Moreover, according to Papias the elders received them from John, who in turn received them from the Lord. One may infer from this that these ideas were very ancient and originated in the early Christian community, explaining the degree of respect they were given by a figure of the stature of Irenaeus.[89]

The millenarian outlook also explains the relation of this description as a whole to paradise, since according to this view the messianic eschatological kingdom is described as a return to paradise. Adam's life span in the garden of Eden was meant to be a thousand years, but was not completed because of his sin.[90]

---

[88] On Papias's millenarian outlook see Eusebius, *Hist. eccl.* 3.39.11–12 (LCL 153:295). Papias quoted other stories that reached him verbally, together with several unknown proverbs of the Lord and other things of an allegorical character. He says that after the resurrection of the dead there will be a period of one thousand years during which the kingdom of Christ will be founded upon earth in a corporeal manner. For further testimonies concerning Papias's outlook, see Daniélou, *Theology of Jewish Christianity,* 382.

[89] Daniélou (*Theology,* 383–84) brings additional testimony to the existence of these views. The researchers learn from the concrete description of the abundance of fruit of the earth that the Asiatic millenarian outlook described the kingdom of a thousand years as an earthly kingdom founded upon the earth in Zion. Those who rise in the first resurrection will continue to eat material food, and only thereafter will the second, fuller transformation come about (see Irenaeus, *Haer.* 5.33.1 [SC 153]; Eusebius, *Hist. eccl.* 3.39.11–12 [LCL 153:295]; Augustine, *Civ.* 20:7, 9 [LCL 6:285, 287, 305]; Stanton, *The Jewish and Christian Messiah,* 310–16; Charles, *Revelation of St. John,* 2:144ff.; Russell, *The Method and Message of Jewish Apocalyptic,* 294–95).

[90] *Jub.* 4:29–30; Irenaeus, *Haer.* 5.23.2 (SC 153:291). The description of the millennium in terms of paradise is based upon Isa 65:17ff., specifically in light of the exegesis given to it by the LXX (65:22), which adds "like the days of the tree of life shall

150   PART TWO: THE IDEA OF ESCHATOLOGICAL REDEMPTION

A millenarian faith is also reflected in *Syriac Baruch* in the division of the Messiah's appearance into two stages. By this distinction, made by the author, the Eucharist constitutes the beginning of the Messiah's revelation—that is, the first stage of the resurrection, and only after a period of a thousand years will the full appearance of the Messiah arrive.[91]

This period of time is also known in Christian sources as rest (κατά-παυσις; ἀνάπαυσις),[92] in which Christ will reign together with the martyrs and the saints who came to life in the first resurrection. This term associates the millennium with the seventh day of the cosmic week: the six days in which God created the world correspond to the six thousand years of this world, after which everything comes to an end; then will come the Sabbath, in which God completes and rests from his labor of creation, corresponding to the seventh millennium. The eighth day is the commencement of a different world.[93]

---

be the days of my people." This may be a Christian interpolation. On the identification of the millennium with paradise, see Justin, *Dial.* 80.4; 81:3–4 (PG 6:668–69); Charles, *Eschatology*, 315; Daniélou, *Theology*, 393 ("Asiatic millenarianism is derived entirely from speculation on the paradisiacal nature of the messianic age"; on the paradisiacal aspect in this description, see Daniélou, *Sacramentum Futuri*, 14).

[91] Millenarian approaches are also articulated in other apocalyptic works, such as *Ascen. Isa.* 4:13ff.; *Apoc. Elijah* 3:97–99; *Jub.* 23:27–31 ("And the days will begin to increase and grow longer among those sons of men, generation by generation, and year by year, until their days approach a thousand years, and to a greater number of years than days. And there [will be] no old men and none who is full of days [or: "whose days would not be full" (Charles)]. Because all of them will be infants and children, and all their days they will be complete and live in peace and rejoicing and there will be no Satan and evil [one] who will destroy, because all their days will be days of blessing and healing . . . and their bones will rest in the earth, and their spirits will increase joy"). Cf. *Jub* 4:29–30; *2 En.* 32:2–33:2. On the two stages in the appearance of the Messiah, see below.

[92] *2 Bar.* 73:2; cf. Heb 3:11, 18; 4:1, 3, 10, 11; 2 Thess 1:7.

[93] *Barn.* 15: 3–8; Justin, *Dial.* 81 (PG 6:669); 2 Pet 3:8; Irenaeus, *Haer.* 5.28.3 (SC 153:359), in which the seventh millennium is identified with the messianic kingdom. For Hippolytus the Sabbath is the archtype and embodiment of the kingdom of the holy ones in the future, when they will rule with Christ and it is called "the rest," ἀνάπαυσις (*Frag. Dan.* 2.4 [PG 10:645]; cf. Epiphanius, *Pan.* 66.85.9 [GCS; ed. K. Holl; Berlin, 1985; 3:128]; idem, *de Fide* 24.2–3 [p. 525]; Daniélou, *Theology*, 396–97, and on this view among other Christian authors, Daniélou, *Theology*, 400–402). Daniélou attempted to distinguish between two directions of development of this idea. In Asia, the environment in which Revelation was written and of which Papias testifies, this earthly kingdom is painted in paradisiacal colors, making use of the Bible and the apocalypses in order to describe a messianic age of peace among the animals,

CHAPTER 4: Description of the Appearance of Messiah   151

These approaches were rejected by the orthodox Christian church, and found explicit expression in the New Testament only in Rev 20:2–7. However, they are also alluded to in other sources in the New Testament,[94] as well as being testified to by the early Christian authors and church fathers.[95]

4.4. The Full Appearance of the Messiah

The initial appearance of Messiah at the end of days, as described in *Syriac Baruch*, is connected with the holy feast, which will already be conducted in the new world in paradise upon the opening of the millennium. This is the first stage in the full return of the Messiah, the *me'tita demeshiha*, "the coming of Messiah," once the appointed time has been fulfilled and he returns in splendor (*venehefokh beteshbohta*). As in his first appearance upon earth, when Jesus established the sacrament of the Last Supper prior to his full messianic appearance that occurs with his crucifixion,[96] so too in the new creation the holy feast precedes the second full manifestation (*Parousia*), to be revealed to all upon the resurrection of the dead and the final judgment. His first appearance "in the flesh" is an example or prefiguration of his second appearance "in the spirit." So too paradise, which is fully established with the beginning of the second appearance of Christ, is the realization of the paradise that Christ plants and radiates at the beginning of his earthly appearance.[97] The christological

---

extraordinary abundance of the earth, and human life spans of a thousand years. In Syria and Egypt, the messianic kingdom is connected with calculations and astrology related to the cosmic week of seven thousand years. The seventh millennium corresponds to the seventh day of creation, in which God rests, and is connected to the messianic rule that seems like the rest of the saints. However, in *Syriac Baruch* the two approaches appear alongside one another. On millenarianism, see Daniélou, *Theology*, 378ff. Similar calculations appear in talmudic works, especially in *Pereq Ḥeleq* of *b. Sanh.* See the stance of Rav Ketina regarding the duration of the existence of the world and the claim that, just as debts are cancelled one out of every seven years, so does the world rest a thousand years out of seven thousand (*b. Sanh.* 97a; ʿ*Abod. Zar.* 9a; but here too the description of the millennium is not woven within a concrete apocalyptic drama and apocalyptic messianism). These ideas are nowhere mentioned in earlier talmudic literature.

[94] John 5:25–30; 1 Cor 15:23, 25ff.; 51ff.; 1 Thess 4:16, 17; 2 Thess 1:7; 2 Pet 3:8; and cf. Daniélou, *Theology*, 378–79.

[95] Tertullian, *Marc.* 4.24 (PL 2:355–56); Eusebius, *Hist. eccl.* 3.39.11–12 (LCL 153:295); Augustine, *Civ.* 20:7; 9 (LCL 6:285, 287, 305); and see further testimony in Lesètre, "Milléniarisme," 1094–96 and n. 48.

[96] He is identified as such by the Roman centurion: "Truly, this was the Son of God!" (Matt 27:54; Mark 15:39).

[97] Thus the return of paradise is described in the Gospels upon the coming of Jesus. Jesus himself announces it (Matt 11:5; Luke 7:22) and shows by word and deed that his

paradise is in effect a symbol for the eschatological paradise.⁹⁸

The second coming of Messiah is mentioned following the description of the Eucharist. The term *me'tita* is the regular Syriac word for Parousia; hence the expression *zabna deme'tite demšiḥa* refers to the period of the second coming of Jesus, that is, the Parousia.⁹⁹ The same word appears in a similar context in an early version of the Eucharist described in 1 Corinthians 11:26—"For as often as you eat this bread and drink the cup, you proclaim the Lord's death *until he comes (deme'tite)*." The expression, "and he shall return in glory" (*venehefokh betešboḥta*), depicting the glorious coming of the Christian Messiah, also appears in the same context.¹⁰⁰

Two features are emphasized in the description of the full coming of Messiah:

1. The Messiah described in this passage is a preexistent heavenly messiah.

The phrase, "and he returns in glory," is to be understood as a return to heaven, implying that this is a Messiah who previously existed in the heavens prior to his coming and who returns to the place from whence he came.¹⁰¹ The

---

announcement is the realization of the description of paradise according to Isa 35:5ff. Mark's version of the tests of Christ also portrays Jesus as bringing humanity back to the time before the creation, and to the status of paradise. In Mark 7:37, the multitude praise him, using quotations from Gen 1:31 and Isa 35:5. According to John, Jesus embodies in his personality both the bread and the water of life, the ancient symbols of the garden of Eden. All these passages express the certainty that Jesus is the one who will bring paradise and that this restoration is already visible in his incarnation on earth.

⁹⁸ Daniélou, "Terre et Paradis," 456.

⁹⁹ The Greek word *parousia* is derived from the root πάρειμι, "to come." Thus Matt 24:3, 27, 37, 39; 1 Cor 15:23; 1 Thess 2:19, 3:13; 4:15; 5:23; 2 Thess 2:1; 1 John 2:28; 2 Pet 1:16; 3:4; Jas 5:7, 8.

¹⁰⁰ Matt 16:27; Rom 6:4; 1 Pet 4:11; 2 Pet 1:3, 17; 3:18; Rev 1:6; 4:9, 11; 7:12; 19:7. See similar to this, *Life of Jeremiah* 10–12. Many scholars have noted the Christian character of the description of "the coming" of Messiah in *2 Bar.* 30:1. Volz (*Die Eschatologie der jüdischen Gemeinde im neutestamentlichen Zeitalter*, 44) conjectures that 30:1 is "ein christlicher Satz"; according to Oepke ("παρουσία," 863) it is a Christian interpolation (cf. Charles, *The Apocalypse of Baruch*, 56; Lagrange, *Le Messianisme chez les Juifs*," 110 n. 4, 130; idem, "Notes sur le messianisme au temps de Jesus," 503 n. 5; Frey, "L'apocalypse syriaque de Baruch," 1.421; Klijn, "2 (Syriac) Baruch," 631 n. *a*).

¹⁰¹ There is a debate among scholars as to whether the expression *venehofokh betešboḥta* refers to the coming of Messiah upon the earth, in which case the resurrection of the dead will be part of his kingdom upon earth (thus Violet, *Die Apokalypsen des Esra und Baruch*, 246; Charlesworth, "From Jewish Messianology," 246) or whether it signifies the Messiah's return to heaven upon the conclusion of his temporary reign, in

CHAPTER 4: Description of the Appearance of Messiah   153

preexistent nature of Messiah likewise finds expression in the verb *netgala* (revelari), used by the author to describe the beginning of his appearance. One may infer from this that until his appearance the Messiah was hidden and the beginning of his appearance only takes place at the end of days. The author uses the same verb to portray the initial appearance of the Messiah in the vision of the forest, the cedar, the vine and the spring: "and it will happen when the time of its fulfillment is approaching in which it will fall, that at that time the beginning[102] of my Anointed One (רישיתא דמשיחא) which is like the fountain and the vine will be revealed (תתגלא). And when it has revealed itself, it will uproot the multitude of its host" (39:7). As is rightly claimed by De Faye, the use of this specific verb in these two places speaking of the appearance of Messiah indicates that this was a term of special significance, which cannot be replaced by a synonym of more general significance. This is not a simple revelation or appearance of the Messiah before the people; rather, one is dealing here with a movement from one sphere to another. *Revelatur* means that he leaves the invisible world in order to enter into this-worldly existence. This is a messiah who appears from a transnatural world, where he was born and where he stays; a preexistent messiah. His appearance is sudden, and he emerges from a hidden place.[103] The same verb is used by the author of *4 Ezra* to describe the appearance of Messiah at the end of days: "the time . . . when my son the Messiah shall be revealed (*revelabitur*)." His preexistence is depicted as a situation of hiddenness with God: "that the bride shall appear, the city which is now not seen shall appear, and the land which now is hidden shall be disclosed" (*4 Ezra* 7:26–36).[104] Similarly in *1 Enoch*: "For the Son of Man was

---

which case the righteous will enjoy heavenly life (thus Russell, *The Method and Message of Jewish Apocalyptic*, 295; Charles, *The Apocalypse of Baruch*, 56: "this can have only one meaning, and that is that at the close of His reign, the Messiah will return in glory to heaven"; Bogaert, *Apocalypse*, 1:416; 2:65; Cavallin, *Life After Death*, 86). Cf. Klijn, "2 (Syriac) Baruch," 631 n. *b*; Box, *Ezra Apocalyptic*, 113; Volz, *Eschatologie*, 44; Holleman, *Resurrection and Parousia*, 107.

[102] Kahana translated this as ראשות המשיח, "the dominion of . . ."; cf. Klijn, "2 [Syriac Apocalypse of] Baruch," 633. However, ראשית means "the beginning." See Payne Smith, *Compendious Syriac Dictionary*, 540, and de Jonge, "χρίω," 515. And cf. the similar use of this verb in the later talmudic traditions (*b. Sukkah* 52a; *Tg. Ps.-Jon.* to Zech 3:8, 6:12). However, these do not imply a preexistent messiah.

[103] De Faye, *Les Apocalypses Juives*, 124–26; Box, *Ezra Apocalypse*, 113; cf. Mowinckel, *He That Cometh*, 302: "This expression . . . indicates that the Messiah's appearing has a special character"; Klijn, "2 (Syriac) Baruch," 631 n. b. Bogaert raises the possibility that the description of the Messiah here assumed characteristics of a description of the Son of Man (*Apocalypse*, 1:418).

[104] "Revelabitur filius meus Iesus (!)"—the Latin version, as quoted already by

concealed from the beginning, and the Most High preserved him in the presence of his power; then he revealed him to the holy and the elect ones" (62:7; cf. 48:3–6).

There are those who seek the roots of preexistent messianism in Judaism.[105] However, the figure of an apocalyptic messiah connected to the end of time or that of a preexistent messiah are not mentioned in the Bible, in the sources of Judaism from the Second Temple period (such as: Ben-Sira, 1 Maccabees, 2 Maccabees, Tobit, Judith, Josephus, and Philo), or in tannaitic sources. This is lucidly summarized by Joseph Klausner: "During the tannatic period there was not yet a concept of a 'suffering Messiah' nor of a 'messiah who preceded the creation of the world.' He was a mighty king, a person of moral superiority, a political and spiritual leader of the Jewish people in particular and of the human race in general—this and this alone was the messiah of the tannaim" (Klausner, *The Messianic Idea*, 459).

True, the name of the Messiah is included among the six things that preceded the creation: "There were those that were created, and those that arose in [the Divine] thought to be created. The Torah and the throne of glory were created.... The patriarchs and Israel and the temple and the name of the Messiah arose in thought to be created" (*Gen. Rab.* 1.4 [ed. Theodor-Albeck, 6]).[106] But even this tradition only speaks of the *name* of Messiah, of the "idea," but not of the Messiah himself.

Ambrosius (ca. 339–97 CE). Cf. Box, *Ezra Apocalypse*, 114, and Bloch, "Some Christological Interpretations," 90, who claim that this is a Christian interpolation. Cf. *4 Ezra* 12:32; 13:25–26, 51–52; *As. Mos.* 1:14; *1 En.* 46:1–2; 48:3, 6; 62:7.

[105] Charles, *Baruch*, 52; De Faye, *Les Apocalypses Juives*, 125; Schürer, *History* 2:522, based upon Mic 5:1 and Dan 7:13–14. Cf. *Tg. Ps.-Jon.* to Mic 4:8, to Zech 3:8, and to Zech 6:12. However, in none of these places does it refer a preexistent messiah. Micah 5:1 is interpreted as referring to a leader who is an offspring of the house of David. "Before the days of eternity" refers to the historical period in which the Davidic line was established (see Smith, Ward, and Bewer, *Micah*, 104; Vergon, *Sefer Mikha*, 143–44). The figure of the Son of Man in Daniel does not symbolize the Messiah but the Jewish people, "the enslaved and oppressed nation, who shall in the future recover and be raised up to the heights of its human goal and purpose, like the Son of Man who approaches the divine throne 'with the clouds of heaven' and takes the reins of power in the cosmos," see Efron, "Daniel and His Three Friends," 107–8 and nn. 241, 252; idem, "Holy War and Redemptive Goals," 42–43 and n. 22; idem, "The Idea of the Servant of God," 121ff.; Higgins, "Jewish Messianic Belief," 301–2; Roberts, "The Old Testament's Contribution to Messianic Expectations," 39–41; Liver, "Messiah," 508; Hesse, "χρίω," 498–505; Mowinckel, *He that Cometh*, 280–86, 334; Collins, "Messianism in the Maccabean Period," 98.

[106] See parallel traditions: *b. Pes.* 54a; *Ned.* 39b; *Gen. Rab.* 2.4 (ed. Albeck; 6); "And the spirit of God hovered over—this is the spirit of the king Messiah," but in a

CHAPTER 4: Description of the Appearance of Messiah   155

One of the sources invoked to support the Jewishness of this idea is a passage from Justin's *Dialogue with Trypho,* in which the Jew Trypho states that even if the Messiah were created and lived some place or other, he is unknown ἄγνωστος; he himself will not know this until Elijah comes, anoints him, and reveals him to all.[107] In any event, Trypho specifically rejects the idea of a preexistent messiah as paradoxical and foolish, stating that the Jews believe in a human messiah.[108] Belief in a hidden messiah is unknown in any of the Jewish sources written until the middle of the second century CE, the period to which the dialogue is dated.[109] It is reasonable to assume that Justin Martyr, for apologetic reasons, placed in Trypho's mouth a description specifically appropriate to the Christian Messiah. That figure really is meant to be unknown until his revelation by John the Baptist, the embodiment of Elijah the prophet, one of whose central tasks is to reveal the Messiah (John 7:27). In any event, the statement attributed to Trypho by Justin is not to be accepted as a reliable expression of the Jewish beliefs widespread at that time. While Justin was acquainted with the views widespread among Jews of his time, which he at times presents in a correct manner, his zeal as a Christian apologist overtook him whenever a suitable opportunity presented itself, and he attributes to his interlocutor ideas which he could not possibly have held in reality.[110]

The figure of the Messiah bearing eschatological attributes first appears on the amoraitic levels of the Jerusalem Talmud (*y. Ber.* 2.4 [5a]), which allude to a tradition concerning a messiah hidden in heaven, but it finds full and clear expression in the Babylonian Talmud and in the post-talmudic midrashim, which speak of a preexistent messiah who existed before creation and was concealed.[111] These late traditions are already influenced by Christian theology, and were evidently composed under the influence of the polemic with it.

---

metaphoric sense (*Lev. Rab.* 14:1). The fact that these traditions also include Israel proves that there is no preexistent outlook (Mowinckel, *He That Cometh,* 334). And see *Midrash Tehillim* to Ps 90:3: "repentance that preceded the creation of the world"; "the Torah that preceded the creation of the world by two thousand years."

[107] Justin, *Dial.* 8.4 (PG 6:493); 49.1 (ibid., col. 581); 110.1 (ibid., col. 729).

[108] Justin, *Dial.* 48:1; 49:1 (PG 6:580–81).

[109] Goodspeed, *History of Early Christian Literature,* 141; Chadwick, *The Early Church,* 75.

[110] Higgins, "Jewish Messianic Belief," 298–305. Higgins nevertheless accepts Trypho's statement as expressing a contemporary Jewish idea, and this on the basis of John 7:27 (ibid., 300)!

[111] *B. Sanh.* 98b; *Sukkah* 52a; *Pesiq. Rab.* 36 (ed. Ish Shalom; 161–62): "'And God saw the light, that it was good'—We learn that the Holy One blessed be He looked

156   PART TWO: THE IDEA OF ESCHATOLOGICAL REDEMPTION

The concept of a preexistent messiah occupies a central place in the theology of the Logos embodied in Jesus, in the prologue with which the Gospel according to John opens. By the initial phrase, "In the beginning was the Word," the evangelist alludes, not to the beginning of the creation, but to the period prior to creation, thus alluding to a divine sphere.[112] The author of the Fourth Gospel also invokes John the Baptist as witness to the pretemporal nature of Jesus: "This was the one of whom I said, 'He who comes after me ranks before me, for he was before me'" (John 1:15).[113]

2. The appearance of the Messiah in the extant description involves two stages or two secondary periods: the first period is when "the Anointed One will begin to be revealed" and the garden of Eden, with its focus in the holy meal (29:3–8), will be founded. The second period will only take place after the time of the arrival of the Messiah is fulfilled and he returns in glory. At that time all those who believe in Messiah will return to life, the storehouses in which the souls of the righteous are contained will be opened, and the final judgment will take place (30:1–5).[114]

A similar distinction between two stages in the appearance of Messiah, explaining the intentions and significance of the description in *2 Baruch*, is drawn in *4 Ezra* (7:26–36). Following the signs of the End, the church will appear in the form of a bride, and the heavenly Jerusalem will be revealed, together with paradise, "the city," and "the land," which are hidden today. Then Messiah and all those who are with him will be revealed,[115] and a Messianic kingdom will be founded, to continue for four hundred years.[116]

---

upon the Messiah and his deeds *before the world was created,* and hid the Messiah for his generation beneath the throne of Glory." On the date of *Pesiqta Rabbati,* see the introduction to this work and the chapter on the weaving virgins in the temple.

[112] Brown, *Gospel According to John,* 4, 524; cf. 1 John 1:1.

[113] John 1:30; 6:62; 8:58; 17:5, 24; and other places in which this idea is found, albeit not in an overt manner (6:33, 50ff., 58; 7:28ff.; 8:14, 23, 26, 42; 10:36; 16:28). Also 1 Pet 1:[19-]20: "with the precious blood of Christ . . . [who] was destined before the foundation of the world, but was made manifests at the end of the times for your sake" (Budge, *Cave of Treasures,* 246; cf. Brown, *Gospel According to John,* 35; Shnackenburg, *Gospel According to St. John,* 504).

[114] On a similar distinction between two stages in the appearance of the Messiah, see also *2 Bar.* 40:3–4: "And his dominion will last forever until the world of corruption has ended and until the times which have been mentioned before have been fulfilled."

[115] On the saints who will appear with Christ in the Parousia, see 1 Thess 3:13; Jude 14.

[116] The Latin translation and one of the Arab versions uses the number 400. The calculation that the Messiah's kingdom will last for 400 years also appears in *b. Sanh.*

CHAPTER 4: Description of the Appearance of Messiah   157

At the end of this period the Messiah will die, together with all the other people, and the world will revert to primeval silence, to continue for seven days. Thereafter the world will awaken again, the dead will be resurrected, and the final judgment will take place. One Latin version reads *adsumetur* instead of *morietur* (7:29), that is: "ascent" of the Messiah rather than his "death."[117] If we accept this reading, the ascent or death of the Messiah in *4 Ezra* will be fully parallel to the return of Messiah to heaven in glory according to *Baruch*. This will help to clarify the nature and intention of this division into two periods.[118]

How are we to understand the explanation here of two periods in the revelation of Messiah, and what are their sources?

The talmudic tradition likewise distinguishes between "the days of Messiah" and "the world to come," a distinction already found in the Mishnah.[119] But in the *early* talmudic sources these concepts do not involve an apocalyptic drama of the end of the world and the coming of a new world in its place; most important, they do not contain any hint of a Messiah figure, and certainly not the figure of a supernatural and soteriological Messiah who brings an eschatological redemption to his believers.

In my opinion, this concept in *Syriac Baruch* needs to be understood, not against the background of Jewish concepts, but against millenarian approaches that were present among the fringes of the early Christian church and that find clear expression in the book of Revelation. In the descriptions of the apocalyptic drama in Revelation, the angel ties up the sea monster—the primeval snake, who is the denouncer and the Satan—and throws him down into a deep pit

---

99a, which discloses that this calculation is based upon Gen 15:13, and cf. Ps 80:15. The second Arabic version uses the number 1000, based upon what is stated in Revelation, on which see below. The Syriac uses the number 30, in order to adjust it to the life span of Jesus given in Luke 3:23 (thus de Jonge, "χρίω," 516 n. 126; Bloch, "Some Christological Interpretations," 93). The calculation is entirely missing in the Ethiopian and Armenian translations. One Latin version reads 300 (Myers, *I & II Esdras*, 208). According to Box, the original version used the number 400, and all the other versions introduced changes for dogmatic reasons (*Ezra Apocalypse*, 115).

[117] Box, *Ezra Apocalypse*, 117.

[118] On the two periods of Messiah, cf. *2 En.* (long version), 31:1; 42:5. A similar understanding of the two periods appears in *4 Ezra* 6:9–10: "For Esau is the end of this age, and Jacob is the beginning of the age that follows. For the beginning of a man is his hand, and the end of a man is his heel" ("finis enim huius saeculi Esau, et principium sequantis Iacob. Hominis manus inter calcaneum et manum"). See Yisraeli, "The Origin of *4 Ezra,*" 129.

[119] See *m. Ber.* 1.5; *Sanh.* 10.1; and cf. *b. Sanh.* 99a; *Zeb.* 118b; *t. ʿArak.* 2.7. On the distinction in Judaism between the days of the messiah and the World to Come, see Albeck, *Mishnah, Nezikin*, 519–20; Moore, *Judaism*, 2:378.

that is sealed for a thousand years. At that stage the first resurrection of the martyrs and the holy ones, who will live and rule with the Messiah for a thousand years, occurs. At the end of this first stage, Satan will be let out of his captivity, so that the last and final confrontation, in which he will be permanently vanquished by the Messiah and thrown into the pool of fire, may occur with him. At this point the general resurrection and the final judgment will take place. Only thereafter will the new creation, the new heavens and earth which are none other than the heavenly Jerusalem in the form of paradise, be fully established.[120] The idea of two stages of the revelation of Messiah in *Baruch* and *4 Ezra* draws upon the same millenarian approach as in Revelation.

4.5. *The Resurrection of the Dead and the Final Judgment*

With the Parousia, the final stages in the apocalyptic dream—the resurrection of the dead and the final judgment—are described:

> And it will happen after these things when the time of the appearance of the Anointed One has been fulfilled and he returns with glory, that then all who sleep in hope of him will rise. And it will happen at that time that those treasuries will be opened in which the number of the souls of the righteous were kept, and they will go out and the multitudes of the souls will appear together, in one assemblage, of one mind. And the first ones will enjoy themselves and the last ones will not be sad. For they know that the time has come of which it is said that it is the end of times. But the souls of the wicked will the more waste away when they shall see all these things. For they know that torment has come and that their perditions have arrived. (*2 Bar.* 30:1–5 [*OTP* 1:631])

The resurrection of the dead to occur with the Parousia is shown here along clearly Christian lines.

The period between death and resurrection is described as sleep ("then all who sleep in faith of him will arise"),[121] and the author uses the verb ἐγείρω ("to rise"), characteristic of the resurrection in Christianity.[122] Elsewhere

---

[120] Rev 20:1ff. On the two resurrections, see Augustine, *Civ.* 20.6 (LCL; 6:277–81); Moore, *Judaism,* 2:340. For a similar division into two periods in the end of days in the Qumran writings, see Licht, "The Doctrine of Time," 64.

[121] Thus in *Gos. Pet.* 41–42 following the description of the hope for resurrection: "And they heard a voice coming from heaven, saying: Hast thou preached unto them that sleep? And an answer was heard from the cross, saying: Yea" (James, *NT Apocrypha,* 92–93). Cf. Matt 27:53; John 11:11 ("Our friend Lazarus has fallen asleep, but I go to awake him"); Acts 7:60; 1 Cor 15:6, 18, 20; 1 Thess 4:13, 14, 15; Daniélou, *Theology,* 234; *4 Ezra* 7:32. On death as sleep, see appendix.

[122] Matt 9:25; 10:8; 11:5; 14:2; 16:21; 17:9; 26:32; 27:52; 28:6; Mark 12:26; John

CHAPTER 4: Description of the Appearance of Messiah   159

Baruch, on the basis of Dan 12:2, portrays those who will rise to life as the righteous who sleep in the dust (11:4).[123] The righteous ones or saints who sleep in their faith appear in a similar context in additional Christian works. Thus, for example, when Jesus breathed out his spirit and the veil of the temple was rent in two, "the tombs also were opened, and many bodies of the saints who had fallen asleep [RSV: slept in the earth] were raised" (Matt 27:52).[124]

Baruch draws a distinction between the resurrection of those who slept in their faith in him, that is, the holy ones or martyrs, and that of the righteous whose souls are preserved in the storehouses of souls, where they sleep and await their resurrection.[125] These storehouses are called *promtuaria* (*4 Ezra* 4:33–43; 7:32), and also *habitacula* or *habitationes*, "residences" (*4 Ezra* 7:78–80; 95; *1 En.* 22:9; 51:1; 100:5; *L.A.B.* 32:13; 13:8). In these storehouses, located in paradise, sleep the fathers of the nation: Abraham, Isaac, and Jacob, and the like (*2 Bar.* 21:24),[126] together with the chosen righteous ones,

---

2:22; 5:21; etc. Ign. *Magn.* 9.2: "How then shall we be able to live without him of whom even the prophets were disciples in the spirit and to whom they looked forward as their teacher? And for this reason he whom they waited for in righteousness, when he came (παρών) raised (ἤγειρεν) them from the dead." See also Herm. *Sim.* 9.16.5–7: "having fallen asleep in the power and faith of the Son of God." *T. Benj.* 10:6–8; *T. Jud.* 25:1.

[123] See also Isa 26:19; Puech, *La croyance des Esséniens*, 1:137.

[124] Daniélou, *Theology*, 234–36, 239. Similar expressions appear in another early Christian text, the *Apocryphon of Jeremiah*, quoted by Justin, *Dial.* 72.4 (PG 6:645), and by Irenaeus, *Haer.* 3.20.4; 4.22.1, 27.2, 33.1, 33.12; 5.31.1 (SC 211:395–97; 100b:685, 739, 805, 835; 153:391), and cf. SC 100a:255, 687: The Lord God remembers his dead, the holy ones of Israel who fell asleep (κεκοιμημένων) in the dust of the grave, and he descended to them to convey the good news of the salvation that he brought them (cp. 1 Pet 1:3–5).

[125] For a similar distinction, see *4 Ezra* 7:32. Storehouses in heaven also appear in the NT: Matt 6:19–21; 19:21. But there seems to be a distinction between these storehouses and the "storehouses in which are stored the virtues of all those who were righteous in the creation"; cf. *2 Bar.* 24:1 ("also the treasuries in which are brought together the righteousness of all those who have proven themselves to be righteous [will be opened]"); and *4 Ezra* 7:77; 8:33 (where it shall be counted to their credit in the new world); 6:5; 13:23; Luke 12:33; Puech, *La croyance des Esséniens*, 1:153; and similarly in *b. B. Bat.* 11a.

[126] *2 Bar.* 15:7–8; 44:15; 48:22–29; 52:6–7. The righteous are described in *Syriac Baruch* in accordance with the biblical idea of the remnant (Saylor, *Have the Promises Failed?* 115). Similarly in the Apocalypse of Ezra, which enumerates, inter alia, Noah "from whom all the righteous men emerged," Abraham, and Jacob (*4 Ezra* 3:11–16); "The Most High made this world for the sake of many, but the world to come for the sake of few" (*4 Ezra* 8:1); cf. *L.A.B.* 19:12–13; *T. Judah* 25:1; *T. Benj.* 10:7–9. These

for whose sake this world was created, and for whom alone the world to come is reserved. The storehouses are meant to include a fixed number of children to be born, whose number was predetermined at the time of Adam's sin:

> For when Adam sinned and death was decreed against those who were to be born, the multitude of those who would be born was numbered. And for that number a place was prepared where the living ones might live and where the dead might be preserved. No creature will live again unless the number that has been appointed is completed. (*2 Bar.* 23:4–5 [*OTP* 1:629]; cf. 21:9–25)

Only after this predetermined number has been completely fulfilled will the creation be renewed and the resurrection take place. That the number of those to be born is known in advance is consistent with the deterministic approach, widespread in this book, as well as with the belief in the tablets of heaven, or of those books in which are recorded all the deeds of man to take place on the earth for eternity.[127] However, this End must eventually come, like the vision of the End as a whole, because "In Hades the chambers of the souls are like the womb. For just as a women in travail makes haste to escape the pangs of birth, so also do these places hasten to give back those things that were committed to them from the beginning" (*4 Ezra* 4:41–42).

The tradition concerning the righteous sleeping in storehouses located in Sheol (the Underworld) is connected to similar traditions in early Christian works that speak of Jesus descending to Hell in order to inform the righteous who are imprisoned there of the tiding of salvation. Christianity thereby attempted to resolve the theological problem of the destiny of the righteous who died before Christ. Thus, according to Irenaeus, the Lord descended to areas beneath the earth, where he announces his coming and the forgiveness of the sins that will take place for all those who believe in him: "The Lord descended to the regions beneath the earth, tells there of his coming, and brings about the atonement of sins for those who believe in him" (Irenaeus, *Haer.* 4.27.2 [SC 100b:739]).

The *early* Jewish tradition does not know of such storehouses for the souls of the righteous who died or of those who are to be born in the future until the

---

storehouses are located in paradise, where the souls of the patriarchs, the chosen, and the saints are found (*1 En.* 70:4): "And there I saw the first (human) ancestors [or: the first forefathers"; "the original ancestors"; etc.] and the righteous ones of old, dwelling in that place"; see also *1 En.* 60:7, 23; 61:12; *Apoc. Abr.* 21:7. The Christian work, *The Cave of Treasures*, contains a description of a cave in paradise where the patriarchs are buried until the resurrection; this cave is identical to the storehouse of souls (Budge, *Cave of Treasures*, 109–10).

[127] *1 En.* 81:2; *2 En.* 10:8 ("for all the souls have been prepared before the creation"). The number of saints is known in Christianity in advance (Rev 6:11; Justin, *1 Apol.* 45 [PG 6:396]).

CHAPTER 4: Description of the Appearance of Messiah   161

resurrection. There is, however, a similar talmudic tradition according to which "While Adam lay a shapeless mass before Him at whose decree the world came into existence, He [God] showed him every generation and its sages, every generation and its judges, scribes, interpreters, and leaders. . . . This is the Book of the Generation of Adam" and "The royal Messiah will not come until all the souls which [God] contemplated creating have been created. . . . And the souls are those referred to in the book of Adam" (*Gen. Rab.* 24.2 [trans. H. Freedman; London, 1961; 1:201]).[128] Like the tradition in *2 Baruch*, this tradition speaks also on a certain number of souls who have to be born in the future; their number is known from the creation of the world, and the termination of this process has an eschatological feature—it is connected to the appearance of the royal Messiah. However, there are also some differences: the number to be born was not fixed at the time of Adam's sin but was a result of God's free will as part of the creation; notwithstanding the eschatological colour, it is not connected to the resurrection; and the early Midrashic tradition does not refer to a particular place where these souls exist.

The Babylonian sources refer to the concept of a body, interpreted as a storehouse in which are kept all the souls that will be born in the future; the son of David will only come after all the souls in this body have been completed (*b. Nid.* 13b; *'Abod. Zar.* 5a).[129] There also appears a storehouse in which the souls of the righteous are kept after their death (*Qoh. Rab.* 3.21). But even in those sources the storehouse is not seen as the dwelling place of the souls until their resurrection. The storehouse of souls of the talmudic literature is in the world to come, where they will enjoy eternal rest.[130]

Chapters 49–52 express *Syriac Baruch*'s outlook on the resurrection clearly. At the end of time all the dead, both righteous and wicked, will rise with the same appearance and bodily form they had previously:

> For the earth will surely give back the dead at that time; it receives them now in order to keep them, not changing anything in their form. But as it has received

---

[128] Lev. Rab. 15. 1; Sanh. 38b; Ex. R. xl, 2, 3.

[129] According to another view this "body" is the partition before the throne of glory, to which all the souls are drawn (see Ginzberg, *Legends of the Jews* 5:75 n. 19; *b. Yebam.* 62a; 63b; Zeron, "The System of the Author of *Antiquities*," 154. And cf. "The souls of the righteous and the spirits and souls that are to be created are found in the seventh heaven, in 'Araboth" [*b. Ḥag.* 12b]).

[130] Zeron, "The System," 152; *Sifre Bamidbar,* 139 ("His dead soul . . . is in the treasure house"); *Sifre Devarim,* §344 (ed. Finkelstein; 401). And compare *b. Šabb.* 152b ("For the bodies of the righteous he says, "Let them come in peace, and rest at their place of resting").

them so it will give them back. And as I have delivered them to it so it will raise them." (50:2)[131]

Baruch anticipates a transitional period between the bodily resurrection and the changing. After they recognize one another, the judgment will begin and then the bodies of those restored to life will change:[132] the appearance of the sinners will undergo a shocking change for the worse, while that of the righteous, who were justified in their faith and planted in their hearts the root of wisdom, will shine like the radiance of the angels in their "changing" (*shuhlafa*). The appearance of their faces will change to that of radiant light, they will merit eternal life, and time will no longer age them. Paradise, identified with the heavenly Jerusalem that dwells in the "heights of the world" (51:9), will be spread before them, and they will resemble the angels and be compared to the stars.[133]

The resurrection described in these chapters is bodily and individual, displaying much similarity to the Christian outlook as expressed in the 1 Cor 15:35–39:

> "How are the dead raised? With what kind of a body do they come?" You foolish man! What you sow does not come to life unless it dies. And what you sow is not the body which is to be, but a bare kernel, perhaps of wheat or of some other grain. But God gives it a body (σῶμα) as he has chosen, and to each kind of seed its own body. For not all flesh is alike, but there is one kind for men, another for animals, another for birds, and another for fish."[134]

The resurrection described by Paul, like that in *Syriac Baruch*, is a bodily resurrection. But unlike *Baruch*, the dead will not rise in the same body: "What is sown is perishable, what is raised is imperishable. . . . It is sown a physical body (ψυχικόν), it is raised a spiritual body (πνευματικόν)" (1 Cor 15:42, 44). Paul distinguishes between the physical body, which is the earthly body, and

---

[131] See also *2 Bar.* 42:7–8; *1 En.* 51:1; 61:5; *L.A.B.* 3:10; 23:13; *Sib. Or.* 4:182; *4 Ezra* 7:32.

[132] The judgment precedes the "changing," as also follows from *Sib. Or.* 4:182–91. Bauckham (The Fate of the Dead, 283) explains that the first stage is necessary because it provides the means by which the dead can be recognized and thus answers the apologetic problem of how it will be possible to know that it is really the dead who are raised.

[133] Based upon Daniel 12:3. See similarly 1 Cor 15:41; Matt 13:43; *4 Ezra* 7:97, 125; *L.A.B.* 33:5.

[134] 1 Thess 5:23; A. Robertson and A. Plummer, *1 Corinthians*, 368; Russell, *The Method and Message of Jewish Apocalyptic*, 295; Puech, *La croyance des Esséniens*, 267; Cavallin, *Life After Death*, 89. For parallels between *2 Bar.* 49–51 and Christian sources, see Frey, "L'apocalypse syriaque de Baruch," 421.

CHAPTER 4: Description of the Appearance of Messiah   163

the spiritual body, which is not "flesh and blood" but a heavenly entity that is not perishable and that alone may inherit the kingdom of God. The "changing," described in *Baruch* as only taking place at a later stage, occurs, according to the Pauline approach, immediately upon the resurrection of the dead, that is, with the Parousia of Jesus, marked by the final trumpet blast: "we shall not all sleep [die], but we shall all be changed, in a moment, in the twinkling of an eye, at the last trumpet" (1 Cor 15:51–52).[135]

Belief in the resurrection of the dead also developed in Judaism during the Second Temple period. It does not appear in the books of Ben Sira, Judith, Tobit, or 1 Maccabees, but peeks through between the lines of Dan 12:2–3 and is more clearly expressed in 2 Maccabees (7:9, 13–14, 23; 12:43–45; Josephus, *J.W.* 2.163; 3.372; *Ant.* 18.14). Anticipation of personal, bodily resurrection is explicitly expressed in the talmudic sources and is even described in images similar to those in the Christian tradition.[136] But in none of the Jewish sources is it connected with the end of the world and the appearance of the Messiah, nor is it a central pillar of faith. In the Jewish sources, the resurrection is connected to God, who creates life and takes it away; He alone has the power to revive the dead, as stated explicitly in the *Amidah* prayer: "You are mighty for eternity, O Lord, You revive the dead, and do great acts of salvation." And in the blessing recited upon arising from sleep: "O God, the soul which You have given me is pure. You have created it, You have formed it,

---

[135] See also 1 Thess 4:16; Rev 11:15ff.; *4 Ezra* 6:23. The blowing of the shofar also has eschatological significance in the Bible (Fee, *First Epistle to the Corinthians*, 801–2, and n. 26 there).

[136] See esp. *b. Sanh.* 90b. Also *m. Sanh.* 10:11 ("And these are those who have no share in the world to come: he who says that there is no resurrection of the dead . . ."); *m. Ber.* 5.4; *m. Sota* 9.15; *m. 'Abot* 4.22; *b. Ber.* 60b ("Blessed are you, O Lord who returns souls to dead corpses"); *Exod. Rab.* 40.2; *Midr. Zutta* to Eccles, 57 (ed. Buber; 114). Scholars note various biblical passages containing images and expressions that acknowledge the possibility of bodily resurrection, such as Isa 26:17–19; Ezek 37:1–14; Hos 6:2. But against these see the position of Moore (*Judaism*, 2:291) based upon Job 14:7–15. (Cf. Russell, *Method and Message*, 368; Zeron, "The System," 119; Urbach, *Hazal*, 589–93; Schürer, *History*, 2:540; Morissette, "La Condition de Ressuscite," 211ff.; Y. Baer, "To Clarify the Doctrine of the End of Days in Second Temple Times" [Hebrew], *Zion* 23–24 [1958–59]: 3–34.) One needs to distinguish between the anticipation of bodily resurrection and the expectation that the soul alone will survive eternally (after it has left the body to disintegrate in death). This latter outlook characterized Greco-Hellenistic thought in the wake of Plato and found expression in Jewish sources (Wis 3:1–6; 4:17–19; 5:15; 4 Macc 17:5, 18; for this idea in Philo, see Wolfson, *Philo*, 404–5; Josephus, *J.W.* 1.650; Oepke, "ἀνίστημι," 370; Kasher, *Contra Apion* [Jerusalem, 1997], 513–14). On the differences between the two views, see Cullmann, *Immortality and Resurrection*, 13–21; Urbach, *Hazal*, 588.

You have breathed it into me, and You preserve it within me, and You shall take it from me and return it to me in the future. So long as the soul is in me, I thank you, O Lord, God and God of my fathers, Master of all the worlds, Lord of all souls. Blessed art Thou, O Lord, who returns souls to dead corpses" (*b. Ber.* 60b).[137]

The anticipation of bodily and personal resurrection in 2 Baruch is thus consistent with the Christian credo,[138] *which promised its believers the quickening of the flesh with the second appearance of Jesus.* The faith in the bodily resurrection is a basic element in the Christian doctrine concerning man's lot at the End.

---

[137] Cf. *y. Ber.* ch. 4.2 (7d).

[138] Moore, *Judaism,* 2:394. The basic Christian credo unambiguously affirmed the fleshly resurrection; see the Apostolic Creed ("Sarkos Anastasis, Carnis Resurrectio"). On the question as to why resurrection occupied such a central position in the Christian credo, see Dodds, *First Corinthians,* 335–40. The conflict with the Gnostics led to greater emphasis on this subject. Millenarians in every century have anticipated the fleshly coming of Christ and together with him the fleshly reign of the saints upon the earth for a thousand years.

CHAPTER FIVE

The Vision of the Forest, the Cedar, the Vine, and the Spring (*2 Bar.* 36–40)

The description of the Messiah's appearance at the end of days is the focus of the two great apocalyptic visions in *Syriac Baruch* that complement the image of the Messiah as presented in chapters 29–30:
 a. The vision of the forest, the cedar, the vine, and the spring;
 b. The vision of the cloud over the bright waters and the black waters.

In the former, Baruch sees in a night vision a large forest of trees planted on a plain surrounded by high mountains and steep rocks. Opposite the forest grows a vine, beneath which a spring quietly flows. The spring reaches the forest, and the great waves that emerge from it flood the forest, uproot its trees, and wash away the surrounding mountains, apart from one cedar. When that too is knocked down by the spring and the entire forest disappears as if it never existed and its place was not even known, the vine and the spring quietly and calmly approach a place near the cedar, and bring the cedar close to it. The vine chastises the cedar for its wickedness, for imposing its rule upon that which does not belong to it, and for its arrogance and self-confidence, sentencing it to the same destiny as that of the forest as a whole:

> Therefore O cedar, follow the forest which has departed before you and become ashes with it, and let your earth be mixed together. And now, sleep in distress and rest in pain until your last time comes in which you will return to be tormented even more.

After these things, Baruch sees the cedar burning, while the vine grows, and around it a valley filled with flowers that do not wither (*2 Bar.* 36–37).

At Baruch's request, God interprets the vision to him. The great forest surrounded by high and steep mountains are the four kingdoms: the first of these, which destroyed Zion, will be destroyed and subjugated to the one that will come after it. The second kingdom will also be destroyed by a kingdom that will come after it—and so on until the fourth kingdom, which will be harsher and more evil than those that preceded it, and whose reign will last longest. It will lift itself up above the cedars of Lebanon, the truth will be hidden, and all those who polluted by unrighteousness will flee to it.

And it will happen when the time of its fulfillment is approaching in which it will fall, that at that time the beginning of my Anointed One[1] which is like the fountain and the vine, will be revealed. And when it has revealed itself, it will uproot the multitude of its host. And that which you have seen, namely the tall cedar, which remained of that forest, and with regard to the words which the vine said to it which you heard, this is the meaning. The last ruler who is left alive at that time will be bound, whereas the entire host will be destroyed. And they will carry him on Mount Zion, and my Anointed One will convict him of all his wicked deeds and will assemble and set before him all the works of his hosts. And after these things he will kill him and protect the rest of my people who will be found in the place that I have chosen. And his dominion will last forever until the world of corruption has ended and until the times which have been mentioned before have been fulfilled. (39:7–40:3)

The first vision describes the stages of the Parousia, at whose focus is the sacrament of the eschatological meal, the founding of paradise, and the thousand-year period (millennium), symbolized by the abundance of yield of the earth, the vine, and the manna.

The present vision sheds light upon another aspect of the appearance of Messiah: the confrontation with the antichrist, "the last ruler" on Mount Zion, and the victory over him. But here too, as in the first vision, the Parousia is characterized by means of two Christian sacraments: baptism and Eucharist.

The vine and the spring are clearly interpreted in this vision as referring to Messiah, "my Anointed One which is like the fountain and the vine" (*2 Bar.* 39:7). We already noted, in connection with the previous vision, Jesus' role as the true vine that symbolizes the Eucharist. But Jesus is also the spring, a flowing spring and source of living waters; it is related of him that one who drinks from him and believes in him, "Out of his heart shall flow rivers of living water": he will never again be thirsty, but will enjoy eternal life (John 4:10–15; 7:37–38; Rev 7:17, 22:2).[2] Instead of the river that flows in paradise and irrigates the garden (Gen 2:10), and instead of the living water that, according to the Hebrew Bible (Ezek 47:1–12; Joel 4:18; Zech 14:8; Ps 46:5), trickles from beneath the threshold of the temple, in the time of the final salvation there shall be "the river of the water of life, bright as crystal, flowing from the throne of God and *of the Lamb*" (Rev 22:1). The source of the living waters, used in the Hebrew Bible to describe God, is in the Christian approach transformed into a symbol of Jesus. The presentation of Jesus as a spring is

---

[1] Kahana translated here ראשות המשיח (cf. Bogaert, *Apocalypse de Baruch,* 1:488; Klijn," 2 [Syriac] Baruch," 633; Charlesworth, "From Jewish Messianology to Christian Christology," 247). But the word *rishita* means "beginning." See similar to this in *2 Bar.* 29:3; cf. de Jonge, "To Anoint," 515.

[2] Cf. *1 En.* 22:9; 48:1; 96:6; *Odes Sol.* 30; for similar symbolism see *1 En.* 24–26.

consistent with the background of the garden of Eden, in which the author of this vision places the revelation of the Messiah. The description of the broad forest planted in the valley, the high mountains surrounding it, and the steep rocks, allude to the dwelling place of the souls of the sinners who await their judgment in paradise, as portrayed in the *Book of Enoch* (*1 En.* 27:1–2; 22:1ff.). This description also alludes to Ezekiel (47:1–12), where the prophet sees the source of water bursting beneath the threshold of the new temple, from whence they flow down into a stream that is impossible to cross. The river transforms the desert into a paradise, alongside which grow trees whose fruits serve as food and whose leaves serve for healing.[3] This river is also a symbol for baptism that constitutes the act of admission into paradise, embodied in the Christian church.[4]

In the *Odes of Solomon* Jesus is compared to a spring of flowing waters, which is shining and pure and gives rest to the soul. Like the spring that flows in silence in *Baruch*, so too in the *Odes of Solomon* it is invisible:

> Fill for yourselves water from the living spring of the Lord, because it is opened for you. And come all you thirsty and take a drink and rest beside the spring of the Lord. Because it is pleasing and sparkling and perpetually pleases the self. For more refreshing is its water than honey. . . . Because it flowed from the lips of the Lord, and is named from the heart of the Lord. And it came boundless and invisible, and until it was set in the middle they knew it not. Blessed are they who have drunk from it, and have rested by it. (*Odes Sol.* 30)

The combination of vine and spring symbolizes the two main sacraments of Christianity: baptism and Eucharist. The vine is the blood, and the spring symbolizes the baptismal water.[5] These two ancient sacraments are presented alongside one another in the description of the death of Jesus: after he yielded up his spirit, one of the Roman soldiers pierced his side with a spear, and blood and water came out (αἷμα καὶ ὕδωρ; John 19:34). Just as Eve was born from the rib of Adam, so was the Christian church born from the rib of Jesus, the new man, through the two sacraments symbolized by water and blood: "This is

---

[3] Manns, "Le symbolisme du jardin," 64, 74. The symbols of the fountain, the garden, and the trees appear in the description of Jesus' imprisonment in the Fourth Gospel (John 18:1ff.). Details from Ezek 47 are used to allude to the garden of Eden.

[4] Daniélou, *Sacramentum Futuri*, 11, 16–17.

[5] Cf. John 2:1–12, for the miracle at Cana where Jesus turned water to wine. According to Justin (*1 Apol.* 65 [PG 6:428), at the meal, bread is served together with a cup of wine mixed with water (Cullmann, *Early Christian Worship*, 69).

he who came by water and blood, Jesus Christ, not with the water only but with the water and the blood" (1 John 5:6).[6]

The mystery of baptism and the cross are understood in Christianity as one complete unit, according to which the atoning death of Jesus on the cross sanctifies the water of baptism and gives it its revivifying power. Thus, Paul writes:

> Do you not know that all of us who have been baptized in Christ Jesus were baptized into his death? We were buried therefore with him by baptism into death, so that as Christ was raised from the dead by the glory of the Father, we too might walk in newness of life. Or if we have been united with him in a death like his, we shall certainly be united with him in a resurrection like his. (Rom 6:3–5)

Similarly, Ignatius of Antioch states that: "He [Jesus Christ] was born, and was baptized, that by his suffering he might purify the water" (Ign. *Eph.* 18:2).[7]

This idea likewise finds expression in Christian art, in which the tree of life, identified with the cross, is depicted near the source of the rivers in paradise. In the present vision the vine that gives eternal life to the believer may symbolize the tree of life, which is the tree of the cross that lends its revivifying power to the baptismal font.[8] The spring, as symbol of baptism, indicates the antiquity of the present tradition, in which baptism had to be carried out in flowing, "living water."[9]

However, in the vision at hand the combination of vine and spring involves an additional aspect. J. Daniélou, in his discussion of the symbolism of the cross, cites a number of passages in ancient Christian literature in which the symbolism of the cross relates to the material from which it is made, namely, wood. Trees usually appear together with water, so that the context is sacramental: water constitutes the body of the sacrament, while wood

---

[6] Ephraem Syrus, *Commentaire de l'Evangile,* 21.11 (SC 121:380): Adam's rib is his wife, and the blood of the Lord is his church. Death came from Adam's rib, and life from the Lord's rib.

[7] Cf. Ambrose, *Myst.* 4.20 (PL 16:394c); Augustine, *C. Jul.* 6.19.62 (PL 44:861a). This is the source of the custom of affixing a cross in the Jordan River at the place where, according to a tradition, Jesus was baptized (Rahner, *Greek Myth and Christian Mystery,* 78–81, and further testimonies there).

[8] Rahner, *Greek Myth,* 80. On the vine as the tree of life, see Murray, *Symbols of Church and Kingdom,* 97, 118, 119–23.

[9] Acts 8:36; *Ps.-Clem.* 4.32; 6.15; 7.38 (PG; 1:1329, 1355, 1370); *Acts Pet.* 5 (James, *Apocryphal NT,* 308); Cullmann, *Early Christian Worship,* 31.

symbolizes the divine power brought to it.[10] The wood of the cross is identified, among other things, with the tree of life in the garden of Eden.[11] The vine gives eternal life to the believer; hence it may symbolize in this vision the wood of the cross, whose revivifying power is expressed in baptism. Daniélou also notes that in many of these passages emphasis is placed upon the power of the tree contrasted with that of water. We may also understand from this the more active role played by the vine in the present vision.

Water also symbolizes the spirit that Jesus gives through his death and that thereby facilitates entry into the tree of life. His body is the temple. Water and blood flow from this new temple, symbolizing Jesus' sacrificial death and his holy spirit, and recall, by means of the sacraments, those activities by whose means this death is realized in the church.[12]

It is worth noting that a mixture of water and wine, or the use of water instead of wine in the Eucharist, was customary in certain places and among various streams in Christianity.[13]

The symbolism of the vine and the spring indicates the relationship between the theology of *Baruch* and that of the Eastern gnosis of the Mandaean sect.[14] The vine (*gufana*) is widely used in Mandaean religion as a symbol for

---

[10] Daniélou, *Theology of Jewish Christianity*, 276; *Barn.* 11:8; Justin, *Dial.* 86 (PG 6:680); *Sib. Or.* 8:244–47. The term "tree" (ξύλον) in the sense of "wood," is referring to the cross, as opposed to δένδρον, which is a living, growing tree (see Acts 5:30; 10:39; 13:29; Gal 3:13; 1 Pet 2:24; 1 Pet 2:24; Rev 2:7; 22:2).

[11] Justin, *Dial.* 86.1 (PG 6:680); Ign. *Trall.* 9.2 (LCL 24:221). According to *1 En.* 24:4, the tree of life is the palm in Song 7:8–9, where it is the symbol of beauty, and in Ps 92:13, where it is the symbol of the righteous. M. Wilcox, "'Upon the Tree' – Deut 21:22–23 in the New Testament." JBL 96 (1977): 85.

[12] Manns, "Symbolisme," 78–80.

[13] Clement of Alexandria, *Paed.* 2.19.3 (SC 108:49); Justin, *1 Apol.* 66 (PG 6:428–29); R. D. Richardson, "Introduction and Further Inquiry" (in Lietzmann, *Mass and Lord's Supper* [Leiden, 1979]), 245, 246. Marcion used water rather than wine (Richardson, "Introduction," 248, 253, 273).

[14] The Mandaeans belonged to an Eastern Gnostic order that still exists in Mesopotamia. Since the publication of their writings at the beginning of the twentieth century, there has been an ongoing debate within scholarly literature as to the question of the sect's origin and the period of time during which it appeared (for the different views, see Thomas, *Le Mouvement Baptiste*, 210–36; Yamauchi, *Pre-Christian Gnosticism*, 117–39). According to all views, their writings are late and the manuscripts are no earlier than the sixteenth century. But scholars date the sources of the early manuscripts to the seventh century, that is, to the beginning of the Muslim period. If the origin of the sect is prior to this time, it may be possible to see it as part of the great Gnostic movements that emerged in the second and third centuries (see Thomas, *Le Mouvement*

the tree of life, and light and wine were always symbols of fecundity and of germinating life.[15] The entire series of messengers from the world of light are described in terms of a vineyard,[16] and the figure of the prophet of the sect is compared to the true vine.[17] The symbol of the spring, called "living water" or "the fountains of life," is also very widespread and indicates flowing water. These waters are called by the sect "Jordan," whose origin is heavenly and is identical to the world of light.[18]

In comparing the vision to its interpretation, we are struck by its failure to fit the image of the four kingdoms. In the interpretation of the vision, God explains to Baruch that the great forest surrounded by high and difficult mountains must be understood as the four kingdoms that will arise, one upon the ruins of the other. However, the plot of the vision in no way alludes to this change, as the forest, the high mountains surrounding it, and the rocks appear simultaneously, and not one after another. In addition, the identification of the four kingdoms in the vision with the forest, the plain, the mountains, and the rocks, is not at all clear: the forest symbolizes the final kingdom, as from it there remains the cedar, the final ruler. But what are the symbols of the other three kingdoms? Every attempt to draw an analogy between the vision and the four kingdoms is, as Lagrange notes, forced and almost impossible.[19] One of the explanations suggested for this incompatibility is that the vision came from an independent source, composed before the year 70 CE, which the author of the apocalypse of *Baruch* subsequently used, writing for it an interpretation that suited his own tendencies.[20] Others have argued that this separate source does not at all belong to the original work, but was inserted later by a compiler.[21] Bogaert has correctly commented that, even if there are hints that chapters 36–40 were taken from a source prior to the year 70 CE or from

---

Baptiste, 219). In any event, it is not prior to the appearance of Christianity. See Dodd, *The Interpretation of the Fourth Gospel,* 115; Lietzman, *A History of the Early Church,* 1:43–44; Loisy, "Das Mandäertum," 419–32; Puech, "Der Stand des Mandäerproblemes," 433–44.

[15] Rudolph, *Die Mandäer,* 2:35, 44–45; Brown, *Gospel According to John,* 669.

[16] Behm, "Amphelos," 342–43.

[17] Bultmann, *Gospel of John,* 8, 530.

[18] Rudolph, *Die Mandäer,* 2:61–72. On the relationship between *Baruch* and the Mandaeans in ch. 6, below, on the vision of the bright waters and dark waters.

[19] Lagrange, "Notes sur le Messianisme," 504–5.

[20] Bogaert, *Apocalypse de Baruch,* 1:85–86.

[21] De Faye, *Les Apocalypses Juives,* 25.

ancient traditions, they were completely integrated within the composition of the work.[22]

The characterization of the four kingdoms is also rather confused and unclear. The first kingdom is characterized more or less clearly; from the statement that it was the one that destroyed Zion, we may identify it with Babylonia.[23] But nothing specific is said concerning the next two, and it seems as though the author "hastened" to arrive at a depiction of the final kingdom that is at the center of this vision. This kingdom represents the kingdom of evil and will be the harshest and most evil of all its predecessors. It will rise above the cedars of Lebanon, the truth will be hidden in it, and all those contaminated by wickedness will flee to it. All that will remain of it will be the cedar, the final ruler, depicted as evil, who never did any good. He will rule over that which does not belong to him, he lacks compassion, imposes his rule upon those who are distant from him, holds those who are close to him in the snare of his evil, and his heart is constantly haughty. But he will meet a bitter end. He will lie in trouble and tribulation together with the forest until the coming of the final time, when he will awaken therein to further sufferings, but his end will come to him in fire. From whence did the author draw this picture of four kingdoms, and who is this final ruler?

It is generally agreed that this format of four kingdoms is based upon the vision of Daniel (chs. 2, 6–7). The use of the cedar as a symbol for the final ruler is based upon Ezek 31, which provides all of the scenery for the vision of the forest in *Baruch*. In this prophecy, addressed to the king of Egypt, the prophet compares the arrogance of Egypt with that of Assyria, saying that Egypt's final end will be like that of Assyria. The king of Assyria is compared to the cedar of Lebanon, tall of stature and with spreading boughs, that grows in the garden of God, that is, in the garden of Eden. Among its branches nest all the birds of heaven, beneath its boughs all the beasts of the forest will give birth, and in its shadow sit many nations. But its heart is haughty, and therefore God will recompense it *according to its evil*, and it will be expelled. It will be cut off and abandoned in the *mountains*, will descend to *Sheol*, and the deep will cover it. The cedar, which considered itself the most dignified and greatest of all the trees in Eden, will descend together with the other trees into the netherland and will lie down together with the uncircumcised. As in the description in *Syriac Baruch*, so too in this prophecy the cedar will lift itself up above the other trees and its heart will be high and haughty, but their end will

---

[22] Bogaert, *Apocalypse*, 1:86.

[23] Charles, *2 Baruch,* 501; Sayler, "Have the Promises Failed?" 24; De Faye, *Les Apocalypses,* 26–27; Flusser, "The Four Empires," 326 n. 38.

be the same. As in *Baruch*, this cedar too grows in paradise,[24] but the author seems to have combined here images from Ezekiel with the description of Antiochus Epiphanes from Daniel: "he shall exalt himself and magnify himself above every god, and shall speak astonishing things ... and shall prosper. ... He shall not give heed to any other god, for he shall magnify himself above all" (Dan 11:36–37).[25] This conclusion becomes explicit from a parallel tradition in *Fourth Ezra*: in the vision of the eagle in chapters 11–12, the eagle is depicted like the cedar in Baruch: it remains the last of the four creatures, over which it was triumphant. It imposed a rule of fear and evil over the entire world and its heart was arrogant, but like the cedar, its end too will be bitter

---

[24] Due to the importance of the cedar and its beauty, it was included in Eastern legends among the trees of the divine gardens. The cedar is a symbol of strength and size, for which reason it appears in the vision of *Baruch* as the opposite of the vine. It rises to great height with pride and glory, while the vine crawls and stretches along the earth in lowliness and humility (cf. Isa 2:13; 10:33; Amos 2:9; Isa 14, for the descriptions of the kings of Babylonia and Assyria that gave birth to the typology of the king who rises and falls, as referring to the antichrist). See Moore, *Judaism*, 2:333 n. 5; Efron, "Psalms of Solomon," 246–49. A description similar to the present vision appears in the *Thanksgiving Scroll*, 1QH xvi 4–26. This description contains the image of "trees of life in the secret source" and "a plantation of cypresses and elms, together with cedars," contrasted with "trees at the water." The trees of life, whose roots stretch to the spring of water, will sprout a shoot that will open up its trunk to the living water and become an eternal source; beneath its leaves wild animals will graze, its trunk will be tread upon by passers-by, and its branches will provide shelter for every bird. The trees by the water will rise above it and be proud that living trees flourish in their plantings, but these are condemned to disappear, as they do not send forth their roots to the spring and their end will be to be dragged down to the depths by the rapid stream and to sink like lead in the powerful waters, or to be burned and dried up. Like the vision in *Syriac Baruch*, this description is also based upon several biblical passages, and especially upon sections from Isaiah and Ezekiel. The symbol of the trees by the waters is based upon Ezek 31, the same chapter that provides the main features of the description in *Baruch*. Among the water trees that grow in the garden of Eden, the cedar stands out here as beyond compare with any of the other trees of the garden, but because of its haughtiness it will be cut down by strangers and descend to Sheol together with the other trees of Eden that drink water. The present description also depicts the garden of Eden, whose fruits God protects "with the mystery of powerful heroes and spirits of holiness," and the garden is identified with the sect itself (Ringgren, "The Branch and the Plantation," 5; Licht, *Thanksgiving Scroll*, 132). The tree of life that grows in the garden of Eden appears here in the plural (see, similarly, *Pss. Sol.* 14:3; *Odes Sol.* 11; Murray, *Symbols*, 255).

[25] Cf. Dan 4:7–14, 17–20; 7:8, 25. Daniel may have constructed this picture on the basis of Ezek 31; cf. Beale, *The Use of Daniel*, 269. On the place of Antiochus Epiphanes in the development of the image of the antichrist, see Buzy, "Antechrist," 299–303.

and it will disappear. In the interpretation of the vision the author explicitly states from whence he derived the inspiration for this vision:

> The eagle which you saw coming up from the sea is the fourth kingdom, which appeared in a vision to your brother Daniel. But it was not explained to him as I now explain or have explained it to you. (*4 Ezra* 12:11–12)

The identification of the fourth kingdom in Daniel with the Roman Empire was already common at the time of Josephus (*Ant.* 10.276).[26] But unlike the descriptions of the fourth kingdom and the figure of Antiochus Epiphanes in Daniel, and in contrast to the descriptions of the kings of Babylonia and of Assyria in the prophecies of Isaiah and Ezekiel, which are drawn in realistic lines and placed in the reality of their time, the image of the fourth kingdom in *Syriac Baruch,* like that of the final ruler, is drawn in general and typological lines.

The author of the present vision did not intend to describe a concrete historical picture. For him, the four kingdoms are merely a schematic framework, based upon an apocalyptic interpretation of Daniel, which he uses in order to portray the end of days and the appearance of the Messiah who is "the beginning of God's creation" (ἀρχὴ τῆς κτίσεως; Rev 3:14),[27] the firstborn son which will be forever (2 Bar 40:3). He needs to mention the fall of Rome, the fourth kingdom, because, according to the Revelation of John, it is that which precedes the appearance of the antichrist, who corresponds to the "final ruler" here.[28] Like the final ruler in *Baruch,* in the New Testament the

---

[26] M. Wise, M. Abegg Jr., and E. Cooke, *The Dead Sea Scrolls: A New Translation* (San Francisco, 1996), 439. This new interpretation also appears in the talmudic tradition (see *Gen. Rab.* 44:17; and *b. Yoma* 10a). The depiction of the four kingdoms as trees, the last one of which is identified with the Roman kingdom, appears throughout the prophecy, including the vision of the four kingdoms in Qumran (4Q552–553). 4Q553 fr. 4 describes the fourth tree, whose branches reach to the heavens, which has power of rulership, and which, similar to the cedar in *Baruch,* appears in connection with a place of water (see P. Flint, "'Apocrypha' and Previously Known Writings and 'Pseudepigrapha' in the Dead Sea Scrolls," in *The Dead Sea Scrolls After Fifty Years* [ed. P. Flint and J. C. VanderKam; Leiden, 1999], 2:60–61).

[27] Jesus is designated "the beginning" (ἀρχή) or "the creation" (Heb. *Berešit*) on the basis of Gen 1:1; Col 1:15–18; see Daniélou, *The Theology of Jewish Christianity,* 1:166–68.

[28] Scholars identify the last ruler with one of the Roman figures, Pompey or Caligula. Thus Charles, *2 Baruch,* 501; De Faye, *Les Apocalypses,* 27–28; Rowland, *The Open Heaven,* 60, 172. Note that, instead of the "desolating sacrilege" (שיקוץ משומם) that symbolizes Antiochus in Daniel (cf. Matt 24:15; Mark 13:14), 2 Thess 2:3 introduces "the man of lawlessness," who is the antichrist. Thus also in Irenaeus, *Haer.*

antichrist[29] is portrayed as the rival and enemy of the true Messiah, as "the man of lawlessness ... the son of perdition, who opposes and exalts himself against every so-called god or object of worship," with wicked deception, and who is followed by all those who, having fallen into the snare of his evil, are to perish (2 Thess 2:3ff). He is not a figure of flesh and blood, but a dominion and principality, one of the leaders of the darkness of this world who possess evil spiritual powers in heaven (Eph 6:10ff.).

The comparison of Rome to the cedar forest, from which there only remains the last cedar, the antichrist, who will be defeated by the Messiah at the end of days, may also have been based upon an interpretation of Isa 10:34–11:1. These verses likewise speak of a forest (vv. 33–34) whose tall trees are cut down and brought low, and which is to be uprooted and burned (9:17). The cedar in Baruch's vision is consistent with the term "Lebanon" in Isa 13; its depiction as being thrust down to the earth, cut off, and judged by the Messiah may likewise derive from the interpretation of these verses.[30] The identification there of "Lebanon" with Rome was known among Christian exegetes who saw in it a symbol of idolatry and of the powers of evil that oppose God and are therefore judged for destruction.[31]

A similar description is propounded by two *Pesher* passages from Qumran. In the *Isaiah Pesher* (4QpIsa[a] 8–10 = 4Q161)[32] the Messiah from the house of David, "the shoot of David," is described as a militant messiah who at "the end of days" will be victorious over the "Kittim" who will rise up in attack against Jerusalem.[33] The Kittim are identified in the Scrolls with Rome[34] and, as in the

---

5.25.4 (SC 153:319), who identifies antichrist with the "desolating sacrilege," and in his wake Hippolytus (*Frag. Dan.* 2.22 [PG 10:656]); idem, *On Christ and Anti-Christ*, 62–63 (PG; 10:781–83); Tertullian, *Adv. Jud.* 8 (PL 2:612–13; Augustine, *Civ.* 20.8, 13 (LCL 6:292–303, 327–32).

[29] This term appears in the Epistles to John: 1 John 2:18, 22; 4:3; 2 John 7; *Sib. Or.* 3:63–74; *Ascen. Isa.* 4:1–13.

[30] See R. Bauckham ("The Messianic Interpretation of Isa. 34 in the Dead Sea Scrolls, 2 Baruch, and the Preachings of John the Baptist," *DSD* 2 [1995]: 206–10), who connects this prophecy to the Qumran *pesharim* mentioned below, as well as to several sayings attributed to John the Baptist in the Gospels.

[31] Sparks, "The Symbolic Interpretation of 'Lebanon,'" 267.

[32] DJD 5:13–14.

[33] This is hinted at in a previous passage from the same Pesher: 4QpIsa[a] 5–6 (DJD 5:12).

[34] Thus in the *War Scroll, Nahum Pesher, Habakkuk Pesher*, etc. See R. Eisenman and M. Wise, *The Dead Sea Scrolls Uncovered*, 27, 40; Vermes, "The Oxford Forum,"

2 *Baruch,* this host is compared in this *Pesher* to the forest of the cedars of Lebanon. The *Pesher* interprets the "great in height," who are to be hewn down, with the "heroes of the Kittim," while "Lebanon with its majestic ones will fall" refers to "the rulers of the Kittim who shall be given into the hands of his great one,"[35] that is, into the hands of the Messiah. In a similar manner the end-of-days battle of the Messiah with his enemies is described in *Serek hamilhama* (4Q285),[36] which is close in contents and ideas to the *Isaiah Pesher.*[37] The prince of the congregation, who is identified with the shoot of David, conducts a trial of his enemies ("and they judged . . ."),[38] and kills a certain rival ("and he was killed by the prince of the congregation, the sho[ot of David]"), who is evidently mentioned in the truncated section that precedes line 4 in the Pesher.[39] This is almost certainly the leader of the enemies, who is

---

89; Bockmuehl, "A Slain Messiah," 162; Pomykala, *The Davidic Dynasty Tradition,* 199, 203, 205.

[35] This word may be read as גדולי or גדולו, but the word באדיר is to be interpreted in the singular and not in the plural (see Bauckham, "The Messianic Interpretation," 205).

[36] B. Z. Wacholder and M. Abegg, *A Preliminary Edition of the Unpublished Dead Sea Scrolls,* 2:225 (Frg. 5); Eisenman and Wise, *DSS Uncovered,* 29 (Fragment 7). This text includes ten fragments that belong to one manuscript (Pomykala, *Davidic Dynasty,* 203). Wacholder and Abegg (*Preliminary Edition,* 2:xv), suggest that this is to be seen as part of the *Scroll of the War of the Sons of Light and the Sons of Darkness.* On the basis of the similarity between *Serek Hamilhama* and *Isaiah Pesher,* which expound the same verses in the context of an eschatological conflict, one may assume with certainty that in this text too the cedars of Lebanon are identified with the Kittim, even though this is not stated explicitly (see Pomykala, *Davidic Dynasty,* 206).

[37] Pomykala, *Davidic Dynasty,* 198, 204.

[38] Pomykala (*Davidic Dynasty,* 206 n. 149), follows Bockmuehl, "A Slain Messiah," 164.

[39] On this reading, see Vermes, "The Oxford Forum," 85–90; ibid., "The 'Pierced Messiah' Text," 80–82; Gordon, "The Interpretation of 'Lebanon,'" 92–94; Bockmuehl, "A Slain Messiah," 165–66; Wacholder and Abegg, *Preliminary Edition,* 2:xv; Abegg, "Messianic Hope," 88–90; Pomykala, *Davidic Dynasty,* 207–10. On the reading, "the sho[ot of David]," Pomykala, *Davidic Dynasty,* 206 n. 147, as against the reading of Wacholder and Abegg (*Preliminary Edition,* Frg. 5, p. 225). Upon its publication, this text aroused an intense debate among scholars, focused upon the question as to how the word והמיתו is to be read. Eisenman and Wise, who published this text, argued that it is to be understood as a verb in the third person masculine plural. According to this reading, the enemies are those who will put the Messiah to death; if so, this messiah's destiny is identical to that of the Christian Messiah (thus Eisenman and Wise, *DSS Uncovered,* 24–27; Eisenman, "More on the Pierced

also mentioned in fragment 4 as one who is brought to judgment before the Messiah.[40] This leader is known from the *Scroll of the War of the Children of Light and the Children of Darkness* as "the king of the Kittim" (1QM 15 2) and may be identified with the cedar, the "final ruler" mentioned in the present vision.[41]

The confrontation between the Messiah and the community of his believers, on the one hand, and the antichrist and his armies, on the other, will take place on Mount Zion in the heavenly Jerusalem—that is, at the gates of paradise, as is clearly implied by *Fourth Ezra,* which puts forward an extremely similar vision. There the Messiah, whom God had kept for many ages, comes up from the sea in order to redeem his creation. All the nations gather together to do battle with him at the top of Mount Zion. "And Zion will come and be made manifest to all people, prepared and built, as you saw the mountain carved out without hands" (*4 Ezra* 13:36). As in the tradition in *Syriac Baruch,* the war of the Messiah with the antichrist will not be conducted with the sword: the Messiah will reproach the nations who come up for their wickedness and will destroy them like a flame of fire (*4 Ezra* 13:9–11, 38).[42] The Messiah does not battle the antichrist with a sword, even though the descriptions of the war are filled with military terms, but rather chastises him for all the evils he

---

Messiah," 66–67; Tabor, "A Pierced or Piercing Messiah?" 58–59). The reasons given for preferring the first reading are rooted in the context in which the sentence in question appears and in its syntactic structure. The fragment proposes an exegesis to Isa 10:34–11:1. In these verses the prophet describes the fall of the cedars of Lebanon, which are the symbol of the enemies of Israel, and thus he represents the figure of David, the "shoot from the stock of Jesse," the victorious king who "smites the land with the rod of his mouth and in the breath of his lips kills the wicked." One may assume that the interpretation given to these verses fits their original intention and is not the opposite of it. The description of the Davidic Messiah as a militant and victorious Messiah is also consistent with his descriptions in other Qumran texts. In addition, if "the prince of the congregation" is the object of this sentence, the conjunction את should have appeared. For further details on their reasoning, see Vermes, "Oxford Forum," 89; Bockmuehl, "A Slain Messiah," 164–65; Pomykala, *Davidic Dynasty,* 207–10.

[40] Wacholder and Abegg, *Preliminary Edition,* 225; Eisenman and Wise, *DSS Uncovered,* frg. 6, p. 28; Abegg, "Messianic Hope," 87.

[41] Vermes, "Oxford Forum," 89; Bockmuehl, "A Slain Messiah," 165. See also the Targum to Isa 10:34. The identification of "Lebanon" with Rome or with the nations of the world does not appear at all in the early talmudic literature (Vermes, "The Symbolic Interpretation of 'Lebanon'," 7–9). The tradition in the Targum, like that of Qumran, is not prior to Christianity and one may assume that it was even influenced by it, as opposed to what is argued by Vermes ("Symbolic Interpretation," 7).

[42] See Rev 19:15.

has done, in keeping with Isa 11:4: "with the breath of his lips he shall slay the wicked." The antichrist is the embodiment of evil, and the Messiah must kill him with the breath of his mouth, as stated in 2 Thess 2:8: "Then the lawless one will be revealed, and the Lord Jesus will slay him with the breath of his mouth."[43] It is possible that the source of the defeat of Satan with the breath of the lips is related to the view that the mouth of the Lord is the true word and the gate to his light (*Odes Sol.* 12:3). Like *Baruch*, in the Johannine apocalypse there is also a war in which the Messiah, the Lamb, and the congregation of his believers engage the antichrist on Mount Zion (Rev 20:7–10).[44] The final conflict is conducted specifically on Mount Zion, because it is there that the deliverance will take place for all those who call upon the name of the Lord, and it is there that the remnant will be concentrated, according to Joel 3:5: "And it shall come to pass that all who call upon the name of the Lord shall be delivered; for in Mount Zion and in Jerusalem there shall be those who escape, as the Lord has said, and among the survivors shall be those whom the Lord calls."[45] There, according to Zechariah, the Lord sets forth to wage war against the Gentiles: "On that day his feet shall stand on the Mount of Olives which lies before Jerusalem on the east; and the Mount of Olives shall be split in two from east to west by a very wide valley; so that one half of the Mount shall withdraw northward, and the other half southward" (Zech 14:4). This war will be conducted upon Mount Zion, in the heavenly Jerusalem identified with the garden of Eden. There, in the gates of the garden of Eden, Jesus also defeated Judas Iscariot, who embodies Satan, thereby carrying out the divine death sentence against the serpent (John 18:4).

The armies of the antichrist are the nations lacking in faith, which he will gather for battle against the camp of the saints at the end of the millennium. In Revelation, they are called "Gog and Magog" (Rev 20:8).[46] Although this expression is based upon the prophecy of Ezekiel (chs. 38–39), the Christian apocalypse introduced to it new contents and form. Ezekiel portrays an imaginary vision, in which Gog represents a tremendous northern king, identified with Gigas king of Lydda, who reigned in the middle of the seventh

---

[43] See *4 Ezra* 12:32–33; 13:37.

[44] Heb 12:22–24; and cf. Rev 14:1. The Davidic Messiah will arise in Zion according to the Florilegium as well (4QFlorilegium [4Q174], DJD V:53; Pomykala, *Davidic Dynasty*, 213).

[45] Cf. *2 Bar.* 29:2; 40:2; 71:1; *4 Ezra* 13:48, 49.

[46] Similarly, in the Qumran scrolls: "Gog" appears in the *War Scroll* (1QM xi 16); "Magog" in the *Isaiah Pesher* (4QpIsa^a [4Q161] 8–10 [DJD 5:14]), as an eschatological enemy that will be defeated by the shoot of David (Pomykala, *Davidic Dynasty*, 201).

century BCE,[47] who came from Magog[48] and out of sheer lust for destruction attacked Israel, who were dwelling peacefully and without any guilt in their hands. This was an attack of warlike people upon a peaceful kingdom, only with God's counsel its end will be the sanctification of God's name in the world: Gog will be defeated and fall slain upon the mountains of Israel, together with the peoples allied with him, and thereby the name of the Lord will be made known in Israel and in the nations.[49] Ezekiel's prophecy concerning Gog exemplifies how God will protect Israel from the Gentiles, and does not involve any apocalyptic tendency. The defeat of Gog does not herald the end of the world; it does not bring the redemption, nor is there any messianic personality involved in the war with him. Jerusalem is not mentioned in this vision; the people do not besiege it, they do not conquer it, and they do not fall before its walls. Moreover, the prophecy of Ezekiel against "Gog from the land of Magog" was transformed in the Christian apocalypse into "Gog and Magog," a combination which has no basis in the Jewish sources from that period. True, this expression seemingly appears in the Mishnah (*m. ʿEd.* 2.10), where it is listed among the five things of twelve months duration enumerated by Rabbi Akiva: "The future judgment of Gog and Magog shall be for twelve months." However, in *all* the early manuscripts of the Mishnah the reading is "the future judgment of *Gog* shall be for twelve months";[50] this original version

---

[47] Kaufmann, *History*, 3:579 n. 100.

[48] On the basis of Gen 10:2, Magog is the name of a northern people, of the descendants of Japheth. Cf. Ezek 38:1–5.

[49] See Kaufmann, *History*, 3:579–83.

[50] MS Paris 328–29, Pt. II, 298; MS Cambridge, *Matnita de-Talmuda debnei maʿarava* (ed. W. H. Lowe; Jerusalem, 1967), Pt. I, 137b; MS Kaufmann, *Nezikin-Qodashim-Toharot* (Jerusalem, 1968), 323; MS Firma de Russo 138 (Jerusalem, 1970), 216; *Mishnah ʿim Perush ha-Rambam* (translated from the original Arabic manuscript by J. Kapah; Jerusalem, 1964), 300. In the first printed edition of the Mishnah with Maimonides' commentary (*Nezikin-Qodashim-Toharot* [Naples, 1492; Jerusalem, 1970]), ʿEd. 2.10, this sentence does not appear at all! The expression first appears in the JT: "'I love when the Lord has heard their voice'—in the days of Messiah. 'Bind the festal procession'—in the days of Gog and Magog" (*y. Ber.* 2.4 [4d]; *y. Meg.* 2.1 [73a]). This expression appears here, it is true, in an eschatological context and is connected with the days of Messiah, but in a low-key manner and without any explicit apocalyptic significance. In the BT, this expression already appears frequently and in an apocalyptic context (thus *b. Sanh.* 97b, "the wars of Gog and Magog," in the context of those who calculate the End, but as a quotation from an apocalyptic scroll found among the texts hidden away in Rome. And cf. *b. Ber.* 7b, 10a, 13a, 58a; *Šabb.* 118a; *Pesaḥ.* 118a; *Meg.* 11a, 17a; ʿ*Abod. Zar.* 3b).

of Rabbi Akiva's dictum fully corresponds to the intention and contents of Ezekiel's prophecy.

The description of the end of the antichrist in the present vision also displays similarity to its description in Revelation. The cedar is sent off, in the forest's wake, to sleep in trouble and in suffering, but all this only until the coming of the final time, in which it will continue to suffer, finally to be thrown into the pool of fire and consumed (according to Mal 3:19 and Dan 7:11). Here too, as in the previous vision, there is an allusion to the period of the millennium which, according to Rev 20:1–10, will continue between the imprisonment of the serpent, the antichrist, and his release, which will conclude with his confrontation with the Messiah and his being burned.

Upon Satan's final defeat and destruction, paradise is established, characterized by an abundance of flowers that never wither, as described by Ephraem Syrus in his *Hymn on Paradise:* "Seated among the trees, in the fresh air, with flowers beneath them, fruits above them, their heaven—made from the fruits of the earth and with the earth beneath them—a bower of flowers. Who has heard or seen such a thing? A cloud of fruits shades their heads, and a cloud of flowers falls down and is spread beneath their feet."[51]

A number of researchers have connected the idea of the militant messiah who wages war, as in *2 Baruch,* with the Jewish tradition concerning the Messiah son of Joseph or the Messiah son of Ephraim.[52] In this view, Judaism anticipated two chosen anointed messiahs, meant to appear upon the earth at the end of times. One is the son of David, whose reign will be eternal, and the other is the son of Joseph, or the son of Ephraim, who will lead the armies of Israel to victory, but will in the end die in battle before the walls of Jerusalem. However, as in *Baruch* the Messiah does not fall in battle and does not die, he was conflated with the figure of the Messiah in *Fourth Ezra* who, as mentioned, died after a certain period of rule, and there was thereby accepted, so to speak, a picture consistent with the Jewish tradition of Messiah son of Joseph.[53]

---

[51] Ephraem Syrus, *Hymnes sur le Paradis,* 9.5; 10.3 (CSCO, col. 174; Sci. Syri 78, pp. 36, 43).

[52] Torrey, "The Messiah Son of Ephraim," 261–67; Bogaert, *Apocalypse,* 1:414, 417–18.

[53] Torrey, "Messiah Son of Ephraim," 253. In later talmudic sources, this messiah wages war against Gog (or Armilus) and defeats him (see *Tg. Ps.-J.* to Exod 40:12; Even Shmuel, *Midrashei Ge'ulah, Agadat ha-Mashiah, 'Eser Otot, Otot ha-Mashiah,* and elsewhere).

The idea of Messiah son of Joseph first appears in the midrash *Genesis Rabbah* (*b. Sukkah* 52a).[54] In a discussion of Gen 32:6, "And I have oxen and asses," the Rabbis commented that "oxen" alludes to the "one anointed for war," of whom it is said, "his firstling bull has majesty" (Deut 33:17), while "asses" alludes to the King Messiah, of whom it is said, "humble and riding on an ass" (Zech 9:9; see *Gen. Rab.* 75.6 [ed. Theodor-Albeck, 892]). Elsewhere, Joseph is identified with the one anointed for war into whose hands Rome will fall: "By whose hand will the kingdom of Edom fall? By the hand of the one anointed for war, who will be descended from Joseph" (*Gen. Rab.* 99.2 [ed. Theodor-Albeck, 1274]).

In these traditions, Messiah son of Joseph is identified with the one anointed for war, who musters the troops in time of war and is depicted as a victorious hero. But this midrash knows nothing of his defeat and death, which evidently represent a later stage in the development of this tradition and appear first in the Babylonian Talmud. In a tannaitic dispute concerning Zech 12:12 ("The land shall mourn, each family by itself; the family of the house of David by itself, and their wives by themselves"), Rabbi Dosa and the Sages comment concerning the occasion for the mourning: "One said: It was for Messiah son of Joseph who was killed; and the other said: for the Evil Urge that was killed."[55] The death of Messiah son of Joseph is also mentioned further on in the context of that same discussion:

> Our Rabbis taught, [concerning] Messiah son of David, who shall appear in the future speedily: The Holy One blessed be He said to him: Ask of me a thing, and I shall give it, as is said "I will tell of the decree . . . today I have begotten you. Ask of me, and I will make the nations your heritage" (Ps 2:7–8). Once he saw that Messiah son of Joseph had been killed, he said to him: Master of the Universe, I do not ask anything of you but life . . . .

---

[54] Cf. *Pesiq. Rab Kah.* 5.9 (ed. Mandelbaum; 97); *Pesiq. Rab.* 15 (ed. Ish-Shalom; 75a); *Cant. Rab.* 2.13; *Num. Rab.* 14.1.

[55] *B. Sukka* 52a. In the parallel in *y. Sukkah,* 5.2 (55b), the dispute is conducted among the amoraim, and it speaks only of the Messiah, whereas the Bavli expands the discussion and identifies him with Messiah son of Joseph who was killed (see Heinemann, *Aggadot,* 134–35; idem, "Messiah son of Ephraim and the Exodus of the Children of Ephraim Before the End" [Hebrew], *Tarbiz* 40 [1971], 454–55). There are those scholars who explain the death of Messiah in this tradition in the context of the failure of the Bar Kokhba Rebellion (thus H. L. Strack and P. Billerbeck, *Kommentar zum Neuen Testament aus Talmud und Midrasch* (Munich, 1924), 2:294; Klausner, *The Messianic Idea,* 297–98; Heinemann, *Aggadot,* 136–37). In *Pesiq. Rab.* 36–37, he already appears as a figure closer to the Christian Messiah (cf. *Tg Ps.-J.* to Gen 49:11).

CHAPTER 5: The Vision of the Forest

If there is room for any parallel between the figure of Messiah in *Syriac Baruch* and that of Messiah son of Joseph, it is limited to the first and earliest stage of the tradition. However, this attempt to connect the militant Messiah in *Baruch* to the Messiah son of Joseph seems to me entirely without basis. The idea of the Messiah son of Joseph, or of the one anointed for war, who precedes Messiah son of David, remains at the margins of the Jewish messianic approach, and there is only a vague and obscure echo to it in Jewish sources, no earlier than the fifth century CE.[56] It seems reasonable to assume that this tradition developed in Judaism specifically in light of the polemic with Christianity, which connected to Christ the crowns of Joseph and his son Ephraim, based upon the blessings of Jacob and of Moses in Gen 49:22–26 and Deut 33:13–17. In these blessings Joseph is presented as a mighty warrior and fighter: "his horns are the horns of a wild ox; with them he shall push the peoples, all of them, to the ends of the earth." In the figure of Messiah son of Joseph, Judaism wished to prove that these blessings were indeed realized in the past in the seed of Joseph[57] or are realized in a Jewish Messiah.[58] But the main reason for rejecting this speculation is that the figure of the Messiah in *Baruch*, as we have attempted to prove, is consistent with the figure of the Christian Messiah and with the apocalyptic expectation of his appearance. Why, then, must we seek its roots in a vague and weak Jewish tradition that is in any event no earlier than the appearance of Christianity?!

---

[56] On the dating of *Genesis Rabbah*, see Zunz, *Derashot be-Yisra'el*, 77, and esp. 338 n. 50; Albeck, *Mavo le-Bereshit Rabbah*, 96.

[57] "His firstborn ox" is identified in a Jewish tradition with Joshua (thus *Tg. Ps.-J.* to Deut 33:17; *Tg. Yer.* Rashi, "The king who comes out of him, he is Joshua"; Ramban ad loc.; *Gen. Rab.* 6.9; 39.11; 75.12; *Num. Rab.* 2.7; and more). This identification enabled the Christians to attribute these traditions to Jesus, i.e., "Joshua."

[58] For other conjectures as to the origin of this tradition, see Lagrange, *Le Messianisme*, 254–55; Klausner, *Messianic Idea*, 320ff.; Mowinckel, *He That Cometh*, 290–91; van der Woude, "χρέω," 527.

CHAPTER SIX

The Vision of the Bright Waters and the Dark Waters (*2 Bar.* 53, 56–74)

The final vision, involving the cloud and the bright and dark waters, completes the eschatological picture by emphasizing the new heavens and the new earth, the incorruptible world to be established instead of the world that has been destroyed upon the second appearance of the Messiah. In this vision, Baruch sees a single cloud rising from the great sea, filled with bright waters (*hora*) and dark waters. There are many different colors in this water and a figure like a great bolt of lightning is visible at its top. The cloud quickly passes by and covers the entire earth. Thereafter the cloud begins to alternatively rain dark water and bright water upon the earth, twelve times in succession; each time the dark water was more than the bright waters. The last dark waters are darker and thicker than those that came before them and are mixed with fire, raining down destruction and loss. Thereafter the visionary sees the lightning taking hold of the cloud and bringing it down to the earth, illuminating the earth more and more, healing those places that had been destroyed by the dark waters, occupying the whole earth and ruling over it. The visionary then sees twelve rivers ascending from the sea, surrounding the lightning and subjugating it (*2 Bar.* 53:1–12)

Like the two visions that preceded it, this vision also depicts the end of days and the destruction that will precede it, as well as the eschatological redemption that will follow, with the appearance of the Messiah and the founding of a new world. The first vision constitutes a transitional link between the pseudohistorical portion of the work describing the destruction of Jerusalem and the apocalyptic portion. This may be the reason why it is the only one among the three that does not present a complete symbolic picture requiring commentary.[1] The two visions that follow it present a complete apocalyptic scheme, incorporating a historical survey that concludes with the end of time, the coming of Messiah, and the complete redemption. However, in both of these visions the historical surveys were not intended to describe the course of history, and [indeed] their authors were not interested in history as such;

---

[1] On the mystery that characterizes the visions of the Apocalypse and its interpretation, see Dimant, "History according to the Vision of the Beasts," 20–22.

they were subjugated, from beginning to end, to the apocalyptic idea, which they come to serve: they lead to the necessary end of this world and the coming of a new world in its stead.[2]

In the vision of the forest, the cedar, the vine, and the spring, the historical survey is brief and schematic, as it does not serve the main element of the idea in the vision (namely, the Messiah's battle with the antichrist). In order to express this idea, the author only required the final empire and the ruler that will come after it. In the vision of the End discussed here, the historical survey is lengthy and detailed, because it is the very focus of the idea expressed therein.

As we have seen, the author constructs his apocalyptic visions by means of symbolism connected to the two principal Christian sacraments—the Eucharist (the sacrament that expresses the believer's participation in the sacrifice of the crucified Jesus and the eschatological anticipation of his full return at the Parousia) and baptism (through which the one baptized is united with the body of Jesus and his death, as a means of receiving renewed life with his resurrection). In the first vision, the author emphasized the bread, the grape, and the manna as symbols of the Eucharist. In the second, he placed the vine and the spring alongside one another as symbols of the crucifixion and baptism. In this last vision he represents the sacrament of baptism by means of the bright waters and the dark waters.

In the Christian sources, the bright waters are the symbol of the baptismal waters, as the eyes of one who is baptized become filled with light. In ancient terminology, baptism was called φωτισμός, meaning "enlightenment," and the verb φωτισθῆναι is a synonym of βαπτισθῆναι.[3] Baptism in the name of Jesus is called enlightenment because Jesus is the light (φῶς). Justin says the following about Christian baptism:

---

[2] There are similar historical surveys in other apocalyptic works: *1 En.* 85–90; 93:4–10; 91:11–17; *As. Mos.*; *Sib. Or.* 4:47–85. Similar historical surveys appear in Aphraates in his sermon on the grape seed (SC 359:875–86, 900–927). This sermon is based upon Isa 65:8–9 ("Thus says the Lord: As the wine is found in the cluster, and they say, 'Do not destroy it, for there is a blessing in it.' So I will do for my servants' sake, and not destroy them all"). The cluster is the people Israel, and the blessing that was in it is Christ; and despite the sin that began with Adam, the entire cluster is preserved thanks to the blessing until the end of all time. This blessing is preserved by the righteous in each generation, among whom he counts the series of figures that appear also in *Syriac Baruch.*

[3] Cullmann, *Early Christian Worship,* 103; Bultmann, *Theology of the New Testament,* 1:143. Heb 6:4 ("those who have once been enlightened [φωτισθέντας], who have tasted the heavenly gift, and have become partners of the Holy Spirit"); Heb 10:32.

And this bathing is called illumination, because those who learn these things receive an illumination in their understanding. And in the name of Jesus Christ, who was crucified by Pontius Pilate, and in the name of the Holy Spirit, who by means of the prophets made known all of the things of Jesus from the beginning, one who is illuminated—is baptised. (Justin, *1 Apol.* 61.12 [PG 6:421])[4]

Jesus is also called the life: ζωή. Hence the bright waters are also waters of life, and they too symbolize Jesus (John 4:10; 7:38; Rev 22:1).

The alternating appearances of bright and dark waters, interpreted here as historical periods, are none other than a doctrine of the two ways, such as was presented before the candidates for baptism and is known to us from early Christian sources (*Did.* 1–6; *Barn.* 18–20): the way of light and the way of darkness (ὁδοὶ δύο εἰσὶν . . . ἥ τε τοῦ φωτὸς καὶ ἡ τοῦ σκότους; *Barn.* 18:1), or the way of life and the way of death (*Didache* 1:1), which are completely distinct and different from one another.[5] The way of light, or the way of life, is

---

[4] Cf. Justin, *1 Apol.* 65 (PG 6:428); Justin, *Dial.* 122.5 (PG 6:760). We have been enlightened by Jesus: ἐφώτισεν. Clement of Alexandria, *Paed.* 1.6.26.1 (SC 70:159); *Didas. Apost.* 8.2.6 (Funk, 482–83); the term φωτισμός and the verb φωτίζειν are very early and appear in the LXX in translation of the words אור ("light"), להאיר ("to cast light"). The noun appears in the NT in a metaphorical sense, describing Christian faith as illumination (2 Cor 4:4; Eph 1:18; 2 Tim 1:10). But Justin was the first to connect them specifically with baptism (Barnard, *Justin Martyr,* 174–76 n. 377). The image of Jesus as light and the perception of baptism as illumination are connected with the mysteries of Jesus as the sun of righteousness (Rahner, *Greek Myth amd Christian Mystery,* 123–27, 133, 143).

[5] *Didas. Apost.* 7.1–32; *Ps.-Clem.* 7.7. Cf. 1QS iii 13–iv 14; also *T. Asher* 1:3–4; *T. Jud.* 20:1. The idea of the two ways is based upon Deut 30:15–20 ("I call heaven and earth to witness against you this day, that I have set before you life and death, blessing and curse; therefore choose life, that you and your descendants may live"; cf. 11:26–28; Jer 21:8). The choice between them is in human hands (see Moore, *Judaism,* 1:454–56). The instruction concerning the two ways in *Did.* 1–6 belongs to the most ancient stratum in this work, dated to the end of the first century CE (see Lake, *Apostolic Fathers,* 1:307; Audet, *Didache,* 187–89; Michell, "Baptism in the Didache," 227–29; Alon, "Halakhah in the Acts of the Apostles," 274–75; Flusser, "Two Ways," 240). These and other scholars think that the "two ways" was an independent Jewish source, used by the Christian author of the *Didache,* like that of *Barnabas,* within which they interpolated Christian additions, and that it originally had no connection to baptism (Audet, *Didache,* 58, 358–59). This is not the place to polemicize with the principles of this approach, which "judaizes" all of early Christian literature, including the NT itself and the figure of the Messiah that lies in its focus. I certainly do not question the Jewish foundations of Christianity. The question is, rather, what were the lines of separation and division that turned fundamentally Jewish ideas into a new theological-ideological entity. As an ethical religion, Judaism obviously involves a choice between good and

that of faith in Jesus, who is "the light of the world"; one who follows him "will not walk in darkness, but will have the light of life" (John 8:12).[6] He is "the resurrection and the life" and whoever believes in him "shall never die" (John 11:25–26). As opposed to this, the way of "darkness" or "the black way" is the dominion of "blackness" embodied in Satan, "the dominion of darkness," in which those who do not believe in Jesus will walk (John 1:4–5; 8:12).[7] In keeping with this, those who follow Jesus are the sons of light, υἱοὶ φωτός, while the sons of darkness are those who do not walk after him (John 12:35–36; 1 Thess 5:4–5).[8]

The doctrine of the two ways expresses the ongoing process of decision undertaken in this world by one who is baptized. It is true that baptism assures him of eternal life in the heavenly kingdom, but meanwhile he lives with the dangers and temptations that lie in wait for him on earth, and he is required to choose between light and darkness, between life and death, between Christ and Belial. The alternation of periods of bright waters and dark waters concretizes the constant struggle between two paths, that will only cease with the end of days and the triumph of Christ over the forces of darkness and Satan.

---

evil. But there is no connection between this and a dualistic approach that distinguishes between the path of light and the path of darkness as two distinct realities separate from one another, representing the realm of God, on the in hand, and that of Satan, on the other, who struggle with one another until the victory of the divine realm. Such an approach does not exist in Judaism until it develops an apocalyptic literature in the Middle Ages. For our purposes, it is important to note that the doctrine of the two ways is incorporated in explicitly Christian works, the process of its transmission is entirely Christian, liturgical use is made of it in the Christian church, and no expression is given to it in explicitly Jewish sources. Its very presence in the Qumran writings indicates the closeness of this sect to Christianity, as follows also from the present study. As the doctrine of the two ways stands today, it expresses the principles of Christian behavior, which was taught to catechumens prior to baptism (Lake, *Apostolic Fathers*, 1:307). It is also associated with baptism in some of the manuscripts: see Audet, *La Didache*, 358.

[6] Cf. John 9:5; 14:6; 1 John 1:6–7.

[7] Col 1:13; the dominion of darkness: Luke 22:53, Eph 6:12, *Barn.* 4:9; the Black One (ὁ μέλας): *Barn.* 20:1; "the way of the darkness": *Barn.* 14:6.

[8] See similar terminology in Qumran: "ways of light" (דרכי אור); "the light of life" (אור החיים), there too in connection with baptism; also "sons of light" as against "sons of darkness"; "the fount of light"; "the source of darkness"; "ways of darkness" (1QS i 9–11; iii 1–13; iii 18–26; *The Scroll of the War of the Sons of Light against the Sons of Darkness* [1QM]). And see, similarly, *1 En.* 22:9: "and to separate the souls of the righteous therein from the fount of water enlightening them"; Ephrem de Nisibe, *Sermons on the Garden of Eden*, 1.5: *b'nei nehora*.

CHAPTER 6: The Vision of the Waters

These images again indicate the relationship of the present work to the Mandaean religion, which made extensive use of symbolism of bright waters and dark waters.[9] The Mandaean religion valued "living water," that is, flowing water, in which the Mandaean baptism (*maṣbuta*) was carried out, as opposed to "darkish" (i.e., stagnant) water. These "living waters" are closely connected with the heavenly kingdom of light, dominated by "life," which is the source of the earthly waters and the salvation contained therein. The flowing waters are living waters, because they originate in life and are life-giving, and through them alone is the connection to the world of light assured. Mandaeanism makes extensive use of such terms as "the founts of life," "the founts of light," and "the revivifying baptism," which is the hallmark of its baptism. In the Mandaean cult, water assures life, power, and eternity. Just as the world of light is surrounded by water, considered the source of "life" or of the "white" waters, so is the darkness represented as the source of the "muddy," "black," "stinking," and "burning" waters which are the source of evil. The Mandaeans called their flowing baptismal waters "Jordan." They believed that the rivers of the Jordan are fed by the world of light, where the heavenly rivers of Jordan, similar to those upon the earth, flow. The earthly Jordan is merely a sliver of the Jordan of heavenly light. One who immerses himself in the River Jordan comes into direct contact with the world of light and partakes of its salvation, acquiring both external and internal purity from his sins. The Jordan of the world of light is filled with white water, white as milk, cold and tasty, whose fragrance is sweeter than the great seasoned grape. In order to describe these great characteristics of Mandaean baptism, they also speak of participation (*laufa*) in the world of light or in life that takes place in baptism, by whose means the world of light is transformed to be present and active.[10]

The vision of the bright and dark waters expresses an extreme dualistic approach that characterizes both apocalyptic literature and that of Christianity. The struggle between the two dominions is also alluded to in the alternation of periods of light and darkness. The descriptions of the dark waters, that each time increase, expresses a deterministic outlook, according to which the world

---

[9] Bogaert, *Apocalypse de Baruch*, 2:99; Thomas, *Le Mouvement Baptiste*, 192; Rudolph, *Die Mandäer*, 61–68; Dodd, *Interpretation of the the Fourth Gospel*, 117. The central ritual of the Mandaeans was baptism in water, which was considered not only a symbol of life but, in a certain sense, life itself. The water, which reflects the light, was considered a form of light, and the person baptized is described as being "clothed in light"; he is dressed in a white garment symbolizing the garments of light worn among the heavenly beings (Drower, *The Mandaeans of Iraq and Iran*, 100–101).

[10] Rudolph, *Die Mandäer*, 66; idem, "La Religion Mandéenne," 506–7. On the symbolism of light and darkness in Gnosis, see Bultmann, *The Gospel of John*, 342; Gil, "Studies in the Book of Enoch," 175.

needs to come to an end in a cosmic catastrophe and salvation can only come about through a soteriological messiah.

The exegesis of the vision of the bright waters and the dark waters portrays twelve periods in the biblical history of the Israelite people, chosen by the author to exemplify the doctrine of the two ways. According to the descriptions of the way of darkness in ancient Christian sources as the path of eternal death and punishment, the path of Satan, filled with things that destroy the soul, such as idolatry, corruption, arrogance, hypocrisy, adultery, murder, robbery, pride, falsehood, cheating, witchcraft, gluttony, impiety, etc.,[11] the event that opens the black path is the original sin. Following upon the sin of Adam, the first man (*adam barnasha qadmaya*), there came into the world premature death, affliction, illness, labor, pride, and passion,[12] in such a manner as to emphasize the corruptness of this world from the very outset (56:5–8). The point of departure for this survey is clearly Christian, fitting the Pauline approach to primal sin and its place in human history: "Therefore as sin came into the world through one man and death through sin, and so death spread to all men because all men sinned . . ." (Rom 5:12). Adam's sin brought death to the human race as a whole, and the results of his sin were passed on to his descendants.[13] While Judaism also associated the source of death with Adam's sin, it did not see it as the cause for the sins or weaknesses of human beings in succeeding generations. The source of evil lies in the impulse of man's heart, that lies in wait for man in each generation and trips him up, but the choice between good and evil lies in his own hands. As Kaufmann says:

> Evil came into the world because of sin, and the essence of sin is the element of choice, the secret of freedom of the will, with which God has graced the crown of creation—man. There is no primeval divine realm within reality that lies outside of God's dominion. But God created in his world the realm of freedom: man's free will that rules over his deeds. In this freedom lies the crossroad: it leads to good

---

[11] *Barn.* 20; *Did.* 5; *Didas. Apost.* 7:18; 1–2 (Funk, 402–3); ibid. 7:1, 3 (Funk, 386–87).

[12] *2 Bar.* 17:2–3; 18:2; 23:4; 48:45–46; 54:15–19. In 54: 15–19, Adam's sin was the cause of his physical death, but each person has the choice whether or not to accept faith in Messiah and to merit future honor (*tešbuḥta d'atidan*): "For, although Adam sinned first and has brought death upon all who were not in his own time, yet each of them who has been born from him has prepared for himself the coming torment. And further, each of them has chosen for himself the coming glory" (also *4 Ezra* 3:7, 23, 25; 4:30–32; 7:116–29).

[13] On the Christianity of this idea in *Syriac Baruch* and in *4 Ezra*, see M. de Jonge and J. Tromp, *The Life of Adam and Eve* (Sheffield, 1997), 74.

and to evil. If man chooses the path of sin and rebellion against God, then he brings evil to the world.[14]

Just as Paul contrasts Adam's sin with the salvific activity of Christ, the new Adam, who will nullify sin and the death that is its consequence, so too the vision of the dark waters concludes with the appearance of the Christ/Messiah who will bring eternal life and the negation of death and corruptible life. The Christianity of this tradition is also emphasized by the representation of the beginning of sexual lust (*ritha de-abaha*) and birth (*nasba debnaya*) as the result of Adam's sin in the garden of Eden. Indirectly, it is implied here that Adam and Eve did not have sexual relations in the Garden. A similar idea is found in *Jub.* 3:2–13. According to it, Eve was presented to Adam before they entered the garden of Eden, and their initial sexual contact also occurred outside of it. Only after forty days could the man enter the garden, while Eve was required to wait eighty days: "And when she finished those eighty days, we brought her into the garden of Eden, because it is more holy than any land, and every tree which is planted in it is holy" (*Jub.* 3:12). These numbers reflect the duration of the days of purification a woman is required to observe after childbirth (according to Lev 12), during which it is forbidden for her to touch any holy thing or to enter into the temple. In the book of *Jubilees,* the garden of Eden was understood as a prototype of the temple; hence, the same laws of purity and impurity apply to it. Since sexual contact generates impurity (Lev 15:18; 22:4–7), the sexual relations between Adam and Eve must have taken place before they entered the garden of Eden, and they were required to observe a period of purification before entering it. As G. Anderson notes, this is an explicitly Christian approach, according to which the garden of Eden is not seen as a story about the primeval world, but as a metaphor for the future world. In other words, the garden of Eden is understood as a paradigm for the ideal world of the Eschaton, in which marriage will not exist at all (Luke 20:27–40).[15] This approach is absolutely opposed to the Jewish tradition, according to which Adam and Eve had sexual

---

[14] Kaufmann, *History of Israelite Faith,* 2:408. Cf. Moore, *Judaism,* 1:480–96.

[15] Anderson, "Celibacy in the Garden?" 121–48; see also the *Greek L.A.E.* (*Apoc. Mos.*) 1:1–3. In the *Cave of Treasures* (Budge, 69), Adam and Eve remain virgins until their expulsion from the garden. The Christian view, according to which there were no sexual relations in the garden of Eden, is related to the Christian tradition about the future paradise: "now that faith has come. . . . There is neither Jew nor Greek, there is neither slave nor free, there is neither male nor female; for you are all one in Christ Jesus" (Gal 3:28).

relations in the garden of Eden, even emphasizing the blessed results of this contact.[16]

The way of darkness continues in the sin of the angels, who went down to the daughters of man because of their lust and greediness, forfeited a life of eternity and immortality, and suffered imprisonment until their destruction in the waters of the Flood (*2 Bar.* 56:10–16). While this story has its origins in Gen 6:1–8, in the tradition in question it reveals a clear relation specifically to its exegesis in the pseudepigraphic works related to *Baruch* and to the Christian tradition in general. These saw in the angels, who were imprisoned in the depths of the earth, the source of evil and corruption in the world. Despite their imprisonment in the depths of the earth, their evil spirits continue to mislead and to tempt people, in the form of spirits and demons that hover over the face of the earth.[17] The fallen angels imprisoned in Sheol represent Satan, who like them was imprisoned and locked up (according to Revelation), and like them will be destroyed at the end of days, symbolized by the Flood. Jesus descended to them and preached them his message during the three days he spent in the grave (1 Pet 3:19), and he will also struggle with Satan in Sheol in order to free the souls that he is keeping under his staff.[18]

Thus, the path of darkness is opened in two Christian traditions that propound an explanation for the source of the evil in the world. The third period in the path of darkness is not described in sufficient detail and is presented in a schematic way. It is a mixture of all the sins following the death of Abraham and his descendants and the wickedness of the land of Egypt, and it is evidently based upon Gen 15:13.[19]

---

[16] See, e.g., Rashi's interpretation of Gen 4:1: "'And Adam knew (*veha-adam yadaʿ*; i.e., in the pluperfect) his wife.' Already prior to the above matter, before they sinned and were expelled from the garden of Eden, and likewise regarding the pregnancy and birth. For were it written, *veyeda ha-adam* (in the imperfect) this would imply that only after they were expelled did they have children" (*Gen. Rab.* 19.6 [ed. Theodor-Albeck, 171–72]; also 18.3 [168]; and for further bibliography see the above-mentioned article by Anderson).

[17] Thus *1 En.* 6–36, 86–88, which brings the most detailed tradition concerning this matter; *Jub.* 5:1–12; *T. Reub.* 5; *T. Naph.* 3:5; L.A.B. 3:1–2; *Asc. Isa.* 11:23–24; Justin, *2 Apol.* 5 (PG 6:452). See the detailed discussion of the tradition of Enoch in Gil, "Studies in the Book of Enoch," 158–60; Russell, *The Method and Message of Jewish Apocalyptics*, 249–51.

[18] *T. Dan* 5:10–11; *T. Benj.* 9:5; cf. Daniélou, *Theology of Jewish Christianity*, 234–35, 239; Clement of Alexandria, *Strom.* 5.1.10 (PG; 9:24); Tertullian, *Marc.* 5.18 (PL 2:519); idem, *Idol.*, 9 (PL 1:671).

[19] See a similar description in Aphraates, *Les Exposés* 23 (SC 359:885), followed by the deeds of Moses, Aaron, and Miriam.

Chapter 6: The Vision of the Waters

The next period in the path of darkness involves the acts of the Amorites, the whisperings of their incantations, their wicked mysteries, and the mixtures of their pollutions. The Amorites were one of the seven nations of Canaan, against whom the Israelites conducted a war and whom they vanquished. The destruction of Sihon and Og, the Amorite kings who were the great enemy of the Israelites at the time of the conquest of the land, became the symbol of the power of the Israelites and their God. On both occasions that the Amorites appear in the book of Kings—as a symbol of the sin of idolatry—they are mentioned in connection with the acts of Ahab (and Jezebeel) and Manasseh, who appear in this historical survey (1 Kgs 21:26; 2 Kgs 21:11).[20] The sin of idolatry also lies at the focus of the following period, in the figures of Jeroboam and Jezebel, a sin that led to the destruction of Israel (1 Kgs 12:28–33; 1 Kgs 18:1–4). The ninth period is devoted to the figure of a Manasseh, who "acted very wickedly, and killed the righteous, and perverted judgment, and shed innocent blood, and violently polluted married women, and overturned altars, and abolished their offerings, and drove away the priests lest they minister in the sanctuary" (*2 Bar.* 64:2). This description is based upon 2 Kgs 21, in which Manasseh is portrayed as one who did evil in the eyes of the Lord like the abominations of the nations, and one who did more evil than was done by the Amorites before him, spilling much innocent blood until Jerusalem was completely filled with blood. According to 2 Chr 33:10–13, Manasseh regretted his deeds after he was exiled to Babylon and his sins were forgiven, he was restored to his throne, and he ended his life as a righteous man. The Jewish tradition combined the information from Kings with that in Chronicles, and always presents, alongside Manasseh's sins, his repentance at the end of his reign. This tradition also exaggerates his transformation and invokes him as an example of the true penitent.[21] In the survey in *Baruch*, Manasseh exemplifies the evil and sinful king who dies unrepentant. His overall wickedness is emphasized by two statements that appear at the beginning and end of his life story, regarding him as being a sinner and evil-doer. He embodies the path of Satan and therefore his final habitation is within fire (64:1; 65:1).[22]

---

[20] The Amorites occupy an important place in *L.A.B.* 25:9–12; 26:4; 27:9.

[21] Josephus, *Ant.* 10.37–46; *m. Sanh.* 10.2; *t. Sanh.* 12.11; *y. Sanh.* 10 (28c); *b. Sanh.* 102b; *Deut. Rab.* 2.20; *Mek. de-Rabbi Yishma'el, Baḥodesh* §10 (ed. Horowitz-Rabin; 240–41); *Pesiq. Rab Kah.* §24 (ed. Mandelbaum; 364–66). On the importance of repentance in Judaism as a means of atoning for sin, see Moore, *Judaism*, 1:520–34.

[22] Bogaert, *Apocalypse*, 1:303. Manasseh is presented in a similar manner in *Asc. Isa.*: he is seen there as the disciple of Belial who dwells within him and serves Satan, the messenger of Samael. He was the symbol of the pursuer of prophets and the one who killed Isaiah.

Like the way of darkness, so too the way of light is exemplified by means of biblical figures symbolizing the bright waters, the path of life, whose significance is belief in the Lord. Thus they are all invoked as symbols of faith and are in part prototypes of the Christian Messiah.

> The bright waters; that is the fountain of Abraham and his generation, and the coming of his son, and the son of his son, and of those who are like them. For at that time the unwritten law was in force among them, and the works of the commandments were accomplished at that time, and the belief in the coming judgment was brought about, and the hope of the world which will be renewed was built at that time, and the promise of the life that will come later was planted. (*2 Bar.* 57:1–2)

Abraham stands at the top of the list of believers, as in his time faith (*haimnuta*) was born in the world that would be established anew, that is, in the Christian faith—this, even before the giving of the Law and the commandments. On the basis of Gen 15:6 ("And he [Abraham] believed in the Lord, and he reckoned it to him as righteousness"), Paul developed in his letters the idea that Abraham's righteousness lay in his faith even before the giving of the Law, and that by virtue of his faith he was given the promise "that they should inherit the world" (Rom 4:13). According to the Christian outlook, Abraham exemplifies the true Judaism, that is based, not on the laws of the Torah, but on the faith in the heart. The sons of faith, who accepted Christianity upon themselves, are the sons of Abraham, "the father of many nations," and they are blessed together with him against those who rely upon the acts of the Torah and who are under a curse.[23] Abraham appears in the Christian tradition alongside his son and grandson, that is, Isaac and Jacob, who appear after him in the genealogy of Jesus, and the Christian tradition even creates a direct connection between them.[24]

Moses, Aaron, Miriam, Joshua son of Nun, Caleb, and all those like them are taken as examples of faith during the period of conquest and possession of the land, and they exemplify figures of great significance in Christology. Moses and Aaron are prototypes of Jesus: Moses is the model of the prophet-king,[25]

---

[23] Rom 4:1ff.; Gal 3:1–14; Heb 11:8; Jas 2:21–24; John 8:58; and cf. Matt 3:9; Luke 3:8. One who accepts the faith in Jesus is called "a son of Abraham": Luke 19:9; Acts 13:26. Abraham is the father of the believers and hence the founder of the dynasty of Jesus: "Jesus Christ son of David son of Abraham": Matt 1:1–2; Luke 3:34; Matt 1:17. Abraham spoke of Christ: Irenaeus, *Haer.* 4.7.1–4 (SC 100b:455ff.).

[24] Matt 8:11; Luke 13:28; *Jub.* 19:15ff.

[25] Philo, *Mos.* 1.148, 334; 2.1–7, 66ff., 187, etc. Jesus is a prophet like Moses according to Deut 18:15, 18–19; Acts 3:22–24; 7:37; John 5:46; cf. Brown, *Gospel According to John*, 86.

whose ascent to Mount Sinai is understood as an ascent to heaven. The Sinaitic epiphany is connected to his coronation, and the Torah that he received is interpreted as a prefiguration of the New Testament. The Exodus from Egypt that he led and the period of the wilderness become an anticipation of the salvation brought by Jesus to his believers and a model of eschatological expectations. Moses and all the prophets after him prophesied about Jesus,[26] and like Jesus, Moses too, according to the description at hand, was taken before God, who showed him the paths of the Torah, the end of days, the image of Zion and its dimensions, and the image of the heavenly temple.[27] The tendency to make Moses into a prototype for Jesus also evidently underlies the statement that Moses was brought up to God, and "the heavens which are under the throne (altar) of the Mighty One were severely shaken" (59:3). Those who are beneath the altar of God are "the souls of those who had been slain for the word of God and for the witness they had borne" (Rev 6:9; 8:3)—that is to say, the souls of the martyrs who lie beneath the heavenly altar.[28] Thus, Moses is also considered among the martyrs.[29] Like Jesus, Moses

---

[26] Luke 24:27; John 1:45; 5:45. On the unique attitude of the Fourth Gospel to Moses and to Exod in general, see Brown, *Gospel According to John*, lx–lxi; Bultmann, *The Gospel of John*, 90. In the scene of the transfiguration, Moses and Elijah are shown speaking with Jesus (Matt 17:3; Mark 9:4; Luke 9:30). Luke explains that they speaking with him about his death, which was to take place in Jerusalem (Heb 3:2ff.; 11:23ff.; etc.). See Glasson, *Moses*, 20–26, and other parallels there.

[27] Cf. *L.A.B.* 19:10. On the connection between this description and *1 En.* 17–36, see Meeks, *The Prophet-King*, 158. Moses could experience these heavenly visions because his ascent to Mount Sinai is perceived as an ascent to heaven. On the connection of this description to *2 En.* 40:12 and its eschatological character, see also Bauckham, The Fate of the Dead, 60–66.

[28] Elsewhere in the NT the martyrs are considered as sacrifices offered to God (2 Tim 4:6; Phil 2:17; and cf. Ign. *Rom.* 2.2; 4.2; see also Rom 12:1 ["I appeal to you therefore, brethren, by the mercies of God, to present your bodies as a living sacrifice, holy and acceptable to God"] and Rom 6:13). Only in the post-Babylonian Jewish tradition do we encounter a similar idea, that the souls of the righteous are hidden beneath the divine throne (thus ʾ*Abot R. Nat.*, Version A, 26 [ed. Schechter, 82] *b. Šabb.* 152b ["Rabbi Eliezer says: The souls of the righteous are hidden beneath the throne of Glory, as it is said, 'And the soul of my master will be bound in the bundle of life'"]; *Deut. Rab.* 11.9 ["The Holy One blessed be He said to him (to Moses' soul): Go out and do not be late, and I shall lift you to the highest heavens and place you beneath the throne of glory, with cherubs and seraphim and hosts."]). *Midr. Eleh Ezkerah* (in A. Jellinek, *Bet ha-Midrasch*, 66) mentions an altar adjacent to the divine throne, upon which the souls of the righteous are offered every day (cf. *Tosafot* to *b. Menaḥ.* 110a).

[29] Cf. Heb 11:24–26.

too is among the light of the world: "for at that time the eternal lamp which exists forever and ever illuminated all those who sat in darkness." The promise of reward is made known for those who believe, while the punishment of fire is kept for those who deny (59:2). Aaron is also a prototype of Jesus, who like him was chosen and appointed to the high priesthood by God (Heb 5:4–5)—especially since Jesus is an offspring of Aaron, as his mother Mary was a relative of Elizabeth who was "of the daughters of Aaron" (Luke 1:5). Joshua son of Nun is the explicit prototype of Jesus. The Christian tradition emphasizes the fact that his name was changed from Hosea to Joshua by Moses (on the basis of Num 13:16)[30] so that he might embody the figure of Jesus, who like him also needed to deliver the people, to take them over the Jordan, and to give them the land. Caleb is the prince of Judah (Num 13:6; 34:19) and is the son of Hezron, one of Jesus' ancestors (1 Chr 2:9, 18). He is mentioned by Justin alongside Joshua, as one who was sent to spy out the land of Canaan (Justin, *Dial.* 113.1–7 [PG 6:736]).[31] Miriam is the mother of Jesus, while David, Solomon, Hezekiah, and Josiah are all his ancestors (Matt 1:9–10).[32]

6.1. Description of the End and the Appearance of the Messiah

The vision of the clear waters and the dark waters concludes with a description of the end of the world (*shulma dealma*), the apocalyptic drama that will precede it, and the final appearance of the Messiah.

The Second Temple period constitutes the final historical era prior to the end. During it, Zion will be rebuilt, sacrifices will be restored, the priests will return to their service, and the people will again come and praise it. But, in conformity with the outlook of the author, this period is described only briefly, and emphasis is given to the understanding that its glory will be less than that of the period that preceded it (68:6).[33]

The stages of the apocalyptic drama fit those found in the two previous visions: the coming of the End is heralded by the disasters that precede it.

---

[30] Justin, *Dial.* 113 (PG 6:736); and cf. *Dial.* 115 (PG 6:741), where Jesus is identified with Joshua son of Jehozadak, the high priest of Zech 3:1–2, 5; *Barn.* 12:8; Tertullian, *Marc.* 3.7 (PL 2:330–31). Jesus was buried in a grave that was dug for Joshua (Budge, *The Book of the Cave of Treasures*, 236; Daniélou, *Sacramentum Futuri*, 205–16).

[31] Caleb is mentioned by Ephraem Syrus as one who brought the cluster of grapes upon the pole and waited to see the grape, whose wine would comfort all people (*Hnat.* 1.30 [CSCO 186, Syr. 82]).

[32] These people are seen as a prototype of Jesus (Aphraates, *Sermon* 21.8–17 [SC 359:819–30]; *Sermon* 23.4 [SC 359:884–86]; Budge, *Cave of Treasures*, 183, 185).

[33] See, similar to this, *1 En.* 89:73.

When the time is ripe in the world and the harvest of the seed of the evil and the good comes—that is, as the time of the End approaches—the Almighty will bring upon the earth and its inhabitants and its leaders a confusion of spirit and amazement of the heart.

> Behold, the days are coming and it will happen when the time of this world has ripened and the harvest of the seed of the evil ones and the good ones has come that the Mighty One will cause to come over the earth and its inhabitants and its rulers confusion of the spirit and amazement of the heart. (*2 Bar.* 70:2)[34]

As in the first vision (*2 Bar.* 29:2), the holy land (*ara' qadishta*) will protect its inhabitants at that time. After these signs come and the people are all shaken, then will come the time of the Messiah: "after the signs have come of which I have spoken to you before, when the nations are moved and the time of my anointed One comes . . ." (72:2). After he conquers everything in the world and begins to dwell in peace forever upon the throne of his kingdom, then *he will be revealed in a banquet* (bosma) *and rest shall be visible* (73:1).[35]

The author briefly surveys the first stage of his appearance or "the beginning of his appearance," which were discussed extensively in the previous visions. The Messiah will sit upon his royal throne in the heavenly temple[36] with the renewal of creation, the messianic feast (the eschatological Eucharist), and the rest (millennium). But here he emphasizes the background of the garden of Eden even more: healing will descend like dew, and all disease, worry, trouble and sighs will be removed from man. Unlike the case of Adam who sinned, human beings will again enjoy eternal life and will not die before their time. Animals will come from the forest to serve human beings. The serpent and dragons will leave their lairs as if they had become servants of a child.[37] In contrast to the curse of Eve ("with pain shall you bear child"), women will no longer suffer the pains of childbirth when they deliver the fruit of their bodies. In those days the harvesters and the builders will not tire, because that time will be the conclusion of that which is born (corruptible) and

---

[34] This image of the harvest (θερισμός) of weeds and wheat at the End also appears in Matt 13:30, 40–43. The harvest is the end of the world (Matt 13:39; Rev 14:15).

[35] *Bosma* means gladness, delight, felicity, but also banquet (Payne Smith, *Syriac Dictionary*, 38).

[36] See, similar to this, Matt 19:28; Heb 1:8; 8:1; Rev 4:2, 9.

[37] As in Mark 1:13, based on Isa 11:6–8. This prophesy was interwoven within the description of this kingdom of peace (de Jonge, "χρίω," 515, and cf. Isa 65:20–25; Charlesworth, "Jewish Messianism," 247 ["That place and time is *paradise redivivus.*"]). The control over wild beasts represents a return to the Edenic state (Daniélou, "Terre et Paradis," 468).

the beginning of that which is not born (incorruptible). "For that time is the end of that which is corruptible and the beginning of that which is incorruptible" (74:2). In this description, the author continues to rely upon the previously mentioned passage from Irenaeus, upon which he built his description of the fruit of the earth after the beginning of the appearance of the Messiah and the period of a thousand years:

> And all the creatures that enjoy these foods which they receive from the earth will be made peaceful and gentle to one another, and will obey human beings with great obedience. (Irenaeus, *Haer.* 5.33.3 [SC 153:417])[38]

This description of the eschatological redemption integrates well with the two that precede it and completes the description of the Parousia. In the first vision the author describes the End, the disasters that will precede it, the first stage in the appearance of the Messiah, the beginning of his revelation, the messianic Eucharist, the period of a thousand years, his second and final appearance, the resurrection, and the Last Judgment. In the second vision he focuses upon the Messiah's struggle with the antichrist to be conducted before the corruptible world disappears. In the third vision he describes the new heaven and the new earth, the incorruptible and unchangeable world, which will be established upon the Second Parousia. The lightning that takes hold of the cloud and brings it down to earth is the Son of Man, whose coming will be like a thunderbolt that comes from the east and lights up the sky to the west (Matt 24:27; Luke 17:24).[39]

At the conclusion of this vision, the promise given to Baruch by God at the opening of the first vision—that he is about to take away Zion so as to quickly *heal* the world in his time—is realized (20:1–2). With this, he closes the visionary cycle from the literary and conceptual viewpoint. Now, at the end of the third vision, the lightning, which symbolizes the Messiah, takes hold of the cloud, which is the new creation, and brings it down to earth. It lights up the entire world, *heals* all the places that were destroyed by the black waters, and rules the earth. With this, the final victory of the Messiah over death, that is, over Satan, occurs: the curse that had been placed upon Adam and Eve, who were the source of sin, is nullified and nobody dies prematurely. The serpent is enslaved to the child, and women no longer give birth in pain. As in Revelation, there will be eternal life in the creation, and there will no longer be tears, mourning, bereavement, crying, or pain (Rev 21:4).[40]

---

[38] And similarly also in Justin, *Dial.* 81.1–2 (PG 6:668).

[39] The image of the Son of Man is based upon Dan 7:13; cf. Mark 13:26–27; Matt 24:30; Luke 21:27–28.

[40] Cf. 1 Cor 15:25–27, 54.

CHAPTER 6: The Vision of the Waters 197

The twelve rivers that ascend from the sea, surrounding the lightning and submitting to it, symbolize the twelve apostles, to whom Jesus gave the eschatological function of gathering the twelve tribes of the new Israel, who constitute the Christian church in the eschatological age. This church is identified with the heavenly Jerusalem, which will descend from heaven in the future; on its twelve gates are written the names of the twelve tribes of Israel, and on the foundations of its walls are written the names of the twelve messengers of the Lamb, who surround the lightning that symbolizes the new heavenly temple (Rev 21:9ff.; 7:4–8; Matt 19:28; Luke 22:30).[41] With the victory over Satan and the descent of the heavenly Jerusalem, the apocalyptic drama of *Syiac Baruch* attains its full realization.

The three apocalyptic visions present us with the author's view concerning the End and the appearance of the Messiah. But simultaneously, through the symbolism of the vine, the manna, the spring, the messianic feast, and the bright waters, they are intended to arouse in the readers or listeners associations of the two ancient and central sacraments of the Christian church: Eucharist and baptism, both of which bear clear eschatological meaning.

In this respect there is a striking resemblance between *Syriac Baruch* and the Fourth Gospel. Many scholars have noted the sacramental nature of the Gospel of John and its great interest in liturgy. In their opinion, those passages in John that mention water are to be understood in connection with the sacrament of baptism, while those dealing with meals, bread, wine, and the vine are connected with the sacrament of the Eucharist. These two sacraments are represented by symbolic means and are intended to strengthen faith in Christ among the new Christian congregations.[42] This is the reason why, like

---

[41] See twelve baskets miraculously fed five thousand (John 6:13), representing the twelve apostles and the believers (Meeks, *The Prophet-King*, 96; Geyser, "The Twelve Tribes," 397; Charles, "Baruch," 89; Klijn, "Syriac Baruch," 639, ch. 53 n. a). See also the twelve springs in Elim (Exod 15:27; Daniélou, *Sacramentum Futruri*, 149–50). The twelve rivers are incorporated within the typological form of the number 12 that exists in *Syriac Baruch* as a whole (27:1–18; chs. 56–69; cf. Pines, "Notes on the Twelve Tribes in Qumran," 152–54). The members of the Qumran sect are identified with the twelve tribes, as mentioned in the battle of the sons of light with the sons of darkness in an eschatological context, and also in the *Temple Scroll*. Cf. Jaubert, *La Symbolique des Douz*, 457.

[42] Cullmann, *Early Christian Worship*, 37; idem, *The Johannine Circle*, 14, 16; Craig, "Sacramental Interest," 32 ("The Fourth Gospel breathes the intimacy of the cult group"). Brown (*Gospel of John*, cxi-cxiv) mentions the names of those scholars who emphasize this aspect. See also: Dodd, *The Fourth Gospel*, 134–38; Schnackenburg, *Gospel According to St. John*, 160–63; Manns, "Le symbolisme du jardin," 53–54; idem, "Lecture symbolique de Jean 21, 1–11," *Liber Annuus* 36 (1986): 85–89; X. Leon-

the Gospel according to John, *2 Baruch* as a whole, and particularly its final chapters known as the *Epistle of Baruch*, were popular in early Christianity, especially among the Syriac-speaking churches.[43]

Dufour, "Towards A Symbolic Reading of the Fourth Gospel," *NTS* 27 (1981): 444, 451; Daniélou, *Sacramentum Futuri*, 139, 257. Bogaert notes the parallels between Baruch and Revelation, but without drawing any historical conclusion from them (Bogaert, *Apocalypse*, 2:22; cf. 1:231).

[43] L. H. Brockington, "The Syriac Apocalypse of Baruch," in Sparks, *Apocryphal Old Testament*, 835; Charles, *The Apocalypse of Baruch*, xx–xxii; Harris, *The Rest of the Words*, 9–11; Bogaert, *Apocalypse*, 1:160–62. Also significant is the fact that the Ambrosiana Manuscript, which is the only one extant, originated in a Christian milieu, and note also the Arabic MS, which also originated in a Christian milieu and which was written in Christian Arabic (Leemhuise, Klijn, and Gelder, *The Arabic Text*, 4). On the importance of the process of transmission in determining the identity of the work, see R. Kraft, "The Pseudepigrapha in Christianity," in *Tracing the Threads* (ed. J. C. Reeves; Atlanta, Ga., 1994), 57–58; D. Satran, "Biblical Prophets and Christian Legend," 143–49.

Conclusion

An analysis of the traditions describing the destruction of Jerusalem and of the visions portraying the eschatological redemption has revealed the underlying intentions concealed behind the external, pseudobiblical facade of the *Syriac Apocalypse of Baruch* and elucidated those features that connect it to the Christian tradition and set it apart from the Jewish tradition.

The *Syriac Baruch*, in its extant form, is a Christian work, whose internal structure, ideas, and tendencies may only be understood against the background of Christian theology. True, it does not contain any obviously Christian statements, nor is the name of the Christian Messiah mentioned there explicitly; rather, it expresses its outlook in an allusive and subtle way in comparison to other pseudepigraphic works related to it.

But this fact should not mislead us, as it is precisely the absence of explicitly Christian features that may at times serve as the key to the identification and understanding of a work. As D. Satran noted regarding the work *Vitae Prophetorum*:

> Indeed, I have tried to demonstrate . . . that it is precisely the lack of distinctively Christian elements which provides a major clue toward the understanding of the document. There are, nevertheless, indisputably Christian attributes in the work, yet their qualities are diametrically opposed to the concept of "interpolation": they are subtle, confounding simple identification, and so deeply imbedded in the fabric of the texts as to resist extraction. (Satran, *Biblical Prophets,* 76)

Even though the actual historical background against which the plot of *Syriac Baruch* is anchored is the destruction of the Second Temple, and Baruch allegedly expresses the pain of his people over the destruction of Jerusalem and the temple, throughout the entire work there is no real anticipation or longing for the restoration of the temple or for the rebuilding of the historical Jerusalem. The author does not anticipate the restoration of the earthly Jerusalem, as this was by its very nature inferior and intended for destruction. The eternal Jerusalem, which is "engraved upon the hand of God," is not to be found in this world, upon the earth or in the historical Jerusalem, as the prophet Isaiah attempted to portray it in 49:16. This is the heavenly and preexistent Jerusalem, kept with God in the heavens alongside the garden of Eden. It is for the sake of this Jerusalem that the vessels of the temple were also concealed—vessels that will be used in the new temple to be established upon the second coming of Jesus at the end of time. The supernal Jerusalem and the supernal temple are the eternal holy places to be established in the future and for which the author longs. The historical temple is destined for destruction; the true "guardian of the house" abandons it to officiate in the spiritual temple that will be established by God and not by man; its keys are thrown up to heaven so that they may be used in the heavenly temple; the curtain of the temple is the body of Jesus, which was woven by the virgins and which upon its destruction passes over to the nations of the world.

The author of the *Apocalypse of Baruch* presents his eschatological approach in three main visions: the description of the appearance of the Messiah in chs. 24–30; the vision of the cedar, the vine, and the spring in chs. 36–40; and the vision of the cloud with the bright waters and the dark waters in chs. 53, 56–74. These visions depict the apocalyptic drama to take place upon the coming of the End, the disasters that will precede it, the appearance of the Messiah, and the redemption that he will bring in the future to those who believe in him. The three visions complement one another, expressing a consistent and well-formulated apocalyptic approach. They are depicted by means of symbolism connected with the two principal Christian sacraments: the Eucharist, the sacrament based upon the ceremony of the Last Supper, expressing the believer's participation in the sacrifice of the crucified Jesus and the eschatological anticipation of his full return in the Parousia; and baptism, in which the one baptized is united with the death of the Christian Messiah as a means of enjoying renewed life upon his resurrection.

Clear and definite lines separate the approaches and beliefs expressed in *Syriac Baruch* from those of the early Jewish tradition. In the Bible, in the literature of the Second Temple, and in the early layers of talmudic literature there is no apocalyptic messianism; that is to say, there is no drama of the end of days or anticipation of a heavenly Jerusalem that will come in place of the earthly one. The first hints of eschatological messianism appear in the amoraic layers of the Jerusalem Talmud, but it finds fuller expression in the Babylonian Talmud and in the medieval midrashim.

The development of an apocalyptic outlook in Judaism was the result of both internal developments and external influences: the remoteness of the possibility of national redemption in the concrete historical plane fostered the emergence of a supernatural, miraculous messianism bearing apocalyptic characteristics. In addition, the relative weakness of the Jews within Christian society and their tendency to adapt themselves to the milieu and concepts that surrounded them, led in the final analysis to the penetration of Christian influences. These contributed to the increasing distance of Jewish thought in the Middle Ages from its early Palestinian sources and to a blurring of the lines of distinction between it and Christianity regarding the apocalyptic-messianic subject.

This study has confirmed the proximity existing among the various pseudepigraphic and apocalyptic works in terms of worldview, theology, and the concepts used to express this outlook. Literary works reflect the spiritual milieu of the society within which they are composed and from whose conceptual world they derive their symbolism and imagery (Gil, "Studies in the Book of Enoch," 171, 182, 191–192). One may conclude that these works were composed in a close ideological-theological environment, from the same motivations and for the same goals.

There is likewise a definite relationship between *Syriac Baruch* and the literature of the Qumran sect. This proximity indicates the relationship of this literature, whose authors' identity has to date not been sufficiently clarified, to the pseudepigraphic works and to the circle of early Christianity.

The ideological relationship of *Syriac Baruch* to the theology of the Mandaeans and the use it makes of images and symbols that were widespread among them indicate its closeness to certain Gnostic sects. Further testimony to this closeness is provided by the *Paralipomena* (see Appendix), which betrays a close relation to *2 Baruch* in terms of contents and ideology, on the one hand, while expressing definite Gnostic ideas and concepts, on the other.

The connection of *2 Baruch* with the early Christian tradition and its explicit relationship to Christian works, dated from the end of the first century and the first half of the second century CE, confirm the commonly accepted dating of its writing, while its sacramental aspects emphasize its place in the propaganda of the mission conducted by the Christian church during the early centuries of its existence.

APPENDIX

The Tidings of the Christian Resurrection and Its Conditions in *Paralipomena Jeremiae*

Introduction

Paralipomena Jeremiae Prophetae[1] is a pseudepigraphic work that enjoyed great popularity in the Christian world and is exant in numerous manuscripts in various languages, including Greek, Ethiopic, and Armenian.[2] The work was first published in 1866 by A. Dillmann in the Ethiopic version,[3] and two years later M. Ceriani published the text in Greek.[4] In 1889 Rendel Harris published

---

[1] According to the Ethiopic version, "The Rest of the Words of Baruch." The book is sometimes referred to as *4 Baruch, 3 Baruch,* or *2 Baruch.* On the confusion among these names, see Thornhill, "Paraleipomena," 814. References in the following pages will use the designation *P. Jer.*

[2] Opinions differ regarding the original language of the work. Some scholars think that it was written in Greek (thus Charles, *Apocalypse of Baruch,* xviii; Bogaert, *Apocalypse de Baruch* 1:178; Denis, *Introduction,* 71; Wolff, "Irdisches und Himmlisches Jerusalem," 147; Riaud, "Paralipomena," 38). Other scholars posit the existence of a more ancient Hebrew version based, among other things, upon the appearance of the word *Zar* as the title of the strange god in 7:25. (Thus, e.g., Licht, "Paralipomena Jeremiae," 71; Kilpatrick, "Acts vii.52 eleusis," 141; and cf. the list in Wolff, *Jeremia im Frühjudentum und Urchristentums,* 45; and Robinson, "4 Baruch," 414.) The manuscripts are no earlier than the tenth or eleventh century. For a comprehensive list of manuscripts and editions, see the provisional edition in Kraft and Purintun, *Paralipomena Jeremiou;* Bogaert, *Apocalypse,* 1:177–78; Denis, *Introduction,* 71–73, 75. Some of the manuscripts originated in the Eastern church, which used the work in the liturgy for 4 November, the day of commemoration of the destruction of Jerusalem (see Thornhill, "Paraleipomena," 814–15; Riaud, "Paralipomena," 26).

[3] A. Dillmann, "Reliqua Verborum Baruchi," *Chrestomathia Aethiopica* (Leipzig, 1866).

[4] A. M. Ceriani, "Paralipomena Jeremiae prophetae quae in Aetiopica versione dicuntur reliqua verborum Baruchi," *Monumenta sacra et profana ex codicibus praesertim Bibliothecae Ambrosianae* 5.1 (Milan, 1868), 9–18.

the work in a critical edition with an English translation,[5] which remains to this day the most popular edition.

The plot takes place against the background of the conquest of Jerusalem by the Babylonians. God informs Jeremiah of his plan to destroy the city due to the sins of its inhabitants and asks Jeremiah and Baruch to leave before it is besieged by enemies. At God's instruction, Jeremiah conceals the temple vessels and sends the Ethiopian Abimelech outside of the city, to the vineyard of Agrippa (3:10, 15)[6] (εἰς τὸν ἀμπελῶνα τοῦ Ἀγρίππα) to bring back some figs for the sick people in the city. Abimelech does as he is instructed, and thereby earns the privilege of not seeing the conquest of Jerusalem and the exile of the people to Babylonia. After gathering the figs in his basket, Abimelech sits in the shade of a tree to rest a bit. He leans his head upon the basket of figs, falls asleep, and sleeps for sixty-six years. When he awakens, a miracle has taken place for him: the figs in his basket have not dried out nor turned rotten, but are still filled with juice (5:4). He places the basket on his shoulders and returns to Jerusalem, but does not recognize it. He thinks that he has gone the wrong way, but an old man returning from the field assures him that this is indeed Jerusalem, and that Jeremiah had gone into exile with the rest of the people to Babylonia. Abimelech finds it hard to believe that so much time has passed since he was sent to gather the figs, and shows the old man the basket of still-fresh figs. The latter realizes the significance of the miracle and, in order to convince Abimelech of the truth of his words, shows him the fields that have already produced crops[7] while it is not yet the fig season. Abimelech then understands the significance of the things and praises the "God of heaven and of the earth, the rest of the souls of the righteous in every place" (5:32).

An angel leads Abimelech to Baruch, who is lying in his grave, and shows him as well the miraculous figs. In order to tell the exiled Jeremiah of the miracle that befell Abimelech, Baruch composes a letter to Jeremiah in which he specifies the conditions of the return of the exiles: those returning needed to abandon all the acts of the Babylonians and separate themselves from their Babylonian spouses. Whoever does not do so cannot be allowed to enter Jerusalem. The letter is sent via an eagle, together with fifteen figs from Abimelech's basket. The eagle arrives in Babylonia and brings to life a corpse whom Jeremiah and his fellows were burying. At the proper time the exiles

---

[5] Harris, *The Rest of the Words of Baruch: A Christian Apocalypse of the Year 136 A.D.* (London, 1889).

[6] Or to the field ἄγρον, according to MS c from the tenth century.

[7] Thus Harris, *The Rest of the Words*, 5:31, p. 54; Riaud, "Abimeléch," 291. For another reading, "The ripening of the crops *has not* appeared," see Kraft and Purintun, *Paraleipomena Jeremiou*, 27; Robinson, "4 Baruch," 421.

return to Jerusalem. Those who refuse to take upon themselves the specified conditions are not allowed to enter Jerusalem and establish the city of Samaria. The others cross the Jordan River, enter Jerusalem, and offer sacrifices. On the tenth day Jeremiah offers sacrifices by himself, and his soul departs, but is restored to him after three days. Jeremiah sings praises of the coming of Christ, is stoned by the mob, and dies.

Harris considered this to be a Christian work, composed in Jerusalem by a Jewish Christian in the year 136 CE.[8] In his view, it ought to be understood as a call to peace (εἰρηνικόν) towards the Jews on the part of the Christian church in Jerusalem, following the Bar Kokhba rebellion, in light of the prohibition against entering Jerusalem that had been imposed upon them by Hadrian. The Christians proposed that the Jews accept Christian baptism and change their religion, thereby circumventing the prohibition.[9]

Harris's position as to the Christianity of the work was rejected by most scholars. Notwithstanding the presence of patently Christian elements, there was a widespread opinion that the *Paralipomena* was fundamentally a Jewish work. As Jacob Licht observes:

> The *Paralipomena* is a legend concerning the destruction of the First Temple and the Return to Zion. It was written shortly after the destruction of the Second Temple and is suffused with deep pain over the destruction and the exile, and pulses with intense hope for imminent redemption. The subject of the book and the atmosphere reflected therein are adequate proof of its Jewish origin.[10]

---

[8] Cf. A. Dilmann, in his article on the Old Testament Pseudepigrapha (*Encyklopädie für protestantische Teologie und Kirche,* vol. 12 [Leipzig, 1883], 358) already described this work as "christliches Baruch-Büchlein."

[9] Harris (*The Rest of the Words,* 2–5, 11–16) dated it at 136 CE on the basis of the identity found in the work between the destruction of the First Temple and that of the Second Temple in 70 CE with the addition of 66 years that Abimelech slept, after which the return from Exile was expected. A further confirmation of this dating is found in the geographical designation, "the vineyard of Agrippa" (cf. Kohler, "The Pre-Talmudic Haggada," 409). Most scholars, even though they argued with Harris's claims, in the final analysis accepted this approximate dating (Bogaert, *Apocalypse de Baruch,* 1:220). Dennis dates it between 70 and 130 CE (*Introduction,* 75); G. Delling, "Jüdische Lehre und Frömmigkeit," 3; Wolff, *Jeremia im Frühjudentum,* 45; Wolff, "Irdisches und Himmlisches Jerusalem," 145; Kilpatrick, "Acts vii.52 eleusis," 141. Riaud ("Paralipomena," 40), dates it between 118 and 132 CE; this period fits, in his opinion, the sympathetic attitude of the author to the Samaritans and the hope expressed in the work for the rapid reconstruction of the temple, since the end of the period of seventy years of exile was near. See also Riaud, "Les Samaritains," 150–52. Similarly, Herzer (*Die Paralipomena Jeremiae,* 177–78) dates it at 130 CE; Robinson, "4 Baruch," 414.

[10] Licht, "Paralipomena," 66. Harris's stance was rejected from the beginning by

According to this view, the work was later subjected to a certain Christian reworking or editing. The Christian redactor added to the Jewish work his own conclusion (9:10–32), in which he relates how Jeremiah was stoned because he prophesied the death and resurrection of Jesus, and even inserted certain Christian interpolations in the body of the work itself.[11]

Recently, a number of researchers have again come to support Harris's position. While P. Bogaert rejected the explanation proposed by Harris concerning the book's historical background, he accepted his opinion regarding its ideological identity, arguing that it was an esoteric Christian-Gnostic work addressed to Jewish Christians describing the conditions of entry into any Jewish-Christian congregation.[12] Bogaert's approach was continued by M. Philonenko, who examined several of the central concepts and approaches of the work, concluding that its author was a Jewish Christian. He held that the work is to be understood against the background of approaches and concepts that were widespread among Gnostic, baptist, syncretistic and esoteric groups in the East, particularly among the Mandaeans.[13] A similar view was supported by M. de Jonge who called for a new analysis of the work's theological identity and authorship.[14]

In this appendix I examine the theological identity of the work while clarifying one of its central ideas: the resurrection of the dead. The central issue to be discussed here is whether this idea is to be explained against the background of ideas and conceptions that were common in contemporary Judaism, or

---

Schürer, *Geschichte des Jüdischen Volkes*, 3:286; Charles, "Baruch," xviii; and Frey, "L'Apocalypse Syriaque de Baruch," 455. For a list of scholars taking this position, see Wolff, *Jeremia*, 45 n. 1. Cf. Denis, *Introduction*, 74; Notscher, "Paralipomena Jeremiae," 895; Kohler, "The Pre-Talmudic Haggada," 407–9; Wolff, "Irdisches und Himmlisches Jerusalem," 147; Riaud, "Paralipomena," 39; Heller, "Éléments, Parallèles et Origine," 205 no. 1; Kilpatrick, "Acts vii.52 eleusis," 141; Delling, "Jüdische Lehre," 2–3, 68; Robinson, "4 Baruch," 414–16, who divides the Jewish part into three levels; Herzer, *Die Paralipomena Jeremiae*, 30–32.

[11] J. Herzer, "Direction in Difficult Times: How God is Understood in the *Paralipomena Jeremiae*," *JSP* 22 (2000): 9–30; J. Riaud, "The Figure of Jeremiah in the *Paralipomena Jeremiae Prophetae*: His Originality; His 'Christianization' by the Christian Author of the Conclusion (9.10–32), *JSP* 22 (2000): 31–44.

[12] Bogaert, *Apocalypse*, 1:216–17. See also the criticism of Wintermute, "Gerhard Delling, Jüdische Lehre und Frömmigkeit."

[13] Philonenko, "Simples Observations." Against Philonenko see J. Herzer, "Die Paralipomena Jeremiae – eine christlich-gnostische Schrift?" *JSJ* 30 (1999), 25–39.

[14] M. de Jonge, "Remarks in the Margin of the Paper 'The Figure of Jeremiah in the Paralipomena Jeremiae,'" *JSP* 22 (2000): 45–49 [a response to J. Riaud; see n. 11 above].

whether it reflects tendencies and beliefs that were widespread in Christianity of the second century CE—the assumed period of the work's composition.

The Promise of Resurrection

The promise of resurrection to be enjoyed by the believers forms a central axis throughout the length of the work, connecting its various units into a well-structured theological and programmatic unity.

The author exemplifies and concretizes this idea by using four scenes of bodily and personal resurrection.

The resurrection of the Ethiopian Abimelech, which opens the narrative plot, and that of Jeremiah, with which it closes, lies at the focus of the work and constitutes the clearest and most outspoken manifestation of resurrection. Between these two scenes unravels the story of the return from the Babylonian exile, interwoven with the resurrection of Baruch, who rises from his grave, and that of the anonymous dead man whom the eagle raises from death, concretizing the resurrection promised to all.

The Sleep of Abimelech

The figure chosen to be the hero of the story, Abimelech, is a reincarnation of Ebed-melech the Ethiopian, mentioned in the Bible as the one who saved Jeremiah from the pit of mire and whom Jeremiah promised to reward by saving him when Jerusalem fell to its enemies (Jer 38:1–13; 39: 15–18; *P. Jer.* 3:12–13). In accordance with this promise, he is sent outside of the city and does not fall into captivity.

The story of Abimelech's sleep and the accompanying miracle of the figs form the central theme on which all the plot of this work is built and in which its theological tendencies are anchored.

Many scholars have noted the similarity between the story of Abimelech's sleep and similar stories of sleep that were common in the Jewish and Greek tradition; in particular, they noted its similarity to the talmudic traditions telling of the sleep of Honi the Circle Drawer.[15] Abimelech's sleep is interpreted by them as a midrash on Ps 126:1, which is mentioned in the tradition of Honi the Circle Drawer: "When the Lord restored the fortunes of Zion we were like those who dream." For them, the figure of Abimelech in the

---

[15] See *y. Taʿan.* 3.9 (66d); *b. Taʿan.* 23a; *Midrash Shoher Tov* on Ps 126:1; Kohler, "Pre-Talmudic Haggada," 416; Licht, "Paralipomena," 69; Bogaert, *Apocalypse,* 1:196–98; Heller, "Sept Dormants," 203–7 (Heller cites additional parallels to the legend of the long sleep, 190–97, 212, 215–19, 417). Cf. Herzer, *Die Paralipomena Jeremiae,* 92ff.; Riaud, "Abimelech: Le singulier dormant des Paralipomenes de Jeremie le Prophete," 292. For an analysis of the talmudic traditions on the Circle-Drawer and his sleeping, see Efron, "The Hasmonean Kingdom and Simeon ben Shetah," 237–44.

Paralipomena exemplifies the task of the "dreamers," and the exile is understood as sleep. The author wished to console his contemporaries, hinting to them that the period of Jerusalem's desolation and the exile of the Jewish people would pass as quickly as a dream, just like the sleep of Abimelech.[16]

There seems no doubt that the author of the *Paralipomena* utilized, *inter alia*, the tradition of Honi the Circle Drawer. The similarities between the two traditions are obvious. In both, the hero departed the city and was spared seeing the destruction of the temple. Likewise, both Abimelech and Honi fell asleep for about seventy years and, upon awakening, realized that the world had changed. But comparison between the two traditions specifically brings out the difference between them. The early Palestinian tradition in the Palestinian Talmud does not refer to Honi the Circle Drawer, the noted pietist of the Hasmonean period, but to one of his distant ancestors who fell asleep "close to the destruction of the temple" and awoke after it was rebuilt. In reward for his righteousness he was privileged to sleep throughout the seventy dark years of the destruction of the First Temple (Jer 25:11; 29:10), realizing through his personal destiny the verse "When the Lord restored the fortunes of Zion we were like those who dream" (126:1).[17]

Unlike the *Paralipomena*, the Palestinian talmudic tradition reflects the concrete historical background of the destruction of the First Temple, the Babylonian exile, and the return to Zion. In this tradition, unlike that involving Abimelech, Honi's ancestor awakens, not to the destroyed Jerusalem or to the heavenly Jerusalem, but to the earthly Jerusalem of Second Temple times and, at its focus, the Second Temple.

Abimelech's sleep is unrelated to the historical reality of the destruction of the temple and the exile. The author used the motif of a sleep lasting for many years, which he found in the Jewish and pagan tradition, in order to weave round it the idea of the resurrection.

Abimelech's sleep is the Christian sleep of death, the sleep of rest (ἀνάπαυσις), while his awakening from it (ἐξυπνίζειν) symbolizes the resurrection to be enjoyed by the believing righteous upon the Parousia, as

---

[16] Wolff, "Irdisches und Himmlisches Jerusalem," 147–48; Licht, "Paralipomena," 69; Riaud, "Paralipomena," 35.

[17] Efron, "The Hasmonean Kingdom," 240–41. The Babylonian version removed the aggadah from its original roots, erased the figure of the old Honi from the time of the destruction, and conflated his story with the biography of Honi the Circle-Drawer set in the Hasmonean period. Hence its main justification was eliminated: the pleasant homily on the biblical psalm was eliminated, and the seventy years of sleep no longer make sense. It is not clear what aroused Honi's doubt regarding the veracity of the verse, why a carob tree requires seventy years until it yields fruit, and why Honi was punished and died through being lonely and abandoned.

indicated by the terms used in the work, all of which are taken from the Christian lexicon: ἀναπαύω (5:1, 26); κλίνω (5:1, 26); ὑπνόω (5:1, 5, 9, 10); κοιμάω (5:4, 5, 26); ἐξυπνίζω (5:2, 5, 26; 9:13); ἐγείρω (5:10).[18]

The term ἐξυπνίζω is a technical one, indicating the awakening (based upon Dan 12:2) from the sleep of death and the entry into eternal life.[19] This meaning is clearly implied by the blessing recited by Abimelech to the "God of heaven and of the earth, the rest of the souls of the righteous in every place" (ἡ ἀνάπαυσις τῶν ψυχῶν τῶν δικαίων ἐν παντὶ τόπῳ; 5:32). According to the Christian conception, faith in Jesus is considered as rest (based upon Ps 95:11), and the dead who believe in Jesus remain in this intermediate state until they rise to life.[20]

Abimelech is the prototype of the righteous everywhere, as the old man says to Abimelech: "O, my son, you are a righteous man (δίκαιος ἄνθρωπος), and God did not want you to see the desolation of the city, so he brought this stupor upon you" (5:28).[21]

---

[18] See κλίνειν (Matt 8:20; Luke 9:58; John 19:30); ὕπνος (John 11:11–13); κοιμᾶσθαι (Matt 27:52; John 11:11–12; Acts 7:60; 1 Cor 15:18, 20; 1 Thess 4:13–14); and the verb ἐγείρω, which is the usual verb used in the NT for resurrection from the dead (Matt 9: 25; 10:8; 14:2; 16:21; 17:9; Mark 12:26; John 2:22; etc.).

[19] Philonenko, "Paralipomena," 167–68; Riaud, "Abimelech: Le singulier dormant," 293–94; Delling, "Jüdische Lehre," 30; Herzer, *Paralipomena Jeremiae*, 108ff. The reference to God as ἀνάπαυσις is also found in Gnostic writings (e.g., *Ps.-Clem.* H III: 72.1 in Hennecke, *New Testament Apocrypha* [1964], 2:557). This is also the term commonly used for Jesus in the *Gospel of Thomas* (Herzer, *Paralipomena Jeremiae*, 107 n. 337).

[20] Matt 11:28. Thus is depicted also the death of the believers in the Lord (Rev 14:13–14; 6:11). Cf. the parallel term, κατάπαυσις (Heb 3:11–4:12; Acts 7:49); this is the rest prior to the resurrection, as expressed in the wearing of robes that were washed in the blood of the lamb (Rev 7:9–17; *L.A.B.* 3:10; 19:12; 28:10; *4 Ezra* 7:32, 75; *Jub.* 23:31; *1 En.* 91:10; 92:3; 100:5; *2 Bar.* 30:1; 85:11). Death as sleep also appears in the HB (Isa 26:19; Jer 51:39, 57; Ps 13:4; Job 3:13; Dan 12:2, but only as a figure of speech). See Wolff, "Irdisches und himmlisches Jerusalem," 151ff.; Cullmann, *Immortality and Resurrection*, 39 n. 33.

[21] One may assume that his name was changed from Ebed-melech to Abimelech in accordance with his function here as a prototype of Jesus and of the Christian believer in general. The choice of the Ethiopian Abimelech/Ebed-melech as the example and prototype for the Christian believer derives, first of all, from his relation to Jeremiah and to the historical background of the destruction of the First Temple and the Babylonian exile, in which the work is rooted. However, he is also intended to be reminiscent of the Ethiopian eunuch, who was among the first believers in Jesus from among the nations, to whom Philip conveyed the faith in Jesus the Messiah son of God, and whom Philip even baptized (Acts 8:26–39).

Abimelech's sleep of rest and his awakening from it are closely connected with the miracle of the figs. The preservation of the figs symbolizes the physical resurrection and the eternity promised to the body of the righteous in reward for his righteousness. As Baruch says in the prayer that he recites after rising from his grave upon seeing these figs:

> You are the God who bestows a reward [on] those who love you.[22] Prepare yourself, my heart; rejoice and be glad in your tabernacle, saying to your fleshly dwelling, 'Your sorrow has been turned to joy.' For the Mighty One is coming and will raise you [i.e., bring you to life, ἀρεῖ] in your tabernacle, for sin has not taken root in you. Be refreshed within your tabernacle, in your virgin faith,[23] and believe that you will live. Look at this basket of figs; for behold, they are sixty-six years old and they have not withered nor do they stink, but they are dripping with milk. This will it be for you, my flesh, if you do the things commanded you by the angel of righteousness. He who preserved the basket of figs, the same one will again preserve you by his power. (6:5–6)

While the author draws a distinction between the body, the fleshly home (σαρκικός οἶκος), which he compares to the sanctuary (σκήνωμα), and the soul, that is freed with death from its dwelling place (tent; tabernacle), according to the Pauline approach,[24] he also addresses the flesh and promises it eternity, as illustrated by the basket of figs. The figs symbolize bodiliness, the fleshly home, the dwelling place of the soul, which shall neither be worn out nor rot, but will be preserved for the personal resurrection promised to the righteous who love the Lord and have no sin, whose faith is virginal.

---

[22] According to the Ethiopic MS C, τοῖς ἁγίοις αὐτοῦ. For variant readings see Harris, *The Rest of the Words*, 55; Kraft and Purintun, *Paraleipomena Jeremiou*, 29.

[23] Thus Harris, *The Rest of the Words*, 55, or: "in your virgin flock." Eusebius cites the words of Hegesippus, who uses this expression in relation to the Christian church, which remained virginal and uncorrupted until the period of Trianus, when the first heresies emerged (*Hist. eccl.* 3.32.7 [LCL 153:267–77]). The author of *Paralipomena* may be alluding to that virginal aspect (see Bogaert, *Apocalypse*, 1:210–11). This expression relates to the polemic that possibly exists in this work with the heretical sects. On the Christianity of the expression, see also Robinson, "4 Baruch," 415. In *Odes Sol.* 33, the "complete virgin" is Wisdom or Christ who speaks as Wisdom and is considered as light. The belief in a virgin of light is attributed to Bardesanes (see Harris and Mingana, *Odes and Psalms of Solomon*, 375–76). See further on virginity below.

[24] 1 Cor 15:42–54; 2 Cor 5:1–10; 2 Pet 1:13, 14 ("I think it right, as long as I am in this body [Gk: tent], to arouse you by way of reminder, since I know that the putting off of my body [Gk: tent] will be soon, as our Lord Jesus Christ showed me"); *Epistle to Diognetus* 6:8 (LCL 25:363); Eusebius, *Hist. eccl.* 3.31.1 (LCL 153:268). On the significance of this passage, see further below.

The figs are the symbol of the eternity embodied in Abimelech, who did not change or age during the course of his sixty-six years of sleep. The old man calls him "my son" (5:31), and Baruch and Abimelech recognize one another immediately as if they had not aged. All those figures in this story who participate in the miracle of the figs are promised resurrection: Abimelech, Baruch, Jeremiah, the anonymous corpse revived by the eagle, as well as the old man who explains to Abimelech what has happened to him. The figs are the guarantors of the bodily resurrection of the holy righteous ones that will take place in the heavenly Jerusalem.

The figs plucked by Abimelech are found in the vineyard or field in which Abimelech also sleeps, and in which he too rises to life. The metaphor of the vineyard (ὁ ἀμπελών) which in Greek is identical to the vine, (ἡ ἄμπελος), alludes to paradise.[25]

The vine or vineyard are symbols of the Christian Messiah and his congregation and occupy an important place in the theological symbolism of the early church. Jesus is the true vine, as he himself declares: "I am the true vine (ἐγώ εἰμι ἡ ἄμπελος), and my Father is the vinedresser" (John 15:1).[26] The vine is identified with the tree of life that was in the garden of Eden (Rev 2:7; 22:2) and constitutes a *topos* for Christ as a source of the life of the church and its sacraments.[27]

---

[25] Even if we accept the reading "field" (ἀγρός), on the basis of the Ethiopic manuscript, the scene could take place in paradise. The field may be identified with paradise. Thus in *4 Ezra* "campus" is identified with paradise, in which flowers and satisfying vegetation grow as foods (9:26), and in the field the heavenly Jerusalem is revealed to the visionary: "Therefore I told you to remain in the field where no house had been built. For I knew that the Most High would reveal these things to you. Therefore I told you to go into the field where there was no foundation of any building, for no work of man's building could endure in a place where the city of the Most High was to be revealed" (10:51–54). On flowers in paradise, see Ephraem Syrus, *Sermons on Paradise*, 9:3–9 (CSCO, 174; Scr. Syri 78, p. 36); *2 Bar.* 37:1.

[26] See also the exegeses connecting the image of the vine with Jesus (based upon Ps 80:9, 18; Ezek 17) in Brown, *The Gospel According to John*, 670–71. Cf. *4 Ezra* 5:23. Ephraem Syrus compares the cluster of grapes brought by the spies upon their return from Canaan (Num 13:23) to Christ on the cross (CSCO 186, Syr. 82, *Hnat.* 1.3; Murray, *Symbols of Church and Kingdom*, 104–30).

[27] Aphraates begins the history of the blessing contained in the grape, based upon Isa 65:8–9, by saying that he is speaking of the garden of Eden. Although not explicitly stated, Aphraates implies that the grape itself comes from paradise (Aphraates, *Sermon* 23 [SC 359:875ff.], "Concerning the Seed of the Grape"). Similarly, Ephraem Syrus describes the cluster of grapes as granting life to all (Ephraem Syrus, *Hymnes sur le paradis*, 6:8 (SC 137:85). Cf. Irenaeus's exegesis connecting the abundance of the fruit

The fig is also connected with the garden of Eden. According to the biblical story, Adam and Eve made themselves loincloths out of fig leaves so as to cover their nakedness (Gen 3:7). For that reason, in Christian tradition the fig tree, and especially the fig leaves, became a symbol of original sin and of the presence of sin in this world generally.

Thus, in the *Apocalypse of Moses,* immediately after Eve violated the prohibition and ate the forbidden fruit, all of the trees except for the fig tree shed their leaves (out of shame); hence, the fig was the only tree from whose leaves Adam and Eve could make themselves belts with which to cover their shame:

> I looked for leaves in my region so that I might cover my shame, but I did not find (any) from the trees of Paradise, since while I ate, the leaves of all the trees of my portion fell, except (those) of the fig tree only. And I took its leaves and made for myself skirts; they were from the same plants of which I ate. (*Apoc. Mos.* 20:4–5)

The fig leaves, which covered up the consequences of the sins of Adam and Eve, became a symbol for sinful Judaism. It is in this sense that the fig tree cursed by Jesus upon his entrance into Jerusalem appears: this is the fig that has only leaves, and that will never again yield fruit (Mark 11:12–14, 20–22; Matt 21:18–20).[28]

The Christian tradition identified the tree of knowledge from whose fruits Adam and Eve were forbidden to eat with the fig tree. Hence the fruit of the fig tree, and not only its leaves, can bring about sin.[29]

---

of the vine and grain to paradise (Irenaeus, *Haer.* 5:33, 3–4 [SC 153:411–19], and also Eusebius, *Hist. eccl.* 3.39 [LCL 153:291]; Cyril of Jerusalem, *Catechesis* 14.11: "his place of burial was a garden. And what was planted [was] a vine" κῆπος ἦν ὁ τόπος τῆς ταφῆς. Καὶ ἄμπελος ἡ φυτευθεῖσα [PG 33:837]).

[28] *Apoc. Pet.* 2 (Elliott, *Apocryphal New Testament,* 600–700). This work is dated to the first half of the second century CE (Ibid., 595). See also Cyril of Jerusalem: "He came at a time when eating food was not available. Who does not know that during the winter the fig does not bear fruit, but only useless leaves? Everyone knows this. Did not Jesus know? But even though he knew he went to seek. He knew that he would not find, but he did so in order that the form of the curse would be upon the leaves alone" (*Catechesis* 13.18 [PG 33:796, A]). On the fig as symbolic of sin in Augustine, see G. Bonner, "The Figure of Eve in Augustine's Theology," *Studia Patristica* 33 (1997): 28.

[29] *Apoc. Mos.* 20; *Testament of Adam* (*OTP* 1:994); Ephraem Syrus, *Hymnen de Paradiso* 12.10 (CSCO 174; Scr. Syri 78; p. 2); J. Riaud, "Abimelech, Personnage-Clé des Paralipomena Jeremiae?" 177 n. 34; C. H. Hunzinger, "σύκη," 752. The dried-out fig tree symbolizes Judaism, which will remain in such a state until the end of the world (Origen, *Comm. Matt.* [PG 13:1460]; Cyril of Jerusalem, *Catachesis* 13.18 (PG 33:793–96). Figs serve in the Bible as a symbol of national redemption in the vision of the two mandrakes seen by Jeremiah after the exile of Jehoiachin (Jer 24:1–10). The fig is also a symbol of peace and security and appears alongside the vine (Isa 34:4; Jer 5:17;

But upon the atonement of the original sin by Jesus, the second Adam, the fig is transformed into a symbol of resurrection and the eternity of the body. In contrast to the weakness of Adam's flesh and its transitory nature, Jesus represents the eternity of the body, which is also symbolized by the fig. The fruit of the fig tree thus bears a double meaning in Christianity: on the one hand it symbolizes sin, but it is also identified with the fruit of the tree that brings about the distinction between good and evil, it has the power to bring healing, and it symbolizes the resurrection.

This double meaning of the fig tree is noted by Ephraem Syrus. He compares the tree of knowledge, identified with the fig, with the inner curtain of the sanctuary, hidden from Adam and Eve:

> Its fruit is the key of righteousness that opens the eyes of the sinners so that they may repent. But their eyes were actually closed, so they might not see the splendor and the depression: thus might not see the splendor of that sanctuary that is within, nor see the shame of their bodies. These are the two signs (notes) that he hid (covered) in the tree and he put it as a judge between the two sides. And when Adam dared to eat it, these two signs quickly spread within him, removing the two veils which were on his eyes. He saw the splendor of the Holy of Holies and was astonished. He saw his own disgrace and was ashamed, groaned, and moaned, because the two signs which had become known to him were a source of pain. (*Hymns on Paradise*, 3.5–7 [*Hymnes sur le paradis*, 55–56])

On the one hand, the tree of knowledge symbolizes holiness, being the veil that covers the Holy of Holies; on the other, its fruit leads to seeing sin in the naked bodies.

The two meanings of the fig tree in Christianity follow from this. It is both a tree symbolizing the curse of the people of Israel, and one whose fruit symbolizes the resurrection. It is in this eschatological sense that one needs to understand the meaning of the figs in the Paralipomena.[30]

8:13; Hos 2:14; 9:10; Joel 1:7; 2:22; Ps 105:33; Cant 2:13 ["The fig tree puts forth its figs, and the vines are in blossom"], which is interpreted as referring to the redemption of Israel and the days of Messiah [Bowman, *The Gospel of Mark*, 221]). Each man sitting under or eating of his own vine and fig tree is a well-known symbol for peace and security (1 Kgs 5:5; Mic 4:4; Zech 3:10); the fig is a symbol of piety (Prov 27:18); and figs have healing qualities (2 Kgs 20:7; Isa 38:21). The identification of the forbidden fruit from which Adam and Eve ate as the fruit of the fig tree also penetrated into Jewish tradition (see *Gen. Rab.* 15:7 [ed. Theodor-Albeck, 140–41]).

[30] Figs appear in a similar sense in the *Book of Adam and Eve* (S. C. Malan, *The Book of Adam and Eve, also called the Conflict of Adam and Eve with Satan* [London-Edinburgh, 1882]). The fig is a divine fruit, bringing blessing from God (ch. 66); it is a holy fruit (ch. 62; cf. T. Kronholm, *Motifs from Genesis 1–11 in the Genuine Hymns of Ephrem, the Syrian* [Uppsala, 1978], 111). It may be in this sense that Jesus mentions

Unlike the fig tree cursed by Jesus when he entered Jerusalem, that would never again bear fruit, in his entry into the heavenly Jerusalem Abimelech presents other figs, that grow outside of Jerusalem and will never again wither.

Like Jesus (Mark 11:13), Abimelech also arrives in Jerusalem before the beginning of the fig season. The blossoming of the fig tree is among the signs of the End, as Jesus says in the Synoptic apocalypse ("From the fig tree learn its lesson: as soon as its branch becomes tender and puts forth its leaves, you know that summer is near" [Mark 13:28–29; Matt 24:32ff.; Luke 21:29–31]),[31] while the ripening of the fruit is already [a sign of] the end of the world (Mark 4:29; Matt 13:39; John 4:35–38; Rev 14:15). But in the present work the figs in Abimelech's basket drip juice and are ripe even before the beginning of the fig season, that is, before the coming of the End. The ripe figs in Abimelech's basket even before the coming of the End emphasize the Christian view, according to which the eschatological age already began upon Jesus' first appearance; this is an eschatology that is already realized in the present, that will only reach its completion in the Parousia. According to this view, the paradise to be established upon Jesus' second coming is the realization of the garden of Eden planted by Christ in his first earthly appearance. As Daniélou says: "The christological paradise is the symbol of the eschatological paradise."[32]

Abimelech's sleep, the intermediary sleep of the Christian believer, like his resurrection, is thus realized in this paradise, in the heavenly Jerusalem, to which God leads not only Abimelech, but also all of the believing saints, including the old man who believed in the miracle of the figs (in exchange for which Abimelech gave him several of the figs and blessed him, saying "May God guide you with [his] light to the city above, Jerusalem" [*P. Jer.* 5:34]), and Jeremiah (who returns with the faithful to the heavenly Jerusalem after he too is sent fifteen figs).

---

the fig tree under which he saw Nathanael, who is called a true Israelite who is without guile (John 1:47–50).

[31] The word קיץ (summer) refers to the harvest of summer fruits, including figs (see Jastrow, *Dictionary*, 1366; *b. B. Bat.* 28a; *t. Ned.* 4.1).

[32] Daniélou, "Terre et Paradis," 456. Consistent with this approach, the Gospels depict the return of the garden of Eden upon the appearance of Jesus. Jesus himself says so (Matt 11:5; Luke 7:22, showing by word and deed that his appearance is the realization of paradise, according to its portrayal in Isa 35:5ff.). The version of Mark concerning the tests also portrays Jesus as returning man to the beginning of his creation and to his status in the garden of Eden. In Mark 7:37 the crowd praises him, citing passages from Gen 1:31 and Isa 35:5. All these passages express the certainty that Jesus is the one who will restore the garden of Eden and that this restoration is already blossoming at his earthly appearance.

These intentions are confirmed by the Christian work known as the *Jeremiah Apocryphon*, which is based upon the *Paralipomena* and clarifies its intentions.[33] Abimelech's sleep is depicted there, not as death, but as a peaceful rest: "Thou shalt not die, but shalt live until the Lord turns away His wrath. The sun shall nurture thee and the firmament shall rear thee, and the earth on which thou shalt sleep shall give thee rest, and the stone shall protect thee from the cold of the winter and the heat of the summer, and thy soul shall be in joy and pleasure for seventy years until thou seest Jerusalem in its glory and rebuilt as it was before" (Mingana, "New Jeremiah Apocryphon," 363).

That the new Jerusalem seen by Abimelech after he awakes is the heavenly Jerusalem follows from the description of the ascent of Jeremiah and his people to the city after their return from exile. Jeremiah rides on his horse while dressed in royal raiment and wearing a crown on his head. He is accompanied by horses, mules, camels, and supplies for the journey, and by twelve servants and all the Hebrews, who *go up* with him to Jerusalem with their mouths filled with prayers and songs of thanksgiving. They arrive in Jerusalem in the month of Nissan, that is, on the eve of Passover, and enter Jerusalem with palm fronds and carrying cuttings of fragrant bushes and olive branches. The description of Jeremiah's entrance into Jerusalem is based upon Jesus' festive and royal entrance to Jerusalem during the Passover festival, according to John 12:13–15, riding on an ass surrounded by his twelve disciples while palm branches waved to greet him.

The temple entered by Jeremiah is not the historic temple, as that was destroyed by the Babylonians, but the heavenly temple in the heavenly Jerusalem, established after the end of the world. This fact follows explicitly from Jeremiah's words to Abimelech in their meeting in Jerusalem: "The Lord has overshadowed you with his holy arm and placed you in a refreshing sleep till you saw Jerusalem reconstructed and glorified for the second time" (Mingana, 391).

In the *Paralipomena*, Abimelech's sleep continues for sixty-six years, from the conquest of Jerusalem until the eve of the return of the exiles from Babylonia, headed by Jeremiah. How are we to understand this number? R. Harris suggested that one may infer from this number the date of the composition of the book (i.e., the period of time that had passed between the

---

[33] Mingana, "New Jeremiah Apocryphon." This work is dated to the second–seventh centuries. This work refers explicitly to the Christian Messiah and to the belief in the Trinity, and incorporates ideas from the NT. It was also the Christian church that preserved this work. The extant Coptic version was copied in a Christian monastery and became part of the Christian liturgy (R. Harris, in Mingana, "New Jeremiah Apocryphon," 331; Kuhn, "A Coptic Jeremiah Apocryphon," 102; Wolff, *Jeremia*, 54). For more on this work, see above, chs. 2.4; 3.2.

destruction of the Second Temple and the writing of the book in 136 CE: viz., 70 + 66 years), at which time the author anticipated the realization of the redemptive tidings expressed in his work.[34] Harris is correct in the theological significance that he attributes to this number. The duration of Abimelech's sleep is clearly based upon Jeremiah's prophecy of seventy years,[35] and it is possible that the author altered the period of time of seventy years until the redemption, which is anchored in both the Jewish and Christian tradition, in order to adjust it to the date of writing of his work.[36] However, this change may have been done for other reasons. The *Paralipomena* has an explicit missionary-propaganda purpose: it calls upon pagans to accept the Christian faith while promising the resurrection of the dead. But it simultaneously hints that the time for this resurrection, which is meant to take place at the End, has not yet arrived. While it is true that sixty-six years have passed and the fruit is ripe—that is, the beginning of the end has arrived—the season of the figs, whose ripening indicates the actual End, has not yet come.

Abimelech's resurrection, like that of Jeremiah, occurs during the month of Nisan, that is, at the time of Passover, as implied by the old man's reply to Abimelech (5:34).[37] It thus fits in well with the author's tendency to build the plot as a prefiguration of the new Exodus, like the association of the Exodus with the christological drama in the New Testament, anticipating the making of the new covenant with the sacrifice of Jesus and the resurrection on Passover.

Baruch's Resurrection

The centrality of the assurance of individual, bodily resurrection finds clear expression further on. Abimelech leaves the city, and an angel comes and takes him to where Baruch is lying in his grave. Baruch is the second figure to be restored to life in this work and, like Abimelech and the old man, is likewise

---

[34] Harris, "Paralipomena," 13; and cf. other suggestions in J. Herzer, *Paralipomena*, 95.

[35] Jer 25:11; 29:10; Zech 1:12; 7:5; Dan 9:2; 2 Chr 36:21; Josephus, *Ant.* 10.184; 11.2; 20.233; *J.W.* 5.389.

[36] In several versions of the *Paralipomena* the number is changed to 70 years. See Harris, *The Rest of the Words*, 5, 13; Denise, *Introduction*, 70 n. 4; and Mingana, "New Jeremiah Apocryphon," 340, 389; but they all agree that the number 66 is original and is found in the earliest and most reliable manuscripts (cf. Licht, "Paralipomena," 70).

[37] The old man answers Abimelech's question as to what month of the year it is by saying that it is the month of Nissan—according to several MSS, the twelfth of the month of Nissan (Harris, *The Rest of the Words*, 54; Herzer, *Die Paralipomena*, 111 n. 357; cf. Neh 2:1). The number 12 may appear here as a symbol of the twelve tribes.

seen as an example of the Christian believer: he is referred to by the eagle as "the steward of the faith" (*P. Jer.* 7:2) and by Jeremiah as "the righteous" (7:23). Like Abimelech and the old man, he too participated in the miracle of the figs; after Baruch saw the figs covered in Abimelech's basket, he understood the significance of the miracle. In his prayer, he interprets the vision of the fresh figs as a sign of the recompense (μισθαποδοσία) that God gives to the righteous who love him: he preserves their bodies until the resurrection, just as he preserves the figs.

Baruch's grave symbolizes the dwelling place of the Christian believer, who awaits the occurrence of the resurrection that is to take place, according to early Christian sources, after the separation that Christ will make by means of his sword between the dead and the living.[38] Baruch is counted among the "congregation of the living among the dead," in the words of the *Odes of Solomon* (42:14). These are the souls that are imprisoned in Sheol, whom Christ will free and separate them from the dead: "And [your right hand] chose them from the graves, and separated them from the dead" (*Odes Sol.* 22:8–10). The belief in Christ's dividing sword that will distinguish at the end of days between the living who believed in him and the dead is based upon Matt 10:34 and Luke 12:51, and appears in similar contexts in other early Christian sources. Thus, for example, in the *Pseudo-Clementines,* Peter speaks of Christ as "the true prophet" who will separate those who are living from among the dead by means of his Logos, which is like a sword:

> When he stretches forth the Logos like a sword he destroys ignorance by means of knowledge, as when he cuts and separates the living from the dead.[39]

Similarly in Aphraates:

> When the time comes for the end of the world and the time of the resurrection will come, the Holy Spirit that has been preserved in its purity will receive great power, in accordance with its nature. And it will come before Christ and stand next to the gate of the grave yard, where those people are buried who preserve in purity and await the trumpet. (Sixth Sermon, *De Monachis* 4.4 [PS 1:296])

---

[38] Based upon Ezek 37:12 ("Thus says the Lord God: Behold, I will open your graves, O my people; and I will bring you home into the land of Israel").

[39] *Ps.-Clem.* H XI 19.2 (*Die Pseudoklementinen* [ed. B. Rehm; GCS 42; 2d ed., ed. F. Paschke; Berlin, 1969], 1:164; *New Testament Apocrypha* [ed. W. Schneemelcher; Cambridge, 1991], 2:532). In *Paralipomena* 6:14 and similarly in the *Pseudo-Clementines,* the separation is interpreted as acquisition of "knowledge." On Christ's dividing sword as the basis for the demand to separate from their Babylonian marriage partners, see further below.

Ephraem Syrus likewise compares the water of baptism to the sword of the Lord that separates between the living and the dead: "See the sword of the Lord in the water which separates sons and fathers; this is a living sword, for it separates between the living and the dead" (*Epiphanea* 8.16 [CSCO 186; Scr. Syri 82, p. 173].[40]

The Resurrection of the Anonymous Dead

At the angel's advice, Baruch sends a letter to Jeremiah via an eagle, together with fifteen figs from Abimelech's basket.[41] Upon arriving in Babylon, the eagle sees a corpse; he orders Jeremiah to gather the people together so that they may hear the contents of the letter and the message contained therein. Jeremiah gathers all the people, including the women and children, and in the sight of all those present the eagle swoops down to the body and revives it. The author specifically comments that this was done so that they might believe (ἵνα πιστεύσωσιν [*P. Jer.* 7:17]). The eagle is the symbol of the resurrection and represents Christ.[42] The scene as a whole is evidently based upon the obscure statement in the New Testament: "Wherever the body is, there the eagles will be gathered together" (Matt 24:28), which is likewise stated in an apocalyptic context.[43]

---

[40] See Murray, "The Exhortation to Candidates," 73. Cf. in Aphraates, *Sermon* 11, "On Circumcision," 501, 12. As in the *Paralipomena,* so also in Aphraates and Ephraem Syrus, separation is connected to baptism and virginity; see further below.

[41] The number fifteen may bear some eschatological significance, on the basis of Mic 5:5, who describes the eschatological war against Assyria and mentions "seven shepherds and eight princes of men," together making fifteen. The eschatological meaning of this verse is also implied by the fact that it follows the declaration of the birth of a king from the Davidic house from Bethlehem, which is also connected to messianic meanings (thus in 1QS viii 1; *b. Sukkah* 52b; *Cant. Rab.* 8.10; and cf. Jaubert, "La Symbolique des Douze," 457–58).

[42] In Christianity the figure of the crucified eagle was the symbol of the resurrection, and the eagles are the believers. This image is based in part upon Ps 103:5 ("who satisfies you with good as long as you live, so that your youth is renewed as like the eagle's") and Isa 40:31 ("But they [that] wait for the Lord shall renew their strength, they shall mount up with wings like eagles, they shall run and not be weary, they shall walk and not faint"). In Christian literary and archeological sources, Jesus is described as an eagle, and is portrayed at times carrying seals upon his neck (see M.-J. Pierre's supplementary note on "the eagle" in Aphraates, *Sermons* [SC 349:512–13]). Cf. Exod 19:4; Deut 32:11. On similar traditions in Egyptian mythology, see Philonenko, "Simples Observation," 170.

[43] And in Luke 17:37 ("And they said to him: 'Where, Lord?' He said to them, "Where the body is, there the eagles will be gathered together"). This is an enigmatic

The picture as a whole is portrayed as an analogy to the Sinaitic revelation, as stated explicitly: "Is this the god who appeared to our fathers in the wilderness through Moses [who] has now also appeared to us through this eagle?" (7:18),[44] and is intended to exemplify the promised resurrection of all the anonymous righteous, to all believers in every place. The tiding sent by Baruch and Abimelech to Babylon was the news of the resurrection; by means of the figs carried on the neck of the eagle, it is demonstrated to the entire people that the miracle of the physical resurrection is indeed taking place everywhere throughout the world.

Jeremiah's Resurrection

The tiding of the resurrection reached its climax with the resurrection of Jeremiah. Those returning with Jeremiah from exile to Jerusalem rejoiced and offered sacrifices (ἀναφέροντες θυσίας) for nine days.[45] On the tenth day Jeremiah alone offered sacrifices, and while still praying next to the altar his soul seemingly left him. Baruch and Abimelech wept along with the rest of people, thinking that he was dead. But when they went to bury him they heard a voice prohibiting them from doing so, because he was still alive and his soul would return to his body. Every one gathered around his grave for three days in anticipation of his resurrection. And indeed, after three days, his soul returned to his body, and he even recited a song of praise to the Christian Messiah.

Jeremiah, the prophet and priest, is the prototype of Jesus,[46] while his return to life after three days is the clearest prefiguration of the resurrection of the Christian savior and of the resurrection promised to the Christian believer. The latter, like Jeremiah, must acknowledge and give thanks that, upon his resurrection, the promises involved in accepting the Christian faith were realized.

---

statement which has not been properly explained by exegetes. According to Allen, the sense here is that the Parousia will occur at a fixed time when evil will have reached its height. Just as when life departs the body and it becomes a corpse eagles immediately descend upon it, so too when the world becomes corrupt with evil, the Son of Man will come with his angels to carry out the divine judgment (see Allen, *The Gospel According to St. Matthew*, 257–58).

[44] Wolff, *Jeremia*, 50, 80; Riaud, "Paralipomena," 27–29; idem, "Les Paralipomena Jeremiae dependent-ils de ii Baruch?" 116–18; Delling, "Jüdische Lehre," 10; Herzer, *Die Paralipomena*, 121.

[45] In the *Jeremiah Apocryphon* (Mangina, "A New Jeremiah Apocryphon," 391), the people arrive at Jerusalem carrying palm fronds, bunches of fragrant bushes, and olive branches, as in Jesus' entrance to Jerusalem in John 12:13.

[46] See Matt 16:14.

Everyone agrees that this description was written by a Christian scribe or redactor.[47] But there are some who separate this section (*P. Jer.* 9:10–32) from that which precedes it, on the assumption that the death of Jeremiah at the altar belongs to the Jewish portion of the work and depicts Jeremiah's natural death, to which the Christian author appended the account of his resurrection after three days.[48]

In my opinion, there is no basis for this view. The author may have made use in this chapter of an independent source or tradition; the fact that the description focuses, not on the miracle of Abimelech's figs but upon the prophecy of Jeremiah concerning the descent of the Son of God and the reaction aroused by this prophecy among his opponents, supports this possibility. However, even if he did make use of such a source it was well integrated within the plot of the work as a whole and its theological tendencies. If we separate Jeremiah's death from his resurrection we also cut short the continuity of the plot, stripping the scene of its entire significance. While it is true that Jeremiah's resurrection is clearer than all of its predecessors in terms of its Christianity, the previous scenes are also, as we have seen, based upon Christian approaches and terms.

Moreover, even the so-called Jewish part, describing the "natural" death of Jeremiah, cannot be understood except in a Christian context. Some scholars saw in the description of the offering of sacrifices by Jeremiah and those accompanying him, upon their entrance into Jerusalem, as an expression of the Jewish anticipation present in the work for the restoration of the temple and its cult in Jerusalem.[49] The sacrifice offered by Jeremiah alone in the Holy of Holies on the tenth day was identified by all as the sacrifice of the Day of Atonement which, according to the Torah, falls "in the seventh month, on the tenth day of the month" (Lev 16:29; Num 29:7).[50] However, this scene contains no reference to the Jewish rite of Yom Kippur, at whose center lies the

---

[47] Denis, *Introduction*, 71, 74; Bogaert, *Apocalypse*, 1:212; Delling, "Jüdische Lehre," 13–14; Riaud, "Jeremie, Martyr chrétien," 232; Kohler, "Pre-Talmudic Haggada," 412; Robinson, "4 Baruch," 415; Herzer, *Die Paralipomena Jeremiae*, 147.

[48] Delling, "Jüdische Lehre," 13–14; Riaud, "Les Paralipomena jeremiae dependent-ils?" 125; Herzer, *Paralipomena*, 30; Wolff, *Jeremia*, 89–95. Riaud sees the Christian portion beginning already in 9:7, and the end of the Jewish portion in Jeremiah's prayer ("Paralipomena," 29). Robinson ("4 Baruch," 415) begins the Christian part from 8:12.

[49] Robinson, "4 Baruch," 416; Delling, "Paralipomena," 65, 69.

[50] Bogaert, *Apocalypse*, 1:212; Riaud, "Paralipomena," 36; Riaud, "Les Paralipomena dependent-ils?" 125; Herzer, *Paralipomena*, 144; Philonenko, "Simples Observations," 171.

fast, the expatiatory offering, the sprinkling of the blood, and the sending of the goat to Azazel in the wilderness.[51] The nine days prior to Yom Kippur, during which Jeremiah offered sacrifices together with all the people, have no basis in Jewish law, according to which "seven days before the Day of Atonement the High Priest is separated from his home" (*m. Yoma* 1.1).

The sacrifice described in the *Paralipomena* is the sacrament of the Eucharist, described in early Christian sources as a sacrifice (θυσία)[52] and symbolizing the atoning sacrifice of Jesus which comes in place of the Jewish sacrifice. For that reason the Friday on which Jesus was crucified became a fast day, the Christian equivalent of Yom Kippur.[53] The death of Jeremiah, that takes place on Yom Kippur, is thus consistent with its description in this work as a prototype of Jesus, whose death and resurrection alongside the altar allude to the establishment of the true sanctuary and altar.

Similarly, the prayer uttered by Jeremiah in the Holy of Holies has nothing in common with the Jewish prayers of Yom Kippur, in whose center lies the High Priest's confession of sins and the asking of forgiveness.[54] Rather, this is a Christian prayer in the spirit of the prayers recited in the Eucharistic ceremony (*Did.* 8.2; 10.1–6).[55] The prayer is based in part upon Isa 6, but instead of the call of the seraphim to one another—"Holy, holy, holy is the Lord of Hosts; the whole earth is full of his glory" (Isa 6:3)—the doxology refers, not to God, but to the "incense of the living trees, true light that enlightens me until I am taken up to you" (9:3).

The fragrance (θυμίαμα) of the trees of life is characteristic of paradise in the Christian tradition,[56] and the trees of life are the pious ones (*Pss. Sol.* 14:3).

---

[51] Josephus, *Ant.* 3.240–43; Philo, *Mos.* 23–24; *Mishna, Tractate Yoma*.

[52] *Did.* 14.1–3 portrays the gathering for the breaking of bread and the celebration of the Eucharist on the Day of the Lord as a sacrifice (Justin *Dial.* 41.3; 117.1); in *Apocalypse of Paul* 29, the sacrifice is the body and blood of Christ (James, *Apocryphal New Testament*, 541). Cf. Bultmann, *Theology of the New Testament*, 1:149–50; Bogaert, *Apocalypse* 1. 212.

[53] This idea is already alluded to in the NT (Mark 2:19; Matt 9:15; Luke 5:34–35, which make use of the verb νηστεύω [to fast] in connection with the death of Jesus). Cf. Heb 9; *Barn.* 7; Origen, *Hom. Lev.* (PG; 12:525–28); Venerable Bede, *In Matthaei Evangelium Expositio* 9 (PL 92:47); F. Cabrol, "Jeunes," *DACL* VII.2498.

[54] On the High Priest's prayer in the temple on the Day of Atonement see *m. Yoma* 5.1; *y. Yoma* 5 (42c-d); *b. Yoma* 53b; *Lev. Rab.* 20.3ff.

[55] Bogaert, *Apocalypse*, 1:212; Philonenko, "Paralipomena," 171–72.

[56] The garden of Eden contains trees, including the tree of life, whose leaves and fruits do not wither, produce a pleasant fragrance the likes of which is unknown, and serve as "a healing to the nations" (Rev 22:2). The fragrance that characterizes the trees

The mention of fragrance in the Yom Kippur rite is associated with the incense altar, which is reminiscent of the garden of Eden and plays a central role in the Christian liturgy. While it is true that the incense plays a role in the Jewish Day of Atonement ritual (Lev 16:12), its main components are the sin offering, the sprinkling of blood, and the sending away of the scapegoat.

The "true light" is consistent with the portrayal of Jesus in the Christian tradition, and particularly in the Fourth Gospel, in which Jesus is compared to the true light (John 3:21; 8:12; 11:9; 1 John 2:8) that illuminates the path of the believer, "when the day shall dawn upon us from on high, to give light to those who sit in darkness and in the shadow of death" (Luke 1:78), and, like Jesus, Jeremiah will ascend (ἀναλαμβάνω)[57] after his resurrection to heaven. Jeremiah's prayer prior to his death, that the Lord illuminate the path of the righteous to the heavenly Jerusalem, fits in well with the blessing given by Abimelech to the old man, who believed in the miracle of the figs: "May God guide you with [his] light to the city above, Jerusalem" (*P. Jer.* 5:35) and to the blessing of Baruch (*P. Jer.* 6:9–10): "Our power (ἡ δύναμις), Lord God, [thou] chosen light, [is] that which proceeds from your mouth."[58]

These expressions, like the titles given to the Lord in the prayer of Jeremiah, who is "unbegotten" (ἀγέννητος) and "incomprehensible" (ἀπερινόητος; 9:6) have no basis in contemporary Jewish sources, but are rooted in Christian and Gnostic sources of the second and third century CE.[59]

---

of the garden of Eden is connected with Jesus, who heralds the new garden of Eden. Thus, Mary anoints his feet with rare and precious nard, and the house is filled with the fragrance of perfume (John 12:3), because she anoints his body in preparation for his death, upon which his messiahhood is made known (Mark 14:8). For that reason Jesus is buried together with the spices in his new grave in the garden (κῆπος) that opens the new world, the heavenly paradise that is established upon his resurrection (John 19:39–40). Cf. *1 En.* 24:3–5; 25:4–6; 28; 29; 30; 32:3–4; *T. Levi* 18:11; *2 En.* 5:1–6; *Apoc. Mos.* 28–29; 40:7; Ephraem Syrus, *Sermons on Paradise*, 9:17. This terminology also appears among the Mandaeans, where the supreme power is called "the perfume of life" (Philonenko, "Paralipomena," 172). On the perfume and its relation to water and to light in the Mandaeans, see W. Sundberg, *Kushta: A Monograph on a Principal Word in Mandaean Texts*. Vol. 1: *The Descending Knowledge* (Lund, 1953), 84–88.

[57] This verb describes Jesus' heavenwards ascent (Mark 16:19; 1 Tim 3:16; Acts 1:11; Wintermute, "Gerhard Delling [Review]," 444).

[58] Like Jeremiah and Abimelech, Baruch is also a prototype of Jesus; hence he is referred to by the angel as "the Lord, the messenger of light": σύμβουλος τοῦ φωτός (6:15).

[59] Herzer, *Die Paralipomena Jeremiae*, 154; Sundberg, *Kushta*, 82. The expression "precious light" appears in Mandaean texts (see Drower and Macuch, "nhura," *A Mandaic Dictionary*, 291). Similarly, "messenger of light" (Philonenko, "Simples

The description of Jeremiah's death, as one whose soul left him, is based upon the description of the death of Jesus on the cross, that "he bowed his head and gave up his spirit" (John 19:30; Luke 23:46).

The scene of the offering of the sacrifice, and of the death and resurrection of Jeremiah, all of which occurred after the return from Exile and the crossing of the Jordan, are based upon the description of the Exodus in which Jeremiah exemplifies the figure of Moses, who is in turn a prototype of Jesus.[60] Like the resurrection of Abimelech, this scene is also a prefiguring of the new Exodus that will also take place on Passover and that will lead to the making of a new covenant with the sacrifice of Jesus, who substitutes for the paschal offering. But the significant point is that the Jerusalem to which the exiles return is not the ruined earthly Jerusalem, but the heavenly Jerusalem, identified in Christianity with paradise, in which the action of the work as a whole takes place.

Immediately after his resurrection, Jeremiah utters a song of praise to God and to his son, like that of a Christian preacher: "All [of you] glorify God, and the son of God who awakens us (ἐξυπνίζοντα),[61] Jesus Christ the light (τὸ φῶς) of all the aeons, the inextinguishable lamp (ὁ λύχνος), the life (ἡ ζωή) of faith" (*P. Jer.* 9:14). He prophesies the two appearances of Jesus, his rejection by the Jews (who are compared to the trees which Jesus will cause to wither),[62] his acceptance by the Gentiles,[63] a warning concerning the judgment to be conducted at the end of time, the election of the twelve apostles to preach his message among the nations, and his second appearance on the Mount of Olives.[64] As soon as Jeremiah says that he has seen the Son of God, whose

---

Observations," 164–65). The light emanating from the Lord appears in *Odes Sol.* 12:3 ("because the mouth of the Lord is the true word, and the door of his light"; [Harris and Mingana, *Odes and Psalms,* 1:12]).

[60] Wolff, *Jeremia,* 50; Herzer, *Die Paralipomena Jeremiae,* 156–58, and additional parallel points there.

[61] As in John 1:11: ἵνα ἐξυπνίσω αὐτόν, based on Dan 12:2.

[62] Riaud, "Jeremie, Martyr chrétien?" 234: the trees without fruit, which he prophesies will yield fruit, are the Gentiles, while the withered trees that had previously given fruit are the Jews. Harris, *The Rest of the Words,* 46; Robinson, "4 Baruch," 415.

[63] *P. Jer.* 9:17, based on Isa 42:4.

[64] According to Zech 14:4. Jesus' ascent heavenward from the Mount of Olives and his return are alluded to in the NT only in Luke 24:50 and in Acts 1:12. The *Paralipomena* is evidently the earliest work containing explicit testimony to this expectation (see Bogaert, *Apocalypse,* 1:214; Eusebius, *Dem. ev.* IV [PG; 22:457]; Jerome, *Comm. Zach.* 14.3, 4 [CCSL 76a, p. 879]). The view that the Messiah will be

father honors him, and that he will come to the world, the people are infuriated, because they see his words as a repetition of the words of Isaiah, who supposedly claimed that he had seen God and the son of God. They decide to kill him, not in the same manner in which they had killed Isaiah, but rather to stone him (9:21–22).

In order to tell Baruch and Abimelech the mysterious things that he had seen, a stone was miraculously transformed to look like Jeremiah and the people stoned it, thinking that it was the real prophet. Only after Jeremiah finishes describing to Baruch and to Abimelech what he has seen does the stone cry out and say: "'O stupid children of Israel, why do you stone me, thinking that I am Jeremiah? Behold, Jeremiah stands in your midst!' And when they saw him, they immediately ran at him with many stones, and his stewardship was fulfilled" (9:30–31).

The Christianity of this description needs no proof. However, as against the widespread assumption that this is a late Christian addition, this description is in my opinion connected in an integral way to the plot and to the tendencies upon which the work as a whole is based.

The tradition concerning Jeremiah's stoning by the people is a Christian tradition mentioned in the Christian work, *Vitae Prophetorum*,[65] and was well known to the church fathers, from Hippolutus and Tertullian on.[66] Jeremiah's death by stoning is well rooted in Christian theology, and is seen as exemplifying the death of the prophets, who were persecuted and killed by the Jews "[because they] announced beforehand the coming of the Righteous One" (Acts 7:52), whose death was a prefiguration of the death of Jesus. Jeremiah had to die in Jerusalem, "for it cannot be that a prophet should perish away

---

revealed on the Mount of Olives does not appear in early Jewish sources (W. Foerster, ὄρος, *TDNT*, 5:484).

[65] *Life of Jeremiah*, 1–2 (in Torrey, *Lives of the Prophets*, 21, 35). Unlike in the *Paralipomena*, there Jeremiah is stoned at Tafnes (Tahpanhes) in Egypt, and is buried at the place where Pharaoh's palace had stood. See similar to this the late Jewish tradition in an aggadic midrash to Numbers 30:15 (*Midrash Aggadah ʿal Hamisha Humshei Torah*, ed. Buber, 157), dated in the twelfth century (see Herr, "Midrash," 1511–12).

Everyone agrees that *Liv. Pro.* as extant includes Christian interpolations, the most striking of which appear in the *Life of Jeremiah*, particularly the belief in the virgin and her son in the manger (*Life of Jeremiah*, 7–8), who are clearly Mary and Jesus. According to Satran, this is a fourth century Christian work (Satran, "The Lives of the Prophets," 60, 96–97; *Biblical Prophets in Byzantine Palestine*, 76, 120; "Biblical Prophets and Christian Legend," 143–49).

[66] Hippolytus, *Comm. Dan.* 1.12 (SC; Paris, 1947; p. 80): idem, *Antichr.* 31 (PG 10:752); Tertullian, *Scorp.* 8.3 (PL 2:137); Delling, "Jüdische Lehre," 17; Ginzberg, *Legends of the Jews*, 6:399–400 n. 42; Herzer, *Paralipomena*, 167.

from Jerusalem" (Luke 13:31–35); and this death needed to be by stoning, because Jerusalem is known for "killing the prophets and stoning those who are sent to you" (Matt 23:37).[67] The stone that appears in the image of Jeremiah (*P. Jer.* 9:24–31) and cries out against the stupidity of the Israelites is the same stone that, according to the Christian tradition, will cry after the crucifixion and upon the coming of the End, based upon Hab 2:11: "For the stone will cry out from the wall, and the beam from the woodwork respond."[68]

Jeremiah died as a Christian martyr, witnessing to his faith in Jesus Christ, the Son of God, who has come to the world. It is possible that, underlying Jeremiah's martyrdom may be the actual historical background of persecutions of Christians during the first centuries CE. Jeremiah is an a example for Christians who are persecuted for their faith, who may be consoled in the victory of the tree of life (according to Jer 11:19), that is, the cross that Jeremiah prophesies to them.[69]

The reference in the *Paralipomena* to Isaiah's death indicates the relationship of the *Paralipomena* to the work *The Martyrdom of Isaiah* or *The Ascent of Isaiah* (*Ascensio Isaiae*). This work relates the death of Isaiah, which occurred, among other things, because he claimed that he had seen God and the son of God; he was thus killed by being sawn in half with a wood saw. Even though this work evidently made use of a Jewish tradition concerning the sawing of Isaiah by Manasseh,[70] the *Ascent of Isaiah* is an early

---

[67] Heb 11:37; 1 Thess 2:15. Cf. the stoning of Stephen, the first Christian martyr, in Acts 7:58 and the death of Jesus' brother Jacob (St. James): Eusebius, *Hist. eccl.* 2.23.16 (LCL 153:175), who cites a tradition in the name of Hegesippus; in Josephus, *Ant.* 20.200, this is a Christian interpolation. Cf. Efron: "The Great Sanhedrin in Vision and Reality," 334–36.

[68] See *4 Ezra* 5:5 ("Blood shall drip from wood, and the stone shall utter its voice [de ligno sanguis stillabit et lapis dabit vocem suam]; the peoples shall be troubled, and the stars shall fall)." Harris (*The Rest of the Words*, 20) argues that the author knew this passage from *4 Ezra* and that this gave him the idea to create the story of the rock in the image of Jeremiah. The catalyst for this story was this isolated verse in *4 Ezra* (cf. *Life of Jonah* [Torrey, *Lives of the Prophets*, 28: "And he gave a portent concerning Jerusalem and the whole land, that whenever they should see a stone crying out piteously the end was at hand. And whenever they should see all the gentiles in Jerusalem, the entire city would be razed to the ground"]; Luke 19:40 ["if these were silent, the very stones would cry out"]; Jeremias, "λίθος," 270; Wolff, *Jeremia*, 51).

[69] On the attitude of the Romans to Christians at the end of the first century and the beginning of the second, see Knight, *Disciples of the Beloved One*, 210–12.

[70] On the basis of what is related in 2 Kgs 21:16: "Moreover, Manasseh shed very much innocent blood, till he had filled Jerusalem from one end to the other." Cf. *y. Sanh.* 10 (28c); *b. Yebamot* 49b; cf. *b. Sanh.* 103b; *Pesiq. Rab.* 4 (ed. Ish Shalom; 14).

Christian work[71] composed at the end of the first century or the beginning of the second century CE in the area of Syria.[72]

Evidently Josephus also knew this tradition (*Ant.* 10.38; A. Shalit, *Josephus's Antiquities of the Jews* [Hebrew] (Jerusalem, 1973), n. 51; Ginzberg, *Legends of the Jews*, 6:374 n. 103). In the Jewish tradition the wood saw is not mentioned, which is a characteristic detail in the Christian tradition as a whole, and Isaiah is put to death because he criticized Manasseh for his sins. On the features common to the talmudic tradition, see A. Caquot, "Bref Commentaire du 'Martyre d'Isaïe,'" *Semitica* 23 (1973): 86. On the Christianity of the Jewish material included in this work, see Knight, *Disciples of the Beloved One*, 289.

[71] Until recently, the predominant scholarly opinion was that this work is composed of at least two independent stories. The story of the martyrdom of Isaiah that occupies the first half of *The Ascent of Isaiah* (chs. 1–5), is according to most a work of Jewish origin. The openly Christian passages in this part of the work (e.g., 1:3–4, 5–6, 7; 2:9; 3:13–31), which speak of incarnation, crucifixion, resurrection, the early history of the church, and the events leading to the End and the Last Judgment, are explained as the additions of a Christian editor who interpolated this Christian apocalypse within a Jewish document (3:13–22) and even made several additions and adjustments (thus: Charles, *The Ascension of Isaiah*, xi, xliv, xlvi; Tisserant, *Ascension d'Isaïe*, 42; Denis, *Introduction*, 71; Delling, "Paralipomena," 13–14; Nickelsburg, "Paralipomena of Jeremiah," 52; Knibb, "Martyrdom and Ascension of Isaiah," 2:143, 147). Regarding the other parts of the work, there is no doubt that their author was Christian (see Denis, *Introduction*, 174–75; Barton, "The Ascension of Isaiah," 275). In recent years the view claiming the integrity and Christianity of the work as a whole has become more widely held. Knight opposes an approach that breaks the work down into various literary sources and layers. He sees the author as a creator who shaped the apocalypse from various sources, rather than an editor who merely combined earlier sources (*Disciples of the Beloved*, 31). In his view this is a Christian work, shedding light on Christianity in the second century, composed in the Christian community of Syria about 120 CE (J. Knight, *The Ascension of Isaiah* [Sheffield, 1995], 9–10, 14). Cf. Burkitt, *Jewish and Christian Apocalypses*, 45–48; Ginzberg, *Legends of the Jews*, 6:375 n. 103; Harris, "Paralipomena," 20–22; Torrey, *The Apocryphal Literature*, 133–35; Laurence, who published the *editio princeps* of the Ethiopic text, in Tisserant, *Ascension d'Isaïe*, 42. Flusser ("The Apocryphal Book of Ascensio Isaiae") connects the work to the circles of the Qumran sect, and in his wake also Philonenko, "Le Martyre d'Esäie," 1–10.

[72] Harris, *The Rest of the Words*, 22; Burkitt, *Jewish and Christian Apocalypses*, 46; Charles, *The Ascent of Isaiah*, xi, xlvi, xliv; Tisserant, *Ascension d'Isaïe*, 59–60; Daniélou, *Theology of Jewish Christianity*, 13; Barton, "The Ascension of Isaiah," 779–80. On the origins of this work, see Knight, *Disciples of the Beloved*, 39; idem, *The Ascension of Isaiah*, 23; Flemming and Duensing, "The Ascension of Isaiah," 643; Hall, "The Ascension of Isaiah: Commentary, Situation, Date and Place," 289, 300, 303; Denis, *Introduction*, 175; Flusser, "The Apocryphal Book of Ascensio Isaiae," 31; M. A. Knibb,

Like Jeremiah's prophecy in the *Paralipomena* about seeing God and his son, the descent to the world of the Son of God and the election of the twelve apostles to declare the tidings among the Gentiles, so too Isaiah in the *Martyrdom and Ascension of Isaiah* anticipates Christianity. Among other things, he states that he has seen God and the coming of the Beloved from the seventh heaven, his transfiguration and descent upon earth in the form of flesh and blood, his persecution, his call and instructions to the twelve disciples, his crucifixion upon a cross together with criminals, his burial, his resurrection on the third day, and the sending forth of apostles to spread the faith in the resurrection of the beloved and the salvation that will come to those who believe in him (*Ascen. Isa.* 3:13–31).

Both these figures saw in a vision, while their souls left their bodies and they seemed as if dead, what goes on in the upper firmaments (*Asc. Isa.* 6:11–13, 17). Like Jeremiah, Isaiah too was held to account for this and was executed by sawing. Like the tradition of Jeremiah's death in the *Paralipomena*, so too the tradition of Isaiah's death is well rooted in Christian theology. One may assume that the mention in the Epistle to the Hebrews (11:37) of the prophets who were "sawn in two" (ἐπρίσθησαν) refers first and foremost to Isaiah, just as the reference to those who were "stoned" (ἐλιθάσθησαν) refers to Jeremiah, a tradition that was well known to the church fathers.[73] In both works the prophets of Israel are invoked to witness to the coming of Jesus, and are meant to be persecuted and executed in Jerusalem because they openly declared the coming of "the Righteous One." Like Jeremiah, Isaiah too dies as a Christian martyr.[74]

In recent years, several studies have been published linking the *Martyrdom of Isaiah* to circles of Christian prophets who engaged in polemic at the beginning of the second century CE, either with the leaders of the church (bishops,

---

"Martyrdom and Ascension of Isaiah," in *OTP* 2:149; Herzer, *Die Paralipomena Jeremiae*, 165.

[73] Justin, *Dial.* 120.5 (ed. M. Marcovich; PTS 47; Berlin, 1997; 277); Tertullian, *Pat.* 13 (PL 1:1270); *Scorp.* 8 (PL 2:137). See also the testimonies in Barton, "The Ascension of Isaiah," 775–78; Caquot, "Bref Commentaire," 85. In all of these traditions, Isaiah is sawn by a wood saw: πρίονι ξυλίνῳ, that alludes to the tree of the crucifixion. Cf. Budge, *Book of the Cave of Treasures*, 184–85. From the description there it is clear that the sawing of Isaiah into two, from head to foot, between two pieces of wood is an analogy to the crucifixion of Jesus and the rending of the veil of the temple in two, from above to below (Mark 15:38). The source of the wood saw has been sought even in the Iranian tradition (Caquot, "Bref Commentaire," 87–89).

[74] Knight, *Disciples of the Beloved*, 210. Melito of Sardis invokes these two prophets as examples of martyrs who preceded Christ (*On Pascha* [ed. S. G. Hall; Oxford, 1979), 63–64, 69, pp. 33, 37).

deacons) or with other prophetic streams that held views different from their own.[75] According to Hall, the background of the *Ascension of Isaiah* was in a prophetic stream that believed in the possibility of visionaries ascending heavenwards and seeing God, and that also believed in the doctrine of the descent and ascent of the Beloved. This stream engaged in heated controversy with other circles, that rejected this possibility.[76]

The author of the *Paralipomena* may have belonged to the same prophetic-apocalyptic stream that placed at the center of its belief the anticipation of the descent of Christ (the "Son of Man" or the "Beloved") to the world and his ascent back to heaven, and that also expressed belief in the possibility of the visionary seeing God's face in heaven. The fact that these two prophets were persecuted because of these beliefs may reflect the polemic conducted against them by other early Christian circles, which denied the descent of the Son of Man to the world and his ascent back to heaven[77] and the possibility of literally seeing God,[78] and hence persecuted them mercilessly.

The Test at the Jordan Waters

How can human beings enjoy that bodily and personal resurrection symbolized by the resurrection of Abimelech and the miracle of the figs? The answer to this question is spelled out in the letter carried by the eagle to Jeremiah in Babylon, whose importance may be inferred from the fact that the author repeats it on three separate occasions (*P. Jer.* 6:13–14; 6:17–23; 8:2–4).

Entrance into the heavenly Jerusalem is only permitted to those who are prepared to hear the voice of God, while one who does not obey will become a stranger in both Babylon and Jerusalem. The test of loyalty is by means of the waters of the Jordan, which are "the sign of the great seal": (τοῦτο τὸ σημεῖον τῆς μεγάλης σφραγῖδος [6:17–23]). "Let him who desires the works of the

---

[75] Knight, *Disciples of the Beloved*, 186–88.

[76] Hall, "The Ascension of Isaiah," 289–99.

[77] Possibly Docetic streams. A similar polemic against Docetism appears in John 1:14; 6:53; 19:34. See Borgen, *Bread from Heaven*, 191–92. See also *Apocalypse of Paul* 41, where those who do not acknowledge that Christ came in the flesh and that the Virgin Mary gave birth to him are punished, as are those who argue that the bread and wine of the Eucharist are not the blood and flesh of Jesus (in Eliot, *Apocryphal NT*, 637). This work is dated to the middle of the third century (ibid., 616).

[78] Such views are reflected in the Gospel of John, who rejects the possibility of seeing the Father apart from his Son: "Not that any one has seen the Father except him who is from God; he has seen the Father" (John 6:46; cf. 1:18; 5:37; 1 John 4:12, 20). "No one has ascended into heaven but he who descended from heaven, the Son of Man" (John 3:13. Ign. *Trall.* 10.1; *Smyrn.* 2:1–2).

Lord leave the works of Babylon behind.... And the men who took wives from them, and the women who took husbands from them [shall leave them], let those who hear you cross over, and take them up to Jerusalem.... No man who cohabits with Babylonians may enter this city!" (6:13–14; 8:3, 7).

The demand to annul mixed marriages is based in part upon the well-known struggle of Ezra and Nehemiah during the period of the return to Zion.[79] However, this concrete historical background is merely an external associative pretext, a prefiguration, for the author's entirely different theological tendencies.

The test by means of the waters of the Jordan symbolizes Christian baptism and is the test for those who believe. "The sign (τὸ σημεῖον) of the great seal (σφραγίς)" is Christian baptism, as stated in the Shepherd of Hermas:

> So these also who had fallen asleep received the seal of the Son of God and entered into the kingdom of God. For before ... a man bears the name of the Son of God, he is dead. But when he receives the seal he puts away mortality and receives life. *The seal, then, is the water* (ἡ σφραγὶς οὖν τὸ ὕδωρ ἐστίν). They go down then into the water dead, and come up alive. This seal, then, was preached to them also, and they made use of it, to enter into the kingdom of God." (Herm. *Sim.* 9.16.3–4 [Lake, *The Apostolic Fathers* (LCL) 2:262–63]).

Similarly, in the *Odes of Solomon* we read:

> Raging rivers [are like] the power of the Lord; they bring headlong those who despise them. And entangle their paths, and destroy their crossings. And catch their bodies, and corrupt their natures.... But those who cross them in faith shall not be disturbed. And those who walk on them faultlessly shall not be shaken. Because the sign on them is the Lord, and the sign is the Way for those who cross in the name of the Lord. Therefore, put on the name of the Most High and know him, and you shall cross without danger; because the rivers shall be obedient to you. The Lord has bridged them by his word, and he walked and crossed them by foot. And his footsteps were standing firm upon the water, and were not destroyed; but they are like a beam (of wood [*i.e., the cross*]) that is constructed on truth. On this side and on that the waves were lifted up, but the footsteps of our Lord Messiah were standing firm. And they are neither blotted out, nor destroyed. And the Way has been appointed for those who cross over after him, and for those who adhere to the

---

[79] Ezra 9:1ff.; Neh 13:23–27, etc.; Delling, "Jüdische Lehre," 12–13; Riaud, "Les Samaritains," 136–37; Herzer, *Die Paralipomena Jeremiae*, 146, in whose opinion the scene of offering the sacrifice in the *Paralipomena* is also based upon Ezra and Nehemiah, although there it refers, not to Yom Kippur, but to the festival of Sukkot (see Ezra 3:4; Neh 8:13–18; and cf. Herzer's explanation concerning the Samaritans, *Paralipomena*, 129–43).

path of his faith; and who adore his name. Hallelujah. (*Odes Sol.* 39 [*OTP* 2:768; bracketed addition mine])[80]

Later the seal came to refer to the sign of the cross impressed upon the forehead of the Christians in the framework of the ceremony of baptism, symbolizing their belonging to the chosen congregation.[81] Such a test in the Jordan would have had no meaning from a Jewish viewpoint, because the waters of the Jordan as such are of no particular significance in Judaism. On the other hand, the Jordan provides the background for the establishment of the Christian sacrament of baptism, with Jesus' baptism by John the Baptist (Matt 3:13; Mark 1:9; Luke 4:1). The crossing of the Jordan symbolizes Christian baptism, by whose means the believer identifies with the destiny of Christ, and it assures him a portion in his death and in his resurrection. As Paul says: "Do you not know that all of us who have been baptized into Christ Jesus were baptized into his death? We were buried therefore with him by baptism into death, so that as Christ was raised from the dead by the glory of the Father, we too might walk in newness of life. For if we have been united with him in a death like his, we shall certainly be united with him in a resurrection

---

[80] Cf. Eph 1:13; 4:30; 2 Cor 1:22. In baptism the believer is sealed with the Holy Spirit. *Barn.* 9:6–8. In Herm. *Sim.* 8.2.4 the angel of the Lord provides clothing and the seal before he brings them to the tower, which is the heavenly church (also in 8.6.3; 9.17.4; 9.31.1). Cf. *Odes Sol.* 6:8; *Ep. Apos.* 41, in James, *NT Apocrypha*, 500. On the term "baptismo consignari" see *Ps.-Clem., Rec.* 6.8 (PG; 1:1352); *Acts Thom.* 25: the Lord recognizes his flock via his seal (Elliott, *The Apocryphal New Testament*, 457); the woman asks Thomas to give her the seal of the Lord and he goes to a nearby river and baptizes her in the name of the Father, the Son, and the Holy Spirit (W. Wright, *Apocryphal Acts of the Apostles* [Amsterdam, 1968], 188, Syriac part, p. 206; *Apoc. Mos.* 42:1). On baptism as a seal, see Lampe, *Patristic Greek Lexicon*, 1356; Bultmann, *Theology of the New Testament*, 1:137–38.

[81] *Odes Sol.* 8:15: "I . . . imprinted a seal on their faces," based upon Ezek 9:1–6. Harris, *The Rest of the Words*, 14; Daniélou, *Theology of Jewish Christianity*, 327–30; Cullmann, *Baptism in the New Testament*, 45–46, 56–57, 64; Bogaert, *Apocalypse* 1:220. The words σημεῖον and δοκιμάζειν are also incorporated in a natural way in the context of baptism (Bogaert, *Apocalypse* 1:207; Robinson, "4 Baruch," 415). The sign of the great seal is connected to the "seven seals" with which the earth is sealed (*P. Jer.* 3:7–8) which will be opened after the "seven times." In both passages, this is an expression for the eschatological scheme of salvation that will take place with the coming of the End. The seven seals also appear in this sense in the Revelation to John (5:1, 2, 5, 9; 6:1; 8:1; 10:4; 22:10) and in other Christian works. The seven seals are identical to the seven times (Herzer, *Die Paralipomena Jeremiae*, 121; Charles, *Revelation of St. John*, 138, 158–59; G. Fitzer, "σφραγίς" 950). The expressions "great seal," "this is the sign of the great seal," and the "sign" (*rusumu*) appear among the Mandaeans (see Philonenko, "Simples Observations," 160–62).

like his" (Rom 6:3–5).⁸² Hence, the tiding carried to the pagan world by means of this letter is that the condition for resurrection of the dead and for entering the supernal Jerusalem is to accept Christian baptism. Baptism signifies attachment to Jesus and entrance into the promised land, to the garden of Eden, to the heavenly Jerusalem.⁸³

This significance of the seal also explains why Baruch tells Jeremiah about the miracle of the figs that happened to Abimelech by way of describing the conditions for crossing the Jordan. The figs that did not rot are reflected in baptism, which is the sign of the great seal that symbolizes the resurrection, as stated in the Shepherd of Hermas: "For before a man bears the name of the Son of God he is dead, but when he receives the seal he puts away mortality and receives life" (Herm. *Sim.* 9.16.3 [Lake, *Apostolic Fathers* (LCL) 2:263]). Like the sleep of Abimelech, so too in this passage from the Shepherd of Hermas the discussion of the seal is related to sleep:

> These apostles and teachers, who preached the name of the Son of God, having fallen asleep (κοιμηθέντες) in the power and faith of the Son of God, preached (ἐκήρυξαν) also to those who had fallen asleep (προκεκοιμημένοις) before them and themselves gave to them the seal of the preaching. (ἔδωκαν αὐτοῖς τὴν σφραγῖδα τοῦ κηρύγματος). They went down therefore with them into the water and came up again, but the latter went down alive and came up alive, while the former, who had fallen asleep before, went down dead but came up alive. Through them, therefore, they were made alive, and received the knowledge of the name of the Son of God (Herm. *Sim.* 9.16.5–7 [Lake, *Apostolic Fathers* (LCL) 2:162–63]).

However, Baruch and Jeremiah's call to the people to separate from their Babylonian spouses and to cross the Jordan would seem to have an additional meaning.

The understanding of the water as "waters of testing" or "waters of proof," by whose means it is possible to test those joining the Christian congregation, lies at the focus of an early liturgical text⁸⁴ related to the ceremony of baptism incorporated within the seventh sermon of Aphraates, "On the Penitents" (*De Paenitentibus*).⁸⁵ In this sermon those who wish to join the covenant (*qyama*)

---

⁸² Daniélou, *Sacramentum Futuri*, 233–56.

⁸³ Daniélou, "Terre et Paradis," 458.

⁸⁴ On the antiquity of the text and its liturgical nature, see A. Vööbus, *A History of Asceticism in the Syrian Orient*, 1:93; Murray, "The Exhortation to Candidates for Ascetical Vows," 60; Anderson, "Celibacy or Consummation in the Garden?" 141.

⁸⁵ Aphraates' sermons are dated to the years 337–45 CE (Vööbus, *History of Asceticism*, 18; Brock, "Early Syrian Asceticism," 9).

and to be included among the members of the covenant (*benei qyama*)[86] are called upon to conduct an ascetic way of life as a condition for receiving baptism. This way of life includes sexual celibacy and virginity,[87] refraining from marriage, and is described (using terms borrowed from Deut 20:5–8) as a holy war. Only the "single ones" (μοναχοί), the unmarried, young people, holy ones, and virgins,[88] who turned their faces toward what lies before them and do not remember what is behind them—they alone are able to stand up to the spiritual battle that awaits them, the Christian's battle of monastic life and asceticism.

This sermon includes warnings to those candidates who devote themselves to a life of asceticism. These will be tested by the "waters of testing," which have the power to determine who are the brave ones, who can stand up to this battle and be numbered among the "single ones," and who are the weak and

---

[86] Scholars disagree concerning the interpretation of the terms *qyama* and *benei qyama*. The question is to what the term *benei qyama* relates. Who were the members of the *qyama*, and what was their status? Do these terms relate to the early Christian Syrian congregation as a whole, which demanded all those who had themselves been baptized and who joined them to conduct a life of asceticism, or do they perhaps refer to a select group of Christians, an elite of the baptized and virgins who enjoyed a special status in the early Syrian church? Most scholars interpret *qyama* as "covenant"; hence *benei qyama* are members of the covenant, a select group of people who keep the vow or covenant connected with baptism (cf. Brock, "Early Syrian Asceticism," 7; Vööbus, *History of Asceticism*, 25; Connolly, "Aphraates and Monasticism," 523, 529, 535–37; Nedungatt, "The Covenanters of the Early Syriac-Speaking Church," 203). For an opposing view see Burkitt, "Aphraates and Monasticism: A Reply," 10–11, who thinks that during the early stages of the Syrian church no one was allowed to receive baptism unless he was prepared to conduct a life of asceticism, and that this did not refer to a select status alongside which a regular Christian congregation existed. On a possible connection between this term and the terms used in Qumran, see Vööbus, *History of Asceticism*, 1:100ff.

[87] Anderson, "Celibacy or Consummation?" 142. This text enumerates those that are unable to take part in the struggle demanded of those joining the *qyama*. One of these was one who had betrothed a woman but not yet married her. This law is based upon Deut 24:5. The newly married man needs to "rejoice" his wife whom he has taken. The expression "to rejoice" or "to be happy with" (ושמח) is interpreted as referring to the receiving of pleasure from the sexual union (Anderson, ibid., 133–36). The Syriac text integrates this expression with Deut 20:7. This combination of images emphasizes the fact that the danger to the Christian lies in sexual experience, and not just in the married state.

[88] Vööbus, *History of Asceticism*, 1:108; the holy ones are married people who abandoned married life and began to practice sexual purity (Vööbus, *History*, 1:105–6).

hesitant ones who will go back on their tracks and be counted among the members of the regular Christian congregation.

> O, those who prepared themselves for the battle [i.e., of the ascetic life], hear the sound of the horn and strengthen yourselves, and to you too I speak, those who hold the horns. Priests and scribes and sages, call out and say to all the people:
> Let him who is afraid turn back from the battle, lest he break the heart [spirit] of his brothers like his own heart [spirit]. And he who has planted a vineyard, let him return to working the soil, least he think of it, and fail in the struggle. And he who has betrothed a woman and wishes to marry her, let him turn back and rejoice with his wife. And he who has built a house, let him return to it, lest he remember his house and not fight with all his heart.
> This battle is fitting to the single people, for their faces are turned toward what is before them, and they do not remember what is behind them. . . . and let there be brought down to the waters of testing those whose souls have been chosen for the struggle. For the waters test him who is brave, but those who are weak are separated from there. (Aphraates, *Sermons,* 7.19–21 [PS 1:344–48])

The test by means of water is based upon the manner in which Gideon chose his fighters when he set out to wage war against Midian (Judg 7:5): "So he brought the people down to the water; and the Lord said to Gideon, 'Everyone that laps the water with his tongue, as a dog laps, you shall set by himself; likewise everyone that kneels down to drink." Out of 10,000 men, Gideon chose those three hundred people who lapped the water with their tongues.

Gideon's action is interpreted by Aphraates as a foreshadowing of Christian baptism: "Great is this mystery, my friend, that Gideon anticipated and showed the model of baptism, and the mystery of the struggle and the example of the single ones"[89] (Aphraates, *Sermons,* 7.19–21 [PS 1:344–348]).

Like Aphraates, so too in the *Paralipomena* the test in the waters of the Jordan is intended to determine those who are prepared to devote themselves to the struggle of asceticism and virginity. Hence, the demand to leave the Babylonian spouses is understood as a demand to eschew or abrogate marriage ties in general, as a condition for baptism and entry into the heavenly Jerusalem. Only the "individuals" who are prepared to abandon everything for the sake of Christ are deserving of baptism, and the baptismal waters are able to separate out those few who are truly deserving of the struggle that confronts

---

[89] In Ephraem Syrus, Gideon's act is also interpreted as a test of readiness for battle and as a symbol for baptism that creates "virgins" and "holy ones." "From the water, Gideon chose men who were victorious in battle. You have descended to the water pure; ascend, and be victorious in battle. Receive from the water atonement, and from the battle a laurel" (*Epiphania* 7, 8 [CSCO, 186; Scr. Syri 82; p. 164]; Murray, "Exhortation," 64).

them.⁹⁰ Abimelech, Baruch, and Jeremiah are the models for the single ones, the virgins, who sacrifice marital life and devote themselves to the Lord, as implied by Baruch's prayer:

> You are the God who bestows a reward [on] those who love you. Prepare yourself, my heart; rejoice and be glad in your tabernacle, saying to your fleshly dwelling, "Your sorrow has been turned to joy." For the Mighty One is coming and will raise you in your tabernacle, for sin has not taken root in you. Be refreshed within your tabernacle, in your virgin faith, and believe that you will live. (*P. Jer.* 6:4)

In order to conduct this struggle, God will free the holy believer from the fetters of flesh, in which there is hidden sin and lust, and then he will be able to live his virgin faith whole and compete.⁹¹

In the seventh sermon, Aphraates does not connect the "waters of testing" with the Jordan, but he does so in another sermon which likewise relates to baptism, as well as giving expression to ancient liturgical motifs.⁹² In the eleventh sermon, "On Circumcision" (*De Circumcisione*), Aphraates expounds the verses depicting the circumcision Joshua performed on the Israelites by means of flint knives after crossing the Jordan (Josh 5:2–3): "Hosea son of Nun circumcised the people a second time with knives of flint when he crossed the Jordan, he and the people. And Jesus our savior promised the land of the living to whoever will cross the River Jordan, and in so believing will circumcise the foreskin of his heart" (Aphraates, *Sermon* 11 [SC 359:567]).

The new circumcision spoken of by Aphraates, the circumcision of the foreskin of the heart, is none other than baptism:

> For in him the whole fullness of deity dwells bodily, and you have come to fullness of life in him, who is the head of all rule and authority. In him also you were circumcised with a circumcision made without hands, by putting off the body of flesh in the circumcision of Christ; and were buried with him in baptism, in which you were also raised with him through your faith in the working of God, who raised him from the dead. (Col 2:9–12)⁹³

---

⁹⁰ Vööbus, *Celibacy,* 50–58.

⁹¹ Jeremiah is depicted as the model for the monk who has taken the oath of virginity and singleness in Ephraem Syrus's hymns concerning virginity, which are extant only in Armenian (Graffin, "Hymnes Inédites de Saint Ephraem," 213–42). In the *Paralipomena,* Jeremiah is shown as a Christian messenger who preaches the gospel, as the old man explicitly says to Abimelech: "Jeremiah is in Babylon with the people . . . to preach to them and to teach them the word" (5:21).

⁹² Murray, "Exhortation," 66.

⁹³ Cf. Rom 4:11–12; in the NT the seal of baptism is the realization of the biblical sign of circumcision. "Abraham . . . received circumcision as a sign or seal of the

As in the *Paralipomena,* so too in the above-mentioned passage from Aphraates those who wish to walk in the way of Christ and to enter the promised land by means of Jesus need to cross "the true Jordan," which is the test, and to be circumcised in the new circumcision, that is, to be baptized. In order to participate in the *qyama* (covenant) they need to submit to the dividing sword of Christ[94] that separates them from their spouses and their families and to become "single ones" who live a life of sexual celibacy and singleness. In both these works the testing waters and the demand to separate oneself from one's partner needs to be understood against the background of the ascetic atmosphere within which these works were composed.[95] The demand to abandon one's Babylonian marriage partners is consistent with what is related about Jeremiah, who tells the people to refrain from the abominations of the Gentile nations of Babylonia: "and he continued teaching them to keep away from the pollutions of the gentiles of Babylon" (*P. Jer.* 7:37). This demand likewise makes sense in light of the Christian approach, which identified

---

righteousness . . ." (Rom 4:11).

[94] The sword referred to by Aphraates is the same sword that divides between the living and the dead, connected in the *Paralipomena* to the resurrection of Baruch from the grave. On the dividing sword, cf. *The Gospel of Thomas,* 16 (Elliott, *Apocryphal NT,* 137); also A. Guillaumont et al. (eds.), *The Gospel According to Thomas* (Leiden, 1959), 83:32–84, pp. 10–14: "Men possibly think that I have come to throw peace upon the world, and they do not know that I have come to throw divisions upon the earth, fire, sword, war. For there shall be five in a house; three shall be against two and two against three, the father against the son and the son against the father, and they will stand as solitaries (μόναχος)." The Gospel of Thomas is dated to the mid-second century or earlier, and originated in Edessa. See Elliott, *Apocryphal NT,* 124; *Die Pseudoklementinen,* I, Hom. XI, 19.

[95] Philonenko, "Simples Observations," 163. The demand for celibacy and separation from one's spouse as a condition of Christian baptism finds clear expression in the work *Acts of Thomas,* which evidently belongs to the same ascetic milieu as did Aphraates, Ephraem Syrus, and the *Paralipomena.* Thus, e.g., according to the Greek version, Thomas preached to those who came to hear his teaching from him that they would not be privileged to enjoy eternal life unless they separate from their spouses (Elliott, *Apocryphal NT,* 485). According to the Syriac version, he taught them a new doctrine of asceticism and said that a man cannot live unless he separates from all that he owns, and becomes an ascetic and a wanderer like himself (W. Wright, *Apocryphal Acts of the Apostles; The Syriac Part,* 267). In wake of this preaching of Thomas, Mygdonia took upon herself a life of asceticism, refused to have relations with her husband, sought the seal of Jesus, was baptized, and participated in the Eucharist. Other persons in this story did likewise (Elliott, *Apocryphal NT,* 497, 502–5). The *Acts of Thomas* is dated to the third century (Elliott, 442).

the pagan kingdoms generally as the dominion of Satan and saw in Babylon the home of Satan, embodied in the figure of Nebuchadnezzar himself.[96]

The refraining from the pollutions of the pagans corresponds to the decision of the apostolic assembly in Jerusalem "to abstain from the pollutions of idols" (Acts 15:19), which similarly implies the demand to separate from members of one's own family. A demand in similar spirit is expressed in other ascetic sources. Thus, in *Pseudo-Clementine* Sermon 13.4, Peter explains the Christian way of life to the woman:

> We do not live with all indiscriminately; nor do we take our food from the same table as Gentiles, inasmuch as we cannot eat along with them, because they live impurely. But when we have persuaded them to have true thoughts and to follow a right course of action, and have baptized them with thrice-blessed invocation, then we dwell with them. For not even if it were our father or mother, or wife or child, or brother, or any other one having a claim by nature on our affection, can we venture to take our meals with him; for our religion compels us to make a distinction.[97]

This text reflects the interrelationship among all of the elements noted thus far: separation from strangers, the dividing sword of Jesus, and baptism.[98]

Those who did not want to separate from their spouses dwelt in the desert place and built a city and call it Samaria. The desert place evidently symbolizes this world, the world of sin, as Gregory of Nyssa says:

> Go in wake of Jesus, son of Nun, carry the gospel as he carried the holy ark. Abandon the desert, the sin. Cross the Jordan. Hasten towards life according to Jesus, to till the soil which bears its fruits of joy. This is the land flowing with milk and honey, according to the promise.[99]

---

[96] See Origen, *Hom. Jer.* I.3 (SC 232; vol. 1, 200–201); Origen, *Hom. Ezech.*, XI.5 (SC 352:373). Nebuchadnezzar is presented there as Satan. Cf. Jerome's interpretation and translation of Origen's homilies (Jerome, *Orig. Jer. Ezech.* [PL 25:614–15, 639, etc.]).

[97] *The Clementine Homilies* (*ANF* 8; ed. A. Roberts and J. Donaldson; Cambridge, Mass., 1995), 300–301.

[98] The *Pseudo-Clementines* are dated to the beginning of the third century (Cross, *Oxford Dictionary of the Christian Church*, 304; T. Smith, *The Ante-Nicene Fathers*, 8:74. An opposed view that possibly expresses an internal dispute within early Christianity is taken by Paul, who allows mixed marriages (1 Cor 7:12–16).

[99] Gregory of Nyssa, *On the Baptism of Christ* (PG 46:420d–421a). See also the *Acts Thom.*: Mygdonia describes to Judah Thomas life in this world before accepting Christian faith as "a site of ruins," "like beasts which have not the Logos we are carried" (Wright, 256; Elliott, 481).

The community described in the *Paralipomena* was an ascetic community that demanded of those joining it abstention from marriage, that is, bachelorhood, as a necessary condition of baptism. In this community, baptism was a special privilege of the ascetic elite, and was taken as the sign of those who had the courage to take upon themselves the difficult decision to march forward in the path of their new life and to turn their backs decisively on the world they had left behind. This is a community that refrains from contact with Gentiles and takes particular care not to dine with them, considering them impure so long as they have not taken upon themselves Christianity and the faith in Christ. These aspects are consistent with what is known to us concerning many of the early Christian communities, but they particularly characterize the Syriac-speaking churches of the second and third centuries CE. This community is assured entrance into the heavenly Jerusalem and the resurrection of the dead manifested in the figs from Abimelech's basket.

ABBREVIATIONS

ANF	Ante-Nicene Fathers
ANRW	Aufstieg und Niedergang der römischen Welt
BAR	Biblical Archaeology Review
BR	Biblical Research
CBQ	Catholic Biblical Quarterly
CSCO	Corpus Scriptorum Christianorum Orientalium
DACL	Dictionnaire d'archéologie chrétienne et de liturgie
DB	Dictionnaire de la Bible
DBS	Dictionnaire de la Bible, Supplément
DJD	Discoveries in the Judaean Desert
DSD	Dead Sea Discoveries
EncJud	Encyclopaedia Judaica
EncBib	Encyclopaedia Biblica [Hebrew]
ETL	Ephemerides theologicae lovanienses
FJB	Frankfurter Judaistische Beiträge
GCS	Die griechischen christlichen Schrifsteller der ersten Jahrhunderte
HTR	Harvard Theological Review
HUCA	Hebrew Union College Annual
ICC	International Critical Commentary
IDB	The Interpreter's Dictionary of the Bible
IEJ	Israel Exploration Journal
JAOS	Journal of the American Oriental Society
JBL	Journal of Biblical Literature
JE	The Jewish Encyclopedia
JJS	Journal of Jewish Studies
JPT	Jahrbücher für protestanische Theologie, Leipzig, Braunschweig 1875–1892
JQR	Jewish Quarterly Review
JSJ	Journal for the Study of Judaism
JSP	Journal for the Study of the Pseudepigrapha
JTS	Journal of Theological Studies
JZWL	Jüdische Zeitschrift für Wissenschaft und Leben
KNT	Kommentar zum Neuen Testament
LCL	Loeb Classical Library
LTK	Lexikon für Theologie und Kirche
NovT	Novum Testamentum

NTS	*New Testament Studies*
OTP	*Old Testament Pseudepigrapha,* edited by J. H. Charlesworth, 2 vols., New York, 1983
PG	Patrologia graeca, edited by J. P. Migne
PL	Patrologia latina, edited J. P. Migne
PS	Patrologia syriaca
PVTG	Pseudepigrapha Veteris Testamenti Graece
RB	*Revue biblique*
REJ	*Revue des études juives*
RHPR	*Revue d'histoire et de philosophie religieuses*
RevQ	*Revue de Qumran*
SC	Sources chrétiennes
Scr. Syri	Corpus Scriptorum Christianorum Orientalium Scriptores Syri
TDNT	*Theological Dictionary of the New Testament*
TU	Texte und Untersuchungen
VT	*Vetus Testamentum*
ZAW	*Zeitschrift für die alttestamentliche Wissenschaft*
ZDMG	*Zeitschrift der deutschen morgenländischen Gesellschaft*
ZNTW	*Zeitschrift für die neutestamentliche Wissenschaft*

BIBLIOGRAPHY

Abegg, M. G., Jr. "Messianic Hope and 4Q285: A Reassessment." *Journal of Biblical Literature* 113 (1994): 81–91.

Abot de-Rabbi Nathan. Edited by S. Schechter. New York, 1967.

Abravanel, D. I. *Perush ha-Torah.* Edited by A. Schottland. Jerusalem, 1997.

Acts of Peter. Pages 304–36 in *The Apocryphal New Testament,* edited by M. R. James. Oxford, 1975.

Acts of Thomas. Pages 439–511 in *The Apocryphal New Testament,* edited by J. K. Elliott. Oxford, 1993.

Aland, K., M. Black, C. M. Martini, B. M. Metzger, and A. Wikgren, eds. *The Greek New Testament.* 2d ed. New York: United Bible Society, 1969.

Albeck, H. *Mishnah.* See *Mishnah.*

———. "Introduction to Bereshit Rabbah" [Hebrew]. Pages 1–138 in *Midrash Bereshit Rabbah,* edited by J. Theodor and H. Albeck. Jerusalem, 1965.

———. "Midrash Vayiqra Rabbah." In *Sefer ha-yovel likhevod Levi Ginzberg,* edited by S. Leiberman et al. New York, 1946.

Allegro, J. M. "Further Messianic References in Qumran Literature." *Journal of Biblical Literature* 75 (1956): 174–87.

———. "More Isaiah Commentaries from Qumran's Fourth Cave." *Journal of Biblical Literature* 77 (1958): 215–21.

———. "Fragments of a Qumran Scroll of Eschatological Midraṣim." *Journal of Biblical Literature* 77 (1958): 350–54.

———. *Discoveries in the Judaean Desert,* vol. V [= Commentary on Isaiah]. Oxford, 1968.

Allen, W. C. *Critical and Exegetical Commentary on the Gospel According to Saint Matthew.* International Critical Commentary. Edinburgh, 1907.

Alon, G. *Toldot ha-Yehudim be-Eretz Yisra'el betequfat ha-Mishnah veha-Talmud.* 2 vols. Tel-Aviv, 1976.

———. "The Halakhah in the Epistle of Barnabas" [Hebrew]. Pages 295–312 in *Mehqarim be-Toldot Yisra'el,* I. Tel Aviv, 1967. (= *Tarbiz* 11 [1940]: 25ff.)

———. "Halakhah in the Doctrine of the Apostles" [Hebrew]. Pages 274–94 in *Mehqarim be-Toldot Yisra'el*, I. Tel Aviv, 1967.

Ambrose. *De Mysteriis*. PL 16.

Amélineau, E. *Contes et romans de l'Égypte chrétienne*. 2 vols. Collection des contes et chansons populaires 13, 14. Paris, 1888.

Andersen, F. I., trans. "(Slavonic Apocalypse of) Enoch." Pages 91–222 in vol. 1 of *Old Testament Pseudepigrapha*, edited by J. H. Charlesworth. 2 vols. London, 1983–85.

Anderson, G. "Celibacy or Consummation in the Garden? Reflections on Early Jewish and Christian Interpretations of the Garden of Eden." *Harvard Theological Review* 82 (1989): 121–48.

Aphraates, the Persian Sage. *Demonstrationes*. Patrologia syriaca, 1. Edited by R. Graffin. Paris, 1894.

———. *Sermons*. See: Aphraate le Sage Persan. *Les exposés*. 2 vols. Edited by M.-J. Pierre. Sources chrétiennes 349, 359. Paris, 1989.

Apocalypse of Peter. Pages 600–700 in *The Apocryphal New Testament*, edited by J. K. Elliott. Oxford, 1993.

Apocalypse of Paul. Pages 616–44 in *The Apocryphal New Testament*, edited by J. K. Elliott. Oxford, 1993.

Aptowitzer, V. "The Heavenly Temple in the Aggadah" [Hebrew]. *Tarbiz* 3 (1931): 137–53, 257–87.

Arndt, W. F., and F. W. Gingrich. *A Greek-English Lexicon of the New Testament and Other Early Christian Literature. A Translation and Adaptation of Walter Bauer's Griechisch-Deutsches Wörterbuch zu den Schriften des Neuen Testaments und der übrigen urchristlichen Literatur*. Chicago, 1957.

Ascension of Isaiah. See Barton, *Ascension of Isaiah*.

Assis, M. "On the History of the Text of Tractate Shekalim" [Hebrew]. Pages 141–56 in *Proceedings of the Seventh World Congress of Jewish Studies, Section C*. Jerusalem, 1981.

Audet, J. P. *La Didachè; Instructions des apôtres*. Paris, 1958.

Augustine (Saint). *The City of God; Against the Pagans*. Loeb Classical Library. London and Cambridge, Mass., 1960.

———. *Contra Julianum*. PL 44.

Avi-Yonah, M. "The Second Temple" [Hebrew]. Pages 392–418 in *Sefer Yerushalayim*. Jerusalem and Tel Aviv, 1956.

Baars, W. "Neue Textzeugen der Syrischen Baruch." *Vetus Testamentum* 13 (1963): 476–78.

Babylonian Talmud. See *Talmud Bavli.*

Bacher, W. "Notes Critiqes sur la Pesikta Rabbati." *Revue des etudes juives 33* (1898): 40–46.

Baer, Y. "The Manual of Discipline: A Jewish Document of the Second Century CE" [Hebrew]. *Zion* 29 (1964): 1–60.

———. "To Clarify the Doctrine of the End of Days in Second Temple Times" [Hebrew]. *Zion* 23–24 (1958–59): 3–34.

———. "Pesher Habakkuk and Its Period" [Hebrew]. *Zion* 34 (1969): 1–42.

———. *Yisra'el ba-'Amim.* Jerusalem, 1955.

Baillet, M., J. T. Milik, and R. de Vaux, *Les Petites Grottes de Qumran.* Discoveries in the Judaean Desert 3. Oxford, 1962.

Balz, H., and G. Schneider, eds. *Exegetical Dictionary of the New Testament.* Grand Rapids, Mich., 1993.

Baraita de-Melekhet ha-Mishkan. Edited by M. Ish-Shalom. Vienna, 1908.

Barnabas. *The Epistle of Barnabas.* Pages 335–409 in vol. 1 of *The Apostolic Fathers,* edited by K. Lake. Loeb Classical Library. London, 1965.

Barnard, L. W., trans. *St. Justin Martyr: The First and Second Apologies.* Ancient Christian Writers 56. New York and Mahwah, N.J., 1997.

Barrett, C. K. "The Eschatology of the Epistle to the Hebrews." Pages 363–93 in *The Background of the New Testament and Its Eschatology: In Honour of C. H. Dodd,* edited by W. D. Davies and D. Daube. Cambridge, 1964.

Barton, J. M. T. "The Ascension of Isaiah." Pages 775–812 in *The Apocryphal Old Testament,* edited by H. F. D. Sparks. Oxford, 1984.

Basset, R. *Le Livre de Baruch et la Légende de Jérémie, dans Les Apocryphes Éthiopiens.* Paris, 1893.

Bauckham, R. *The Fate of the Dead.* Leiden, Boston & Köln, 1998.

Baumgarten, J. M. "The Qumran Sabbath Shirot and Rabbinic Merkabah Tradition." *Revue de Qumran* 13 (1988) 199–213.

Beale, G. K. *The Use of Daniel in Jewish Apocalyptic Literature and in the Revelation of St. John.* Lanham, 1984.

Beard, M. "Evocatio." Page 580 in *The Oxford Classical Dictionary.* Oxford and New York, 1966.

Bede, the Venerable. *In Matthaei Evangelium Expositio.* PL 92.

Behm, J. "ἄμπελος." Pages 342–43 in vol. 1 of *Theological Dictionary of the New Testament.*

Ben-Menahem, N. "Two Elegies from the Genizah" [Hebrew]. Pages 144–46 in vol. 4 of *Eretz Yisra'el; Mehqarim beyedi'at ha-aretz va-atiqoteha*. Jerusalem, 1967.

Ben Shalom, M. "Selected Historical Issues in *Aboth de-Rabbi Nathan*" [Hebrew]. Master's Dissertation. Tel Aviv, 1987.

Ben Shalom, Y. "Processes and Ideology During the Yavneh Period as Indirect Causes Factors in the Bar-Kokhba Rebellion" [Hebrew]. Pages 1–12 in *Mered Bar-Kokhba: Mehqarim Hadashimi*. Jerusalem, 1984.

———. "The Support of the Sages for Bar-Kokhba's Revolt." [Hebrew]. *Cathedra* 29 (1984): 13–28.

Berenheimer, R. "Vitae Prophetarum." *Journal of the American Oriental Society* 55 (1935): 200–203.

Bereshit Rabbah. See Albeck.

Bet ha-Midrasch. See Jellinek.

Betz, H. D. *Galatians*. Philadelphia, 1979.

Bietenhard, H. *Die himmlische Welt im Urchristentum und Spätjudentum*. Tübingen, 1951.

Black, M. *The Book of Enoch, or I Enoch*. Leiden, 1985.

———. "Qumran Baptismal Rites and Sacred Meal." Pages 91–117 in *The Scrolls and Christian Origins*. Chico, Calif., 1961.

Bloch, J., "Some Christological Interpretations in the Ezra-Apocalypse." *Harvard Theological Review* 51 (1958): 87–94.

Bockmuehl, M. "A 'Slain Messiah' in 4Q Serekh Milhamah (4Q285)?" *Tundale Bulletin* 43 (1992): 155–69.

Bogaert, P. *Apocalypse de Baruch, Introduction, Traduction du Syriaque et Commentaire*. 2 vols. Paris, 1969.

———. "Les Apocalypses Contemporaines de Baruch, d'Esdras et de Jean." Pages 47–68 in *L'Apocalypse Johannique et l'Apocalyptique dans le Nouveau Testament*, ed. J. Lambrecht. Louvain, 1980.

Bohl, F. "Die Legende vom Verbergen der Lade." *Frankfurter Judaistische Beiträge* 4 (1976): 63–80.

Bonner, C. "Two Problems in Melito's Homily on the Passion." *Harvard Theological Review* 31 (1938): 175–90.

Bonner, G. "The Figure of Eve in Augustine's Theology." *Studia Patristica* 33 (1997): 22–34.

Borgen, P. *Bread from Heaven*. Leiden, 1965.

———. "Philo of Alexandria." Pages 280–333 in *Jewish Writings of the Second Temple Period*, edited by M. E. Stone. Assen, 1984.

Botterweck, G. J., and H. Ringgren, eds. *Theological Dictionary of the Old Testament*. 11 vols. Grand Rapids, Mich., 1975.

Bousset, W. *Antichrist Legend*. London, 1896.

———. *Die Offenbarung Johannis*. Göttingen, 1966.

Bousset, W., and H. Gressmann. *Die Religion des Judentums im Späthellenistischen Zeitalter*. Tübingen, 1966.

Bowman, J. *The Gospel of Mark*. Leiden, 1965.

Box, G. H. *The Ezra-Apocalypse*. London, 1912.

Braude, W. G. *Pesikta Rabbati*. New Haven and London, 1968.

Briggs, E. G. *A Critical and Exegetical Commentary on the Book of Psalms*. International Critical Commentary. Edinburgh, 1906–1907.

Brock, S. P. *Isaiah; The Old Testament in Syriac*. Leiden, 1987.

———. "Early Syrian Asceticism." *Numen* 20 (1973): 1–19.

Brockelman, C. *Lexicon Syriacum*. Göttingen, 1928.

Brockington, L. H. "The Syriac Apocalypse of Baruch." Pages 835–95 in *The Apocryphal Old Testament*, edited by H. F. D. Sparks. Oxford, 1984.

Brooks, O. S. "The Johannine Eucharist." *Journal of Biblical Literature* 82 (1963): 293–300.

Brown, F. *The New Brown-Driver-Briggs-Gesenius Hebrew and English Lexicon*. Peabody, Mass., 1979.

Brown, R. E. *The Gospel According to John*. Anchor Bible. New York, 1970.

———. "The Johannine Sacramentary Reconsidered." *ThS* 23 (1962): 183–88.

———. *The Birth of the Messiah*. New York, 1979.

Brownlee, W. H. "Messianic Motifs of Qumran and the New Testament." *New Testament Studies* 3 (1957): 195–210.

Büchler, A. "Die Schauplatze des Bar-Kochbakrieges, und die auf diesen bezogenen jüdischen Nachrichten." *Jewish Quarterly Review* (OS) 16 (1904): 143–205.

Budge, E. A. W. *The Book of the Cave of Treasures*. London, 1927.

———. *The History of the Blessed Virgin Mary and the History of the Likeness of Christ*. London, 1899.

Bultmann, R. *The Gospel of John, A Commentary.* Oxford, 1971.

———. *Theology of the New Testament.* London, 1952.

Burkitt, F. C. *Jewish and Christian Apocalypses.* The Schweich Lectures, 1913. London, 1914.

———. "Aphraates and Monasticism: A Reply," *Journal of Theological Studies* (1905) 10–15.

Burrows, M. *More Light on the Dead Sea Scrolls.* London, 1958.

Burton, E. D. W. *A Critical and Exegetical Commentary on the Epistle to the Galatians.* International Critical Commentary. Edinburgh, 1962.

Buzy, D. "Antechrist." Pages 297–305 in vol. 1 of *Dictionnaire de la Bible, Supplément.* Paris, 1928.

Cabrol, F. "Jeunes." *Dictionnaire d'archéologie chrétienne et de liturgie* 7:2483–2501.

Calmet, A. *Commentaire litteral sur tous les livres de l'Ancien et du Nouveau Testament.* 8 vols. Paris, 1924–26.

Caquot, A. "Bref Commentaire du 'Martyre d'Isaïe.'" *Semitica* 23 (1973): 65–93.

———. "Léviatan et Béhemoth dans la Troisième 'Parabole' d'Hénoch." *Semitica* 25 (1975): 111–22.

Cassius Dio. See Dio Cassius.

Cassutto, M. D. *ha-Elah 'Anat.* Jerusalem, 1951.

———. *Perush 'al Sefer Shemot.* Jerusalem, 1954.

———. "Leviathan" [Hebrew]. *Encyclopaedia Biblica* 4:485.

Causse, A. "De la Jerusalem Terrestre a la Jerusalem Celeste," *Revue d'histoire et de philosophie religieuses* 27 (1947): 12–36.

Cavallin, H. C. *Life After Death: Paul's Argument for the Resurrection of the Dead in I Cor. 15. Part 1: An Inquiry into the Jewish Background.* New Testament Series, 7/1. Lund, 1974.

Ceriani, A. M. "Apocalypsis Syriaca Baruch." Pages 113–80 in vol. 2.iv of *Monumenta Sacra et Profana ex Codicibus Praesertim Bibliothecae Ambrosianae.* Milan, 1871.

———. "Paralipomena Jeremiae Prophetae quae in Aetiopica Versione Dicuntur Reliqua Verborum Baruchi." Pages 9–18 in vol. 5 of *Monumenta Sacra et Profana.* Milan, 1868. 9–18.

Chadwick, H. *The Early Church.* London, 1967.

Charles, R. H. *The Book of Enoch.* Oxford, 1893.

———. *The Apocalypse of Baruch.* London, 1896.

———. *The Ascension of Isaiah.* London, 1900.

———. *The Apocrypha and Pseudepigrapha of the Old Testament.* 2 vols. Oxford, 1913.

———. *A Critical and Exegetical Commentary on the Revelation of St. John.* 2 vols. International Critical Commentary. Edinburgh, 1920.

———. *Eschatology: The Doctrine of a Future Life in Israel, Judaism and Christianity.* New York, 1963.

———. "II Baruch." Pages 470–526 in vol. 2 of *The Apocrypha and Pseudepigrapha of the Old Testament.*

Charlesworth, J. H. "The Concept of the Messiah in the Pseudepigrapha," *Aufstieg und Niedergang der römischen Welt* 19.1 (1979): 188–218.

———. "From Jewish Messianology to Christian Christology: Some Caveats and Perspectives," Pages 225–64 in *Judaisms and Their Messiahs at the Turn of the Christian Era,* edited by J. Neusner, W. S. Green, and E. S. Frerichs. Cambridge, 1987.

———. "Jesus as the 'Son' and the Righteous Teacher as 'Gardener,'" Pages 146–47 in *Jesus and the Dead Sea Scrolls,* edited by J. H. Charlesworth. New York, 1992.

———. *The Old Testament Pseudepigrapha.* 2 vols. London, 1983–85.

Cheyne, T. K. *Prophecies of Isaiah.* London, 1898.

Chronis, H. L. "The Torn Veil: Cultus and Christology in Mark 15:38–39." *Journal of Biblical Literature* 101/1 (1982): 97–114.

Clement I, II. Pages 3–163 in vol. 1 of *The Apostolic Fathers,* edited by K. Lake Loeb Classical Library. London, 1965.

Clement of Alexandria. *Le Pédagogue.* Sources chrétiennes 70, 108, 158. Paris 1960–1970.

———. *Stromata.* PG 9.

Clifford, R. J. *The Cosmic Mountain in Canaan and the Old Testament.* Cambridge, Mass., 1972.

Collins, A. Y. "Aristobulus." Pages 830–36 in vol. 2 of *Old Testament Pseudepigrapha,* edited by J. H. Charlesworth. 2 vols. London, 1983–85.

Collins, J. J. *The Apocalyptic Imagination.* New York, 1987.

———. *Apocalypticism in the Dead Sea Scrolls.* Leiden-New York, 1997.

———. "Messianism in the Maccabean Period." Pages 97–109 in *Judaisms and their Messiahs at the Turn of the Christian Era,* edited by J. Neusner et al. Cambridge, 1987.

Collins, M. F. "The Hidden Vessels in Samaritan Traditions." *Journal for the Study of Judaism* 3 (1972): 97–119.

Connolly, R. H. *Didascalia Apostolorum.* Oxford, 1969.

———. "Aphraates and Monasticism," *Journal of Theological Studies* 6 (1904): 522–38.

Cook, S. L. *Prophecy and Apocalypticism.* Minneapolis, 1995.

Cooke, G. A. *A Critical and Exegetical Commentary on the Book of Ezekiel.* International Critical Commentary. Edinburgh, 1967.

Coppens, J. "Eucharistie." *Dictionnaire de la Bible, Supplément* 2:1146–1215.

Cothenet, E. "Le Protévangile de Jacques: Origine, genre et signification d'un premier midrash chrétien sur la nativité de Marie." Pages 4253–69 in *Aufstieg und Niedergang der römischen Welt,* Teil II: Principat; Band 25.6: Religion. Berlin and New York, 1988.

———. "Protévangile de Jacques." *Dictionnaire de la Bible, Supplément* (Paris, 1972) 7:1374–84.

Craig, C. T. "Sacramental Interest in the Fourth Gospel." *Journal of Biblical Literature* 58 (1939): 31–41.

Cross, F. L., ed. *The Oxford Dictionary of the Christian Church.* Oxford, 1983.

Cross, F. M. *The Ancient Library of Qumran and Modern Biblical Studies.* The Haskell Lectures, 1956–1957. New York, 1958.

Cullmann, O. *Baptism in the New Testament.* London, 1964.

———. *Early Christian Worship.* London, 1966.

———. *Immortality and Resurrection.* New York, 1965.

———. *The Johannine Circle.* London, 1976.

Cyril of Jerusalem. *Hymni et Sermones.* [Syriac.] Edited by G. Bickell. *Zeitschrift der deutschen morgenländischen Gesellschaft* 27 (1873): 566–98.

Daniélou, J. *Primitive Christian Symbols.* London, 1961.

———. *Sacramentum Futuri.* Paris, 1950.

———. "Terre et Paradis chez les Peres de L'Eglise." *Eranos Jahrbuch* 22 (1953): 433–72.

———. *The Theology of Jewish Christianity.* History of Early Christian Doctrine Before the Council of Nicaea, 1. Translated and edited by J. A. Baker. London, 1964.

Davies, W. D. *Paul and Rabbinic Judaism.* London, 1962.

Day, J. *God's Conflict with the Dragon and the Sea.* Cambridge, 1985.

Dedering, S. *Apocalypse of Baruch.* Peshitta Institute, Part IV, Fasc. 3. Leiden, 1975. Pages i-iv; 1–50.

De Faye, E. *Les apocalypses juives: exxai de critique littéraire et théologique.* Paris, 1892.

De Jonge, M. *Jewish Eschatology, Early Christian Christology, and the Testaments of the Twelve Patriarchs: Collected Essays.* Supplements to Novum Testamentum 63. Leiden, 1991.

———. "Remarks in the Margin of the Paper 'The Figure of Jeremiah in the Paralipomena Jeremiae.'" *JSP* 22 (2000): 45–49.

———. "The So-called Pseudepigrapha of the Old Testament and Early Christianity." Pages 59–71 in *The New Testament and Hellenistic Judaism.* Peabody, Mass., 1997.

———. "The Testaments of the Twelve Patriarchs." Pages 505–600 in *The Apocryphal Old Testament,* ed. H. F. D. Sparks. Oxford, 1984.

———. *The Testaments of the Twelve Patriarchs: A Critical Edition of the Greek Text.* Pseudepigrapha Veteris Testamenti Graece, 1.2. Leiden, 1978.

———. "Two Interesting Interpretations of the Rending of the Temple-Veil in the Testaments of the Twelve Patriarchs." Pages 220–31 in *Jewish Eschatology, Early Christian Christology, and the Testaments of the Twelve Patriarchs.* Supplements to Novum Testamentum 63. Leiden, 1991.

———. "χρίω." *Theological Dictionary of the New Testament* 9:511–517.

De Jonge M., and J. Tromp. *The Life of Adam and Eve.* Sheffield, 1997.

De Jonge M., and A. S. van der Woude, "11Q Melchizedek and the New Testament." *NTS* 12 (1966): 301–26.

Deissmann, G. A. *Bibelstudien; Beitrage zumeist aus den Papyri und Inschriften, zur Geschichte der Sprache, des Schrifttums und der Religion des hellenistischen Judentums und des Urchristentums.* Marburg, 1895.

Delling, G. *Jüdische Lehre und Frömmigkeit in den Paralipomena Jeremiae.* Berlin, 1967.

Denis, A. M. *Fragmenta Pseudepigraphorum Quae Supersunt Graeca.* Pseudepigrapha Veteris Testamenti Graece 3. Leiden, 1970.

———. *Introduction aux pseudépigraphes grecs d'Ancien Testament.* Edited by A. M. Denis and M. de Jonge. Studia in Veteris Testamenti Pseudepigrapha, 1. Leiden, 1970.

Deubner, L. *Attische Feste.* Hildesheim, 1962.

De Young, J. C. *Jerusalem in the New Testament.* Kampen, 1960.

Dicuntur Reliqua Verborum Baruchi. Pages 9–18 in vol. 5 of *Monumenta Sacra et Profana.* Milan, 1868.

Didache. Pages 303–33 in *The Apostolic Fathers,* ed. K. Lake. Loeb Classical Library. Cambridge, Mass., 1965.

Didascalia et Constitutiones Apostolorum. See Funk.

Dilmann, A. "Pseudepigraphen des Alten Testaments." Pages 341–67 in vol. 12 of *Encyclopädie für protestantische Theologie und Kirche.* Leipzig, 1883.

Dillmann, A. "Reliqua Verborum Baruchi." *Chrestomathia Aethiopica.* Leipzig, 1866.

Dimant, D. "4QFlorilegium and the Idea of the Community as Temple." Pages 165–89 in *Hellenica et Judaica,* edited by A. Caquot, M. Hadas, J. Lebel, and J. Riaud. Leuven and Paris, 1968.

———. "History According to the Vision of the Beasts (Ethiopic Enoch 85–90)" [Hebrew]. *Mehqerei Yerushalyim be-mahshevet Yisra'el* 2 (1982): 18–37.

———. "Jerusalem and the Temple According to the Animal Apocalypse (*1 Enoch* 85–90) in Light of the Ideology of the Dead Sea Sect" [Hebrew]. *Shnaton la-Miqra ule-heqer ha-Mizrah ha-Qadum* 5–6 (1981–82): 177–93.

———. "The Apocalyptic Interpretation of Ezekiel at Qumran." Pages 31–51 in *Messiah and Christos, Studies in the Jewish Origins of Christianity, Presented to D. Flusser.* Tübingen, 1992.

Dio Cassius. *Roman History.* Edited by E. Cary. 9 vols. Loeb Classical Library. London and Cambridge, Mass., 1954–55.

Diodorus of Sicily, ed. C. H. Oldfather. Loeb Classical Library. Cambridge, 1933.

Diqduqei Soferim. Edited by S. Z. Rabinowitz. Jerusalem, 1960.

Dodd, C. H. *The Interpretation Of The Fourth Gospel.* Cambridge, 1968.

Dods, M. *The First Epistle to the Corinthians.* London, 1890.

Doran, R. "Narrative Literature." Pages 287–310 in *Early Judaism and Its Modern Interpreters,* edited by R. A. Kraft and G. W. E. Nickelsburg. Atlanta, Ga., 1986.

Driver, S. R., and G. B. Gray, *The Book of Job.* Edinburgh, 1921.

Drower, E. S. *The Mandaeans of Iraq and Iran.* Leiden, 1962.

Drower, E. S., and R. Macuch, *A Mandaic Dictionary.* Oxford, 1963.

Efron, J. "Daniel and His Three Friends in Exile." Pages 67–112 in *Studies on the Hasmonean Period*. Leiden, 1987.

———. "Holy War and Visions of Redemption in the Hasmonean Period." Pages 33–66 in *Studies on the Hasmonean Period*. Leiden, 1987.

———. "Simeon ben Shatah and Alexander Jannaeus." Pages 143–218 in *Studies on the Hasmonean Period*. Leiden, 1987.

———. *Studies on the Hasmonean Period*. Leiden, 1987.

———. "The Bar-Kokhba War in Light of the Palestinian Talmudic Tradition as Against the Babylonian" [Hebrew]. Pages 47–105 in *Mered Bar-Kohkhba; Mehqarim Hadashim*, edited by A. Oppenheimer and U. Rappaport. Jerusalem, 1984.

———. "The Great Sanhedrin in Vision and Reality." Pages 286–338 in *Studies on the Hasmonean Period*. Leiden, 1987.

———. "The Hasmonean Kingdom and Simeon ben Shetah" [Hebrew]. Doctoral Dissertation. Jerusalem, 1962.

———. "The Idea of the Servant of God in the Book of Daniel." Pages 113–42 in *Studies on the Hasmonean Period*. Leiden, 1987.

———. "The Psalms of Solomon, The Hasmonean Decline, and Christianity." Pages 219–86 in *Studies on the Hasmonean Period*. Leiden, 1987.

Ego, B. *Im Himmel wie auf Erden*. Tübingen, 1989.

Eichhorn, J. G. *Einleitung in die apokryphischen Schriften des Alten Testaments*. Leipzig, 1795.

Eisenman, R. "More on the Pierced Messiah Text from Eisenman and Vermes." *Biblical Archaeology Review* 19:1 (1993) 66–67.

Eisenman, R., and M. Wise. *The Dead Sea Scrolls Uncovered*. New York and London, etc., 1992.

Eldridge, M. D. *Dying Adam with His Multiethnic Family*. Leiden, Boston & Köln, 2001.

Elliott, J. K. (ed.), *The Apocryphal New Testament*. Oxford, 1993.

Enzeqlopedya Talmudit. Edited by M. Bar-Ilan, S. Y. Zevin. Jerusalem, 1947–1989.

Ephraem Syrus. *Carmina Nisibena*. Edited by E. Beck. 2 vols. in 4. Part I: Corpus Scriptorum Christianorum Orientalium 218–219, 240–41, Syr. 92–93, 102–103. Louvain, 1961–1963.

———. *Commentaire de l'evangile concordant ou Diatessaron Traduit du Syrien et de l'Armenien*. Edited by L. Leloir. Sources chrétiennes 121. Paris, 1966.

———. *Hymnen de Nativitate [Hnat].* Edited by E. Beck. 2 vols. Corpus Scriptorum Christianorum Orientalium 186–187; Corpus Scriptorum Christianorum Orientalium. Scriptores Syri, 82–83. Louvain, 1959.

———. *Hymnen de Paradiso und Contra Julianum.* Edited by E. Beck. Corpus Scriptorum Christianorum Orientalium 174; Corpus Scriptorum Christianorum Orientalium Scriptores Syri, 78. Louvain, 1957.

———. *Hymnen de Virginitate.* Edited by E. Beck. 2 vols. Corpus scriptorum Christianorum Orientalium, 223–224. Louvain, 1962.

———. *Hymnes sur le paradis.* Translated from Syriac by R. Lavenant. Introduction and notes by F. Graffin. Sources chrétiennes 137. Paris, 1968.

Epiphanius. *Panarion (Panarium) Adversus Haereses.* Patrologiae cursus completus: Series graeca, 41. Edited by J.-P. Migne. Turnholti, 1860.

———. *Panarion (Panarium) Adversus Haereses.* Die griechischen christlichen Schriftsteller der ersten Jahrhunderte, 25 & 31. Edited by K. Holl. Berlin, 1985.

Epstein, Y. N. *Mavo le-Nusah ha-Mishnah.* Jerusalem, 1948.

———. "On Fine Points of the Jerusalem Talmud" [Hebrew], *Tarbiz* 5 (1934): 257–72.

Eusebius. *Demonstratio Evangelica.* Patrologiae cursus completus: Series graeca, 22. Edited by J.-P. Migne. Paris, 1857.

———. *Ecclesiastical History.* Edited by J. E. L. Oulton and K. Lake. Loeb Classical Library. London and Cambridge, Mass., 1953–1957.

Even Shmuel, Y. *Midrashei Ge'ulah.* Jerusalem and Tel Aviv, 1954.

Ewald, H. *Geschichte des Volkes Israel bis Christus,* III, Letzte Hälfte. Göttingen, 1852.

Exodus Rabbah. See *Midrash Rabbah.*

Fabricius, J. A. *Codex Pseudepigraphus Veteris Testamenti, Collectus, Castigatus Testimoniisque, Censuris et Animadversionibus Illustratus.* 2 vols. Hamburg, 1722–1723.

Fallon, F. "Eupolemus." Pages 862–871 in vol. 2 of *Old Testament Pseudepigrapha,* edited by J. H. Charlesworth. 2 vols. London, 1983–85.

Fee, G. D. *The First Epistle to the Corinthians,* ed. F. F. Bruce. (New International Commentary on the New Testament) Grand Rapids, Mich., 1988.

Feldman, L. H. "Prolegomenon." Pages IX-CLXIX in M. R. James, *The Biblical Antiquities of Philo* (New York, 1971).

Fitzer, G. "σφραγίς." *Theological Dictionary of the New Testament* 7:939–53.

Flemming, J., and H. Duensing, "The Ascension of Isaiah." Pages 642–63 in E. Hennecke, *New Testament Apocrypha*, vol. II. Great Britain, 1974.

Flint, P. "'Apocrypha' and Previously Known Writings and 'Pseudepigrapha' in the Dead Sea Scrolls" Pages 60–61 in vol. 2 of *The Dead Sea Scrolls After Fifty Years*, edited by P. Flint and J. C. VanderKam. Leiden, 1999.

Flusser, D., ed. *Sefer Yossipon.* Jerusalem, 1978.

———. "The Apocryphal Book of Ascensio Isaiae and the Dead Sea Sect." *Israel Exploration Journal* (1953): 30–47.

———. "Two Notes on the Midrash on Sam. Vii." *Israel Exploration Journal* 9 (1959): 99–109.

———. "Jerusalem in Second Temple Literature" [Hebrew]. Pages 263–294 in *Ve-em begevurot*, edited by A. Even-Shushan, A. H. Elhanani, A. Beer, A. M. Haberman, and S. Shalom. Reuven Mass Festscrift. Jerusalem, 1974

———. "The *Isaiah Pesher* and the Idea of the Twelve Apostles in Early Christianity" [Hebrew]. Pages 283–304 in his *Yahadut u-meqorot ha-Nazrut.* Tel Aviv, 1979.

———. "There are Two Paths" [Hebrew]. Pages 235–52 in his *Yahadut u-meqorot ha-Nazrut.* Tel Aviv, 1979.

———. "The Last Supper and the Essenes" [Hebrew]. Pages 115–19 in his *Yahadut u-meqorot ha-Nazrut.* Tel Aviv, 1979.

———. "The Four Empires in the Fourth Sibyl and in the Book of Daniel." Pages 317–44 in his *Judaism and the Origins of Christianity.* Jerusalem, 1988.

———. "Apocalypse." *Encyclopaedia Judaica* 3:179–81.

Foerster, W. "ὄρος." *Theological Dictionary of the New Testament* 5:475–78.

Ford, J. M. *Revelation.* (Anchor Bible) New York, 1975.

———. "The Heavenly Jerusalem and Orthodox Judaism." *Donum Gentilicium; New Testament Studies in Honor of David Daube* (edited by E. Bammel et al; Oxford, 1978) 215–226.

Frey, J. B. "L'apocalypse syriaque de Baruch." Pages 418–23 in vol. 1 of *Dictionnaire de la Bible, Supplément*, edited by L. Pirot, A. Robert, U. Cazelles, A. Feuillet. Paris, 1928.

Fritsch, C. T. "Apocrypha." *The Interpreter's Dictionary of the Bible* 1.161–66.

Funk, F. X. *Didascalia et Constitutiones Apostolorum.* Vol. I. Torino, 1970.

Furst, J. *Handwörterbuch über das Alte Testament.* Leipzig, 1876.

Gallois, R. P. "L'apocalypse de Saint Jean." *Revue biblique* 2 (1893) 384–430.

García Martínez, F. "L'interpretation de la Torah d'Ezechiel dans les MSS. de Qumran." *Revue de Qumran* 13 (1988) 441–452.

———. "The 'New Jerusalem' and the Future Temple of the Manuscripts from Qumran." *Qumran and Apocalyptic* (Leiden, 1992) 180–213.

García Martínez, F., and E. J. C. Tigchelaar, eds. *The Dead Sea Scrolls Study Edition*. Leiden, New York & Koln, 1997.

García Martinez, F., and A. S. van der Woude, "A Groningen Hypothesis of Qumran Origins and Early History." *RQ* 14 (1990): 521–41.

Gartner, B. *The Temple and the Community in Qumran and the New-Testament; A Comparative Study in The Temple Symbolism of the Qumran Texts and the New-Testament*. Cambridge, 1965.

Gaster, M. *The Chronicles of Jerahmeel*. New York, 1971.

Gaster, T. H. *The Dead Sea Scriptures*. New York, 1976.

Gaston, L. *No Stone On Another*. Leiden, 1970.

Geiger, A. "Erbsünde und Versöhnungstod: Deren Versuch in das Judenthum einzudringen." *Jüdische Zeitschrift für Wissenschaft und Leben* 10 (1872): 166–71.

Geyser, A. "The Twelve Tribes in Revelation, Judean and Judeo Christian Apocalypticism." *New Testament Studies* 28 (1982) 388–399.

———. "Some Salient New Testament Passages on the Restoration of the Twelve Tribes of Israel." *l'Apocalypse Johannique et l'Apocalyptique dans le Nouveau Testament* (ed. J. Lambrecht; Louvain, 1980), 305–310.

Giblet, J. "Eupolème et l'Historiographie du Judaïsme Hellénistique." *Ephemerides theologicae lovanienses* 39 (1963) 539–554.

Gil, M. "Studies in the Book of Enoch" [Hebrew], in *Dor le-Dor; Qovez Mehqarim likhevod Yehoshua Efron* (eds. A. Oppenheimer and A. Kasher; Jerusalem, 1995) 155–200.

Ginzberg, L. *Legends of the Jews*. 7 vols. Philadelphia, 1909.

———. *Perushim ve-Hiddushim ba-Yerushalmi*. New York, 1941–61.

———. "Baruch, Apocalypse of (Syriac)." *The Jewish Encyclopedia* 2 (1903): 551–56.

———. "Some Observations on the Attitude of the Synagogue Towards the Apocalyptic-Eschatological Writings." *Journal of Biblical Literature* 41 (1922) 115–36.

Ginzberg, L., ed. *Yerushalmi Fragments from the Genizah (= Seridei ha-Yerushalmi [from the Genizah])*. New York, 1909.

Glasson, T. *Moses in the Fourth Gospel.* London, 1963.

Golden, M. *Childhood in Classical Athens.* Baltimore and London, 1990.

Goldstein, J. A. *II Maccabees.* (The Anchor Bible) New York, 1983.

Goodblatt, D. *The Monarchic Principle.* Tübingen, 1994.

———. "Suicide in the Sanctuary: Traditions on Priestly Martyrdom." *Journal of Jewish Studies* 46 (1995) 10–29.

———. "Tannaitic Support or Priestly Influence" [Hebrew]. *Cathedra* 29 (1984): 6–12.

Goodspeed, E. J. *A History of Early Christian Literature.* Chicago, 1942.

Goppelt, L. *Typos: The Typological Interpretation of the Old Testament in the New.* Grand Rapids, Mich., 1978.

Gordon, R. P. "The Interpretation of 'Lebanon' and 4Q285." *Journal of Jewish Studies* 43 (1992) 92–94.

Gospel of Peter. Pages 90–94 in *The Apocryphal New Testament,* edited by M. R. James. Oxford 1975.

Gospel of Thomas. Pages 123–47 in *The Apocryphal New Testament,* edited by J. K. Elliott. Oxford, 1993.

Graffin, F. "Hymnes Inédites de Saint Ephraem sur la Virginité." *L'Orient Syrien* 6 (1961), 213–242.

Gregory of Nyssa. *De Baptismo.* Patrologiae cursus completus: Series graeca, 46.

Grenfell, B. P., and A. S. Hunt, *The Oxyrhyncus Papyri.* London, 1903.

Grinz, Y. M. "Apocrypha and Pseudepigrapha." *Encyclopaedia Judaica* 3. 181–186.

Gry, L. "La Date de la Fin des Temps, selon les Révélations ou les Calculs du Pseudo-Philon et de Baruch (Apocalypse Syriaque)." *Revue biblique* 48 (1939) 337–356.

———. "Le Papias des Belles Promesses Messianiques." *Vivre et Penser* 3 (1944), *Revue biblique* 52 (1943/44), 112–124.

———. "La Ruine du Temple par Titus; Quelques Traditions Juives Plus Anciennes et Primitives à la Base de *Pesikta Rabbati* xxvi." *Revue biblique* 55 (1948) 215–226.

Guttmann, J. *Ha-Sifrut ha-Yehudit ha-Hellenistit.* Jerusalem, 1963.

———. "Leviathan, Behemoth and Ziz: Jewish Messianic Symbol in Art." *Hebrew Union College Annual* 39 (1968) 219–230.

Gvaryahu, H. M. I. "The Vision of the Temple Mount in the End of the Days" [Hebrew]. Pages 88–124 in vol. 1 of *Studies in the Book of Isaiah*, edited by B. Z. Luria. Jerusalem, 1976.

Hadot, J. "La Datation de l'Apocalypse Syriaque de Baruch." *Semitica* 15 (1965), 79–95.

Hall, G. R. "The Ascension of Isaiah: Community Situation, Date, and Place in Early Christianity." *Journal of Biblical Literature* 109/2 (1990) 289–306.

Hall, S. G. (ed.). *On Pascha*. Oxford, 1979.

Hameiri, M. *Perush ha-Mishnah leha-Meiri, le-Rabbenu Menahem be-Rav Shlomo le-Beit Meir*. (ed. M. M. Meshi-Zahav), Jerusalem, 1971.

Hamerton-Kelly, R. G. "The Temple and the Origins of Jewish Apocalyptic." *Vetus Testamentum* 20 (1970) 1–15.

Hanson, P. "Prolegomena to the Study of Jewish Apocalyptic." Pages 389–413 in *Magnalia Dei: The Mighty Acts of God*. New York, 1976.

Haran, M. *Bein Rishonot la-Ḥadashot*. Jerusalem, 1963.

———. "The Disappearance of the Ark." *Israel Exploration Journal* 13 (1963): 46–58.

Hare, D. R. A. "The Lives of the Prophets." Pages 379–399 in vol. 2 of *Old Testament Pseudepigrapha*, edited by J. H. Charlesworth. 2 vols. London, 1983–85.

Harofe (Troki), Y. Pages 145–46 of *Hizzuk Emuna* [Hebrew]. Ashdod, 1975.

Harnack, A. *History of Dogma*. New York, 1961.

Harnisch, W. *Verhängnis und Verheissung der Geschichte: Untersuchungen zum Zeit- und Geschichtsverständnis im 4 Buch Esra und in der Syr. Baruchapokalypse*. Göttingen, 1969.

Harrington, D. J. "Pseudo-Philo." Pages 297–377 in vol. 2 of *Old Testament Pseudepigrapha*, edited by J. H. Charlesworth. 2 vols. London, 1983–85.

Harrington, W. H. *Understanding the Apocalypse*. Washington and Cleveland, 1969.

Harris, R., and A. Mingana. *The Odes and Psalms of Salomon*. Oxford, 1916.

Harris, R. J. *The Rest of the Words of Baruch: A Christian Apocalypse of the Year 136 A.D.* London, 1889.

———. "A New Jeremiah Apocryphon" (Woodbrooke Studies 1), *Bulletin of the John Rylands Library* 2 (Manchester, 1927), 329–342.

Hartman L. F., and A. A. Di Lella, *The Book of Daniel*. Anchor Bible. New York, 1978.

Hartom, A. S. *Qadmoniyut ha-Miqra.* Tel Aviv, 1969.

Hatch, E., and H. A. Redpath. *A Concordance to the Septuagint.* Graz, 1954.

Heinemann, Y. *Aggadot ve-Toldotehen.* Jerusalem, 1974.

Heller, B. "Éléments, Parallèles et Origine de la Légende des Sept Dormants." *The Jewish Encyclopedia* 48 (1904) 190–218.

Hengel, M. *Judaism and Hellenism: Studies in Their Encounter in Palestine During the Early Hellenistic Period.* Philadelphia, 1974.

Hennecke, E. *New Testament Apocrypha.* Edited by W. Schneemelcher. Translated by R. McL. Wilson. 2 vols. London, 1963–1965.

Herodotus. Edited by A. D. Godley. Loeb Classical Library. Cambridge, Mass., and London, 1946.

Herr, M. D. "Midrash." *Encyclopaedia Judaica* 12. 1507–1514.

Herzer, J. "Direction in Difficult Times: How God is Understood in the *Paralipomena Jeremiae*." *Journal for the Study of the Pseudepigrapha* 22 (2000): 9–30.

———. *Die Paralipomena Jeremiae.* Tübingen, 1994.

———. "Die Paralipomena Jeremiae – Eine christlich-gnostische Schrift?" *Journal for the Study of Judaism* 30 (1999): 25–39.

Hesiod. *Works and Days.* Edited by M. L. West. Oxford, 1978.

———. *Theogony.* Edited by H. G. Evelyn White. Leob Classical Library. London & Cambridge, Mass., 1959.

Hesse, F, "χρίω." *Theological Dictionary of the New Testament* 9:496–509.

Higgins, A. J. B. "Jewish Messianic Belief in Justin Martyr's Dialogue With Trypho." *Novum Testamentum* 9 (1967) 298–305.

Hippolytus. *Christ and Antichrist.* Patrologiae cursus completus: Series graeca, 10.

———. *Commentaire sur Daniel.* Sources chrétiennes 14. Paris, 1947.

———. *Fragmenta in Danielem.* Patrologiae cursus completus: Series graeca, 10.

Hirshberg, A. S. *Hayyei ha-Tarbut be-Yisra'el be-tequfat ha-Mishnah veha-Talmud.* Warsaw, 1924.

Hoenig, S. B. *The Great Sanhedrin.* New York, 1953.

Holladay, W. *Jeremiah.* Philadelphia, 1986.

Hollander, H. W., and M. de Jonge, *The Testaments of the Twelve Patriarchs.* Leiden, 1985.

Holleman, J. *Resurrection and Parousia.* Leiden, New York & Köln, 1996.

Homer, *The Iliad.* Loeb Classical Library. Cambridge, Mass., 1999.

———. *The Odyssey.* Loeb Classical Library. Cambridge, Mass., 1995.

Hooker, M. *The Son of Man.* London, 1967.

Huet, P. D. *Demonstratio Evangelica.* Leipzig, 1694.

Hunzinger, C. H. "συκῆ." *Theological Dictionary of the New Testament* 7:751–57.

Hüttenmeister, F. G. *Übersetzung des Talmud Yerushalmi; Sheqalim.* Tübingen, 1990.

Hyman, A. *Toldot Tanna'im ve-Amoraim.* Jerusalem, 1964.

Ignatius, *The Apostolic Fathers,* vol. 1, edited by K. Lake. Loeb Classical Library. Cambridge, Mass., 1965.

Ilan, T. "The Status of the Jewish Woman in Palestine in the Hellenistic-Roman Period" [Hebrew], Doctoral Dissertation, Jerusalem, 1991.

Irenaeus of Lyons. *Contre les Hérésies,* ed. A. Rousseau. 10 vols. Sources chrétiennes 263, 264, 293, 294, 210, 211, 100a, 100b, 152, 153. Paris 1969.

Isaac, E. "1 (Ethiopic Apocalypse of) Enoch." Pages 5–89 in vol. 1 of *The Old Testament Pseudepigrapha,* edited by J. H. Charlesworth. 2 vols. London, 1983–85.

Ish-Shalom, M., ed., *Pesiqta Rabbati.* Tel Aviv, 1967.

Israeli-Taran, A. *Aggadot ha-Hurban.* Tel Aviv, 1997.

Jacobs, I. "Elements of Near-Eastern Mythology in Rabbinic Aggadah." *Journal of Jewish Studies* 28 (1977): 1–11.

Jacobson, H. *A Commentary on Pseudo-Philo's Liber Antiquitatum Biblicarum.* Leiden, New York, and Köln, 1996.

James, M. R. *The Apocryphal New Testament.* Oxford, 1966.

———. *The Biblical Antiquities of Philo.* New York, 1971.

Jastrow, M. *A Dictionary on the Targumim, the Talmud Babli and Yerushalmi, and the Midrashic Literature.* New York, 1950.

Jaubert, A. *La Date de la Cène; calendrier biblique et liturgie chrétienne.* Paris, 1957.

———. "La Symbolique des Douze." Pages 453–60 in *Hommages à André Dupont-Sommer.* Paris, 1971.

Jellinek, A. *Bet ha-Midrasch.* Vols. 4–6. Jerusalem, 1967.

Jeremias, J. "κλείς." *Theological Dictionary of the New Testament* 3:744–53.

———. "λίθος." *Theological Dictionary of the New Testament* 4:265–80.

———. "παράδεισος." *Theological Dictionary of the New Testament* 5:765–73.

Jerome. *Commentariorum in Zachariam.* Corpus Christianorum: Series Latina 76a. Turnhout, 1970.

Jerusalem Talmud. See *Talmud Yerushalmi.*

Johnson, S. F. "Notes and Comments." *Anglican Theological Review* 22 (1940): 330–31.

Jonge, H. J. de. See de Jonge, H. J.

Josephus. *The Jewish War.* Trans. H. St. Thackeray. Loeb Classical Library. Cambridge, Mass., 1927–1928.

———. *Jewish Antiquities.* Translated by H. St. J. Thackeray, R. Marcus, A. Wikgren, and L. H. Feldman. Loeb Classical Library. Cambridge, Mass., 1961–1965.

———. *The Life; Against Apion.* Translated by H. St. J. Thackeray. Loeb Classical Library. Cambridge, Mass., 1966.

Justin Martyr. *I, II Apologies.* Patrologiae cursus completus: Series graeca, 6.

———. *Dialogus cum Tryphone.* Edited by M. Markovich. Patristische Texte und Studien 47. Berlin, 1997.

Kabisch, R. "Die Quellen der Apokalypse Baruch," *Jahrbücher für protestantische Theologie,* 18 (1892): 66–107.

Kahana, A. *Ha-Sefarim ha-Ḥizonyim.* 2 vols. Jerusalem, 1970.

———. *Yehudei Mizrayim ha-Hellenistit veha-Roma'it.* Tel Aviv, 1979.

Kahouth, H. *'Arukh ha-Shalem.* 8 vols. New York, 1892.

Kalimi, I. and D. J. Purvis, "The Hiding of the Temple Vessels in Jewish and Samaritan Literature." *Catholic Biblical Quarterly* 56 (1994): 679–85.

Kappler, W., and R. Hahart. *Maccabaeorum Liber II.* Göttingen, 1959.

Kasher, A. *Yehudei Mizraym ha-Hellenistit veha-Romit* [Hebrew]. Tel Aviv, 1979.

Kasher, M. M. *Torah Shlemah* [Hebrew]. 10 vols. New York, 1994–.

Kasovsky, Ḥ. Y. *Thesaurus Talmudis. [Otsar leshon ha-Talmud.]* 41 vols. Jerusalem, 1954–84.

———. *Thesaurus Mishnae. [Otsar leshon ha-Mishnah.]* 4 vols. Jerusalem, 1960.

Kasovsky, M. See Kosovsky.

Kaufmann, Y. *Toldot ha-Emunah ha-Yisra'elit.* 8 vols. in 4. Jerusalem and Tel Aviv, 1976.

Kee, H. C. "Testaments of the Twelve Patriachs." Pages 775–828 in vol. 1 of *Old Testament Pseudepigrapha,* edited by J. H. Charlesworth. 2 vols. London, 1983–85.

Keuls, E. C. *The Reign of the Phallus; Sexual Politics in Ancient Athens.* New York, 1985.

Kilpatrick, G. D. "Acts vii.52 eleusis." *Journal of Theological Studies* 46 (1945): 136–45.

Kiraz, G. A. *Concordance to the Syriac New Testament.* Leiden, New York, and Köln, 1993.

Kissane, E. J., and O. D. Litt, *The Book of Isaiah.* Dublin, 1960.

Kister, M., ed. *Aboth de-Rabbi Nathan* (S. Z. Schechter Edition [Hebrew]). New York & Jerusalem, 1997.

Koch, K. *The Rediscovery of Apocalyptic.* London, 1972.

Klausner, J. *The Messianic Idea in Israel.* New York, 1955.

Klijn, A. F. J. "The Sources and Redaction of the Syriac Apocalypse of Baruch." *JST* 1 (1970): 65–76.

———. "2 (Syriac Apocalypse of) Baruch." Pages 615–52 in vol. 1 of *Old Testament Pseudepigrapha,* edited by J. H. Charlesworth. 2 vols. London, 1983–85.

Kmosko, M. "Liber Apocalypseos Baruch Filii Neriae Translatus de Graeco in Syriacum." Pages 1056–1305 in *Patrologia Syriaca,* Pars. Prima, T. II. Paris, 1907.

Knibb, M. A. *The Ethiopic Book of Enoch.* Oxford, 1978.

———. "Martyrdom and Ascension of Isaiah." Pages 143–76 in vol. 2 of *Old Testament Pseudepigrapha,* edited by J. H. Charlesworth. 2 vols. London, 1983–85.

Knight, J. *Disciples of the Beloved One, The Christology, Social Setting and Theological Context of the Ascension of Isaiah.* Sheffield, 1996.

———. *The Ascension of Isaiah.* Sheffield, 1995.

Koehler, L., and W. Baumgartner, *Lexicon in Veteris Testamenti Libros.* Leiden, 1958.

Koester, C. R. *The Dwelling of God; The Tabernacle in the Old Testament, Intertestamental Jewish Literature, and the New Testament.* Washington, D.C., 1989.

Kohler, K. "The Pre-Talmudic Haggada & The Second Baruch, or Rather the Jeremiah Apocalypse." *Jewish Quarterly Review* 5 (1893): 407–19.

———. "Eschatology." *The Jewish Encyclopedia* 5:209–18.

Komlosh, Y. *Ha-Miqra be-or ha-Targum.* Tel Aviv, 1973.

Kosovsky, M. *Concordance to the Talmud Yerushalmi. [Otsar leshon Talmud Yerushalmi.]* <7 vols.> Jerusalem, 1979–<1999>.

Kraft, R. A. "The Multiform Jewish Heritage of Early Christianity." Pages 174–99 in *Christianity, Judaism, and Other Greco-Roman Cults,* edited by J. Neusner. FS Morton Smith. Leiden, 1975.

———. "The Pseudepigrapha in Christianity." Pages 55–86 in *Tracing the Threads; Studies in the Vitality of Jewish Pseudepigrapha.* Edited by J. C. Reeves. Atlanta, Ga., 1994.

———. "Reassessing the 'Recensional Problem' in Testament of Abraham." Pages 121–37 in *Studies on the Testament of Abraham,* edited by G. W. E. Nickelsburg. SBL Septuagint and Cognate Studies 6. Missoula, Mont., 1976.

Kraft, R. A., and G. W. E. Nickelsburg, eds. *Early Judaism and its Modern Interpreters.* Atlanta, Ga., 1986.

Kraft, R. A., and A. E. Purintun. *Paraleipomena Jeremiou.* Missoula, Mont., 1972.

Krauss, S. "Sklavenbefreiung in den jüdisch-griechischen Schriften aus Südrussland." Pages 52–66 in *Festschrift zu Ehren des Dr. A. Harkavy.* Petersburg, 1908.

———. "Addenda et Corrigenda." Page 177 in *Festschrift zu Ehren des Dr. A. Hakavy.* St. Petersburg, 1908.

———. *Synagogale Altertumer.* Berlin and Wien, 1922.

Krochmal, N. *Moreh Nevukhei ha-Zeman.* Lemberg, 1851.

Kronholm, T. *Motifs from Genesis 1–11 in the Genuine Hymns of Ephrem, the Syrian.* Uppsala, 1978.

Kuhn, K. G. "The Lord's Supper and the Communal Meal at Qumran." Pages 65–93 in *The Scrolls and the New Testament,* ed. K. Stendahl (New York, 1957).

Kuhn, K. H. "A Coptic Jeremiah Apocryphon." *Le Museon* 83 (1970): 95–135, 291–339.

Kuhnel, B. *From the Earthly to the Heavenly Jerusalem.* Rome, Freiburg, and Wien, 1987.

Lacoque, A. *The Book of Daniel.* Atlanta, 1979.

Ladd, G. E. *A Commentary on the Revelation of John.* Grand Rapids, 1972.

Lagrange, M. J. *Le Messianisme chez les Juifs.* Paris, 1909.

———. "Notes sur le messianisme au temps de Jesus." *Revue biblique* 14 (1905): 481–514.

Lake, K. *The Apostolic Fathers.* Loeb Classical Library. Cambridge, Mass., 1965.

Lampe, G. W. H. *A Patristic Greek Lexicon.* Oxford, 1968.

Leclercq, H. "Encencoir." *Dictionnaire d'archéologie chrétienne et de liturgie* 5.i (Paris, 1922): 21–33.

———. "Pâques." *Dictionnaire d'archéologie chrétienne et de liturgie* 13 (Paris, 1938): 1522–74.

———. "Paradis." *Dictionnaire d'archéologie chrétienne et de liturgie* 13 (Paris, 1938): 1578–1615.

———. "Soleil." *Dictionnaire d'archéologie chrétienne et de liturgie* 15 (Paris, 1953): 1577–1585.

Leemhuis, F., A. F. J. Klijn, G. J. H. Van Gelder, *The Arabic Text of the Apocalypse of Baruch.* Leiden, 1986.

Lefkowitz, M. R. *Women in Greek Myth.* Baltimore, 1990.

Lehmann, M. R. "The Temple Scroll as a Source of Sectarian Halakhah." *Revue de Qumran* 36 (1978) 579–87.

Leloir, L. See Ephraem Syrus, *Commentaire de l'evangile.* . . .

Leon-Dufour, X. "Towards a Symbolic Reading of the Fourth Gospel." *New Testament Studies* 27 (1981): 439–56.

Leqah Tov. See *Midrash Lekah Tov.*

Lesêtre, H. "Manne." *Dictionnaire de la Bible* 4.i (Paris, 1912): 656–63.

———. "Milléniarisme." *Dictionnaire de la Bible* 4.ii (Paris, 1912): 1090–97.

Lévi, I. "Apocalypses dans le Talmud." *Revue des études juives* 1 (1880): 108–14.

———. "Notes Critiques sur la Pesikta Rabbati." *Revue des études juives* 35 (1897): 224–29.

———. "Bari dans la Pesikta Rabbati." *Revue des études juives* 32 (1896): 278–82.

Levin, B. A. "The Prophet Isaiah and His Relation to the Temple" [Hebrew]. Pages 145–68 in *'Iyyunim be-Sefer Yeshayahu, I,* ed. B. Z. Luria. Jerusalem, 1976.

Leviticus Rabbah. Wayiqra Rabbah. Edited by M. Margalioth. Jerusalem, 1972.

Levy, J. *Wörterbuch über die Talmudim und Midraschim.* 4 vols. 2d ed. Berlin and Vienna, 1924.

———. "Tacitus's Words on the Antiquities of the Jews and Their Attributes" [Hebrew]. Pages 115–96 in *'Olamot Nifgashim.* Jerusalem, 1960.

Lewis, A. S. (ed.), "The Protevangelium Jacobi." Pages 1–12 in *Studia Sinaitica,* no. xi. Apocrypha Syriaca. London, 1902.

Licht, J. "An Ideal Town Plan from Qumran—The Description of the New Jerusalem." *Israel Exploration Journal* 29 (1979): 45–59.

———. *Megillat ha-Hodayot.* Jerusalem, 1957.

———. "The Book of the Deeds of Jeremiah" [Hebrew]. Pages 66–80 in *Bar Ilan: Sefer Hashana* 1. Hurgin Memorial Volume. Ramat Gan, 1963.

———. "The Doctrine of Time of the Judaean Desert Sect and of Other 'Figurers of the End" [Hebrew]. Pages 63–70 in *Eretz Yisra'el; Mehqarim be-yedi'at ha-aretz va-'atiqoteha* 8. Jerusalem, 1967.

———. "The End [*Qez*]" [Hebrew]. *Encyclopaedia Biblica* 7:211–12.

Liddell, H. G., and R. Scott. *Greek-English Lexicon.* Oxford, 1978.

Lieberman, S. *Greek and Hellenism in Palestine* [Hebrew]. Jerusalem, 1984.

———. *Hellenism in Jewish Palestine.* New York, 1950.

———. "Introduction to the Leiden Manuscript" [Hebrew]. Pages 230–35 in vol. 4 of *Mehqarim be-Torat Eretz Yisra'el.* Edited by D. Rosenthal. Jerusalem, 1991.

Lietzmann, H. *A History of the Early Church.* London, 1967.

———. *Mass and Lord's Supper.* Leiden, 1979.

Liver, J. "Messiah" [Hebrew]. *Encyclopaedia Biblica* 5: 507–25.

Loewenstamm, S. A. "Sanctuary" [*Mishkan*]" [Hebrew]. *Encyclopaedia Biblica* 5: 532–47.

Lohse, E. "Σιών." *Theological Dictionary of the New Testament* 7: 319–38.

Loisy, A. "Das Mandäertum und die Ursprünge des Christentums." Pages 419–32 in *Der Mandäismus,* edited by G. Widengren. Darmstadt, 1982.

Luria, B. Z. *Megillat ha-Nehoshet mi-Midbar Yehudah.* Jerusalem, 1964.

Luzzatto, S. D. *Perush Shada"l 'al Sefer Yeshayahu.* Tel Aviv, 1970.

MacCulloch, J. A. "Eschatology." Pages 378–91 in vol. 5 of *Encyclopaedia of Religion and Ethics.* New York, 1951.

Mach, M. "Are There Jewish Elements in the Protevangelium Jacobi?" Pages 215–22 of *Proceedings of the Ninth World Congress of Jewish Studies, Division A.* Jerusalem, 1986.

Maier, J. "The Temple Scroll and Tendencies in the Cultic Architecture of the Second Commonwealth." Pages 67–82 in *Archaeology and History in the Dead Sea Scrolls: The New York University Conference in Memory of Y. Yadin,* edited by L. H. Schiffman. Sheffield, 1990.

Maimonides, Moses. See Moses ben Maimon.

Malan, S. C. *The Book of Adam and Eve, also called the Conflict of Adam and Eve with Satan.* London & Edinburgh, 1882.

Mangenot, E. "Fin du mond." *Dictionnaire de la Bible* 2 (Paris, 1912): 2262–78.

Mann, J. *The Jews in Egypt and in Palestine under the Fatimid Caliphas.* Vol. I. Oxford, 1969.

Manns, F. "Lecture symbolique de Jean 21, 1–11." *Liber Annaus* 36 (1986): 85–110.

———. "Le symbolisme du jardin dans le récit de la passion selon St. Jean." *Liber Annuus* 37 (1987): 53–80.

———. "Une ancienne tradition sur la jeunesse de Marie." Pages 106–14 in *Essais sur le Judéo-Christianisme.* Jerusalem, 1977.

Margaliot, M. *Mavo Nispahim u-maftehot la-Midrash Vayiqra Rabbah.* Jerusalem, 1972.

Marmorstein, A. "Die Quellen des neuen Jeremiah-Apocryphons." *Zeitschrift für die neutestamentliche Wissenschaft* 27 (1928): 327–37.

Maspero, G. *The Dawn of Civilization.* London, 1894.

Mazar, B. "The Prophet Isaiah and His Attitude to the Temple: Discussion" [Hebrew]. Pages 163–64 in vol. 1 of *'Iyyunim be-Sefer Yeshayahu,* edited by B. Z. Luria. Jerusalem, 1976.

McKane, W. *A Critical and Exegetical Commentary on Jeremiah.* International Critical Commentary. Edinburgh, 1986.

McKelvey, R. J. *The New Temple.* Oxford, 1969.

McNeile, M. H. *The Book of Exodus,* London, 1908.

Meeks, W. A. *The Prophet-King.* Leiden, 1967.

Megillat ha-Miqdash. See Yadin, *Megillat ha-Miqdash.*

Meiri. See Hameiri.

Mekhilta d'Rabbi Simon b. Jochai. Edited by J. N. Epstein and E. Z. Melamed. Jerusalem, 1956.

Mekhilta de-Rabbi Yishma'el. Edited by H. S. Horowitz and Y. A. Rabin. Jerusalem, 1960.

Melito of Sardis [Méliton de Sardes]. *Sur la Pâque.* Introduction, texte critique, traduction et notes par O. Perler. Sources chrétiennes 123. Paris, 1966.

Meyer, R. "Μάννα." *Theological Dictionary of the New Testament* 4:462–66.

Meyers, C. L., and E. M. Meyers, *Haggai, Zechariah 1–8.* Anchor Bible. New York, 1987.

Michaelis, W. "σκηνή." *Theological Dictionary of the New Testament* 7:368–81.

Michell, N. "Baptism in the Didache." Pages 226–55 in *The Didache in Context,* edited by N. J. Clayton. Leiden, New York, and Köln, 1995.

Midrash 'Eser Galuyot. See A. Jellinek, *Bet ha-Midrasch.*

Midrash Leqah Tov, hamekhuneh Pesiqta Zutrata, 'al Hamisha Humshei Torah. Edited by S. Buber. Jerusalem, 1960.

Midrash Mishlei. Edited by Wissotzky. New York, 1990.

Midrash Rabbah 'al ha-Torah ve-Ḥamesh Megillot. New York and Berlin, 1927.

Midrash Tanḥuma. Edited by S. Buber. Jerusalem, 1964.

Midrash Tehillim. Edited by S. Buber. Vilna, 1891.

Mikraot Gedolot. Tel Aviv, 1954–1956.

Milhemet B'nai Or. See Yadin, *Megillat Milhemet B'nai Or.*

Milik, J. T. *The Ethiopic Book of Enoch, Aramaic Fragments of Qumran Cave 4.* Oxford, 1976.

———. "Le Testament de Lévi en Arméen; Fragment de la Grott 4 de Qumrân (P1 IV)." *Revue de Qumran* 62 (1955): 389–406.

———. "Notes de l'épigraphie et topographie palestiniennes." *Revue biblique* 66 (1959): 550–75.

———. "The Dead Sea Scrolls Fragment of the Book of Enoch." *Biblica* 32 (1951): 393–400.

Mingana, A. "A New Jeremiah Apocryphon." Woodbrooke Studies. Pages 352–95 in vol. 11 of *Bulletin of the John Rylands Library.* Manchester, 1927.

Mishnah (Albeck). *Shishah Sidrei Mishnah,* with commentary by H. Albeck. 6 vols. Jerusalem and Tel Aviv, 1952–1959.

Mishnah 'im Perush ha-Rambam. Facsimile of first edition. Naples, 1492. Jerusalem, 1970.

Mishnah 'im Perush Rabbenu Moshe ben Maimon. Jerusalem, 1964.

Mishnah, based on MS Kaufmann. Jerusalem, 1968.

Mishnah. *Matnita de-Talmuda devnei Ma'arava.* Mishnah based on MS Cambridge, edition of William Low. Facsimile. Jerusalem, 1967.

Mishnah. MS Paris 328–29. Jerusalem, 1973.

Mishnah. *Shishah Sidrei Mishnah.* MS Farma, de Rossi 138. Jerusalem, 1970.

Mishnah. *Sidrei ha-Mishnah: Zera'im, Mo'ed, Nashim.* Unknown imprint (Pissaro or Constantinople). Jerusalem, 1971.

Mitchell, H. G., J. M. P. Smith, and J. A. Bewer. *A Critical and Exegetical Commentary on Haggai, Zechariah, Malachi, and Jonah.* International Critical Commentary. Edinburgh, 1912.

Moffatt, J. *A Critical and Exegetical Commentary on the Epistle to the Hebrews.* International Critical Commentary. Edinburgh, 1924.

Montgomery, J. A. *A Critical and Exegetical Commentary on the Book of Daniel.* International Critical Commentary. Edinburgh, 1964.

Moore, G. F. *Judaism in the First Centuries of the Christian Era. The Age of the Tannaim.* 2 vols. Cambridge, 1917–1939.

Morissette R. "La condition de ressuscité. 1 Corinthiens 15, 35–49: Structure litteraire de la péricope." *Biblica* 53 (1972): 208–28.

Moses ben Maimon, *Moreh Nevukhim le-Rabbenu Moshe ben Maimon.* Translated by Ibn Tibbon. Jerusalem, 1981.

Mowinckel, S. *He That Cometh.* Oxford, 1956.

Murphy, F. J. *Pseudo-Philo.* Oxford, 1993.

———. *The Structure and Meaning of Second Baruch.* Atlanta, Ga., 1985.

———. "The Temple in the Syriac Apocalypse of Baruch." *Journal of Biblical Literature* 106 (1987): 671–83.

Murray, R. *Symbols of Church and Kingdom.* Cambridge, 1975.

———. "The Exhortation to Candidates for Ascetical Vows at Baptism in the Early Christian Church." *New Testament Studies* 21 (1974–75): 59–80.

———. "Martyrdom and Ascension of Isaiah." Pages 143–76 in vol. 2 of *Old Testament Pseudepigrapha,* edited by J. H. Charlesworth. 2 vols. London, 1983–85.

Myers, J. M. *I & II Esdras: Introduction, Translation, and Commentary.* Anchor Bible, 42. Garden City, N.Y., 1974.

Nedungatt, G. "The Covenanters of the Early Syriac-Speaking Church." *OCP* 39 (1973): 190–215, 419–44.

Nestle, E. "Die dem Epiphanius Zugeschriebene Vitae Prophetarum in doppelter griechischer Rezension." Pages 1–64 in *Marginalien und Materialien*. Tübingen, 1893.

Newsom, C. *Songs of the Sabbath Sacrifice: A Critical Edition*. Atlanta, Ga., 1985.

Nickelsburg, G. W. E. "Narrative Traditions in the Paralipomena of Jeremiah and 2 Baruch." *Catholic Biblical Quarterly* 35 (1973): 60–68.

———. "Paraleipomena of Jeremiah." Pages 56–59 in *Jewish Writings of the Second Temple Period*, edited by M. E. Stone. Assen, 1984.

———. "The Book of Biblical Antiquities." Pages 107–9 in *Jewish Writings of the Second Temple Period*, edited by M. E. Stone. Assen, 1984.

Niemark, D. Ben Shlomo, *Toldot ha-'Iqqarim be-Yisra'el*. Odessa, 1919.

———. *Toldot ha-Filosofyah be-Yisra'el*. New York, 1921.

Nir, R. "The Aromatic Fragrance of Paradise in the *Greek Life of Adam and Eve* and the Christian Origin of the Composition." *Novum Testamentum* (forthcoming).

———. "The Image of John the Baptist" [Hebrew]. Master's Thesis. Tel Aviv, 1986.

Notscher, F. "Paralipomena Jeremiae." Page 309 in *Lexikon für Theologie und Kirche*. Freiburg im Breisgau, 1933.

Numbers Rabbah. See *Midrash Rabbah*.

Odes of Solomon. See Harris and Mangina.

Oepke, A. "παρουσία." *Theological Dictionary of the New Testament* 5:858–873.

———. "ἀνίστημι." *Theological Dictionary of the New Testament* 1:368–372.

Oesterley, W. O. E. *The Books of the Apocrypha: Their Origin, Teaching and Contents*. London, 1915.

———. "Introduction." Pages vii–xxxiii in *The Apocalypse of Baruch*, edited by R. H. Charles. London, 1918.

Oppenheimer, A. "The Messiahhood of Bar-Kokhba" [Hebrew]. Pages 153–65 in *Messianism and Eschatology*. Jerusalem, 1984.

Optowitzer. See Aptowitzer.

Origen [Origène]. *Commentaire sur l'Évangile Selon Matthieu.* Edited by R. Girod. Vol. 1. Sources chrétiennes 162. Paris, 1970.

———. *Contre Celse: Introduction, text critique, traduction et notes.* Edited by M. Borret. 5 vols. Sources chrétiennes. Paris, 1967.

Oxford Dictionary. See Cross.

Palestinian Talmud. See *Talmud Yerushalmi.*

Paraleipomena Jeremiou. Edited by R. A. Kraft and A. E. Purintun. Missoula, Mont., 1972.

Payne Smith, R., ed. *A Compendious Syriac Dictionary.* Oxford, 1903.

Payne Smith, R. *Thesaurus Syriacus.* London, 1901.

Pennington, A. "The Apocalypse of Abraham." Pages 363–91 in *The Apocryphal Old Testament,* edited by H. F. D. Sparks. Oxford, 1984.

Perles, F. "Notes Critiques sur le Texte des Apocryphes et des Pseudépigraphes." *Revue des Etudes Juives* 73 (1921): 177–85.

Perrot, C., and P. M. Bogaert. *Les Antiquités Bibliques.* Paris, 1976.

Pesikta de-Rav Kahana. Edited by B. Mandelbaum (Y. Y. Mandelboim). New York, 1987.

Pesikta de-Rav Kahana: R. Kahana's Compilation of Discourses for Sabbaths and Festal Days. Tr. by W. G. Braude and I. J. Kapstein. Philadelphia, 1975.

Pesiqta Rabbati. See Ish-Shalom.

Petit, M. "La Cachette de l'Arche d'Alliance: A Partir de la 'Vue de Jérémie' 9–15 dans les 'Vitae Prophetarum,'" Pages 119–31 in *La Littérature Intertestamentaire; Colloque de Strasbourg.* Paris, 1985.

Philo. Translated by F. H. Colson, G. H. Whitaker, and R. Marcus. Loeb Classical Library. Vols. I–V, VII. Cambridge, Mass., 1929–1951.

Philonenko, M. "Simples observations sur les Paralipomènes de Jérémie." *RHPHR* 76 (1996/2): 157–77.

———. "Le martyre d'Esäie et l'histoire de la secte de Qumran." *Cahiers de la Revue d'histoire et de philosophie religieuses* 41 (1967): 1–10.

Pines, S. "Notes on the Twelve Tribes in Qumran, Early Christianity, and Jewish Tradition." Pages 151–54 in *Messiah and Christos, Studies in the Jewish Origins of Christianity, Presented to D. Flusser.* Tübingen, 1992.

Pirqei de Rabbi Eliezer. Jerusalem, 1970.

Polycarp. In vol. 1 of *The Apostolic Fathers,* edited by K. Lake. Loeb Classical Library. London, 1965.

Pomeroy, S. B. *Goddesses, Whores, Wives, and Slaves.* New York, 1975.

Pomykala, K. E. *The Davidic Dynasty Tradition in Early Judaism*. Atlanta, Ga., 1995.

Pope, M. H. *Job*. Anchor Bible. New York, 1965.

Priest, J. "A Note on the Messianic Banquet." Pages 222–38 in *The Messiah*, edited by J. H. Charlesworth. Minneapolis, 1992.

Priest, J. F. "The Messiah and the Meal in 1QSa." *Journal of Biblical Literature* 82 (1963): 95–100.

Pseudo-Jonathan. Edited by M. Ginsburger. Berlin, 1903.

Pseudo-Clement. *Die Pseudoklementinen*. Edited by B. Rehm. Die griechischen christlichen Schriftsteller der ersten Jahrhunderte, 42. Berlin, 1953.

Puech, E. *La croyance des Esséniens en la vie future: immortalité, résurrection, vie éternelle?* Paris, 1993.

———. "Der Stand des Mandäerproblems." Pages 433–44 in *Der Mandäismus*, edited by G. Widengren. Darmstadt, 1982.

———. "Préséance sacerdotale et messie-roi dans la regle de l'congregation." *Revue de Qumran* 63 (1994): 351–65.

Qimron, E. "On the Text of the Temple Scroll" [Hebrew]. *Leshonenu* 42 (1978), 83–98.

Qoheleth Rabbah. See *Midrash Rabbah*.

Rabinowitz, L. I. "Talmud Jerusalem." *Encyclopaedia Judaica* 15: 772–79.

Rabinowitz, Z. M. *Mahzor Piyyutei Yannai*. Jerusalem, 1985.

Rad, G. von. See Von Rad, G.

Radak [Rabbi David Kimhi], on the Bible: see *Mikraot Gedolot*.

Rahner, H. *Greek Myths and Christian Mystery*. London, 1963.

Ratner, B. *Ahavat Zion ve-Yerushalayim*. Jerusalem, 1967.

———. *Sefer Ahavat Zion ve-Yerushalayim*. Jerusalem, 1967.

Renan, E. *Histoire des origines du christianisme*. 7 vols. Paris, 1877.

Renard, P. "Autel." Pages 1271–77 in *Dictionnaire de la Bible*. Paris, 1912.

Rengstorf, K. H. "'Ιορδάνης." *Theological Dictionary of the New Testament* 6: 608–23.

Riaud, J. "Abimeléch: Le singulier dormant des Paralipomènes de Jérémie le Prophète." Pages 289–296 in *Frontières terrestres, frontières célestes dans l'antiquité: études réunies et présentées par Aline Rousselle*. Paris, 1995.

———. "Abiméléch, Personnage-Clé des Paralipomena Jeremiae?" *Dialogues d'Histoire Ancienne* 7 (1981): 163–78.

———. "Jérémie, martyr chrétien paralipomènes de Jérémie IX, 7–32." Pages 231–35 in *Kecharitōmenē: mélanges René Laurentin*. Paris, 1990.

———. "Les paralipomena jeremiae dependent-ils de II Baruch?" *Sileno* 9 (1983): 105–28.

———. "Les Samaritains dans les "Paralipomena Jeremiae," Pages 150–52 in *La littérature intertestamentaire, Colloque de Strasbourg*. Paris 1985.

———. "Paralipomena Jeremiae Prophetae." *Folia Orientalia* 27 (1990): 25–41.

———. "The Figure of Jeremiah in the *Paralipomena Jeremiae Prophetae:* His Originality; His 'Christianization' by the Christian Author of the Conclusion (9.10–32)." *JSP* 22 (2000): 31–44.

Richardson, R. D. "Introduction and Further Inquiry." Pages IX–XXVI and 219–697 in *Mass and Lord's Supper: A Study in the History of the Liturgy*, by H. Lietzmann. Translated by D. H. G. Reeve. Leiden, 1953 (repr. 1979).

Riggs, J. W. "The Sacred Food of Didache 9–10 and Second Century Ecclesiologies." Pages 256–83 in *The Didache in Context*, edited by Clayton N. Jefford. Leiden, New York, and Köln, 1995.

Ringgren, H. "The Branch and the Plantation in the Hodayot." *Biblical Research* 6 (1961): 3–9.

Rist, M. "Apocalypticism." *The Interpreter's Dictionary of the Bible* 1:157–61.

———. "Baruch, Apocalypse of." *The Interpreter's Dictionary of the Bible* 1:361–63.

Roberts, J. J. M. "The Old Testament's Contribution to Messianic Expectations." Pages 39–51 in *The Messiah*, edited by J. H. Charlesworth. Minneapolis, 1992.

Robertson, A., and A. Plummer, *A Critical and Exegetical Commentary on the First Epistle of St. Paul to the Corinthians*. International Critical Commentary. Edinburgh, 1971.

Robinson, S. E. "4 Baruch." Pages 413–25 in vol. 2 of *Old Testament Pseudepigrapha*, edited by J. H. Charlesworth. 2 vols. London, 1983–85.

Rosenthal, F. *Vier apokryphische Bücher aus der Zeit und Schule R. Aqiba's: Assumptio Mosis, Das Vierte Buch Esra, Die Apocalypse Baruch, Das Buch Tobi*. Leipzig, 1885.

Rowland, C. *The Open Heaven*. New York, 1982.

Rowley, H. H. *The Relevance of Apocalyptic. A Study of Jewish and Christian Apocalypses from Daniel to the Revelation.* London, 1963.

Rowley, H. H. *The Servant of the Lord and Other Essays on the Old Testament.* London, 1952.

Rudolph, K. *Die Mandäer.* Vol. 2: *Der Kult.* Göttingen, 1961.

———. "La Religion Mandéenne." Pages 498–522 in vol. 2 of *Histoire des Religions.* Paris, 1972.

Russell, D. S. *The Method and Message of Jewish Apocalyptic.* London, 1971.

Safrai, S. "The Heavenly Jerusalem." *Ariel* 23 (1969) 11–16.

Safrai, Z., and H. Safrai. "The Holiness of the Land of Israel and Jerusalem" [Hebrew]. Pages 344–71 in *Yehudim ve-Yahadut biyemei Bayit Sheni ha-Mishnah veha-Talmud,* edited by A. Oppenheimer, Y. Gafni, and M. Stern. Jerusalem, 1993.

Satran, D. "Biblical Prophets and Christian Legend: The Lives of the Prophets Reconsidered." Pages 143–49 in *Messiah and Christos: Studies in the Jewish Origins of Christianity Presented to D. Flusser,* edited by I. Gruenwald, S. Shaked, and G. G. Stroumsa. Tübingen, 1992.

———. *Biblical Prophets in Byzantine Palestine.* Leiden, 1995.

———. "The Lives of the Prophets." Pages 56–60 in *Jewish Writings of the Second Temple Period,* edited by M. E. Stone. Assen, 1984.

———. "Qumran and the Origins of Christianity" [Hebrew]. Pages 152–59 in *Megillot Midbar Yehudah: Arba'im Shenot Mehqar,* edited by M. Beroshi, S. Talmon, S. Yefet, and D. Schwartz. Jerusalem, 1992.

Saylor, G. B. *Have the Promises Failed? A Literary Analysis of 2 Baruch.* Society of Biblical Literature Dissertation Series, 72. Chico, Calif., 1984.

Schermann, T., ed. *Prophetarum Vitae Fabulosae. Indices Apostolorum Discipulorumque Domini Doretheo. Epiphanio. Hippolito Aliisque Vindicata.* Leipzig, 1907.

———. *Propheten und Apostellegenden nebst Jüngerkatalogen des Dorotheus und verwandter Texte.* Texte und Untersuchungen 31.3. Leipzig, 1907.

Schiffman, L. H. *Halakhah, Haklikhah u-Meshihiyut be-Kat Midbar Yehudah.* Jerusalem, 1993.

———. "The Furnishings of the Temple According to the Temple Scroll," Pages 621–34 in vol. 2 of *The Madrid Qumran Congress,* edited by J. T. Barrera and L. V. Montaner. Leiden, 1992.

Schiller, G. *Iconography of Christian Art.* London, 1966.

Schlier, H. "ἀνατέλλω"; "ἀνατολή." *Theological Dictionary of the New Testament* 1: 351–53.

Schmithals, W. *The Apocalyptic Movement.* Nashville & New York, 1975.

Schnackenburg, R. *The Gospel According to St. John.* New York, 1980.

Schneemelcher, W. *Neutestamentliche Apokryphen in deutscher Übersetzung.* 5th ed. 2 vols. Tübingen, 1987, 1989.

Schneemelcher, W. *New Testament Apocrypha.* 2 vols. Cambridge, 1991.

Schneider, C. "καταπέτασμα." *Theological Dictionary of the New Testament* 3:628–30.

Scholem, G. "The Messianic Idea in Kabbalah." Pages 37–48 in *The Messianic Idea in Judaism and Other Essays.* New York, 1971.

Schrenk, G. "ἱερεύς." *Theological Dictionary of the New Testament* 3:221–47.

Schürer, E. *Geschichte des jüdischen Volkes im Zeitalter Jesu Christi.* Leipzig, 1898.

———. *The History of the Jewish People in the Age of Jesus Christ (175 B.C.– A.D. 135).* A new English version, revised and edited by G. Vermes and F. Millar. Edinburgh, 1987.

Schwemer, A. M. *Studien zu den frühjüdischen Prophetenlegenden Vitae Prophetarum.* Tübingen, 1995.

Séd, N. "Les Hymnes sur le Paradis de Saint Ephrem et les Tradition Juives." *Muséon* 81 (1968): 455–501.

Seder Eliyahu Rabbah. Edited by M. Ish-Shalom. Jerusalem, 1960.

Seder Olam Rabbah. Edited by Ratner. Vilna, 1894.

Seeligmann, I. L. "Jerusalem in Hellenistic Jewish Thought" [Hebrew]. Pages 192–208 in *Yehudah ve-Yerushalayim; ha-kinus ha-shneim asar le-yediʿat ha-ʾarez.* Jerusalem, 1957.

Sefer Yossipon. See Flusser, *Sefer Yossipon.*

Sela, S. "The Book of Josippon and Parallel Sources in Arabic and Judeo-Arabic" [Hebrew]. Doctoral Dissertation. Tel Aviv, 1991.

Septuaginta. Vetus Testamentum Graecum Auctoritate Societatis Litterarum Gottingensis Editum. Göttingen, 1936 etc.

Septuaginta. Isaias. Edited by J. Ziegler. Göttingen, 1939.

Shadal. See Luzzatto, Solomon David.

Shalit, A. *Josephus' Antiquities of the Jews* [Hebrew (Yosef ben Mattityahu, Qadmoniot ha-Yehudim)]. Jerusalem, 1973.

Shepherd of Hermas. Pages 7–305 in vol. 2 of *The Apostolic Fathers,* edited by K. Lake. Loeb Classical Library. Cambridge, Mass., 1913.

Shishah Sidrei Mishnah. See Mishnah.

Shlomo Adani. *Melekhet Shlomo le-Masekhet Sheqalim, Sisha Sidrei Mishnayot Vilna ha-Shalem im shemonim ve-ahat Hosafot.* Jerusalem, 1960.

Sifrei 'al Sefer Devarim. Edited by L. Finkelstein. New York, 1969.

Sifre Bamidbar [Sifrei to Numbers]. Edited by H. S. Horovitz. Jerusalem, 1966.

Simon, M. "Retour du Christ et reconstruction du temple dans la pensee chretienne primitive." Pages 9–19 in *Recherches d'Histoire Judeo-Chretienne.* Paris, 1962.

Sivan, D. *Ugaritic Grammar* [Hebrew]. Jerusalem, 1993.

Smith, J. M. P., W. H. Ward, and J. A. Bewer, *A Critical and Exegetical Commentary on Micah, Zephaniah, Nahum, Habakkuk, Obadiah, and Joel.* International Critical Commentary. Edinburgh, 1911.

Smith, M. "On the History of ἀποκαλύπτω and ἀποκάλυψις." Pages 9–19 in *Apocalypticism in the Mediterranean World and the Near East,* edited by D. Hellhom. Tübingen, 1983.

Smith, R. Payne. See Payne Smith, R.

Sokoloff, M. *A Dictionary of Jewish Palestinian Aramaic.* Ramat Gan, 1990.

Sparks, H. F. D. *The Apocryphal Old Testament.* Oxford, 1984.

———. "The Symbolical Interpretation of *Lebanon* in the Fathers." *Journal of Theological Studies* 10 (1959): 264–79.

Stanton, V. H. *The Jewish and Christian Messiah.* Edinburgh, 1886.

Steinberg, Y. *Milon ha-Tanakh.* Tel Aviv, 1961.

Stemvoort, P. A. "The Protevangelium Jacobi, The Sources of Its Theme and Style and Their Bearing on Its Date." Pages 410–26 in *Studia Evangelica* III. Texte und Untersuchungen 88. Berlin, 1964.

Stern, M. *Greek and Latin Authors on Jews and Judaism.* Jerusalem, 1976.

———. "The Suicide of Eleazar ben Yair and His People at Massada and the 'Fourth Philosophy'" [Hebrew]. Pages 313–43 in *Mehqarim be-toldot Yisra'el beyemei ha-Bayit ha-Sheni,* edited by D. Schwartz. Jerusalem, 1991.

Steudel, A. "אחרית הימים in the Texts from Qumran." *RQ* 16 (1993/95): 225–46.

Stinespring, W. F. "Testament of Isaac." Pages 903–11 in vol. 1 of *Old Testament Pseudepigrapha,* edited by J. H. Charlesworth. 2 vols. London, 1983–85.

———. "Testament of Jacob." Pages 913–918 in vol. 1 of *Old Testament Pseudepigrapha,* edited by J. H. Charlesworth. 2 vols. London, 1983–85.

Stone, M. E. "Apocalyptic Literature." Pages 383–437 in *Jewish Writings of the Second Temple Period.* Assen, 1984.

———. "Categorization and Classification of the Apocrypha and Pseudepigrapha." *Abr-Nahrain* 24 (1986): 167–77.

———. "Reactions to Destruction of the Second Temple." *Journal for the Study of Judaism* 12 (1981): 195–204.

———, ed. *Jewish Writings of the Second Temple Period.* Assen, 1984.

Strack, H. L., and P. Billerbeck. *Kommentar zum Neuen Testament aus Talmud und Midrash.* Munich, 1924.

Strack, H. L., and G. Stemberger. *Einleitung in Talmud und Midrasch.* Munich, 1982.

Strobel, A. *Ursprung und Geschichte des Fruhchristlichen Osterkalenders.* Berlin 1977.

Strycker, E. D. *La forme la plus ancienne du Protévangile de Jacques.* Brussels, 1961.

———. "Le Protévangile de Jacques problèmes critiques et exégétiques." Pages 339–59 in *Studia Evangelica,* III. Texte und Untersuchungen 88. Berlin, 1964.

Sundberg, W. *KUSHTA.* Lund, 1953.

Sussman, Y. "Traditions of Study and Tradition of Versions of the Talmud Yerushalmi (Masekhet Sheqalim)" [Hebrew]. Pages 12–76 in *Meḥqarim be-Sifrut ha-Talmudit: Yom 'Iyyun limlot shmonim shanah le-Shaul Lieberman.* Jerusalem, 1983.

———. "Study of the History of the Halakhah and the Dead Sea Scrolls" [Hebrew], *Tarbiz* 59 (1990): 11–76.

Sutcliffe, E. F. "The Rule of the Congregation (IQSa) II,11–12: Text and Meaning." *Revue de Qumran* 2 (1959/60): 541–47.

Swete, H. B. *The Apocalypse of St. John.* Grand Rapids, 1968.

Sweet, J. *Revelation.* London, 1979.

Tabor, D. T. "A Pierced or Piercing Messiah? The Verdict Is Still Out." *Biblical Archaeology Review* 18/6 (1992): 58–59.

Tacitus. *Histories and Annals*. Edited by C. H. Moore and J. Jackson. Loeb Classical Library. London and Cambridge, Mass., 1951–1952.

Talmud Bavli, Codex Florence. Jerusalem, 1972.

Talmud Bavli, Facsimile of Vilna (Rom) edition. Jerusalem, 1968.

Talmud Bavli. Facsimile of first printed edition, Venezia, 5280 (1520). Jerusalem, 1970.

Talmud Bavli, MS München (95). Jerusalem, 1971.

Talmud Bavli, Masekhet Ḥullin. MS Hamburg 169. Jerusalem, 1972.

Talmud Yerushalmi, based upon first printed edition (Venice, 1522). Jerusalem, 1969.

Talmud Yerushalmi. MS Leiden. COD SCAL 3. Facsimile of original manuscript. Jerusalem, 1971.

Tanḥuma. See *Midrash Tanḥuma*.

Targum Yerushalmi. See *Pseudo-Jonathan*.

Taylor, V. *The Gospel According to St. Mark*. London, 1955.

Teicher, J. L. "Priests and Sacrifices in the Dead Sea Scrolls." *Journal of Jewish Studies* 5 (1954): 93–99.

———. "The Christian Interpretation of the Sign x in the Isaiah Scroll." *Vetus Testamentum* 5 (1955): 189–98.

———. "The Damascus Fragment and the Origin of the Jewish-Christian Sect." *Journal of Jewish Studies* 2 (1951): 115–43.

———. "The Dead Sea Scrolls – Documents of the Jewish-Christian Sect of Ebionites." *Journal of Jewish Studies* 2 (1951): 67–99.

———. "The Habakkuk Scroll." *Journal of Jewish Studies* 5 (1954): 47–59.

———. "The Teaching of the Pre-Pauline Church in the Dead Sea Scrolls." *Journal of Jewish Studies* 3 (1952): 111–18, 139–50; 4 (1953): 1–13, 49–58, 93–103, 139–53.

Tepler, Y. "The Teacher of Righteousness in the Qumran Scrolls" [Hebrew]. Master's Thesis. Tel Aviv, 1990.

Tertullian. *Adversus Gnosticos Scorpiace*. PL 2.

———. *Adversus Marcionem*, Patrologia Latina, vol. II. Paris, 1844.

———. *Apologeticus*. PL 1.

———. *Liber de Patientia*. PL 1.

Thackeray, H. St. J. See Josephus Flavius.

Thayer, J. H. *Greek-English Lexicon of the New Testament*. Grand Rapids, Mich., 1987.

Theodor-Albeck. = *Midrash Bereshit Rabbah,* edited by J. Theodor and Ḥ. Albeck. Jerusalem, 1965.

Thomas, J. *Le Mouvement Baptiste en Palestine et Syrie*. Gembloux, 1935.

Thornhill, R. "The Paraleipomena of Jeremiah." Pages 813–34 in *Apocryphal Old Testament,* edited by H. F. D. Sparks. Oxford, 1984.

Tischendorf, C. D. *Evangelia Apocrypha*. Hildesheim, 1966.

Tisserant, E. *Ascension d'Isaie*. Paris, 1909.

Torrey, C. C. "Apocalypse." *The Jewish Encyclopedia* 2:669–75.

———. *The Apocryphal Literature*. New Haven, 1953.

———. *The Lives of the Prophets*. Journal of Biblical Literature Monograph Series 1. Philadelphia, 1946.

———. "The Messiah Son of Ephraim." *Journal of Biblical Literature* 66 (1947): 253–77.

Tur-Sinai, N. H. "Beasts" [*Behemot*] [Hebrew]. *BibEnc* 2 (1950): 39–40.

Uffenheimer, B. "The Prophecy Concerning Hillel ben Shahar" [Hebrew]. *Beit Miqra* 41 (1996): 1–13.

Unger, M. F. *Zechariah*. Grand Rapids, Mich., 1963.

Urbach, E. E. *The Sages; Their Concepts and Beliefs*. Jerusalem, 1975.

———. "Supernal Jerusalem and Earthly Jerusalem" [Hebrew]. Pages 156–71 in *Yerushalayim ledoroteha,* edited by Y. Aviram. Jerusalem, 1969.

Vaulx, J. de, "Notes *Brèves* sur 1 Co. 15, 35–56." Pages 111–16 in *Le corps et le corps du Christ dans la première épître aux Corinthiens, Présenté par V. Guénel*. Paris, 1983.

Vergon, S. *Sefer Mikha*. Ramat Gan, 1994.

Vermes, G. *Jesus the Jew*. Philadelphia, 1981.

———. "The Impact of the Dead Sea Scrolls on the Study of the New Testament." *JJS* 27 (1976): 109.

———. "The Oxford Forum for Qumran Research Seminar on the Rule of War from Cave 4 (4Q285)." *Journal of Jewish Studies* 43 (1992): 85–90.

———. "The 'Pierced Messiah' Text: An Interpretation Evaporates." *Biblical Archaeology Review* 18/4 (1992): 80–82.

———. "The Symbolical Interpretation of LEBANON in the Targums: The Origin and Development of an Exegetical Tradition." *Journal of*

Theological Studies 9 (1958): 1–12 (= *Scripture and Tradition in Judaism* [Leiden, 1973], 26–39).

Vilk, R. "The Jews of Slavonic Syria" [Hebrew]. Doctoral Dissertation. Tel Aviv, 1987.

Violet, B. *Die Apokalypsen des Esra und Baruch.* Unit Textvorschlagen von H. Gressmann. Die griechische christliche Schrifsteller der ersten drei Jahrhunderte 32. Leipzig, 1924.

Volz, P. *Die Eschatologie der jüdischen Gemeinde im neutestamentlichen Zeitalter.* Tübingen, 1934; repr. Hildesheim, 1966.

Von Rad, G. "οὐρανός." *Theological Dictionary of the New Testament* 5:502–9.

Vööbus, A. *Celibacy, A Requirement for Admission to Baptism in the Early Syrian Church.* Stockholm, 1951.

———. *A History of Asceticism in the Syrian Orient.* Louvain, 1988.

Wacholder, B. Z. *Eupolemus.* Cincinnatti, 1974.

———. *The Dawn of Qumran.* Cincinnatti, 1983.

———. "The Letter From Judah Maccabee to Aristobulus: Is 2 Maccabees 1:10b–2:18 Authentic?" *Hebrew Union College Annual* 49 (1978): 89–133.

Wacholder, B. Z., and M. Abegg. *A Preliminary Edition of the Unpublished Dead Sea Scrolls.* Washington, 1992.

Weinfeld, M. "Jeremiah and the Spiritual Metamorphosis of Israel." Pages 244–78 in *Zer le-Gevurot: Qovetz Mehqarim likhvod Shazar,* edited by B. Z. Luria. Jerusalem, 1973.

Weinfeld, M. "Theology and Wisdom in the Third Millennium BCE Mesopotamian Tradition in Relation to the Bible" [Hebrew]. Pages 285–87 in *Shenaton la-Miqra ul-heqer ha-Mizrah ha-Qadum* 4. Jerusalem & Tel Aviv, 1980.

Weiss, A. H. *Dor dor ve-Dorshav* I. Jerusalem & Tel Aviv.

Werblowsky, R. J. Z. "Metropolis of All the Lands" [Hebrew]. Pages 172–78 in *Yerushalayim ledoroteha* [25th National Congress for Knowledge of the Land]. Jerusalem, 1969.

Westerholm, S. "Tabernacle." Pages 699–704 in *The International Standard Bible Encyclopedia.* Grand Rapids, Mich., 1988.

Widengren, G. *Mesopotamian Elements in Manicheanism.* Uppsala & Leipzig, 1946.

Wilcox, M. "'According to the Pattern (*tbnyt*) . . .': Exodus 25,40 in the New Testament and Early Jewish Thought." *Revue de Qumran* 13 (1988): 648–56.

Wilcox, M. "'Upon the Tree' – Deut 21:22–23 in the New Testament." JBL 96 (1977): 85–99.

Wilkinson, J. "Jewish Influences on the Early Christian Rite of Jerusalem." *Le Museon*, 92 (1979): 347–59.

Willett, T. W. *The Eschatologies in the Theodocies of 2 Baruch and 4 Esra*. Sheffield, 1989.

Wintermute, O. S. "Gerhard Delling, Jüdische Lehre und Frömmigkeit in den Paralipomena Jeremiae" [Book Review]. *Catholic Biblical Quarterly* 30 (1968): 442–45.

Wise, M. O. *A Critical Study of the Temple Scroll from Qumran Cave 11*. Chicago, 1990.

———. "4QFlorilegium and the Temple of Adam." *Revue de Qumran* 15 (1991–1992): 103–32.

Wise, M., M. Abegg, and G. Cooke. *The Dead Sea Scrolls*. San Francisco, 1996.

Wolff, C. *Jeremia im Frühjudentum und Urchristentum*. Texte und Untersuchungen zur Geschichte der altchristlischen Literatur, 118. Berlin, 1976.

———. "Irdisches und himmlisches Jerusalem—Die Heilshoffung in den Paralipomena Jeremiae." *ZNW* 82 (1991): 145–58.

Wolfson, H. A. *Philo: Foundations of Religious Philosophy in Judaism, Christianity and Islam*. 2 vols. Cambridge, Mass., 1968.

Woude, A. S. van der. "χρέω." *Theological Dictionary of the New Testament* 9:521–27.

Wright, W. *Apocryphal Acts of the Apostles*. Amsterdam, 1968.

Yadin, Y. *Megillat Milhemet B'nai Or uv'nai Hoshekh*. Jerusalem, 1955.

———. *Megillat ha-Miqdash*. Jerusalem, 1977.

———. *The Temple Scroll*. Jerusalem, 1983.

———. "A Midrash on 2 Sam. vii and Ps i–ii (4Q Florilegium)." *Israel Exploration Journal* 9 (1959): 95–98.

———. "Some Notes on the Newly Published Pesharim of Isaiah." *Israel Exploration Journal* 9 (1959): 39–42.

Yalqut Shim'oni. Jerusalem, 1960.

Yamauchi, E. M. *Pre-Christian Gnosticism*. Grand Rapids, Mich., 1973.

Yeivin, S. *Milhemet Bar Kokhba.* Jerusalem, 1967.

Yellin, D. *Hiqrei Miqra: Yeshayahu.* Jerusalem, 1939.

Yerushalmi Skalim (ed. Sofer) = *Shekalim Treatise,* Bodleian MS. edited by A. Schreiber-Sofer. New York, 1954.

Yisraeli, E. "The Origin of 4 Ezra (The Vision of Ezra) in Light of Its Relation to Christianity" [Hebrew]. Master's Thesis. Tel Aviv, 1989.

———. "Labor [Melakhah]" [Hebrew]. *Encyclopaedia Biblica* 4:998–1010.

Zahn, Th. *Die Offenbarung des Johannes.* Kommentar zum Neuen Testament 18. 2 vols. Leipzig, 1924–26.

Zeitlin, S. *The Second Book of Maccabees.* New York, 1954.

Zeron, A. "The System of Pseudo-Philo" [Hebrew]. Doctoral Dissertation. Tel Aviv, 1973.

Zunz, L. *Ha-Derashot be-Yisra'el vehishtalshelutan ha-historit.* Jerusalem, 1974.

INDEX OF SOURCES

1. Hebrew Bible

Genesis
1:11	139
1:14	40
1:21	133
2:9	139
2:10	32, 166
2:11	74
3:7	212
3:22	139
4:1	190
6:1–8	190
6:13	127
10:2	178
14:18–20	146
15:4	30
15:6	192
15:13	190
27:28	138, 147
32:6	180
49:1	127
49:22–26	181

Exodus
12:2	24
12:7	86
12:13	86
13:21	70
15:17	35
16:4	140
16:33–34	45
19:9	70
23:10	138
24:11	134
24:16	70
25:8–9, 40	23
25:10–22	43, 45
25:23–39	46
26:30	23, 25
26:31	112
26:33–35	46
26:36	112
27:1	38
28:6–34	114
28:15–21	74
28:16	38
28:17–21	41, 44, 72
30:1–10	47
30:2	38
30:13	24
30:22–31	45
32:32–33	122
33:9–10	70
35:25	103, 140
36:35	112
37:25–28	47
39	114
39:9	38
39:10–13	41
39:22–29	114
40:34–38	70

Leviticus
6:4	46
16:12	222
16:29	220
17:5ff.	146
23:39	138
25:19ff.	138
26:4–5	138

Numbers
8:4	23
12:5	70

17:23–25 45
24:14 127
29:7 220

Deuteronomy
4:30 127
10:1ff. 45
11:14 138
18:15, 18–19 192
28:51 138
30:15–20 185
31:29 127
32:14 146
32:25 91
33:13–17 .... 180, 181
33:28 138

Judges
7:5 233

2 Sam
21:6 91

1 Kings
5:20ff. 93
6:20 .... 37, 40
7:2 93
8:4 52
8:9 45
12:28–33 191
18:1–4 191
18:32 140
21:26 191
31:15 70

2 Kings
18:32 138
21:11 191
21:16 225
24:12–16 88
25:1–7 79
25:13–17 48
25:18–21 .... 88, 92

Isaiah
2:2 .... 28, 127
4:3 122
5:1–9 142
5:2 37
7:15 140
9:1 86
9:6 127
9:17 174
10:5–7 88
10:34–11:1 .... 85, 174, 176
11:4 177
13:24–27 126
14:13 28
22:1–2 .... 89, 93
22:22 87
23:4 91
24–27 10
25:6 134
26:19 .... 65, 128
27:1 134
27:2–6 142
28:16 62
30:23 .... 138, 140
35 140
36:17 .... 138, 140
40–66 127
40:31 218
42:1 91
43:20 91
44:5 20
45:4 91
49:16 .... 19ff., 30, 199
51:3 140
51:9 134
52:1 39
52:15 75
53 8
54:11 41
54:11–12 .... 74, 76
55:1–3 134
60:1–3 85
60:19 75
61:5–6 39
64:3 75
65:11–13 134

65:17–18	34, 35, 75, 127
66:7–8	131
66:20–21	39
66:22	34

Jeremiah

2:21	142
3:16	52
4:23	126
5:10	142
6:9	142
11:19	225
12:4	133
12:7	79
12:10–11	142
22:29	44
23:5	85
23:20	127
24:1–10	212
25:8–14	65, 208, 216
27:20	88
29:10	65, 208, 216
30:24	127
32	1
34:4	212
36	1
37:1	88
38:1–13	207
38:3	88
39:1–9	79, 88
39:14	52
39:15–18	207
40:3–4	52, 88
43	1
43–44	68
45	1
48:47	127
49:39	127
51:22	91
51:39, 57	65
52:4–11	79
52:17–23	48
52:24–27	88, 92

Ezekiel

7:2–8	127
10:4	70
11:23	79, 82
15:1–6	142
16:10	112
16:13	112
17:5–10	142
19:10–14	142
21:30	127
21:34	127
28:13, 14	28, 29, 41, 74
28:16	28
29:3	134
32	126
32:2	134
35:5	127
36:35	140
37:12	217
38–39	10, 126, 177
38:8	127
38:16	128
40–48	40, 41
40:1–2	28, 41
41:21	38
42:14	46
43:16	38
44:19	46
45:2	38
47:1–12	32, 166, 167
47:12	139
48:18	140
48:20	38
48:31	75

Hosea

2:24	138, 140
3:5	127
7:14	138
9:1	138
10:1	142
11:9	27

12:9 141
13:13 131
14:8 .... 138, 142
Joel
2:1–11 10
3–4 10
3:1 81
3:1–5 .... 81, 112, 126, 177
3:3 130
4:9–16 126
4:17 39
4:18 .... 32, 166
Amos
8 126
8:2 127
9:13–14 140
Obadiah
1:17 39
Micah
4:1 .... 27, 127
4:9–10 131
5:1 154
5:2 131
5:5 218
5:7 133
7:15 141
Habakkuk
2:3 127
Zephaniah
1:15 126
Haggai
1:11 138
Zechariah
1:12 216
3:4 114
3:8 85
3:9 73
4:7 73
6:12 85
7:5 216
9:9 180

9:15 134
11:1 93
11:2 94
12:12 180
14:4 .... 28, 82, 177, 223
14:8 .... 32, 166
14:21 39
Malachi
3:11 138
3:16 122
3:19 179
3:20 .... 85, 138
Psalms
8:8 133
13:4 65
19:6–7 85
46:5 166
48:3 28
50:10 .... 133, 135
69:29 122
72:5 85
72:17 85
74:14 134
78:25 140
80:9–17 142
84:12 85
85:13 138
89:4 91
89:11 134
90:4 125
95:11 .... 65, 209
99:7 70
103:5 218
104:6–9 134
104:19 85
104:26 134
105:40 140
106:23 91
107:37 138
110:4 146
118:22 62
118:26 82

119:96 127
122:3 27
126:1 .... 207, 208

Proverbs
14:5 128
14:25 128
19:5 128
19:9 128
31:19 103

Job
3:8 134
3:13 65
3:40 134
7:12 134
9:13 134
12:7 133
22:5 127
26:12–13 134
28:3 127
35:11 133
40:15–24 133
40:25–41:26 .... 133, 134

Song of Songs
2:13 213
8:6 20

Lamentations
2:20 92

Ecclesiastes
4:16 127
12:12 .... 7, 127

Daniel
7:9–10 122
7:11 179
8:17 128
8:19 128
9:2 216
9:24–26 125
9:27 126
10:14 127
11:13 128

11:40 128
11:36–37 172
12:2–3 163
12:1 122
12:2 65
12:4 128
12:9 128
12:11–13 128

Ezra
9:1ff. 229

Nehemiah
9:36–37 138
13:23 229

1 Chronicles
4:21 .... 103, 114

2 Chronicles
3:14 112
5:5 52
5:10 45
24:20–22 92
32:28 138
33:10–13 191
36:21 216

2. Septuagint

Genesis
4:16 136

Exodus
28:4 114
28:9 70
28:21 .... 43, 70
25:6 70
29:5 114
35:9 70

1 Samuel
14:18 43

Deuteronomy
32:15 58
33:5 26 58

2 Chronicles
2:6, 13 70
Isaiah
26:19 138
65:22 150
Psalms
78:25 141

3. Targumim

Tg. Ps.-J.
Genesis
2:8 22
3:24 22
15:12 22
Leviticus
16:21–22 136
Deuteronomy
33:17 180
Isaiah
5:2 37
Psalms
50:10 134
122:3 25
Micah
4:8 154

Tg. Esther II
1:3 .... 92, 95

Peshitta
Ezek 27:16 113
Esth 1:6 113

4. Old Testament Apocrypha

1 Maccabees
1:21 53
4:46 55
4:47–52 .... 45, 53
2 Maccabees
1:10–2:18 50
2:1–8 .... 51, 53
2:18 53
4:11 51
7:9 163
7:13–14, 23 163
8:17ff 51
10:3–4 45
12:43–45 163
Tobit
13:16–18 .... 27, 41
14:5 27
Ben Sira
36:1–2 26
36:10 128
36:18–19 26
51:12 25
Wisdom of Solomon
9:8 24
16:20 140
18:23 114
1 Baruch
5:5–9 27

5. Old Testament Pseudepigrapha

Apocalypse of Abraham
9:29 29
10:4 73
10:9 73
16:11 73
29 122
29:1–12 124
Apocalypse of Elijah
3:97–99 150
Apocalypse of Moses (G.L.A.E)
15:3 136
20:4–5 212
22:4 29
28–29 139
40:7 139

Index of Sources

Ascension Isaiah
1:3, 7 58
3:13, 18 58
3:22–31 124
3:13–31 227
4:6 58
4:13ff. 150
6:11–13, 17 227
8:7ff. 84
9:22–27 123

Ascension of Moses
1:1 125
7:2 124
10 124
10:12 125

Baruch, Syriac Apocalypse of (2 Bar.)
1:1 41
4:1–7 .... 19ff., 34, 36ff., 69
6:1–7 44
6:4 41
6:7–10 .... 43–78, 86, 98
7:52 58
8:1–5 79
10:18–19 .... 83, 101
11:4 159
15:7–8 159
17:2–3 188
18:2 188
19:5 126
20:1–2 .... 34, 122, 196
21:21 58
21:24 159
23:4–5 .... 160, 188
24–30 121
24:1 .... 122, 159
25:3–4 123
27–29 33
27:1–18 124
28:1–2 124
29:1 126
29:2 .... 177, 195
29:3–30:6 .... 65, 123, 131, 152, 156, 158, 166
30:1 209
32:1–6 .... 32, 36, 122
35:1–5 .... 21, 47
36–40 165–181
40:2 177
40:3–4 156
42:7–8 162
44:15 159
48:22–29 159
48:34–42 .... 122, 124
48:45–46 188
49–52 .... 161ff.
52:6–7 159
53 .... 124, 183–198
53:1–12 183
53:9 122
53:56–74 86
54:1 122
54:15–19 188
56–74 .... 124, 183–198
56:10–16 190
57:1–2 192
59:4 .... 37, 41
64:2 191
65:1 191
67–68 33
68:6 194
70–74 .... 33, 34, 124
70:2 195
71:1 177
72:2 195
73:1 195
73:2 150
77:13–14 126
80:3 44
83:1 122
83:6 122
85:10–13 122
85:11 .... 65, 209

3 Baruch
11:2 87
Book of Adam and Eve
62, 66 213
1 Enoch
1:4 69
2:3–20 84
6–36 190
10:4 136
10:19 148
10:16–20 138
17–36 193
18:6–8 76
22:1ff 167
22:9 .... 159, 166, 186
24–25 135
24:3–5 139
24:4 169
24:4–25:7 29
25:4–6 139
26:1–3 29
28–30 139
32:3 136
32:3–4 139
33–36 37
36:1 139
39:3 29
45:4–5 35
47:1–12 .... 122, 167
48:1 166
51:1 159
60:6 136
60:7–9 .... 69, 135, 136, 137
60:23 136
60:24–25 .... 69, 136
61:1–4 29
62:7–16 .... 135, 137, 154
70:3 29
70:4 160
72:1 35
77:3 .... 29, 136
80:2 122
81:1–2 .... 123, 160
86–88 190
89:61ff 122
89:73 194
90:17 122
90:20 122
90:26–29 .... 28, 37, 69
90:32–35 40
91:10 .... 65, 209
91:16 .... 35, 123
92:3 .... 65, 209
92:12–17 124
93:2 123
93:4–10 124
96:6 166
97:5–6 122
98:7–8 122
100:5 .... 65, 159, 209
104:7 122
(Slavonic) Enoch (2 Enoch)
5:1–6 .... 29, 139
10:8 160
17:4 122
31:1 157
32:–33:2 150
42:5 157
55:2 28
4 Ezra
3:6 28
3:7, 23, 25 188
3:11–14 .... 29, 159
4:30–32 188
4:33–43 159
4:40 123
4:41–42 160
5:1–12 .... 123, 124
5:5 225
5:23 143
6:9–10 157
6:18–28 123
6:20 123
6:49–52 135

7:26–36 .... 28, 35, 122, 154, 156
7:29 157
7:30 64
7:31 ff. 123
7:32, 75 .... 65, 159, 159, 162, 209
7:36–38 28
7:75 .... 35, 209
7:77 159
7:78–80 159
7:116–129 188
7:123 138
8:1 159
8:33 159
8:52 .... 28, 139
9–10 115
9:1–12 123
9:26 211
10:51–54 211
12:11–12 173
13:9–11, 38 176
13:36 .... 28, 176
13:29–31 124
10:54 28
14:10–11 126
14:29–38 69

Jubilees
1:26–29 35
3:2–13 189
3:12 29
4:17–19 123
4:24–26 28
4:29–30 .... 148, 150
5:1–12 190
5:11–12 138
8:19 29
19:15 ff. 192
22:4 145
22:24 87
23:27–31 150
23:31 .... 65, 209
29:17 86
29:19 86

31:4 87
31:22 145
32:22 87
45:5 145
50:4–5 125

Liber Antiquitatum Biblicarum (L.A.B.)
3:10 .... 65, 138, 162, 209
11:15 29
13:8–9 .... 29, 159
19:10 .... 29, 139, 193
19:12 .... 65, 209
19:13 122
19:14–15 125
23:6 29
23:13 162
25:11 74
26:6 29
26:11 74
26:12 44
26:12–15 73
28:1 74
28:8 125
28:10 .... 65, 209
32:13 159

Odes of Solomon
3:5 58
8:15 230
11:13 86
11:13–16 138
12:3 .... 177, 223
15:2–3 86
22:8–10 217
30 .... 166, 167
35:1 138
35:5 138
36:7 138
39 230
42:14 217

Paraleipomena Jeremiou
3:7–8 .... 57, 86, 230

3:12–13	207
3:14	57
4:4–5	84ff.
5:18	85
5:21	234
5:28	209
5:31	211
5:32	209
5:34	214, 216
5:35	222
6:4	234
6:5–6	210
6:9–10	222
6:13–14	228, 229
6:17–23	228
7:2	217
7:18	219
7:23	217
7:37	235
8:2–4	228, 229
9:1–3	139
9:2	85
9:3	139, 221
9:8	85
9:10–32	206, 220, 223
9:14	223
9:17	223
9:20	48, 68, 82
9:21–22	224
9:24–31	225
9:30–31	224

Psalms of Solomon
14:3	221

Sibylline Oracles
2:6ff.	124
3:619–23	138
3:702–96	139
3:743–60	138
3:796–807	123
4:47	126
4:182	162
4:182–91	162
5.414–33	28
7:96ff.	124
7:149	139

Testaments of the Twelve Patriarchs
Testament of Levi
10:3	81, 109
10:5	37
18:3–4	85
18:10–11	87, 139

Testament of Judah
20:1	185
24:1	85

Testament of Zebulun
9:8	85

Testament of Dan
5:10–11	190
5:12	28

Testament of Naphtali
5:4	131

Testament of Asher
1:3–4	185

Testament of Benjamin
7:1–5	58
9:3–4	80, 109
9:5	190

Lives of the Prophets (Vitae Prophetarum)
Life of Isaiah
1	67

Life of Jeremiah
1–2	224
5–9	66
7–8	67, 224
10–12	152

Life of Habakkuk
1	66
10–14	70
12–14	69, 81

6. New Testament

Matthew
1:9–10 194
2:2 85
3:12 142
3:13 230
3:17 58
6:11 140
6:28 100
7:10 71
8:11ff. 144, 192
8:20 209
9:15 221
9:25 158
10:22 .... 70, 130
10:34 217
11:5 .... 152, 214
11:28 .... 65, 209
12:18 58
12:38 130
13:30 142
13:39 .... 70, 214
13:40 70
16:14 219
16:19 87
16:27 152
17:5 58
18:5 70
19:4 34
19:28 .... 34, 131, 197
19:29 70
21:18–20 212
21:33–46 34
21:42 62
23:37 225
23:38–39 82
24 129
24:1 82
24:2ff. 82
24:3 .... 70, 130
24:5 70
24:6 130
24:8 131
24:22 130
24:27 .... 85, 196
24:29 143
24:30 .... 68, 70
24:32ff. 214
24 34
24:38–39 69
26:26–29 .... 144, 146
27:50 80
27:51 .... 70, 71, 110
27:52 .... 159, 209
27:53 158
27:54 151
27:60 68
28:20 70

Mark
1:3–4 69
1:9 230
1:11 58
1:13 195
2:1–12 34
2:19 221
4:29 214
6:30–44 145
6:38ff. 140
6:42 145
7:27 140
7:37 .... 152, 214
8:1–10 145
8:4–8 140
8:11–12 130
9:7 58
9:38 70
10:6 34
11:12–14 .... 212, 214
11:17 83
11:20–22 212
12:1–12 83
12:6 58
12:10 62

13	129
13:2ff	82, 130
13:5	130
13:8	131
13:20	130
13:26	70
13:28–29	214
13:32	130
14:5	143
14:8	139
14:22–25	140, 144, 146
14:58	31
15:38–39	40, 71, 80, 110, 151
15:46	68
16:5	66
16:18	71

Luke

1:9ff	47
1:30ff	110
1:78–79	85, 86, 222
3:22	58
3:23–38	131
4:1	230
5:34–35	221
7:22	152, 214
9:58	209
10:19	71
11:3	140
11:11	71
12:27	100
12:51	217
13:28	192
13:29	144
13:31	225
13:35	82
14:15	144
17:20	130
17:24	196
17:27	69
17:37	218
19:40	225
20	34
20:13	58
20:18	62
20:27–40	189
21	129
21:5ff	82
21:7ff	130
21:12	70
21:27	70
21:29–31	214
22:17–20	146
22:30	131
22:18	143, 144
22:28–30	145, 197
22:53	71, 186
23:35	69
23:45	71, 80, 110
23:46	223
23:53	68
24:27	193
24:30	146
24:47	70
24:50	82, 223

John

1:4–5	186
1:11	223
1:14	39
1:15	156
1:18	70
1:19	86
1:45	193
1:47–50	214
2:1–12	167
2:4	145
2:11–18	130
2:21	40
3:3	30
3:7	30
3:19	71
3:21	222
3:31	30
4:10–15	166, 185
4:35–38	214

5:21	70
5:25–30	151
5:35	145
5:45	193
5:46	192
6:4	142
6:5–14	145
6:27–35	141
6:39	130
6:48	141
6:51	141
6:54–58	141
7:27	155
7:37–38	166, 185
8:12	186, 222
8:23	30
11:9	222
11:11–13	209
11:25–26	186
12:3	222
12:13–15	65, 215
12:35–36	186
14:13	70
15:1–6	143, 211
16:28	68
18:4	177
19:23	114
19:30	209, 223
19:34	167
19:39–40	222
20:15	82
20:31	70

Acts
1:9	70
1:12	82, 223
2:1–4	112
2:3	81
2:11	145
2:17	81, 112
2:19	130
2:21	70
2:42	140, 146
2:46	140, 144
3:6	70
4:7	70
3:22–24	192
4:11	62
4:12	70
4:30	70
5:30	68, 169
7:37	192
7:44–50	30, 31, 48
7:49	65
7:52	58, 224
7:58	225
7:60	209
8:26–39	209
8:36	168
9:27	70
10:39	68
10:43	70
10:45	81, 112
12:3	139
13:29	68
15:19	236
16:34	145
17:24	31
19:39–40	139
20:7	140
20:11	140, 146
26:7	131
26:18	71
27:35	140

Romans
1:20	34
2:19	71
4:1ff.	192
4:11–12	234, 235
4:13	192
5:12	188
6:3–5	168, 231
6:4	152
8:19–22	34

9:20 61
10:13 70
11:5 133
13:12 71
16:15 69

1 Corinthians
1:8 130
2:9 75
3:16–17 40
5:4 70
6:11 70
6:19 40
7:34 111
10:3–4 .... 68, 141, 144
10:9 71
10:16–21 .... 140, 144
11:23–26 .... 140, 144, 146, 152
15:18 209
15:23 151
15:24 130
15:25–27 196
15:35–39 162
15:42, 44 162
15:42–54 210
15:51–52 163
15:54 196
16:22 144

2 Corinthians
4:6 71
5:1–10 210
11:2 111
11:3 71
5:1 ....31, 32
6:14 71
6:16 40
13:12 69

Galatians
2:9 71
3:1–14 192
3:13 68
3:16, 18, 19 30
3:28 189

4:1–7 30
4:19 131
4:21–31 ....30, 32
6:15 34

Ephesians
1:6 58
2:10 34
2:11 31
2:19–22 40
4:9–10 68
4:22–24 34
5:8 71
5:11 71
6:10ff. 174
6:12 .... 71, 186

Philippians
2:10 70
3:14 30
3:20 ....32, 40
4:22 69

Colossians
1:13 186
2:9–12 234
2:11 31
3:1 30
3:12 58

1 Thessalonians
1:4 58
2:15 225
4:13–14 209
4:15 133
4:17 .... 70, 133
5:1ff. 130
5:3 131
5:4–5 .... 86, 186
5:5 71

2 Thessalonians
2:2 130
2:3 .... 173, 174
2:8 177
2:13 58

Titus
3:5 34

Hebrews
1:1–2 130
2:11 225
2:17 114
3:1 114
3:6 130
3:11—4:12 65
4:14–15 114
5:1–6 114
5:4–5 194
5:10 114
6:4 184
6:19–20 .... 110, 114
7 62
7:14 85
7:15–17 114
7:21 114
7:24 114
7:26–28 114
8–10 30
8:1–4 114
8:2–6 .... 31, 84
8:5 31
8:13 62
9:2, 3, 4, 6, 7, 8 46
9:11ff. 30, 31, 47, 114
9:25 114
9:26 70
10:19–20 ....46:110
10:21 114
10:32 184
11:5 12
11:7 69
11:10 32
11:24–26 194
11:37 225
12:22 32
12:23 30

12:22–24 .... 40, 177
13:14 .... 30, 14

1 Peter
1:20 130
2:4–10 .... 39, 40, 62, 69, 75, 110
2:24 68
3:19 190
3:20 69
4:7 130
4:11 152
4:13 145

2 Peter
1:13, 14 210
1:17 58
1:19–20 .... 85, 156
3:3 130
3:8 150
3:10–13 34

1 John
1:6–7 71
2:8 222
2:12 70
2:18 130
5:6 168

Jude
1 58
1:14 12

Revelation
1:7 70
1:16 85
1:18 87
2:3 70
2:7 .... 68, 139, 142, 143, 211
2:17 .... 70, 142
2:26 130
3:7 87
3:12 .... 32, 71
3:14 173
5:1, 2, 5, 9 58
6:1 58
6:9 193

6:11	65, 66, 160, 209
7:1–2	43, 85
7:4–8	197
7:9–10	65
7:9–17	65, 66, 209
7:17	166
8:1	58, 64
8:2	46
8:3	193
9:1	87
9:14–15	43
10:4	58
11:19	47, 69
12:1	85
12:9	71
12:13–18	69
12:22–24	85
14:1	177
14:13–14	65, 70, 71, 209
14:15	71, 214
16:12	85
18:12	113
19:9	145
19:12–13	70
19:17–18	145
20:1–10	34, 69, 137, 151, 158, 177, 179
20:11	34
20:11–15	123
21	75
21:3	48, 110
21:4	196
21:6	130
21:9ff.	197
21:11	75
21:16	40
21:18–20	70
21:22	34, 39
21:23–25	75
22:1–5	32, 39, 68, 138, 139, 143, 166, 185, 211, 221
22:6–21	82
22:10	58
22:16	87
22:17–20	144

7. Qumran Scrolls

1QM (1QWar Scroll)
ii 5	47
xi 16	177

1QS (1QRule of the Community)
i 9–11	186
ii 11–12	146
iii 1–13	47, 186
iii 13–iv 14	185
iii 18–26	186
v 6–7	39, 110
vi 2–5	147
viii 5–10	39, 110
viii 9	47
viii 13	69
ix 3–9	39, 110

1Q28a (1QRule of the Congregation)
i 27–ii 3	147

4QFlorilegium
DJD V:53	35, 85, 110, 177

4QShirShabb 36, 47
15 ii–16	113

11QTemple (Temple Scroll)
vii 13–14	113
xiv 7	47
xv 13	47
xvi 10	47
xxii 8	47
xxxiv	47
xlv 13–14	37
xlvii 3–6, 10–11	37

Index of Sources

5Q New Jerusalem 38

4QpIsa [=4Q164] Isaiah Pesher 76
8–10 .... 85, 174, 177
11–24 85

4QSerek HaMilhamah (4QSM=4Q285) 175
5 1–6 85

Thanksgiving Scroll (1QH)
viii 4–11 82
xvi 4–26 172

Pesher Bereshit (4QpGen)
5 1–7 85

The Scroll of Melchizedek (11QMelch)
l. 7 124

Pesher Habakkuk (1QpHab)
ii 5 146
ix 6 146

Damascus Covenant (CD)
iv 4 146
vi 11 146

4Q552–553 173

War Scroll (1QM)
15 2 176

8. Mishnah (m)

Berakot
1.5 157

Kilʾayim
9.2 112

Pesaḥim
10.6 .... 25, 26

Šeqalim
5.1 103
6.1 48
8.5 101

Yoma
1.1 221
1.7 92
3.4 114
3.6–7 114
6.8 136

Taʿanit
4.8 25

Ketubbot
2.8 101
13.1 94

Nazir
9.5 146

Soṭah
8.1 146

Sanhedrin
9.6 92
10.2 191
10:11 163

ʿEduyyot
2.10 178

ʾAbot
3.1–2 94
3.5 94
3.16 135

Zebaḥim
5.8 39

Menaḥot
11.9 101

Tamid
1.1 92
7.3 25

Middot
3.8 143
4.6 38

Kelim
1.6–9 39
2.4 103

Nega'im
2.4 103

Niddah
1.4 104

9. Jerusalem Talmud (y)

Berakot
2.4 (4d) 178
2.4 (5a) 155
4.2 (7d) 164
4.3 (8a) 27
4.5 (8c) 25

Šabbat
6.1 (7d) 20
4.3 (8a) 24

Yoma
3.6 (40c) 114
6.3 (43c) 94

Šeqalim
4.3 (48a) 101, 103
4.8 (68d–69b) 91
5.1 (49a) 103
6.1 (49c) 48, 49
6.3 (50a) .... 88ff.
8.4 (51b) 101

Sukkah
5.2 (55b) 180

Taaniot
1.1 (63d) 128
2.1 (65a) 49
2.13 (66a) 37
3.9 (66d) 207
3.10 (66d) 65
4.2 (69a) 89
4.8 (69a) 92
7.8 (69a) 103

Megillah
1.3 (72b) 135
2.1 (73a) 178
3.2 (74a) 135

Yebamot
9.1 (10a) 104

Soṭah
3.4 (19a) 103
8.3 (22c) 48

Sanhedrin
10.1 (28a) 12
10.6 (29c) 88, 135

Niddah
1.1 (48d) 102
1.4 (49a) 104
1.5 (49b) 102

10. Babylonian Talmud (b)

Berakot
18b 102
43b 91
60b 163

Šabbat
20b 113
104b 111
105a 91
118a 132, 178
127b 102
152b 161, 193

Pesaḥim
54a 141, 154
87a 91
106a 146
118a 132, 178
119b 135

Yoma
5a 113
9b 91
21b 49
31b 114
34b 114
39b 94
52b 48, 49
53b 48
75b 141

Sukkah
41a 25
52a 153, 155, 180
52b 218

Beṣah
5b 25

Roš Haššanah
16b 122
30a 25
31a 79

Taʿanit
4a 20
5a 27
9a 141
23a 207
29a 91, 92
29b 101

Ḥagigah
4b 111
12b 27, 84, 161
14a 8

Yebamot
59b 102
61b 102
62a 161
63b 161

Ketubbot
66b 102
106a 101, 103
111a 132

Nedarim
39b 22, 154

Soṭah
9a 52

Giṭṭin
56b 93
57b 91

Baba Batra
74b 135, 136
75a 135
75b 27

Sanhedrin
10.1 157
38b 8, 22, 161
43a 8
62b 91
82b 92
90b 163
92b 91
96b 92, 96
96b–99a 129
97a 125, 128, 151
97b 125, 178
98a 8, 132
98b 8, 155
99a 156
100a 7
109b 102

'Abodah Zarah
5a 22, 161
9a 151

Niddah
9b 102
13b 161

Horayot
12a 48

Zebaḥim
88b 44

Menaḥot
29a 24, 25

Ḥullin
80a 134
90b 101, 104, 105

Keritot
5b 48

Tamid
29b 101, 105

11. *Tosefta (t)*

Šeqalim
2.6 .... 101, 103

Yoma
3.7 .... 48, 49

Soṭah
11.10 141
13.1 .... 48, 52

Šebi'it
3.14 104

Niddah
1.9 102

12. Midrashim and Related Works

Midrash Genesis Rabbah (Berešit Rabbah)
1.4 .... 22, 154
2.4 154
6.9 181
7.4 136
19.6 190
24.1–7 .... 22, 161
39.11 181
44.21 22
75.6 180
75.12 181
76.1 91

Exodus Rabbah
51.7 22
33.4 25
35.6 25
38.8–9 72

Leviticus Rabbah
13.3 135
14.1 155
15.1 161
19.6 90
22.9 135

Numbers Rabbah
2.7 .... 72, 181
11.2 141
12.1 25
12.8 .... 24, 25
14.3 25
15.10 .... 49, 50
21.18 135

Deuteronomy Rabbah
2.20 191
11.9 193

Index of Sources

Canticles Rabbah
2.9 141
2.13 180
3.6 .... 101, 103
4.4 25
3.11 25
8.6 20
8.10 218

Lamentations Rabbah
1.5 93
2.4 103
4.16 92
Petihta 1.25 79

Ecclesiastes Rabbah
3.11 22

Qohelet Rabbah
1.9 141
3.21 161

'Abot de Rabbi Natan
 Version I
4 .... 93ff.
26 193
31 22
34 79
37 84
41 .... 49, 52
 Version II
6 93
7 .... 93ff.
8 22

Mekhilta de Rabbi Yishmael
 Shirah
10 25
 Ba-Hodesh
7 146
9 22
 Beshalah
3 141

5 50

Mekhilta de Rashbi
16.15 50
17.14 93

M Midrash Tanḥuma
 Beshalah
22 141
 Vayaqhel
7 25
 Pequdei
1 .... 20, 27
5 22
7 25
 Naso
19 .... 22, 25
24 84
 Bahaalotkha
11.44–45 50
 Behuqotai
5 25

Midrash Leqah Tov
Exod 25 24

Midrash Bereshit Rabbati
27.17 39

Midrash Aggadah al Hamisha
 Humshei Torah
Num 30:15 224

Midrash Shoher Tov
23:7 135
126:1 207

Midrash Tehillim
16.7 22
90.3 155
93.2 22
114 84

Midrash Mishlei
8 22

Pirqe Rabbi Eliezer
3.2 22
11 135

Pesiqta de-Rab Kahana
1.3 25
5.2 22
5.9 180
6 135
13 82
13.11 79
17.8 20

Parasha Aheret
Mandelbaum 455–57 135

Pesiqta Rabbati
5 .... 25, 84
13 82
15 .... 22, 141, 180
16 135
26 .... 79, 95, 101, 115, 116
27 20
36–37 .... 115, 155

Seder Elyahu Rabbah
23 141
29 22

Sifre Bamidbar
Behaalotkha 61 24

Sifre Devarim
43 27
344 161

Baraita de-Mlekhet ha-Mishkan
4 113
7 .... 48, 113

Yalkut Shimoni
1.20 22
1.422 113

2.249 91
2.421 91
2.471 20

13. Christian Writings

Acts of Paul 3:5–6 111

Ambrose
  De Mysteriis 4.20 168

Augustine
  De civitate Dei
  17.3 30
  17.8 39
  17.13 40
  20:6 158
  20:7, 9 .... 149, 151
  20.8, 13 174
  Contra Julianum
  6.19.62 168

Aphraates
  Sermons
  6.6 145
  7.19–21 .... 231ff.
  21.8–17 194
  23 .... 143, 144, 190, 211
  11.12 .... 218, 234
  Sixth sermon, *De Monachis* (Patrologia Syriaca) 4.4 217

Barnabas, Epistle of
  3:6 58
  4.9 186
  9:6–8 230
  15:3–8 150
  18–20 185
  20.1 186

1 Clement
  17:1 58

Index of Sources

Clement of Alexandria
Paed.
2.19.3 169
1.6.26.1 185

Pseudo-Clementine Homilies (Ps.-Clem.)
4.32 168
6.15 168
7.7 185
7.38 168
13.4 236
14.1 146
19.2 217

Cyril of Alexandria
On Easter 148

Cyril of Jerusalem
Catechesis
13 212
14.11 212

Didache
1–6 185
5 188
8.2 221
9–10 142
9.2–4 146
9.2 143
9.4 142
9.5 146
10.1–6 221
10.2 144
10.6 144
14.1–3 221
16.6 68

Didascalia Apostolorum
7.1–32 185
8.2.6 185
23.5.7 81
30 113

Eusebius
Historia Ecclesiastica
2.23.16 225
3.8.1–9 80
3.31.1 210
3.32.7 210
3.39 .... 148, 149, 151, 212
Demonstratio Evangelica
4.10 85
7.3 85
Commentarius in Isaiam
PG 24:92–93 81
PG 24:436–37 30
Commentarius in Lucam
PG 24:605b 80
Praeparatio Evangelica
PG 21, ix, col. 757 51

Ephraem Syrus
Hymnen de Paradiso
1.4 29
2.2 87
3.5–7 213
6.7–9 66
6.8 .... 144, 211
7.1 87
9.5 179
9.3–9, 17 .... 140, 211
10.3 179
12.10 212
15.7–8 47
Hymnen de Nativitate (Hnat.)
1.3 .... 143, 211
1.30 194
3.15 138
Hymnen de Virginitate
31.13 128
Commentaire de l'Evangile Concordant
21.4–6 81
21.11 168

Epiphanea
7, 8 233
8.16 218

Epiphanius
Panarion (Adversus haereses)
66.85.9 150
de Fide
24.2–3 150

Epistle to Diognetus
6:8 210

Gregory of Nyssa
On the Baptism of Christ 236

Hermas, *Shepherd*
Visions
3.2.4 86
Similitudes
8.2.4 230
9.14.5 .... 70, 86
9.16.3–4 .... 229, 231
9.16.5–7 .... 159, 231
13 37

Hippolytus
Commentarium in Danielem (SC)
1.12 224
Fragmenta in Danielem (PG)
2.6 69
2.4 150
2.20 87
2.22 174
Christ and Antichrist
11 148
31 224

Ignatius
Magnesians
9.1 85
9.2 159

Ephesians
18:2 168
20:2 .... 138, 144
Romans
7.3 143
Philadelphians
4.1 143
Smyrnians
7.1 143
Trallians
9.2 169

Irenaeus
Adversus haereses
1.2 58
3.20.4 159
4.27.2 160
5.23.2 149
5.25.4 174
5.28.3 150
5.33.3–4 ...... 138, 148, 149, 196, 212

Jerome
Commentariorum in Isaiam
PL 24:469–71 30
Comentariorum in Zachariam
14.3.4 223

Justin Martyr
Dialogus cum Tryphone Judaeo
8.4 155
41.3 221
48.1 155
49.1 155
72.4 159
80.4 150
81.1–2 196
81.3–4 150
86.1 169
100 85
106 85
110.1 155

111:4	86
113.1–7	194
115	194
117.1	221
120.5	227
121	85
122.5	185
126	85
138	69

Apologia I
61.12	185
65	167, 185
66	144, 169
67	86

Melito of Sardis
Frg. VIIIb 4	85
Sur la Pâque 98	109

Origen

Homiliae in Exodus 9 (*de Tabernaculo*) PG 12:363 31

Homiliae in Jeremiam I.3 236

Homiliae in Ezechielem XI.5 236

Commentariorum in Matthaeum
10.17	111
52.2 PG 13:163	109

Contra Celsum
1.32	111

Protevangelium of James
1:1	131
8:2	107
10	106
11:2	110
12:3	107
19:3–20:1	108

Rabanus Maurus

Commentaria in Ezechielem
PL 110:645	82

Tertullian

Adversus Marcionem
3.7	194
4.24	151
4.42	81, 109
5.18	190

Apologeticum
16	86

Scorpiace
8.3	224, 227

De Paenitentia
13	227

Visio Pauli
21–22	148

14. Josephus

Jewish War
1.650	163
2.163	163
3.372	163
5.5	46
5.210–17	45
5.210	142
5.212	112
5.216	53
5.219	45
5.231	114
5.232–34	43, 45
5.234	72
5.237	46
5.389	216
6.280	93
6.293–300	79
6.310	38
6.387–91	45
6.389	44
7	38

Jewish Antiquities
3.30	140
3.99–101	24

3.125–26 113
3.147 46
3.153–56 114
3.166 44
3.168 72
3.215–18 75
3.216 44
8.72 .... 112, 113
10.37–46 191
10.140 .... 87, 92
10.149–50 .... 87, 92
10.184 216
10.276 173
11.2 216
12.415 51
14.106–7 103
15.395 142
15.403–8 46
18.14 163
18.85–87 54
18.93 46
20.6–16 46
20.233 216

Against Apion
2.106 46

15. Philo

De Vita Mosis
1.148, 334 192
2.1–7, 66ff., 187 192
2.74–76 24
2.87–88 112
2.101–5 46

Quaestiones et Solutiones
52 24
82 24

De Specialibus Legibus
1.12, 66 24
1.86–87 72
2.86 141
3.176 141

Mutatione Nominum
258–60 141

Quod Deterius Potiori insidiari soleat
118 141

De Fuga et Inventione
137 141

16. Greek and Latin Authors

Cassius Dio
66.6.3 93

Homer
Iliad 6.490 102
Odyssey 10.223ff. 102

Hesiod
Theogony 573–75 102
Works and Days 64 102

Tacitus
Histories 5.13 80

INDEX MODERN AUTHORS

Abegg, M. G., Jr., 173, 175, 176
Aland, K., 8
Albeck, H., 90, 102, 128, 135, 154, 157, 181, 190, 213
Allegro, J. M., 35, 76, 94, 96, 109
Allen, W. C., 219
Alon, G., 4, 25, 102, 107, 185
Amélineau, E., 59
Andersen, F. I., 139
Anderson, G., 29, 41, 29, 31, 189, 190, 231, 232
Aptowitzer, V., 23, 29
Assis, M., 103
Audet, J. P., 185, 186
Avi-Yonah, M., 113
Baars, W., 2
Bacher, W., 115
Baer, Y., 13, 25, 163
Baillet, M., 38, 40
Balz, H., 130
Barnard, L. W., 185
Barrett, C. K., 27
Barthélemy, D., 146, 147
Barton, J. M. T., 226, 227
Basset, R., 57
Bauckham, R., 12, 162, 174, 175, 193
Baumgarten, J. M., 113
Baumgartner, W., 23
Beale, G. A. K., 172
Behm, J., 170
Ben-Menahem, N
Ben Shalom, M., 49
Ben Shalom, Y., 25, 89
Betz, H. D., 20, 30
Bewer, J. A., 73, 154
Bietenhard, H., 20, 21, 27

Billerbeck, P., 180
Black, M., 8, 135, 136, 137, 145, 147, 135, 136, 137, 145, 147
Bloch, J., 154, 157
Bockmuehl, M., 175, 176
Bogaert, P., 1, 2, 3, 4, 9, 21, 33, 41, 43, 44, 58, 71, 72, 73, 74, 83, 84, 86, 107, 115, 116, 121, 123, 125, 131, 153, 166, 170, 179, 187, 191, 198, 203, 205, 206, 207, 210, 220, 221, 223, 230
Bohl, F., 68, 69
Bonner, C., 109
Bonner, G., 212
Borgen, P., 141, 142, 146, 228
Botterweck, G. J., 23
Bousset, W., 113, 121
Bowman, J., 213
Box, G. H., 28, 124, 126, 134, 153, 154, 157
Braude, W. G., 115, 116
Briggs, E. G., 23, 143
Brock, S. P., 231, 232
Brockington, L. H., 1, 3, 4, 9, 71, 72, 198
Brooks, O. S., 142
Brown, F., 23
Brown, R. E., 131, 142, 143, 156, 170, 192, 193, 197, 211
Brownlee, W. H., 87
Büchler, A., 102
Budge, E. A., 29, 32, 47, 68, 69, 106, 139, 156, 160, 189, 194, 227
Bultmann, R., 142, 170, 184, 187, 193, 221, 230

Burkitt, F. C., 226, 232
Burrows, M., 147
Burton, E. D. W., 30
Buzy, D., 172
Cabrol, F., 221
Calmet, A., 2
Caquot, A., 133, 136, 226, 227
Cassutto, M. D., 23, 134
Cavallin, H. C., 153, 162
Ceriani, A. M., 2, 203
Chadwick, H., 111, 155
Charles, R. H., 1, 3, 4, 21, 23, 29,
    43, 44, 58, 121, 123, 125,
    126, 134, 136, 149, 150, 152,
    153, 154, 171, 173, 197, 198,
    203, 206, 226, 230
Charlesworth, J. H., 3, 82 , 134,
    152, 166, 195
Clifford, R. J., 23
Collins, A. Y., 50
Collins, J. J., 4, 13, 41, 44, 154
Collins, M. F., 55, 58, 68
Connolly, R. H., 81, 232
Cook, S. L., 10
Cooke, G. A., 40, 173
Coppens, J., 142
Cothenet, E., 108, 111, 114
Craig, C. T., 142, 197
Cross, F. L., 61, 145, 236
Cross, F. M., 145
Cullmann, O., 142, 144, 144,
    145, 146, 163, 167, 168, 184,
    197, 209
Daniélou, J., 11, 33, 47, 48, 66,
    69, 70, 81, 84, 86, 112, 138,
    149, 150, 151, 152, 158, 159,
    167, 168, 169, 197, 173, 190,
    194, 195, 198, 214, 226, 230,
    231
Day, J., 133, 134
De Faye, E., 3, 153, 154, 170,
    171, 173
De Jonge, M., 5, 11, 12, 14, 80,
    81, 109, 110, 112, 124, 157,
    166, 188, 195, 206
De Vaux, R., 38
De Young, J. C., 27, 44
Dedering, S., 2, 123
Deissmann G. A., 2
Delling, G., 44, 58, 205, 206,
    209, 219, 220, 224, 226, 229
Denis, A. M., 2, 203, 205, 206,
    216, 220, 226
Deubner, L., 103
Dillmann, A., 203, 205
Dimant, D., 23, 35, 37, 38, 39,
    110, 183
Dodd, C. H., 164, 170, 187, 197
Driver, S. R., 23, 133
Drower, E. S., 187, 222
Duensing, H., 226
Efron, J., 7, 8, 10, 13, 49, 51, 65,
    89, 93, 94, 95, 128, 154, 172,
    207, 208, 225
Ego, B., 23, 36
Eisenman, R., 110, 174, 175, 176
Eldridge, M. D., 14
Elliott, J. K., 8, 60, 68, 111, 212,
    228, 230, 235
Epstein, Y. N., 102, 103, 105, 128
Even Shmuel, Y., 27, 39, 50, 129,
    179
Ewald, H., 2
Fabricius, J. A., 2
Fallon, F., 51
Fee, G. D., 163
Feldman, L. H., 71, 72, 73
Fitzer, G., 58, 230
Flemming, J., 226
Flint, P., 173
Flusser, D., 9, 21, 27, 29, 54, 76,
    110, 146, 171, 185, 226
Foerster, W., 224
Ford, J. M., 29
Frey, J. B., 4, 152, 162, 206
Fritsch, C. T., 9

Funk, F. X., 81
Furst, J., 23
García Martínez, F., 13, 33, 38, 39, 76, 110
Gartner, B., 39, 110
Gaster, M., 73
Gaston, L., 39
Geiger, A., 8
Gelder, G. J. H. van, 3, 19, 83, 138
Geyser, A., 131, 197
Giblet, J., 51
Gil, M., 12, 29, 187, 190, 201
Ginzberg, L., 3, 7, 10, 26, 43, 44, 50, 73, 88, 90, 91, 128, 129, 226
Glasson, T., 193
Golden, M., 103
Goldstein, J. A., 51, 55, 68
Goodblatt, D., 90ff., 97
Goodspeed, E. J., 111, 155
Goppelt, L., 131
Gordon, R. P., 175
Graffin, F., 234
Gray, G. B., 133
Grenfell, B., 2
Gressmann H., 121
Grinz, Y. M., 9
Gry, L., 9, 115, 116, 123, 125
Guttmann, J., 51, 134, 135
Gvaryahu, H. M. I., 127
Hadot, J., 9, 121
Hahart, R., 51
Hall, G. R., 226, 228
Hameiri, M., 135
Hamerton-Kelly, R. G., 23
Hanson, P., 9
Haran, M., 39, 48
Hare, D. R. A., 66
Harofe (Troki), Y., 10
Harrington, D. J., 71, 73

Harris, R. J., 1, 4, 57, 58, 60, 61, 84, 86, 198, 203, 204, 205, 206, 210, 215, 216, 223, 225, 226, 230
Hartman, L. F., 128
Hatch, E., 70
Heinemann, Y., 180
Heller, B., 206, 207
Hengel, M., 51
Hennecke, E., 8, 60, 106, 108, 111, 209
Herr, M. D., 224
Herzer, J., 55, 57, 58, 59, 205, 206, 207, 209, 216, 219, 220, 222, 223, 224, 227, 229, 230
Hesse, F., 154
Higgins, A. J. B., 154, 155
Hirshberg, A. S., 100
Hoenig, S. B., 88
Hollander, H. W., 109
Holleman, J., 153
Hooker, M., 137
Huet, P. D., 2
Hunt, A. S., 2
Hunzinger, C. H., 212
Hüttenmeister, F. G., 88
Hyman, A., 101
Ilan, T., 102, 103
Isaac, E., 136
Ish-Shalom, M., 114
Israeli-Taran, A., 97, 99
Jacobs, I., 133
Jacobson, H., 9, 72
James, M. R., 8, 9, 60, 61, 71, 106, 107, 108, 111, 158, 221
Jastrow, M., 102, 103, 104, 105, 135, 214
Jaubert, A., 13, 131, 197, 218
Jellinek, A. (Bet ha-Midrash), 27, 113, 129, 135, 193
Jeremias, J., 62, 87, 225
Johnson, S. F., 123

Kabisch, R., 3
Kahana, A., 43, 125, 136, 153, 166
Kahouth, H., 102, 103
Kalimi, I., 49, 53, 54, 58
Kappler, W., 51
Kasher, A., 50, 163
Kasher, M. M., 103
Kasovsky, H. Y., 103, 104
Kaufmann, Y., 23, 80, 127, 140, 178, 188, 189
Kee, H. C., 81
Keuls, E. C., 103
Kilpatrick, G. D., 58, 203, 205, 206
Kiraz, G. A., 133
Kister, M., 49, 95, 99
Klausner, J., 8, 21, 132, 136, 154, 181
Klijn, A. F. J., 3, 4, 19, 83, 125, 138, 152, 153, 166, 197
Kmosko, M., 2
Knibb, M. A., 136, 226
Knight, J., 225, 226, 227, 228
Koch, K., 12
Koehler, L., 23, 220
Koester, C. R., 69
Kohler, K., 123, 205, 206, 207
Komlosh, Y., 96
Kosovsky, M., 104
Kraft, R. A., 5, 11, 12, 14, 50, 57, 198, 203, 204, 210
Krauss, S., 107, 111
Krochmal, N., 7
Kronholm, T., 213
Kuhn, K. G., 144, 145, 147
Kuhn, K. H., 60, 61, 62, 64, 66, 215
Kuhnel, B., 21, 27, 33, 81
Lacoque, A., 128
Lagrange, M. J., 4, 152, 170, 181
Lake, K., 185, 186
Lampe, G. W. H., 86, 230

Leclercq, H., 47, 64
Leemhuis, F., 3, 19, 83, 138
Lefkowitz, M. R., 111
Lehmann, M. R., 113
Leon-Dufour, X., 197–98
Lesètre, H., 142
Levi, I., 114, 116, 129
Levin, B. A., 23
Levy, J., 80, 91, 105
Licht, J., 38, 58, 60, 123, 127, 128, 130, 146, 158, 172, 203, 205, 207, 208, 216
Liddell, H. G., 23
Lieberman, S., 102, 103, 105, 107
Lietzmann, H., 68, 145, 146, 169, 170
Liver, J., 154
Loewenstamm, S. A., 23
Lohse, E., 20, 27
Loisy, A., 170
Luria, B. Z., 55
MacCulloch, J. A., 123
Mach, M., 103, 107, 108
Macuch, R., 222
Malan, S. C., 213
Mangenot, E., 126
Mann, J., 115, 116
Manns, F., 102, 107, 109, 167, 169, 197
Margaliot, M., 90
Marmorstein, A., 60
Martini, C. M., 8
McKelvey, R. J., 21, 27, 29, 31, 110, 131
McNeile, M. H., 23
Meeks, W. A., 193, 197
Metzger, B. M., 8
Meyer, R., 142
Meyers, C. L., 73
Meyers, E. M., 73
Michaelis, W., 31
Michell, N., 185

Milik, J. T., 11, 29, 38, 50, 136, 146, 147
Mingana, A., 59, 60, 61, 62, 64, 66, 86, 87, 210, 215, 216, 219, 223
Mingana, A., 61, 215
Mitchell, H. G., 73, 185
Moffatt, J., 23, 31, 46, 110
Montgomery, J. A., 128
Moore, G. F., 10, 113, 127, 128, 132, 140, 164, 157, 158, 163, 172, 185, 189, 191
Morissette, R., 163
Mowinckel, S., 127, 153, 154, 155, 181
Murphy, F. J., 20, 21
Murray, R., 86, 138, 143, 168, 211, 218, 231, 233, 234
Myers, J. M., 157
Nedungatt, G., 232
Nestle, E., 66
Newsom, C., 36, 47, 113
Nickelsburg, G. W. E., 44, 50, 57, 71, 72, 226
Niemark, D. Ben Shlomo, 24
Nir, R., 47
Notscher, F., 206
Oepke, A., 163
Oesterley, W. O. E., 4
Payne Smith, R., 43, 112, 153, 195
Perles, F., 12
Perrot, C., 71, 72, 73
Philonenko, M., 59, 84, 206, 209, 218, 221, 222, 226, 230, 235
Pierr M. J., 218
Pines, S., 131, 197
Plummer, A., 162
Pomeroy, S. B., 103
Pomykala, K. E., 86, 175, 176, 177
Pope, M. H., 133

Priest, J. F., 143, 147
Puech, E., 147, 159, 162, 170
Purintun. A. E 57, 203, 204, 210
Purvis, D. J., 49, 53, 54, 58
Qimron, E., 36
Rabinowitz, L. I., 105
Rabinowitz, Z. M., 113
Rahner, H., 86, 168, 185
Ratner, B., 102
Redpath, H. A., 70
Renan, E., 9
Renard, P., 46, 47
Riaud, J., 58, 203, 204, 205, 206, 208, 209, 212, 219, 220, 229, 223
Richardson, R. D., 169
Riggs, J. W., 142
Ringgren, H., 23, 172
Rist, M., 4
Roberts, J. J. M., 154
Robertson, A., 162
Robinson, S. E., 57, 84, 203, 204, 205, 206, 210, 220, 223, 230
Rosenthal, F., 3
Rowland, C., 21, 126, 173
Rowley, H. H., 125
Rudolph, K., 170, 187
Russell, D. S., 9, 33, 128, 134, 149, 153, 162, 163, 190
Safrai, S., 21, 23, 27, 29
Satran, D., 11, 12, 13, 67, 198, 199, 224
Saylor, G. B., 3, 4, 126, 159, 171
Schermann, T., 66
Schiffman, L. H., 113, 147
Schiller, G., 85
Schlier, H., 110
Schmithals, W., 10
Schnackenburg, R., 156, 197
Schneemelcher, W., 8, 106, 107, 108
Schneider, C., 130

Scholem, G., 127
Schrenk, G., 29
Schürer, E., 4, 9, 11, 35, 38, 125, 130, 154, 163, 206
Schwemer, A. M., 67, 68, 69
Scott, R., 23
Séd, N., 87
Seeligmann, I. L., 23, 26
Sela, S., 54
Shalit, A., 226
Simon, M., 41
Sivan, D., 128
Smith, J. M. P., 9, 73, 154
Smith, M., 9
Sokoloff, M., 102, 105
Sparks, H. F. D., 174
Stanton, V. H., 138, 149
Steinberg, Y., 23
Stemberger, G., 115
Stemvoort, P. A., 108, 109
Stern, M., 51
Steudel, A., 127, 130
Stone, E. M., 9, 12, 20
Strack, H. L., 115, 180
Strobel, A., 64
Strycker, E. D., 106, 108, 114
Sundberg, W., 222
Sussman, Y., 88, 91, 103, 105
Sutcliffe, E. F., 147
Swete, H. B., 40
Tabor, D. T., 176
Teicher, J. L., 13
Tepler, Y., 86
Thackeray, H. St. J., 38
Thayer, J. H., 70
Thomas, J., 169, 187
Thornhill, R., 57, 58, 203
Tigchelaar, E. J. C., 76
Tischendorf, C. D., 106
Tisserant, E., 226
Torrey, C. C., 9, 66, 68, 70, 81, 179, 224, 225, 226
Tromp, J., 188

Tur-Sinai, N. H., 133
Unger, M. F., 74
Urbach, E. E., 26, 27, 29, 126, 127, 128, 163
Vergon, S., 154
Vermes, G., 131, 174, 175, 176
Vilk, R., 88
Violet, B., 3, 9, 152
Volz, P., 21, 152
Von Rad, G., 23
Vööbus, A., 108, 231, 232, 234
Wacholder, B. Z., 38, 50, 51, 175, 176
Ward, W. H., 154
Weinfeld, M., 23, 24
Weiss, A. H.
Werblowsky, R. J. Z., 30
Westerholm, S., 46
Widengren, G., 82
Wikgren, A., 8
Wilcox, M., 169
Wilkinson, J., 30
Willett, T. W., 2, 9
Wintermute, O. S., 206, 222
Wise, M. O., 29, 35, 36, 38, 39, 110, 173, 174, 175, 176
Wolff, C., 44, 47, 50, 53, 60, 61, 62, 68, 73, 116, 203, 205, 206, 208, 209, 215, 219, 220, 225
Wolfson, H. A., 23, 163
Woude, A. S. van der, 13, 123, 181
Wright, W., 111, 230, 235
Yadin, Y., 35, 36, 38, 76, 113
Yamauchi, E. M., 169
Yisraeli, E., 103, 157
Zahn, Th., 4
Zeitlin, S., 68
Zeron, A., 9, 29, 47, 71, 73, 74, 125, 163
Zunz, L., 20, 39, 54, 90, 113, 114, 116, 181

SUBJECT INDEX

Aaron, 45, 48, 61, 62, 67, 141, 192
Abimelech, 65, 66, 204ff.
'Abot de Rabbi Nathan, 93–100
Abraham, 21, 22, 29, 30, 36, 86, 87, 101, 192
Abravanel, 25, 128
Acts of Peter, 168
Acts of Thomas, 230, 236
Adam, 19, 21, 22, 29, 35, 36, 39, 66, 71, 109, 145, 149, 161, 188, 189, 195, 212, 213
Akiva, Rabbi, 2, 7, 27
Alexander Polyhistor, 51
Altar, 24, 30, 38, 50, 53, 58, 63, 72, 96, 221
Ambrosian MS, 1, 2
Amorites, 191
Angels' sin, 190
Anointing oil, 45, 48
Antichrist, 137, 166, 172, 173, 174, 176, 179, 184, 196
Antiochus Epiphanes, 50, 53, 172, 173
Apocalypse of Paul, 221, 228
Apocalyptic, 1, 5, 6, 9, 10, 11, 13, 14, 23, 34, 38, 41, 44, 74, 121ff., 183, 184, 187, 195
Apocryphal books, 6, 8, 12, 54, 108
Aristobulus, 50, 51
Ark of the covenant, 43, 45, 46, 47, 48, 49, 50, 52, 55, 60, 61, 62, 63, 66, 67, 68, 69, 73
Ascension of Isaiah, 15, 225ff.
Azazel, 136, 137, 221
Babylonian exile, Babylonians, 1, 6, 19, 29, 40, 43, 48, 49, 50, 51, 57, 59, 63, 64, 65, 79, 88, 89, 90, 92, 204ff.
Baptism, 58, 69, 166ff., 184ff., 200, 205, 229
Baruch son of Neriah, 1, 2, 10, 50, 204ff.
Baruch, Apocryphal book of, 1
Behemoth, 69, 133ff.
Ben Sira, 6, 7, 10, 12, 26, 163
Bread, 138, 140ff., 146, 152, 167, 184, 197, 221, 228
Breastplate, 38, 40, 43, 45, 47, 70, 72, 73, 76, 114
Caleb, 192

SUBJECT INDEX

Cave of Treasures, Book of, 29, 32, 47, 68, 69, 156
Christ, 11, 33, 38, 39, 40, 48, 58, 59, 86, 106, 108, 111, 130, 156, 143, 149, 150, 168, 174, 182, 185, 186, 189, 197, 211, 233, 234, 235
Christian church, 1, 11, 30, 31, 32, 33, 46, 48, 60, 61, 69, 71, 75, 81, 84, 86, 110, 111, 112, 131, 138, 141, 151, 157, 163, 167, 190, 192, 194, 197, 199, 201, 205, 210, 215, 236
Christian tradition, theology, 5, 8, 11, 12, 29, 30, 31, 36, 41, 44, 47, 49, 61, 65, 69, 63, 66, 71, 77, 82, 84, 86, 100, 109, 129, 131, 199
Christian writings, literature, 4, 5, 8, 29, 150
Covenant, 21, 29, 31, 43, 45, 46, 61, 62, 64, 72
Cross, 32, 68, 69, 71, 82, 86, 168, 169
Crucifiction, 30, 80, 110
Cyrus, 63, 66
Daniel, Book of, 6, 10, 128, 171
Daphne of Antioch, 88, 92
David, 35, 50, 87, 106, 108, 111, 175
Day of the Lord, 126ff.
Eagle, 172, 207, 217, 218, 228
Elijah, 54, 155
End of days (Eschaton), 1, 9, 11, 28, 33, 34, 37, 55, 56, 57, 58, 59, 61, 63, 67, 69, 71, 73, 74, 76, 82, 121ff., 183ff., 214, 216
Enoch, Book of, 1, 10, 12, 13, 29, 37
Ephod, 43, 45, 70
Epistle (of Baruch), 1, 2
Epistle of Hanukkah (2 Macc), 50, 56
Eschatological anticipation, expectations, 13, 26, 145, 184, 193, 196, 200
Eschatological meal (feast), 14, 36, 132ff., 166, 195
Eschatological redemption, 5, 14, 143, 157, 183, 199
Eschatological Sabbath, 125, 150
Eschatology, 23, 24, 33, 34, 37, 39, 44, 45, 48, 49, 52, 53, 54, 55, 59, 63, 68, 70, 73, 76, 98, 121, 131, 134, 135, 161, 163, 183, 197, 200, 213, 214, 218, 230
Eucharist, 36, 137ff., 166, 167, 169, 184, 200, 221
Eupolemus, 51, 52, 71
Figs, 204ff.
Garden of Eden (see Paradise), 11, 21, 22, 28, 29, 32, 41, 74, 75, 76, 82, 136ff., 167ff., 189, 199, 211, 212, 222
Gnostic Sects, gnosis, 29, 59, 70, 169, 201, 206
Gog and Magog, 177–179
Golgotha, 30
Gospel of Peter, 58, 59, 158, 212
Gospel of Thomas, 209, 235
Greek Apocalypse of Baruch (*3 Baruch*), 1

Subject Index

Hanna and Joachim, 111
Hanukkah, 50, 53
Hasmonean (Mccabees) Period, 29, Rebellion 6, 10, 55, book (Maccabees) 6, 12, 50–53, 54, 55, 68, 163
Holy of Holies, 29, 37, 38, 40, 43, 45, 46, 47, 56, 80, 81, 109, 220
Honi the Circle-Drawer, 65, 207, 208
Ibn Ezra, 25, 128, 134, 135
Incense, altar, 43, 45, 46, 47, 50, 52, 222
Isaac, 30
Isaiah, 224ff.
Israel, the land of, 9, 10, 19, 20, 27, 30, 40, 41, 55, 63, 98, 114, 116, 217
Jehoiachin King, 41, 88, 89, 90, 92, 100
Jeremiah Apocryphon, 59–66, 61, 71, 73, 76, 86ff., 215
Jeremiah, 1, 19, 51, 52, 54, 55, 56, 57, 58, 59, 60, 63, 64, 65, 66, 68, 69, 85, 204ff.
Jerusalem, 5, 12, 13, 20, 30; conquest of, 1, 2, 51, 59, 60, 63, 71, 204; destruction of, 1, 5, 14, 19, 21, 33, 57, 80, 121, 199; heavenly, 9–117, 176, 197, 214, 215, 223, 228, 233
Jewish Hellenistic Tradition, 50–53, 55, 70, 77
Jewish Tradition, 5, 6, 8, 20, 22, 25, 26, 44, 48–56, 70, 77, 79, 88–100, 108, 115, 127, 129, 134, 136, 148, 160, 179, 182, 189, 191, 193, 199, 213, 224, 225
Jordan, 59, 170, 187, 194, 205, 223, 228ff.
Joseph of Arimathea, 68
Josephus, 2, 7, 12, 24, 71, 79, 80
Joshua b. Hananiah, 4
Joshua son of Nun, 192, 194
Josiah, 33, 36, 48, 51, 52, 55, 56, 73
Josippon book, 53, 54
Kenaz, 72, 73, 74
Keys of the temple, 14, 63, 83–100, 115, 200
Kittim, 174, 175
Lebanon, 93, 171, 174
Leviathan, 133ff.
Leviticus Rabbah, 7, 90ff., 97, 98, 99, 100
Liber Antiquitatum Biblicarum (L.A.B.) (Pseudo-Philo), 9, 66, 71–76
Life of the Prophets (Vitae Prophetarum), 15, 66–70, 76
Light-darkness, Doctrine of the two ways, 71, 85–86, 183–194, 185ff.
Luzzatto, S. D. (Shadal), 20, 35
Maimonides, 35, 49, 105, 113
Manasseh, 48, 67, 191, 225
Mandaean, 169, 187, 201, 206, 222, 230

Manicheans, 82
Manna, 45, 48, 140ff., 166, 184
Martyr, 137, 159, 193
Mary Magdalene, 82
Mary, Jesus' mother, 106ff.
Masekhet Kelim, 50
Messiah son of Joseph, son of Ephraim, 179–181
Messiah, 1, 5, 8, 9, 10, 14, 22, 33, 46, 53, 58, 60, 68, 69, 71, 75, 85, 107, 111, 115, 116, 121ff., 165ff., 183ff., 199, 200, 219
Midrash 'Abot de Rabbi Nathan, 93ff.
Midrash Pesiqta Rabbati, 93, 95ff., 114–117
Midreshei Geula, 27, 50
Millenarianism, millennium, 149–50, 166
Moses, 21, 22, 24, 25, 29, 30, 31, 35, 36, 37, 47, 50, 51, 64, 67, 68, 69, 72, 73, 181, 192, 193, 219, 223
Mount Gerizim, 54
Mount Nebo, 54
Mount of Olives, 48, 68, 82, 177, 223, 224
Mount Sinai, 67, 69, 71, 193
Mount Zion, 166, 176, 177
Nebuchadnezzar, 1, 51, 59, 60, 63, 88, 92, 236
Nehemiah, 50, 229
Nobles of Judaea, 88, 91, 92
Obadiah of Bartenura, 135
Oxyrhyncus Papyri, 2
Papias, 148
Paradise, 11, 20, 21, 22, 36, 41, 84, 87, 138, 139–40, 149, 151ff., 166ff., 214, 221
Paralipomena Jeremiou, 1, 9, 15, 56–59, 61, 66, 67, 76, 84ff., 92, 96, 97, 98, 99, 203–237
Parousia, 32, 56, 58, 59, 68, 70, 82, 84, 151ff., 166, 184, 200, 208, 214
Passover, 27, 65, 66, 142, 215, 216, 223
Pentecost, 79, 81, 112
Peplos, 102
Plato, 23, 31
Priest, high priest, 14, 39, 43, 45, 46, 47, 49, 60, 62, 83, 84, 92, 93, 95, 97, 107, 114, 221
Priestly garments, 43, 44, 45, 46, 47, 49, 60, 62, 63, 66, 114
Pseuepigrapha, 1, 6, 9, 11, 12, 13, 35, 93, 96
Qumran sect, scrolls, 13, 29, 35, 37, 39, 41, 69, 76, 110, 146–147, 174, 201
Rabban Simeon the son of Gamaliel, 101
Rabbi Eliezer b. Hyrkanus, 129
Rabbi Hananiah the Vice Priest, 94, 101

Subject Index

Radak, Rabbi David Kimhi, 20, 35, 128
Ramban, 181
Rashi, Rabbi Shelomoh Ben Yitzhak, 20, 24, 25, 101, 105, 113, 134, 181, 190
Redemption, 10, 11, 20, 26, 34, 35, 46, 47, 59, 63, 65, 77, 121, 122, 125, 129, 183, 196, 200
Repentance, 22, 129, 191
Resurrection, 9, 30, 65, 67, 69, 71, 130, 133ff., 144, 151, 158ff., 168, 184, 186, 200, 203, 206ff., 227, 231
Sages, 13, 25, 49, 91, 98, 161, 233
Samaritan, Samaria, 54, 205, 236
Sanctuary, 23, 29, 31, 37, 39, 40, 41, 43, 46, 47, 48, 52, 84, 89, 95, 221
Sanhedrin, 89
Satan, 9, 11, 34, 69, 71, 136, 177, 179, 186, 236
Seals, 58–59, 67, 228
Sefarim Hisonyim, 7
Shekhina, 79
Sheol, 160, 171, 172, 190, 217
Shlomo Adani, 105
Sign, 68, 123, 129, 229
Solomon, 31, 40, 47, 52, 73, 76
Son of man, 8, 68, 70, 137, 153–54, 196, 219, 228
Stephen, 31, 48, 225
Stone, 67, 70, 72, 73, 75, 142, 215, 224
Storehouse, 159ff.
Sun, 61, 62, 63, 64, 73, 84, 85, 86, 88, 138, 185, 215
Tabernacle, 21, 23, 24, 31, 47, 113, 210, 234
Tablets of heaven, 62, 123ff.
Temple: first, second, period, heavenly, 1–117, 123, 124, 140, 142, 155, 162, 169, 189, 193, 195, 199, 200, 205, 208, 222, 227
Tent of meeting, 52, 69, 71
Tetragramaton, 70
Thecla, 111
Tree of Life, 29, 32, 68, 138, 145, 150, 165, 168, 169, 199, 208, 221, 223, 227
Tribs, 1, 43, 48, 70, 131, 198, 216
Urim and Tumim, 73, 75, 76
Veil, 40, 43, 45, 46, 47, 70, 71, 80–82, 101ff., 103, 105, 109, 110, 113, 227
Venerable Bede, 221
Vessels of the temple, 23, 24, 29, 30, 31, 43–78, 204
Virgins, weave, 14, 40, 91, 100–117, 200, 234
Watchman (Guardian of the house), 79–83, 109, 117

Water: bright, black, dark, 14, 86, 122, 124, 152, 184ff., 221
Wine, Vine, Vineyard, grape, 37, 69, 81, 140ff., 165ff., 172, 184, 204, 211, 213
World to come, 7, 33, 124, 135, 157, 160, 163
Yahel, 73
Yom Kippur, Day of Atonement, 94, 213, 220, 221, 222, 229, 233
Zechariah son of Jehoiada, 92, 96
Zedekiah, 50, 60, 79, 80, 88
Zion, 6, 19, 20, 21, 26, 32, 33, 36, 37, 39, 41, 50, 54, 65, 67, 68, 74, 81, 83, 99, 101, 116, 122, 127, 149, 165, 166, 171, 176, 177, 193, 194, 196, 205, 207, 208, 229

www.ingramcontent.com/pod-product-compliance
Lightning Source LLC
Chambersburg PA
CBHW020640300426
44112CB00007B/187